**Equal Treatment for People
with Mental Retardation**

Martha A. Field
Valerie A. Sanchez

Equal Treatment for People with Mental Retardation

Having and Raising Children

HARVARD UNIVERSITY PRESS

Cambridge, Massachusetts, and London, England   1999

Library of Congress Cataloging-in-Publication Data

Field, Martha A.
    Equal treatment for people with mental retardation : having and raising children /
Martha A. Field, Valerie A. Sanchez.
        p.   cm.
    Includes bibliographical references and index.
    ISBN 0-674-80086-9 (alk. paper)
    1. Developmentally disabled—Legal status, laws, etc.—United States.   2. Handicapped
parents—Legal status, laws, etc.—United States.   3. Parent and child (Law)—United States.
4. Sterilization, Eugenic—Law and legislation—United States.   5. Informed consent (Medical
law)—United States.   I. Sanchez, Valerie A., 1960–   . II. Title.
KF480.F54   1999
342.73'087—dc21   99-035786

Contents

Preface

This book is concerned with how law and social policy should address persons who have retardation, and it concentrates on regulations about their producing and raising children. The reason it focuses on those particular "civil liberties" is that they are the most controversial. Reproduction and parenting may be the most difficult issues with which to defend the central thesis: Persons with retardation should be enabled and encouraged to make their own choices. They should not be seen as "other" but should to the greatest possible degree be subject to the same legal rules as everyone else.

More generally, the book seeks to provoke thinking about the extent of society's ethical as well as legal obligations toward persons with mental retardation. It also attempts to help readers experience what life is like for them. Now that their exclusion from the mainstream society through widespread institutionalization is coming to an end and they are becoming part of their varied communities, it is time that we all got to know them better.

Anyone who writes about mental retardation or works in this field faces problems about terminology—in particular, what to call "the mentally retarded." Not only have many varied, and in some cases competing, terms been adopted in an effort not to be pejorative; norms also vary between localities. When Wisconsin's health commissioner transferred to a similar position in Massachusetts, he found that the only acceptable terms in Wisconsin—"developmentally disabled" or "developmentally delayed"—are not the norm in Massachusetts, where it is not deemed necessary (or even desirable) to avoid the "mr" word.[1] Nonetheless, many people prefer that mental retardation, or a reference to other disabilities, not be used to define the whole person. Accordingly, this book does not talk about "the mentally retarded" but instead usually refers to "persons with mental retardation" or "persons who have retardation." Such terms suggest that retardation is only one characteristic, certainly not the only defining feature, of the person.

A more complete description, which some prefer, is persons "who happen to have" retardation. That phrase stresses that retardation, like other conditions, can happen to anyone. Persons without disabilities fool themselves if they see a permanent barrier of difference between themselves and those who have disabilities; thus, the "happen to" is a significant aspect worth thinking about occasionally. Other fashionable terminology—with some groups or in some communities—includes the use of "mentally challenged" or "exceptional" to describe this group. And, as Chapter 3 suggests, "academic retardation" may in fact be a more precise and accurate term than "mental retardation."

The book attempts to convey a sense of how social service agencies actually act and how parents with mental retardation actually function, as well as discussing law and public policy. It results from interviews and field work pursued over a twelve-year period, as well as from legal, medical, and other library research. Even though the book is based on field research, it is in no sense an empirical study (although it does take note of other, limited empirical studies that exist). Particular sources are generally not identified because doing so would have discouraged many legislators, administrators, social workers, special education providers, and clients from talking freely about actual practices and problems.

Acknowledgments

Any acknowledgments must necessarily start with this book's "founding students," who spent a semester in 1985 doing field and library research on "mental retardation and the law" and thereby helped set the book's contours: Dan Daniels, Coleman Gregory, John Fitzpatrick, and Leslie Miller. Thanks are also due then-Dean James Vorenberg, who had the flexibility and imagination to approve an intensive seminar on this subject although it was (and is) not part of traditional law school curricula. In addition, many law students made helpful research and field-work contributions over the past thirteen years, including Stephen Marinko, Georgia Kazakis, Celeste Como, Eileen Minnefor, Jennifer Ault, Laurel Fletcher, Jessica Ladd, Jeanine Poltronieri, Kristin Guyot, Robert Bocchino, Raissa Lerner, Joel McElvain, Lisa Manshel, Kathleen Flaherty, Curtis Miner, Julie C. Lewis, Christopher Papajohn, Lisa Tanzi, James Boswell, Christine Scobey, Ockert Dupper, Rebecca Rosenberg, Isabel Karpin, Jeff Place, Betsy Nevins, Nina Dastur, Rebecca Winters, Gail Brashers-Krug, Terry Mitman, Rob Jancu, Cheryl Hanna, Danny Levin, and Suzanne DeVries.

The authors also wish to thank those residents of Massachusetts who have retardation and their families who shared their stories and their concerns with the Governor's Commission on Mental Retardation during repeated public hearings that started in 1994 and concerned all facets of their life. Listening to self advocates and others who live with retardation and normalization was both educational and inspiring for the commissioners.

In addition, thanks are due to the faculties of Stanford University Law School, Florida State Law School, Arizona State Law School, Harvard Divinity School, and Harvard Law School. Each of those institutions sponsored at least one faculty seminar to explore subjects discussed in this book; the authors profited greatly from insights presented at these discussions. As well,

Zipporah Wiseman sponsored a discussion of the book during its formative stages with the Cambridge Fem-Crits group. Thanks are also due to William Eskridge for reading and commenting on parts of the manuscript; to Christopher Jencks, who read and commented on a draft of parts of Chapter 3; and to Alan Dershowitz, whose insights contributed to discussions in Chapter 13.

The Harvard Law School has continually provided generous support for this project since its inception in 1985. The school has provided two research leaves to enable intensive research and writing during the school year, and it has regularly provided funding for intensive work during the summer months. Our thanks to both Dean James Vorenberg and Dean Robert Clark for their support. And, finally, our thanks to Elizabeth Hurwit, a very fine editor.

**Equal Treatment for People
with Mental Retardation**

PART I

Introduction

CHAPTER 1

Some Families

Until they were young adults, Donna and Ricardo Thornton were confined to institutions for persons with mental retardation. Only because of the success of the civil rights movement have they had the chance to live independent lives. Beginning in the 1960s, our nation turned away from the philosophy of institutionalization of persons with retardation to a philosophy of independent living, and changes in practice have followed changes in philosophy. Throughout the 1970s, a variety of court orders shut down state institutions or set deadlines for their closing.[1]

In 1984, shortly after the Thorntons left their institutions, they married. At the time, Mrs. Thornton was thirty-two and Mr. Thornton twenty-five. Two years later Mrs. Thornton gave birth to their first child, a son, whom they named Ricardo, Jr. At his first birthday party, Mrs. Thornton surveyed the scene with delight—the lemon birthday cake she had baked; the pot of hot dogs she had cooked; the "Happy Birthday" crepe paper draped from the ceiling of her Washington, D.C., townhouse; and her child, "Little Ricky," enlivened by the roomful of friends and crawling from place to place like any other one-year-old.

Mrs. Thornton expressed her profound joy to a newspaper reporter who attended the party: "This is one happy life. When I get old and gray and people say, 'Donna, how was your life?' I'll say, 'It was wonderful' . . . When I was at Forest Haven, I thought I would be there for life. I asked them, 'How do you get out?' They said, 'You have to work your way out. You have to climb the ladder.' That's what I did. I climbed my way out. I wanted to get married, be like everyone else. I wanted a man, a right man, one to help me out and marry me. I got him—and I got my baby . . . That was my dream."[2]

When the Thorntons left their institutions, both obtained full-time jobs. When Donna became pregnant, in anticipation of Ricky's birth they both attended parenting classes. After Ricky was born, they received parenting assistance and instruction in their home from a nonprofit group that assists parents who have mental retardation. One approach of the group was to integrate Ricky, in playgroups for example, with children who had never known anyone with retardation. Moreover, through the playgroups the whole Thornton family met and mixed well with families from a variety of backgrounds.

A community liaison from the District of Columbia's Bureau of Community Services regularly monitored the family. Describing Mrs. Thornton's success, the social worker explained that she had focused on showing her how to hold Ricky and hug him: "[Donna] would watch me . . . picking up the baby and cuddling him . . . and [she would] imitate me. It hit me one day that here is a person who probably never was hugged as a child."

These varied forms of parental assistance worked for the Thorntons. Ricky has shown no signs of mental retardation, and both of his parents are conscientious and understand their child's need for sufficient stimulation. As Mr. Thornton told the reporter at the party, "All I can say to people who are going to be daddies is, it's a challenge. Are they ready to meet that challenge? I was . . . He took me away from a lot of things I like to do, like going to school. He took Donna from working. I've learned a lot of new things, too, like how to put on Pampers! . . . The people at school say he's doing good . . . We're going to school to meet his teachers and they're going to tell us what kind of work they'll be doing with him so we can keep it up at home."[3]

Despite the joys that Mrs. and Mr. Thornton have experienced from their marriage, the birth of their child, and raising him, some people legitimately worry about how parents' mental retardation could adversely affect children like Ricky. At the heart of their concerns lies the question: As he grows up, will it be a terrible experience for a child like Ricky to have parents like Mr. and Mrs. Thornton? Some fear that the intellectual, social, and possibly even physical development of a child may be stymied by such parents' shortcomings as role models and caretakers. They also predict that he will be required at an unusually early age to assume adult responsibilities because his capabilities will exceed his parents' and that such early responsibilities will be bad for him. In addition, they project that he will be stigmatized by his classmates, and later by society, because his parents have mental retardation.

Tammy Woods Bachrach was raised by a parent with mental retardation. She now has a graduate degree in special education and is married to a lawyer. When she was seven years old, Tammy figured out that her parents were different from other parents. Her father had a learning disability, and her mother was referred to by other family members as "a slow learner"; neither could help her with her second-grade math homework. By the time Tammy was ten, her parents had divorced and her mother began to turn to her for advice and assistance with many of life's problems and responsibilities. As a result, Tammy learned at an early age to handle some situations normally reserved for adults, and in the process, she grew closer to her mother. It appears that their relationship was mutually supportive: "I could talk to her real openly because [hers] wasn't a real strong parent role," reported Tammy.[4]

It was not until Tammy was sixteen that her mother was actually diagnosed as having mental retardation. Tammy does not recall feeling any shame or embarrassment when the diagnosis was made. Nor did she feel inhibited, either before or after, about bringing friends home. Instead, she remembers her home as a "warm, welcoming place," and she always "felt real comfortable bringing friends over."[5] The diagnosis changed nothing in her life. She continued to live with her mother and younger brother and had what seems to her a normal adolescence.

Tammy does remember feeling a little anxious when she was eighteen and began to date Mark Bachrach, who later became her husband. Her chief concern then was that he would be put off by the differences between her mother and his parents. Her mother was shy and had relaxed housekeeping habits: she didn't change the kitty litter every day; she didn't always bother to cage the parakeet when visitors arrived; and she casually served Tammy and her boyfriend dinner on paper plates as they sat watching television. Mark's parents, in contrast, were "sophisticated and self-confident" people whose dinner parties were formal affairs, meeting higher standards of social decorum. None of these differences bothered Mark.

The differences between Tammy's mother and society's model mother might have caused concern to social workers and judges had the fact of Mrs. Woods's mental retardation become known earlier than it did, when Tammy was still quite young. Often state authorities move to terminate the parental rights of persons with mental retardation because of generalized fears that retardation makes for parental inadequacy. Often their rights actually are terminated, even though the parents' conduct would have seemed acceptable to state authorities had the parents not been considered "mentally retarded." Mental retardation itself may be perceived as an insurmountable problem, without regard to the parents' actual capabilities and performance.

Often it is deemed best to deprive them of the opportunity to perform by aborting a pregnancy or removing offspring from the home, sending children into foster care, and severing all parental ties.

Ten months after the birth of David and Diane McDonald's twin daughters, the State of Iowa petitioned the state court for permission to remove the girls from home and to terminate the McDonalds' parental rights. It alleged that the McDonalds, both of whom have retardation, were unable to "take proper care of the children, or at least provide them with [the] stimulation . . . they must have to grow into normal, healthy children."[6]

The weight of the evidence suggested that Mrs. McDonald clearly required assistance with parenting but that Mr. McDonald was a competent father. He helped out when he was home and made sure that his wife had reliable assistance in caring for their twins during the day, when he was at work; his mother, who had successfully reared eleven children, was the primary helper for Diane McDonald and the twins.

Nevertheless, the court decided that the children should be removed from home and sent to separate foster homes. It extended the same judgment to a third child born to Diane McDonald shortly before the trial. The court also severed all parental rights of both David and Diane McDonald and all grandparental rights. None of the former caretakers was permitted to visit the three children in foster care. The court reasoned that Diane McDonald seemed unable to improve upon her ability to parent.

The court's sweeping judgment in *McDonald* rested on little evidence of parental unfitness and no separate finding concerning David McDonald's ability to parent. His status as a parent was either ignored or not taken seriously, in apparent violation of constitutional mandates concerning gender discrimination and in great unfairness to him and to other families that depend on male caregivers. When adults other than the mother are ensuring adequate care, the mother's incapacities should not result in breaking up the home. Parents without retardation often rely on caregivers even outside the family, but they are not thereby disqualified from parenting.

In *McDonald* neither the social workers nor the judge saw beyond the differences they perceived between "normal" parents and the McDonalds. Heavily influenced by negative prognostications about parenting by persons with mental retardation, they did not seriously consider how to protect the children's well-being and at the same time allow the McDonald family to stay together.

*   *   *

In 1990 Judge Marie Jackson-Thompson, a family court judge, ordered the Massachusetts Department of Social Services to rewrite its service plan for a family comprised of two parents with mental retardation and their six-month-old daughter. Judge Jackson-Thompson refused to break up the home, saying the state had not made sufficient efforts to keep it together. She instructed the state to rewrite its service plan to focus on teaching essential parenting tasks rather than such nonessential housekeeping skills as folding blankets.

The social worker who first began to monitor the family had reported that the parents occasionally fed the child inappropriately and irregularly. For example, they used pasteurized milk instead of baby formula on occasion and, when out of milk, sometimes used coffee. Moreover, at the end of a month, having spent their welfare money, they skipped a few of the infant's feedings in order to make the food last until they got a new supply.

After making these observations and noting that the family home was not tidy, the social worker had drawn up a fifty-page service plan, to which the parents voluntarily agreed. The plan required the parents, within a fixed period of time, to complete 80 percent of the parenting and housekeeping tasks it set forth. The parents failed to do so, and the state then took the parents to court, seeking custody of the child.

Judge Jackson-Thompson was both experienced in matters of child care and familiar with problems of parents who have mental retardation. She was also wary of inflexible and formulaic social service plans. Unlike many judges, she spoke directly to the parents of the child. She was also forthright with them about their shortcomings.

Using simple language, the judge scolded the parents for feeding their child coffee, which she likened to poison, and for failing to clean the baby's bottles before each feeding. But she understood that they could learn how to take better care of their child. She criticized the state's service plan point by point and ordered a new plan that concentrated on teaching the parents to feed the baby properly. She flatly refused to accept excuses about why the system could not help these parents and ordered the state to find the resources and support staff necessary to make the revised service plan work.

The social worker in this case told a newspaper reporter that she welcomed the judge's approach. It was a "tremendous relief" for the judge to take charge and order the state to do simple things that might keep the family together. The judge's position "outside the bureaucracy" enabled her to "just say, 'Get it done.'"[7]

*   *   *

Clearly, some persons with retardation *can* cope as parents, although how many or what percentage of the population labeled "retarded" can do so is open to question. When persons with mental retardation have children and want to be parents, the resources available to social service providers should be used to keep the family together, rather than breaking it apart. As society is beginning to learn, mental retardation need not prevent a person from experiencing a full life, including child rearing.

Nonetheless parenting by persons with retardation and the related issue of their having children are particularly sensitive subjects. Even many who favor "normalization" and civil rights for persons with retardation draw the line when it comes to parenthood. The underlying assumption is that a person with mental retardation cannot be a good parent and that "it would not be fair to the child" to allow such a parent to try. In other words, it is necessarily terrible for a child to have a parent with mental retardation. The experience of Tammy Bachrach, for one, calls that into question.

CHAPTER 2

Public Policy, Past and Present

Marriage, procreation, and parenthood are experiences that our society values highly but often denies to persons it has labeled "mentally retarded." Some of the hurdles persons with mental retardation face are deeply rooted in the law. Others result from discriminatory and deeply rooted practices that are not embodied in law but that nonetheless pervade social service systems.

Changing Policies toward Mental Retardation

Throughout the nineteenth century persons with retardation were generally free to marry and have and raise children. Most judges ruled that their marriages should not be annulled as long as the participants understood what was involved.[1] In addition, their right to make a will was generally upheld, as was their constitutional right to vote.[2]

In the early 1800s persons considered "retarded" either lived with their parents or other relatives; became wards of the state and lived in almshouses, workhouses, jails, or mental hospitals; or were "auctioned-out" by the state to strangers who were paid by the person's family to "care" for him or her. Those who were cared for at home and had wealthy parents were commonly tutored and trained by private special educators.[3] Various state and local governments also provided financial assistance to families who cared for children or relatives with mental retardation. But the "bidding-out" arrangements often resulted in the private caretaker's abuse or abandonment of the person with mental retardation. And the conditions at the public facilities were "abusive, the inmates often confined to sheds without bedding."[4]

By the mid-1800s numerous social reformers sought to teach persons previously deemed unteachable and founded private experimental residential facilities that organized daily life around constructive training programs.[5] Others spearheaded educational programs that "emphasized object-teaching, imitation, variety, repetition, constant review, sanitary conditions, and physical exercise."[6] Reformers convinced numerous state legislatures to adopt their slogan, "Hope through education," and build specialized educational institutions for school-age persons with mental retardation.[7] By 1880 fifteen such publicly funded institutions existed throughout the United States.[8]

During the 1880s public attitudes toward persons with mental retardation changed drastically, and the "noble experiment" came to an end.[9] One reason was that the school-age population of the newly established institutions had grown to adulthood but still seemed to require institutionalization, making government efforts to educate children with retardation seem futile. Another was the increasing popularity of the eugenics theory that mental retardation was hereditary.[10] It fomented negative myths about persons with mental retardation and encouraged ongoing "custodial care for 'those feeble-minded persons who were a danger to the community, especially women of childbearing age.'"[11] This "custodial care" took place in sexually segregated institutions and encompassed forced sterilization. For most of the twentieth century, sterilization was the social service paradigm for controlling reproduction by "mental defectives."

Society rationalized this harsh program in part by turning victim into villain. Myths abounded about the overactive sexual drives and lack of self-control of persons with retardation.[12] An article written in 1914, for example, stated: "it is a well-known fact that exaggerated sexuality is a marked characteristic of the imbecile," and "wheresoever they come in contact with those of the opposite sex they have no power of controlling the sexual impulse."[13]

Young women with mental retardation especially were no longer viewed with sympathy or as "unfortunates" or "innocents."[14] They were, instead, deemed inherently immoral and even criminal. Since those characteristics, as well as intelligence, were considered hereditary, they were subject to control through a campaign of identification and segregation from the rest of society and particularly from all men. Moreover, with only a few exceptions, the goal of helping them to become independent through education and training was no longer viable. Instead, the dominant state practices became segregation and control.[15]

By the early twentieth century the eugenics campaign was in full swing. American society believed that persons with retardation would produce mentally defective offspring and abuse or neglect their children. Institutionalization became a dominant instrument of public policy. Many states passed laws providing for mandatory and permanent institutionalization of persons considered feebleminded.[16] By 1917, thirty-one states had institutions for persons labeled "retarded," "mentally ill," or "epileptic."[17] Whereas in 1900 only 9,334 persons were institutionalized for mental retardation, by 1930 that number had risen to 68,035.[18]

The eugenics taboos that earlier resulted in rigid sexual segregation within institutions led to continuation of that policy and also adoption of laws allowing compulsory sterilization of institutionalized individuals.[19]

Of course, some persons with retardation were not institutionalized, escaping this form of state interference by living, for example, in their parents' home or with a spouse or friends. But the same eugenics concerns applied to them.[20] State policy to control their reproduction was reflected in laws prohibiting them from marrying in most states.[21] Connecticut passed the first such law in 1896, followed in 1903 by Kansas, and in 1905 by New Jersey, Ohio, Michigan, and Indiana.[22] Within a short period of time, thirty-nine states either prohibited marriage by persons with mental retardation or had established mental retardation as grounds for annulment.[23]

Some such statutes, though not enforced, remain on the books today.[24] Their constitutionality is extremely questionable. The Supreme Court has ruled that "the decision to marry [is] among the personal decisions protected by the right of privacy." The state can regulate or deny access to marriage only to promote important state policies.[25] Marriage is therefore protected from direct and substantial state interference and from regulations interfering with it that do not "support . . . sufficiently important state interests and . . . [are not] closely tailored to effectuate only those interests."[26]

The rule prohibiting persons who have retardation from marrying for eugenics reasons could not accomplish its goals because, then and now, people can and do have children outside marriage. Indeed, as one observer noted as early as 1913, "[r]estrictive marriage laws are unavailing because the unfit reproduce their kind regardless of marriage laws."[27] But even if the state could today prevent persons with retardation from having children, any such prohibition should have to be made directly, without also removing the right to marry. There is no serious argument that a person with retardation cannot be a successful spouse and no reason to deny a person the opportunity to play such an important role. Not only may marriage bring satisfactions in its own right, but for some persons with retardation, living with a spouse may provide a means for them to live in the community, which might not otherwise be available.

Our society's treatment of persons with mental retardation has changed significantly during the past thirty years. The current approach is to "normalize" the lives of individuals with mental retardation.[28] The most significant effect has been vast deinstitutionalization.[29]

An early movement to deinstitutionalize citizens with retardation began in the late 1930s; around 1940 the first community-living alternatives were developed for children and adults who had handicaps. Nonetheless, the trend toward institutionalization continued strong until the 1970s. The number of institutionalized persons with retardation in the United States peaked in 1967. In 1974, 85 of the 384 community-living alternatives then existing were in their first year of operation, 70 were in their second, 50 were in their third; only 94 had been in operation for five years or longer.[30]

The principle of normalization gained world attention in the late 1960s. The Declaration of General and Specific Rights of the Mentally Retarded, which was drafted in 1968 and adopted in 1971 by the United Nations General Assembly, contained its core features: the basic rights "to live [in and] . . . to participate in all aspects of community life" and, for people who needed institutional care, the right to live in circumstances that were "as close to normal living as possible."[31] The United States was among the many countries to adopt the declaration. Subsequently, Benjt Nirje and Wolf Wolfensberger extensively elaborated the principle of normalization, and that policy became the focal point for social reform in the United States. Nirje and Wolfensberger proposed that normalization could be achieved if persons with retardation were offered living conditions at least as good as those of average citizens. They thought it important to enhance the behavior, appearance, experience, status, and reputation of persons with retardation. In 1984 Wolfensberger suggested the term "social role valorization" to replace normalization.

The philosophy of normalization fueled not only deinstitutionalization but also movements to provide special education and create work opportunities for persons with retardation. The aim was to eliminate the dehumanizing effects of social isolation by "making available to . . . mentally retarded people patterns of life and conditions of everyday living which are as close as possible to the regular circumstances and ways of society."[32] A basic tenet of normalization is that society should assist persons with retardation to lead fuller lives.[33] Normalization also embraces the idea that persons who happen to have retardation are legitimate members of society and should be valued as such.

The twin goals of meeting the special needs of persons with retardation and protecting them against discrimination can be in tension. Nonetheless both are accepted as important principles for persons with disabilities such as mental retardation. Government entities on the federal, state, and local levels, as well as many private organizations, have joined in pursuing both objectives in order to remedy historic practices of exclusion and mistreatment: In addition to focusing attention and resources on providing opportunities for persons with retardation, the governments have passed laws prohibiting discrimination against persons with retardation and other disabilities.

One might expect that the Equal Protection clause of the U.S. Constitution would be sufficient to protect against discrimination, and if it did all levels of government would have to comply. But the utility of relying on Equal Protection has been lessened by the U.S. Supreme Court's failure to consider persons with retardation—or with other disabilities—to be a "discrete and insular minority"[34] deserving special protection from the courts. Accordingly, the clause is much less useful in the war against disability discrimination than in the fight against racial, or even gender-based, discrimination.[35] Indeed, the Court has said it would uphold legislation creating special rules for persons with retardation whenever it can find "a rational basis" to justify the rules.[36] This language is what the Supreme Court usually reserves for legislation with the highest presumption of constitutionality, like legislation regulating business practices, and it usually results in the Supreme Court's upholding the legislation against constitutional attack, even when the legislation has the flimsiest justifications.[37]

The 1985 decision that announced this limited scrutiny of special treatments of persons with retardation is Cleburne v. Cleburne Living Center. It involved a challenge to a zoning ordinance requiring special permits for "homes for the feebleminded" but not for most other group homes. The city had denied a permit for the plaintiffs' group home for persons with mental retardation largely because of negative reactions from prospective neighbors.[38]

Despite its declarations that "mere rational basis" was the appropriate standard of review, the Court struck down this application of the ordinance, saying that a government regulation based on "an irrational prejudice against the mentally retarded" cannot stand.[39] It also said that "mere negative attitudes or fear, unsubstantiated by factors which are properly cognizable . . ., are not permissible bases for treating . . . the mentally retarded differently."[40]

These statements by the Court suggest that "intermediate scrutiny" was really used, not the very deferential standard of review that the Court claimed to employ.[41] The rational basis, deferential standard of review would allow legislation to stand if there was any conceivable reasonable basis for it; the fact that it was actually the product of prejudice would not affect the result.[42] Moreover in *Cleburne,* despite rational basis talk, the Court actually exercised considerably more judicial oversight than it did a year later, reviewing classifications discriminating against gays and lesbians. That opinion, Bowers v. Hardwick, was written by the same person as *Cleburne,* Justice Byron White.[43] In *Bowers,* the Court allowed public prejudice against gay people—"the presumed belief of a majority of the electorate in Georgia that homosexual sodomy is immoral and unacceptable"—itself to constitute the rational basis that sustains the legislation. What the Court calls prejudice in *Cleburne,* it calls tradition in *Bowers,* even though both characterizations seem applicable to both. Similarly the legislation in *Bowers* could have been characterized as "mere negative attitudes or fear, unsubstantiated by factors which are properly cognizable."

One way of knowing that scrutiny of classifications involving retardation is not truly minimal, then, is that scrutiny of classifications involving homosexuality is so much less. Nonetheless, the Court's statements about standard of review make any protection of persons with retardation that is more than minimal ambiguous and thus uncertain. Moreover, under Supreme Court doctrine, discrimination against persons with retardation will clearly be subjected to less scrutiny than the "strict scrutiny" accorded racial classifications or even the "heightened" or "intermediate" scrutiny given to discrimination against women.

In addition there is some reason to fear that *Cleburne* may be the high-water mark of the Supreme Court's protection of persons with mental retardation under the Equal Protection clause. In 1993 in Heller v. Doe, the Court held it was all right to extend greater protections in civil commitment proceedings to those with mental illness than to those with retardation, which may suggest a move closer to a true rational basis standard. In addition the

Court's language signaled a retreat: "[A] legislative classification must be upheld against an equal protection challenge 'if there is any reasonably conceived state of facts that could provide a rational basis for the classification.'"[44]

Over its history the Court has not been a protector of persons with developmental disabilities. In Buck v. Bell the Supreme Court upheld forcible sterilization of those deemed mentally deficient. It was half a century later before the Court heard another case bearing on retardation, and it dismissed that case on procedural grounds.[45] Subsequent to *Heller,* the Supreme Court denied certiorari in a significant Pennsylvania case in which the petitioner argued that third party sterilization is unconstitutional unless it is the least restrictive available means of birth control.[46] In short, with the exception of *Cleburne,* the Court has not been receptive to constitutional claims involving mental retardation.

The Americans with Disabilities Act, enacted in 1990, has made it less necessary to rely on constitutional law. That statute, discussed also in Chapter 17, spells out policies of nondiscrimination and inclusion and provides fully for enforcement.[47] Even if the Constitution does not entitle persons with disabilities to any heightened scrutiny of classifications discriminating against them, federal statutory law now offers equivalent or greater protection.

The Current Policy Dilemma concerning Parents with Retardation

Persons with mental retardation, like other people, experience pain and pleasure, suffer through depression, and possess the diversity of personalities and abilities that is the hallmark of the human condition. They share with other individuals an interest in giving birth and in raising their children, if they can do so successfully. The Constitution and at least some aspects of current social policy seem to support protecting those interests for persons with mental retardation. But a dilemma arises because society or government—the various levels of which we sometimes refer to as "the state"—also has another valid and important interest: protecting against incompetent parenting. It is more than legitimate—it is morally required—that society protect children and endeavor to afford them at least a minimally safe and healthy upbringing.

Before considering how to resolve this dilemma, we must look carefully at what the various interests involved actually are. It also is important to consider whether they are necessarily in competition with each other, or whether the interests lend themselves to compromise and accommodation.

The U.S. Constitution has been interpreted to safeguard individual choice in deciding whether to beget or bear a child. Although Buck v. Bell has never been overruled (or reaffirmed), in the 1942 case Skinner v. Oklahoma the Supreme Court said (albeit in *dicta*) that a statute imposing sterilization on some offenders as a punishment for crime violated "one of the basic civil rights of man [and that] . . . [m]arriage and procreation are fundamental to the very existence and survival of the race."[48] The case did not involve mental retardation. Similarly, the Court twenty-three years later, in Griswold v. Connecticut, held that use of contraception was protected, at least for married couples, and in Eisenstadt v. Baird it became clear that this martial privacy extended to unmarried people as well.[49] And again, in Carey v. Population Services, decided in 1977, the Court reaffirmed the constitutional status of reproductive rights: "The decision whether or not to beget or bear a child is at the very heart of [the] cluster of constitutionally protected choices."[50]

Moreover, the constitutional "right to procreate"—or, more precisely, to be free from (undue) state interference with reproductive choice—has been viewed in very broad terms, encompassing even highly controversial subjects like the right to choose abortion free from state interference.[51] The limits of constitutionally protected choice have yet to be defined. Some argue that it even extends to a right to employ a "surrogate" to conceive or gestate a child for an infertile couple, or a right of access to evolving reproductive technology, especially if those are the principal ways a person or a couple can have a child.[52]

Whether or not the right to reproduce will prove to encompass such a broad range of activities, it already extends to a broad range of people. One major group, however, has been excluded from this general "right to procreate": persons with mental retardation. In many states individuals with retardation can sometimes legally be prevented from having children, and the conditions for interfering with their reproductive freedom differ markedly from those applied to other persons.[53]

Not only are choices about reproduction constitutionally protected for most people, but so are the rights of parents to run their family without undue state interference. In the 1930s, for example, the Supreme Court held that states could not prohibit teaching of the German language in the schools and also that the state could not require children to attend public schools rather than private ones.[54] Both those decisions were based in part on the right of parents, rather than the state, to guide their children's up-bringing. As the Supreme Court noted in Ginsburg v. New York, "constitu-tional interpretation has consistently recognized that . . . parents' claim to authority in their own household to direct the rearing of their children is basic in the structure of our society."[55] And again in Wisconsin v. Yoder the Court said: "This primary role of the parents in the upbringing of their children is now established beyond debate as an enduring American tradi-tion."[56] Finally, in Quilloin v. Walcott, the Court said:

> We have recognized on numerous occasions that the relationship between parent and child is constitutionally protected . . . "It is cardinal with us that the custody, care and nurture of the child reside first in the parents, whose primary function and freedom include preparation for obligations the state can neither supply nor hinder" . . . And it is now firmly established that "freedom of personal choice in matters of . . . family life is one of the liber-ties protected by the Due Process Clause of the Fourteenth Amendment."[57]

There are, however, limits to parental autonomy from state intervention in child rearing. The "right to parent," while extremely important, has been much less absolute than the right to procreate. All parents whose conduct endangers the welfare of their children may, in theory at least, be deprived of custody under all fifty states' laws.[58]

Whether individuals with mental retardation should automatically be de-nied the opportunity to parent is still a topic of controversy, and states differ markedly in their approaches. The issue is most clearly raised when state statutes explicitly make retardation a ground for removal of children and when social service agencies petition state courts to remove a newborn from the mother at birth because of the mother's mental retardation. In such cases, the mother is given no opportunity to try to parent; her incapacity is simply presumed because of her retardation. And even parents with retarda-tion who are in the course of raising their children are often subject to a pre-sumption of incapacity when they come to the attention of child welfare in-vestigators.

Yet persons with retardation aspire to be parents for the same reasons that others do. Many of those reasons are intangible; not all of them are fully ra-tional. People generally believe that children will provide their parents with a sense of self-worth and contribute to their parents' happiness.[59] Family may be especially important to persons with retardation. One reason is that they may be most capable of performing the types of tasks associated with living in a family (like washing clothes, keeping house, and caring for children). They also may have fewer agreeable work opportunities in the outside world than other persons do.

Many adults with retardation are stigmatized by society and yearn to be integrated into the community and appear as "normal" as possible.[60] They therefore highly value possessions and experiences that other people regard as commonplace, and value the commonplace *because* it is commonplace.[61] Marriage, childbearing, and parenting represent three of the most commonplace experiences in our society, and in addition are experiences our society values highly. They may be among the most normal and rewarding activities a person with retardation can engage in.

Experiences like marriage and parenting provide people with a sense of "belonging" in society by permitting them to fulfill meaningful and socially valued roles. For many women, motherhood is the most meaningful and rewarding occupation. For a person with retardation who would otherwise work in a sheltered workshop[62] or be unemployed, parenting provides an opportunity for full-time participation in one of the most productive and respected of social endeavors. A child can provide a mother or father with an object of love and a source of emotional support and self-esteem that no social service agency can replicate. Indeed, parenthood can provide a parent who has retardation, like other parents, with a much needed focal point for living.

The person who has retardation does, then, have an important interest in parenting. But it is an interest that exists only if she or he can do it adequately. No one has an interest in persons who have retardation (or others) failing at parenting. And no one is arguing that unfit parents with retardation should be able to parent; only that they should be measured by the same yardstick as others.

People with retardation (like many other people) like to do things they can do well or at least competently. Indeed, to speak in generalizations, they fear their failure and underestimate their own abilities even more than other people do. Studies of children who have mental retardation indicate that an individual's past history of success or failure is the most important variable in determining that individual's attitude toward future endeavors;[63] persons with mental retardation are likely to have experienced more failure in their lives than others have, both because of their more limited abilities and because of societal prejudice. The lower "generalized expectancy for success" they have in turn makes it easy to discourage them from taking on any new experiences.[64] A common technique of educators trying to help their students break this cycle of expecting failure and being unwilling to try new experiences is to provide arenas in which their students are able to succeed.[65]

The fear of failure that is acute among many persons with retardation is one characteristic that makes the group comparatively persuadable. It allows social workers and caretakers easily to convince them not to try. In one sense this ability to persuade women to avoid childbirth or give up their babies is problematic,[66] but it does help smooth the fit between rights for parents with retardation and states' and children's interests.

As a rule, the state will not intervene to remove a child from a parent unless a parent is unfit. The existence of "better alternatives," including better alternative parents, does not become relevant until after an adjudication of unfitness. This system prevents the law from making heavy-handed judgments about which parents are better than others and which styles of parenting are preferable. After all, what criteria would judges use to decide that outsiders would be better parents? Would wealth and education be legitimate factors to take into account, for example, or would our sense of justice rebel at thereby allowing the more privileged to take the children of the less fortunate?

The existing system also enables parents generally to feel a sense of security about their relationship with their child that would not exist in a system that permitted the exploitation of better alternatives. Parents can rest assured that they will be permitted to continue to parent, unless they do something wrong. The resulting sense of security in the family relationships presumably also benefits the children.[67]

Imagine how disruptive it would be if a mother knew she could lose her children simply because someone who appeared to be a "better" parent for them came along. Even if there were a high standard of better parenting, and the transfer would be effected only if a judge considered it to be "in the best interests of the child," the possibility of someone claiming your child would be extremely disturbing. Accordingly, the law permits government to intervene in families—to transfer custody of the children or otherwise—only when it can be shown that there is something disqualifying about the existing parents. Unless the existing parents are disqualified, the existence of "better alternatives" has no legal relevance, and the existing parenting arrangement will continue. Moreover, a high standard of disqualification is generally demanded.

The standard must be high not only to foster family security, but also because people have very different ideas about proper approaches to child rearing. It is important to individual freedom that the state not pick out one "appropriate" way of proceeding and enforce its judgments as an orthodoxy that trumps the variety of views held by different individuals, religions, and subcultures.

Accordingly, the usual state rule prevents intervention in families except when children suffer physical or emotional neglect or abuse at the hands of their parents. The rationale for intervention is that the parents' unfitness threatens the child's welfare. The state then has a duty and power, as *parens patriae,* to protect the child against harm. And, even then, it removes the children from the parents only as a last resort.

For a number of reasons, parents who have mental retardation are often targets of state intervention and may be at a higher risk than other parents of losing their children. First, some states have explicit rules concerning parental fitness for parents with mental retardation,[68] making those parents especially vulnerable. Second, mothers with retardation run greater risks of losing their children because the state is more likely to be aware of them and their problems; the state is much more likely to be in a supervisory relationship already with a person who has retardation than with other parents.[69] Government employees will inevitably measure parents—or parents-to-be—with retardation by whatever standard law or practice has adopted for acceptable parenting, while other persons may simply escape the state's scrutiny.

If the stated standard is either unrealistically high or extremely flexible, state officials will effectively have great discretion. Because parenting is a process, not merely a single action, there often are contradictory factors at work, contributing to decisionmakers' discretion. For example, if there are strong bonds of affection between parent and child, what degree of competence at household tasks should be required? If a person with retardation would be able to function as a parent, but only with a certain amount of assistance with domestic chores, will that person still be deemed an "adequate" parent? How discretion is exercised will often depend on the particular system's, and the particular social worker's, ideas and prejudices about retardation. It is important that when passing judgment on the parent with mental retardation, the decisionmaker not require a standard of behavior higher than is expected of other parents.

The most legitimate fear about letting persons with retardation act as parents is that they may lack the cognitive ability required to protect a child from physical harm. Other concerns are that parents with retardation may have difficulty setting behavioral limits for their children; or that they may lack the attention span required to supervise a child; or that they will provide inadequate intellectual stimulation for their children at home. A related concern is that children born to parents with retardation will be harmed when, at an early age, they surpass the cognitive level of their parents and are forced to assume responsibilities that are generally thought to be inappropriate for children of their age. Alternatively, they may grow up undisciplined, lacking a "competent" authority figure in their home. Another issue sometimes mentioned questions the ability of mothers with retardation to love their children or nurture them emotionally. Finally, there is fear that children reared by individuals who have retardation will be stigmatized, just as our society has traditionally stigmatized their parents.[70]

Clearly, there are many imaginable harms that can befall children of parents who have retardation (and of other parents). Before the state takes steps to sever the parent-child relationship, however, it should ascertain whether the harms attributable to the parents are irremediable and of sufficient gravity to constitute grounds for termination of parenthood. Here too we are fortunate that the state's interest is not ultimately in opposition to that of parents who have retardation. The state's interest is in competent parenting; the interest of the individual with retardation is in parenting if and when he or she can do it competently. There are, of course, tensions between their positions. For example, the state, having less of an affirmative interest in allowing persons with retardation to parent, might be satisfied with measures of competence that eliminate some individuals with retardation who could parent. Or it may not provide services in ways that maximize the opportunity of persons with retardation to parent competently. But at least the ultimate objectives of the state and of the parents it labels "retarded" need not collide.

A fundamental issue is whether individuals with retardation are in fact capable of parenting. Studies of what is known about the actual capabilities and risks of persons with retardation as parents are described in Chapter 14, and more empirical studies are in order. It is important to study not only whether parenting is adequate but also which methods of teaching parenting skills work best.

Current research on the capabilities of parents with retardation is not conclusive, but at a minimum it demonstrates that *some* parents with retardation are capable of effective parenting. In fact, it suggests that many are.

A central problem is that no clear or widely accepted standard of adequate parenting exists. The legal system generally tests parental competence by evaluating an individual's ability to show love and affection, to perform housekeeping tasks, and to attend to a child's physical needs. When parents with mental retardation are involved, courts often consider a fourth factor as well: the parents' ability intellectually to stimulate the child.

Parents with retardation, like others, should be denied custody of their children if they are in fact unfit. Yet there are real risks that the state will underestimate the capabilities of parents who have mental retardation, or that it will not give them proper assistance in succeeding as parents. Part IV considers some policies that might better recognize and develop the capabilities of persons with retardation to parent. It also considers whether the state has a duty—legal or moral—to maximize those capabilities.

Our discussion so far has concerned parents who have mental retardation; the interests and problems discussed relate to men with retardation as much as to women. A man with retardation seeking sterilization, for example, could encounter the same difficulties that a woman with retardation faces in that situation. Or conceivably men might face forced vasectomies, a course that has not been followed in our society to the same extent as the forced sterilization of women.[71]

Men as parents can also come under scrutiny when a woman who has retardation and who lives with a man gives birth to a child. Obviously the character of the man with whom she lives can make an important difference in her ability to provide a satisfactory home. A competent and caring man can improve the prognosis for parenting a great deal; a cruel and abusive man can significantly diminish her chances for effective parenting. And when a woman lives with a man who has retardation, the acceptability of men with retardation as parents is as central an issue as the acceptability of women.

Most of the issues this book discusses, therefore, have obvious implications for men as well as women. But the vast majority of sterilization cases involve women, and a few of the reproductive problems considered, such as hysterectomy or abortion, relate solely to women. The cases involving parenting by persons with retardation also almost invariably involve women.[72] Therefore, this book speaks primarily in terms of reproduction and parenting by *women* with mental retardation.

CHAPTER 3

Who Are Called "Retarded"?

Statistical estimates derived from the U.S. Bureau of the Census, the President's Committee on Mental Retardation, the Arc (formerly the Association for Retarded Citizens in the United States), and other agencies serving people with disabilities suggest that between .67 and 3 percent of the total U.S. population has mental retardation. This percentage amounts to between 1.675 and 7.5 million people. Internationally, the World Health Organization (WHO) estimated in 1996 that approximately 31,361,000 persons, or .55 percent, of the world's population in 1995 had retardation, with the following breakdown in numbers by WHO region:

Africa:	3,627,000	Americas:	5,005,000
Eastern Mediterranean:	2,133,800	Europe:	4,849,600
South-East Asia:	7,837,500	Western Pacific:	8,811,000

Earlier estimates, however, were of considerably larger numbers.

It is difficult to have confidence in any particular number because means of measuring retardation differ.[1] Even in the United States, where widespread intelligence testing is employed, the results are uncertain: individuals from poor socioeconomic environments and those with English as a second language suspiciously often obtain IQ scores indicative of mild mental retardation; many of those persons do not actually have any mental handicap.[2]

Regardless of the precise numbers of persons who have it, mental retardation "knows no boundaries. It cuts across the lines of racial, ethnic, educational, social and economic background. It can occur in any family."[3] This fact is opportune for persons with retardation; many of their most effective advocates have become involved because they happened to have a child or sibling with retardation.[4]

Mental retardation is not a disease or a mental illness; nor is it caused by

23

mental illness. Mental retardation and mental illness are distinct phenomena; persons may have both conditions, but either can exist alone.[5] Frequently, people with mental illness—schizophrenia or depression, for example—are intellectually high-functioning but emotionally damaged or disordered. Conversely, persons with retardation are often emotionally "normal" but intellectually low-functioning.[6] Whereas the behavioral disorders associated with mental illness are often psychiatric in origin,[7] mental retardation is a developmental disorder "associated with difficulties in learning and social adaptation."[8]

Although mental illness and retardation are different, posing quite different problems and calling for different solutions, both law and society have sometimes regarded the two conditions fungibly.[9] One reason for the tendency to associate them is that both conditions are identified with the mind. Another is that both groups have been subjected to institutionalization; they have shared interests in a range of issues, such as controlling the quality of care at institutions, limiting involuntary placements there, and encouraging alternative living situations in the community.[10]

Causes of Mental Retardation

There is great variety in causes, as well as types and degrees, of mental retardation. Retardation is caused by conditions that impair the brain's development before birth, during birth, or in childhood years. When retardation occurs before birth, its causes may be genetic, environmental, or a combination of the two. Retardation occurring during or after birth, by contrast, is almost always environmental.[11] The distinction between genetic and nongenetic conditions is different from the distinction between inherited and environmentally caused distinctions; it is possible for a condition to be genetic but to be environmentally caused, as the following categorization of causes of retardation shows.

There are different ways to categorize the several hundred known causes of retardation; the Arc divides them into four categories:

1. Genetic conditions: These result from abnormality of genes inherited from parents, errors when genes combine, or from other disorders of the genes caused during pregnancy by infections, overexposure to x-rays and other factors. Inborn errors of metabolism which may produce mental retardation, such as PKU (phenylketonuria), fall in this cate-

gory. Chromosomal abnormalities have likewise been related to some forms of mental retardation, such as Down syndrome and fragile X syndrome.

2. Problems during pregnancy: Use of alcohol or drugs by the pregnant mother can cause mental retardation. Malnutrition, rubella, glandular disorders and diabetes, cytomegalovirus, and many other illnesses of the mother during pregnancy may result in a child being born with mental retardation. Physical malformations of the brain and HIV infection originating in prenatal life may also result in mental retardation.

3. Problems at birth: Although any birth condition of unusual stress may injure the infant's brain [such as oxygen deprivation], prematurity and low birth weight predict serious problems more often than any other conditions.

4. Problems after birth: Childhood diseases such as whooping cough, chicken pox, measles, and Hib disease which may lead to meningitis and encephalitis can damage the brain, as can accidents such as a blow to the head or near drowning. Substances such as lead and mercury can cause irreparable damage to the brain and nervous system. [In addition, children may] become mentally retarded because of malnutrition, disease-producing conditions, inadequate medical care and environmental health hazards. Also, children in disadvantaged areas may be deprived of many common cultural and day-to-day experiences provided to other youngsters. Research suggests that such understimulation can result in irreversible damage and can serve as a cause of mental retardation.[12]

There is overlap between the first and second causal categories of retardation listed above; some noninherited *genetic* disorders that cause retardation are attributable to problems during pregnancy. Overexposure to x-rays, for example, can affect the fetus's genes. Similarly, environmental toxins can alter cell development and cause brain damage. But the first and second categories (genetic conditions and problems during pregnancy) are nonetheless distinct from each other, because retardation caused by problems during pregnancy also includes wholly *non*genetic environmental causes—causes that harm the fetus without affecting its genetic makeup, such as fetal alcohol syndrome.[13] Moreover, categorizations differ. A well-known psychiatry textbook, for example, setting out and categorizing known causes, separates "hereditary" rather than "genetic" conditions from others.[14]

It is not surprising that there is a certain imprecision in the statistics about mental retardation and about potentially important issues, such as how much is genetic and to what extent an existing condition is likely to be passed on to the next generation. Not only is the terminology used in imprecise ways, but also in most cases the cause of mental retardation is not known. For children with severe mental retardation, the chance of making a specific causal diagnosis is only 50 percent, and the chance of discovering the origins of milder retardation is even lower. Only about 10 percent of children with mild retardation have specific causal diagnoses.[15] The current medical understanding is that the vast majority of the cases of mild mental retardation are associated with "sociocultural or psychosocial disadvantage" in a child's home environment.[16]

Table 3.1 lists the most common causes of mental retardation, differentiating between genetic and environmentally acquired conditions.

The three most common known causes of mental retardation are Down's syndrome, fetal alcohol syndrome, and the fragile X syndrome. Combined, they occur in three out of every thousand Americans. Fetal alcohol syndrome is nongenetic; it is inborn and results, at least in many cases, from the mother's alcohol consumption during pregnancy. Down's syndrome and the fragile X syndrome are genetic, but only the fragile X is fully inherited and heritable.

Down's syndrome and the fragile X syndrome both occur in chromosomes, which are components of genes. But Down's syndrome is usually a random chromosomal defect that occurs because of nongenetic variables, such as a relatively older mother. One effect of the condition is a low serum testosterone rate in males, commonly resulting in infertility.[17] It is very rare for a Down's syndrome male to father a child. Adult females with Down's syndrome, however, do not have the same fertility problem. They can procreate and have a 50 percent chance of having an offspring who is an (asymptomatic) carrier of Down's syndrome.[18] The rate of procreation by women who have Down's syndrome is not known, but virtually no cases of Down's syndrome are known to be inherited.[19]

After Down's syndrome, the fragile X syndrome is the most common genetic cause of mental retardation,[20] and it is the most common human chromosomal abnormality associated with heritable mental retardation.[21] The fragile X syndrome is caused by an incompletely formed X chromosome, which appears to have a "fragile site" where the chromosome looks unfinished.[22]

Table 3.1   Common causes of mental retardation

Genetic
   Chromosomal disorder (e.g., Down's syndrome)
   Inborn errors of metabolism (e.g., phenylketonuria, or PKU)
   Hereditary degenerative disorders (e.g., Tay-Sachs)
   Hormonal deficiencies
   Primary central nervous system disorders (e.g., microcephaly)
   Malformation syndromes
   Sporadic syndromes with unidentified etiology, possibly genetic

Environmental
   Prenatal
      Infection (e.g., syphilis, rubella, toxoplasmosis, cytomegalic inclusion
         disease)
      Fetal irradiation
      Toxins (e.g., fetal alcohol syndrome, lead poisoning, mercury poisoning)
      Maternal metabolic problems (e.g., maternal PKU)

   Perinatal
      Prematurity
      Asphyxia (e.g., abruptio placentai, cord prolapse, meconium aspiration)
      Infection (e.g., meningitis, encephalitis, TORCH [toxoplasmosis, rubella,
         cytomegalovirus, herpes])
      Trauma (e.g., breech delivery, intracerebral hemorrhage)
      Hypoglycemia
      Kernicterus

   Postnatal
      Brain injury (e.g., trauma, drowning, lightning)
      Poisoning (lead, carbon monoxide)
      Cerebrovascular accidents
      Postimmunization encephalopathy (e.g., pertussis, rabies)
      Infection (meningitis, encephalitis, abscess)
      Early severe malnutrition
      Hormonal deficiency
      Psychosocial deprivation, abuse, or neglect

Source: Adapted from Berini and Kahn (1987).

Many carriers who transmit the gene for fragile X are asymptomatic; about 20 percent of males who carry the fragile X chromosome are not clinically affected, as are up to 50 percent of female carriers. (One hypothesis is that because females have two X chromosomes, the normal one may balance the fragile one.) Moreover, the degree of mental impairment among carriers varies greatly, although there is a particularly high incidence of mental subnormality among female carriers who inherited the fragile X gene from their mothers.[23]

Not surprisingly, the incidence of the fragile X syndrome is greater in populations with retardation than in random populations. The prevalence of the fragile X gene among a control group obtained indiscriminately was between .4 in 1,000 to .9 in 1,000 for males and .2 in 1,000 to .6 in 1,000 for females.[24] Comparatively, screenings of an unselected series of children with an IQ of less than 50 indicated that 7.3 percent of males diagnosed with moderate to severe retardation were fragile X positive, as were 4.5 percent of the males who had mild retardation. But it is not clear that the frequency of cases of fragile X is a function of the severity of a population's mental retardation: although it is higher among males with severe retardation, the frequency of the syndrome is higher among females with milder retardation.[25]

Annually, more than 100,000 children are born with mental retardation in the United States. Down's syndrome and the fragile X syndrome account roughly for 15 and 10 percent of known genetic causes, respectively. Statistics on nongenetic causes that have been diagnosed break down into intrauterine influences, such as infections and fetal alcohol syndrome (10 percent); perinatal complications, such as intracranial hemorrhage or oxygen deprivation (10 percent); postnatal trauma, such as brain injury from falls or automobile accidents (6 percent); environmental toxins, such as lead (3 percent); postnatal infections, such as meningitis and encephalitis (3 percent); and congenital (existing at birth but not hereditary) anomalies, which include spinal and brain malformations such as spina bifida, hydrocephalus, and microcephaly (20 percent).[26]

Defining and Classifying Mental Retardation

The international, multidisciplinary association of professionals known since 1987 as the American Association on Mental Retardation (AAMR) has been defining mental retardation since 1876. After President John F. Kennedy put mental retardation on the national agenda as an issue of "medical and public concern," the organization (then called the American Association of Mental Deficiency, or AAMD) promulgated the first definition of mental retardation that was generally accepted by most disciplines. President Kennedy's initiative, inspired by his own family's experience with mental retardation, marked the beginning of a new "positive philosophical approach to understanding and managing mental retardation as a chronic handicapping disorder."[27]

The 1961 AAMD definition described mental retardation as "significantly subaverage general intellectual functioning which manifests itself during the developmental period and is characterized by inadequacy in adaptive behavior."[28] This definition of mental retardation has undergone numerous alterations. The most recent AAMR definition was promulgated in 1992:

> Mental retardation refers to substantial limitations in present functioning. It is characterized by significantly subaverage intellectual functioning, existing concurrently with related limitations in two or more of the following applicable adaptive skill areas: communication, self-care, home living, social skills, community use, self-direction, health and safety, functional academics, leisure, and work. Mental retardation manifests before [age] 18.[29]

Note that the AAMR definition uses three distinct criteria: (1) the person's intellectual functioning level (IQ) must be below 70–75;[30] (2) he or she must have significant limitations in two or more of the "adaptive skill areas" listed in the quotation above; and (3) the condition must manifest itself during the childhood years—before the subject is eighteen years old.[31] The AAMR also suggests a "system" for applying the definition, in the form of a three-step process: diagnosis, assessment of personal strengths and weaknesses, and identification of needed supports.

The 1992 definition, like that of 1961, relies on IQ tests and the individual's adaptive skills. A diagnosis of mental retardation will only occur if low IQ is accompanied by deficient adaptive functioning; in theory at least, neither is sufficient alone. The novelty of the 1992 definition, however, lies in its requirement of analysis of the support a person needs.[32] Assessments of needed supports are to be made in the person's typical living environment and are based on the individual's capacity to function in that environment. Accordingly, a person is not considered to have retardation even if he or she has an IQ below 70 unless there is also evidence of inadequacy in two or more adaptive skills that are required of the person in his or her particular living context. For example, a person with an IQ below 70 who is living in a simple rural environment such as a farm setting may be self-sufficient and able to cope in that living context. But the same person living in a more complex and demanding urban setting might not be able to be self-sufficient. Under this definition, the person would be considered to have mental retardation in the urban context but not in the rural one.

The current AAMR definition thus diminishes the historically determinative labeling effect of IQ test scores. It also reduces the number of people who will be labeled "retarded." Furthermore, as the AAMR has noted, the diagnostic concept of "mental retardation as constituting low IQ plus adaptive deficits . . . emphasizes that mental retardation is not an innate characteristic of an individual, but a changeable result of an interaction between personal intellectual capacities and the environment."[33]

The importance of relying on adaptive skills along with IQ numbers is critical. Approximately two-thirds of persons labeled mentally retarded "shed their diagnoses in adulthood as adaptive skills increase."[34] The medical profession recognizes that "generally adaptive behavior improves over the course of a lifetime . . . [and t]ypically, the global level of adaptive functioning changes over the course of months or years in response to living arrangements, work opportunities, and parental support."[35]

It is accepted today that any respectable definition of mental retardation must include both subaverage intellectual functioning and deficits in adaptive behavior, but in other respects there is no unanimity. Not all accept the AAMR's definition as the correct one; numerous other definitions of mental retardation, some promulgated earlier and some later, also have adherents. One of the most noticeable differences between the definitions still accepted today concerns when mental retardation must start. For example, the *Merck Manual,* a long-respected physicians' manual of medical diagnoses, states that retardation is "[s]ubaverage intellectual ability present from birth or early infancy, manifested by abnormal development and associated with difficulties in learning and social adaptation."[36] That definition excludes persons with extreme intellectual impairments that result from some trauma, fever, or virus experienced later than "early infancy," even though other definitions like the 1992 AAMR's (and perhaps even the 1961 AAMD definition) would consider such persons "retarded."

On one level, the issue is only one of nomenclature and word usage, but whether a person is labeled "retarded" can have important consequences to that individual. Moreover, the differences show that the term "retarded" does not carry one clear meaning, even in current usage. When persons who have acquired their impairment after the designated age (early infancy for Merck) are not deemed to have retardation, another term is often used to type them. The term "neurologically impaired," for example, is commonly used for at least some in this group. Indeed some special education programs differentiate between students they assess as having retardation and those they consider to have neurological impairments, creating different classrooms for the two groups. In part, the theory is that different teaching and learning techniques may be appropriate for students whose intellectual impairments have different causes and were acquired later in life.

Subcategories

The designers of the IQ tests defined levels of intelligence according to a person's IQ scores, and they also divided intelligence levels into subcategories. Modern examples of such subcategories are "mild," "moderate," "severe," and "profound." Table 3.2 compares the classifications devised by some of the testers.

Historically, the American Association of Mental Deficiency and the World Health Organization (WHO) have loosely adhered to the IQ score ranges set by the testers. Table 3.3 compares the AAMD (1977) and WHO (1980) classifications. The 1992 AAMR definition of mental retardation no longer uses these subclassifications. (It substitutes subclassifications based on "intensity and pattern of support services": intermittent, limited, extensive, or pervasive.)[37] But the old subclassifications are still employed widely in medical and social service literature, such as the American Psychiatric Association's diagnostic and service manual.[38] Moreover, even though the AAMD deleted the "borderline" category as early as 1983, and it is not used in the American Psychiatric Association manual, it continues to be employed by child care and mental health professionals. Descriptions of cases throughout this book will also show judges, lawyers, and laypersons using and misusing the labels.

Characteristics

The Arc describes the characteristics of persons who fall into the mild, the moderate, and the severe and profound categories as follows:

Table 3.2   Wechsler, Stanford-Binet, and Cattell IQ score classifications of intelligence

Wechsler		Stanford-Binet		Cattell	
IQ score	Definition	IQ score	Definition	IQ score	Definition
>130	very superior	140–170	very superior	≥ 122	markedly above average
120–129	superior	120–139	superior	112–122	appreciably above average
110–119	high average	110–119	high average	108–112	high average
90–109	average	90–110	average	92–108	average
80–89	low average	80–90	low average	88–92	low average
70–79	borderline	70–79	borderline defective	78–88	appreciably subaverage
55–69	mild retardation	30–70	mentally defective	50–78	markedly subaverage
40–54	moderate retardation				
25–39	severe retardation				
<24	profound retardation				

Source: Derived From Gottlieb and Williams (1987), 129.

Persons with mild mental retardation may be hard to identify, often being physically indistinguishable from the typical population. In school, they are capable of learning academic skills up to approximately a sixth grade level, and, as adults, they can usually acquire the vocational and social skills necessary for independent living. Of all persons with mental retardation, 89% are mildly retarded.

[For persons who have moderate retardation, a]chievement in academic subjects is significantly impaired, but [such] people . . . can learn self-care, social, and vocational skills. Their language is functional and they can achieve at least partial independence.

[Those who fall within the severe and profound categories are] capable,

Table 3.3 AAMD and WHO classifications of retardation based on IQ scores

Level of retardation	AAMD IQ range	WHO IQ range
Borderline	70–85	71–84
Mild	55–69	50–70
Moderate	40–54	35–69
Severe	25–39	20–34
Profound	<24	<20

Source: Derived from Grossman (1977); World Health Organization (1980).

with special instruction, of a significant degree of self-care and may do useful work in supported employment but will probably require supervision throughout life. Language may be limited, but the person understands more than he or she can express. Only 3.5% of all persons with mental retardation have severe or profound retardation.[39]

This description tells us two important things. First, there is an extreme range of capabilities among "persons who have mental retardation." "Higher functioning" persons with retardation are usually more like ordinary people than like persons who have very serious retardation. Second, the vast majority of persons with retardation have mild mental retardation—89 percent. The moderate category encompasses 7.5 percent, and severe and profound retardation together account for only 3.5 percent of persons with mental retardation.

This proportion might suggest that law's stance toward retardation focus on mild and moderate, but on its face at least the law usually does not distinguish by degree of retardation as much as by whether retardation can be said to exist at all. The law's attention to more serious retardation is understandable, because cases concerning persons with retardation disproportionately involve subjects with very serious problems. But persons with all categories of retardation are sometimes involved as well. What is more disturbing than the law's focus, or the number of cases devoted to one group or another, is that current rules often treat degrees of retardation together, as though differences become slight once the "retardation" label is attached.

Both the Arc categorization and other current studies demonstrate that most people with retardation are capable of achieving self-sufficiency.

Largely as a result of the normalization movement, 80 percent of persons with mild retardation currently hold some kind of job. Furthermore, a 1987 study reported that more than 80 percent of persons with mild retardation get married. Most commonly, their spouse was someone considered to have normal intelligence.[40]

It would be wrong to focus only on the mildest retardation, although it is most common by far. Even those at the other end of the retardation spectrum, who need continual assistance, share with the rest of society an interest in experiencing a full and productive life. And many persons with retardation, though it be mild or moderate, still need help—especially with advocacy to overcome societal and personal barriers to "achieving full citizenship and normal lives":

> They may need advocates to obtain appropriate education, work, social opportunities, and services. They may also need ongoing assistance with practical, everyday matters, such as money management. Many services are available; advocates can assist people with mental retardation in finding appropriate ones. Services include community-based residential facilities, financial assistance, health care, education, and vocational training.[41]

Diagnosing Mental Retardation

Even though elements other than IQ are increasingly part of approved definitions of mental retardation, still it is administering IQ tests that most frequently leads to the diagnosis. In some cases, of course, mental retardation is suspected or presumed from birth, for example when a child is born with Down's syndrome or is subjected to severe oxygen deprivation during birth. But most diagnoses of mental retardation occur later, in early childhood, when psychologists or school officials administer standardized psychological or IQ tests. They do so in preschool and elementary school "screenings" designed to identify children who have below average intellectual ability.[42]

The most commonly used IQ tests are the McCarthy Scales; the Baylay Scales of Infant Development; the Stanford-Binet Intelligence Scale revised for two- to eighteen-year-olds; the Cattell Infant Intelligence Scale; and the Wechsler Intelligence Scales for Adults and Children. The Baylay and McCarthy Scales assess gross motor skills (the ability to walk and sit down without abnormal delays in movement) and fine motor skills (involving among other things the ability to grasp, draw, and write); the McCarthy test also offers a "general cognitive index" that is roughly equivalent to IQ score and is based on testing numerous language and nonlanguage thinking tasks, as well as memory and motor tasks;[43] the Cattell is a version of the Stanford-Binet used for infants between two to thirty months of age; the Wechsler offers test variations for children of various age ranges, each containing numerous subtests of verbal and performance skills. The Wechsler Scales are the preferred psychological tests for children over four-and-one-half years of age because the tests' design, in response to earlier criticisms of the Stanford-Binet tests, allows examiners "to determine a series of IQs in different areas, thereby obtaining a more accurate picture of the child's strengths and weaknesses."[44]

One contemporary textbook on developmental pediatrics explains the rationale for continued standardized testing of children to detect developmental disability:

> Psychological assessment provides an opportunity for observing behavior in an objective, standardized manner. The child performs a series of standardized tasks, from which impressions are formulated on the nature of the child's abilities as well as disabilities. It is important to recognize that psychological tests per se reveal nothing in and of themselves . . . Psychological testing offers a much more expedient approach to acquiring needed information, as it is impractical, or impossible, to follow a child through daily activities for several weeks in order to formulate behavioral impressions. Systematic observations can be made and presented in a standardized manner. The performances are then compared with a normative group and patterns of assets and liabilities derived.[45]

While defending standardized tests as an expedient means of acquiring a sense of the child's strengths and weaknesses, the textbook also warns of the potential for misevaluations by standardized tests: "Tests are sensitive only when administered by a sensitive examiner." Indeed, "[i]nterpretation of the test results represents the crucial aspect in diagnosis," and interpretations of the same case may differ markedly between examiners.[46]

The second half of the diagnostic equation—measurement of the adaptive capacities of individuals with mental retardation—may be accomplished in a variety of ways, but here too standardized tests are used. One example is the Vineland Adaptive Behavior Scales for assessing social maturity and adaptive skills.[47] The Vineland Scales test measures the person's typical performance, rather than optimal ability, in "daily activities required for personal and social sufficiency."[48] It uses five behavioral domains: "communication, daily living skills, socialization, motor skills, and maladaptive behaviors."[49] Table 3.4 specifies the tested adaptive skills in the daily living domain.

As with IQ tests, single measurements of adaptive functioning are likely to oversimplify and undermeasure a person's abilities. It is "rare that a single observer sees a patient in all settings or at all times of the day. This complicates the assessment of adaptive behavior in both standardized and global clinical methods. Clinicians typically use data from multiple sources to draw a composite picture of [the person's] life functioning."[50]

Labels, Past and Present

When the practice of using numerical scores to classify persons began at the turn of the twentieth century, persons now called "retarded" or "developmentally delayed" were labeled "feeble-minded." In 1910, the Committee on Classification of Feeble-Mindedness of the AAMD created the subcategories "idiots," "imbeciles," and "morons." The AAMD defined "idiots" as persons considered to have a mental age of no higher than two years; "imbeciles," those with a mental age of seven or below; and "morons," those with a mental age of no more than twelve.[51] Even as scientific nomenclature, these words carried pejorative baggage that presaged their conversion to the playground insults of today.

Historically these labels both expressed and engendered public fear of persons with retardation. As one writer pointed out, "[t]he alarm with which Americans viewed the feeble-minded resulted in part from an unqualified acceptance of the psychological test as a measure of mental deficiency . . . The mental test became a significant weapon in the [social] caseworker's scientific arsenal."[52] Persons with retardation, so labeled, became pariahs; and with institutionalization, they were physically isolated from mainstream American society.

The labels used at the beginning of this century to classify persons considered "retarded" are relics of the past, but persons with retardation—and their advocates—object to three modes of description still commonly used by professionals: (1) IQ score; (2) level of retardation ("borderline," "mild," "moderate," "severe," or "profound"); and (3) mental age. (Note that all of these are different modes for expressing IQ score.) Their concern is that these modes of reference still foster pejorative, one-dimensional images of

Table 3.4 Vineland Adaptive Behavior Scales: Daily living skills domain, community subdomain

Safety skills
Demonstrates understanding that hot things are dangerous
Looks both ways before crossing street or road alone
Demonstrates understanding that it is unsafe to accept rides, food, or money from strangers
Obeys traffic lights and "Walk" and "Don't Walk" signs
Fastens seat belt in automobile independently

Telephone skills
Answers the telephone appropriately
Summons to the telephone the person receiving a call, or indicates that the person is not available
Uses emergency telephone number in emergency
Uses the telephone for all kinds of calling without assistance
Uses a pay telephone

Money skills
Demonstrates understanding of the function of money
States value of penny, nickel, dime, and quarter
Correctly counts change from a purchase costing more than a dollar
Saves for and has purchased one major recreational item
Earns spending money on a regular basis
Budgets for weekly expenses
Has checking account and uses it responsibly

Time and dates
Demonstrates understanding of the function of a clock, either standard or digital
States current day of the week when asked
States current date when asked
Tells time by five-minute segments

Left-right orientation
Identifies left and right on others

Restaurant skills
Orders own complete meal in restaurant

Job skills
Arrives at work on time
Notifies supervisor if arrival at work will be delayed
Notifies supervisor when absent because of illness
Obeys time limits for coffee breaks and lunch at work
Holds full-time job responsibility

Source: Hales, Yudofsky, and Talbott (1994), adapted from Sparrow, Balla, and Cicchetti (1984).

the person with retardation and thus convey limited understanding of the person's actual range of abilities. The loss to persons with retardation is not only one of dignity. Factual findings based on these shorthand assessments of "intelligence" can have injurious, long-term legal and social consequences for those facing court hearings to assess their legal competence to be their own guardian or to consent to a particular medical procedure or withhold consent.

The concept of mental age is particularly troubling, although it is sometimes reported as though it were a key piece of scientific data to guide decisionmakers. It encourages people to view the adult subject as a child, with the result of frequently making the subject sound more childlike and incapable than he or she is. What could be a more persuasive datum of a woman's unfitness to parent than to say that she has a mental age of only eight? How could an eight-year-old be a mother? Judges often use reasoning like this to support sterilization.

Moreover, mental age scores may be misleading for two reasons. First, a person's mental age number is not likely to increase over the course of his or her life, and may decrease. According to this criterion, an individual may become increasingly handicapped, even though for most people with developmental disabilities, the opposite is true: their adaptive skills and their ability to function will continue to increase over time; and they will continue to demonstrate an ability to learn, though at a slower rate than others.

Mental age is misleading in another way as well: the numbers run low. An average mental age for the general population is sixteen (still not the chronological age one would pick for motherhood!). A mental age of twelve would denote very mild retardation.[53] Frequently misused by decisionmakers, the concept thus is in itself misleading and stacks the deck against the person whose intellectual maturity is being evaluated.

One commentator has explained the lack of correlation between mental age and ability to parent:

An intelligence test may conclude that a woman has intellectual abilities normally associated with a four- or five-year-old. Courts cannot justifiably conclude just from that evidence that she would not be able to look after her child. Certainly four-year-olds do not bear, or, hopefully, have charge of babies. But that is not the point. The court would clearly be in error if it concluded from such a test that the woman had the same physical strength, courage, dexterity or experience as a four-year-old. The intelligence test neither measures these attributes nor the ability to look after babies. It is quite possible that a person with such limited intellectual abilities would be incapable of looking after a child properly. But that needs to be tested by behavioral means rather than to be an inappropriate inference from a test that measures something else.[54]

In addition to the untested attributes listed above, one might add emotional maturity. Surely emotional immaturity is one reason society would not welcome parenting by a four- or eight-year-old, and emotional maturity may be equally or more important than intellectual maturity. Mental age and IQ test scores speak to academic, not emotional, capabilities. Of course a person with a low IQ may be emotionally immature as well, but so may be persons with highly elevated IQ numbers.

"Academic age" might be a preferable term to "mental age"—and "academic retardation" is more precise and accurate than "mental retardation." Whatever one calls it, IQ number (like all other factors that have been examined to predict parenting) does not correlate well with parenting ability. There may be some (weak) correlation between IQ and parenting ability, just as there may be some (weak) correlation between whether a person has finished the fourth grade and his or her parenting ability. Indeed, eliminating parents on the basis of academic achievement might be more defensible than eliminating them because of IQ scores, which are defensible primarily as predictors of academic achievement. Yet no lawmaker has tried to make academic achievement a precondition of parenting. There are many factors that statistically may flag concern for responsible parenting,[55] but none correlates well enough to be determinative of individual parents' relationship with their child.

Most developers of IQ tests never intended the consequences that now flow from them, although the originators did have the foresight to fear an ominous impact on the people whom the tests labeled.

A History of Intelligence Testing

Rightly or wrongly, test numbers carry a lot of weight. Yet a historical survey shows that test results can be arbitrary. The tests have changed over the centuries, but that fact has not.

During the nineteenth and early twentieth centuries, scientists believed that human intelligence was "a single, measurable entity."[56] Early theorists posited a correlation between the size of a person's skull and his or her level of intelligence.[57] The "science of craniometry" thus developed. One result was that apparent differences between the cranial shapes and sizes of persons considered to be of different races led scientists to conclude that "human races were separate biological species" with different levels of innate intelligence.[58] Numerous races were said to exist, though the three principal race classifications were Negroid, Mongoloid, and Caucasian. Caucasian scientists concurred with one another that members of the Negroid and Mongoloid races were inferior to Caucasians.[59]

Theories about the causes and diagnosis of mental retardation developed alongside theories about measuring human intelligence. During the nineteenth century, John Langdon Down, the medical superintendent of the Asylum for Idiots at Earlswood, England, who later owned a private home for young persons with mental retardation, proposed an ethnic classification of mental retardation, encompassing the Caucasian variety, the Ethiopian variety, the Malay variety, the Aztec variety, and the Mongolian variety.[60] His point was not to disparage any particular race.[61] Instead, he wanted to demonstrate that mental retardation "existed before birth and was universal in character, thereby averting parental guilt or avoiding the blaming of others for the child's condition."[62] Most of Down's classifications were rejected by physicians, but "Mongolism" was adopted as a label for the form of mental retardation now known as Down's syndrome (or, alternatively, Down syndrome).[63]

In 1877 William Wetherspoon Ireland, medical superintendent of the Scottish National Institution of Imbecile Children, published the first comprehensive text on mental retardation.[64] He concluded, as had theorists before him,[65] that there were two levels of intellectual functioning in persons with mental retardation: "idiocy" and "imbecility."[66] One of his predecessors, Jean Etienne Dominique Esquirol, had diagnosed these two levels on the basis of the subject's speech and language abilities.[67] Much of Ireland's work attempted to link different types of retardation with different physical considerations and causes, either hereditary or environmental. A more lasting contribution was his suggestion that a "more perfect system of classification would involve different items of intellectual performance based on a comparison with normal persons at different age levels."[68]

A number of nineteenth-century scientists gave their attention to the assessment of "human functioning, both physical and psychological,"[69] but in 1905 the first successful psychological or intelligence test was created. Its designers were two Frenchmen, psychologist Alfred Binet and physician

Theodore Simon, his student. Together they designed the Binet-Simon intelligence test, which compared a child's mental level with his or her chronological age. Their test marked a break from subjective classification of mental retardation and became the basis for other psychological examinations that were designed to provide IQ scores. Their approach of comparing intellectual performance with "normal" persons at different age levels followed the course Ireland had suggested years before.

Earlier in his career, Binet had accepted the theory of craniometry as "incontestable."[70] He became skeptical about its soundness, however, after conducting his own study of the relationship between head size and intelligence:

> The measures . . . ended with the discouraging conclusion that there was often not a millimeter of difference between the cephalic measures of intelligent and less intelligent students. The idea of measuring intelligence by measuring heads seemed ridiculous . . . I was on the point of abandoning this work, and I didn't want to publish a single line of it.[71]

Between 1905 and 1911, Binet and Simon further developed their alternative method for objectifying and measuring human intelligence, which became the Binet-Simon IQ tests.[72] Their test was a psychological, not physical, method of measuring intelligence. Its principal aim was to test the ability to reason.[73]

The Binet-Simon IQ tests had been commissioned by the French Ministry of Public Education "to predict accurately those children who would fail in school" so as to place them in specialized schools.[74] This goal was consistent with the historical perception that persons with below average intelligence "could be rendered more capable."[75] The tests, administered individually by "trained examiners," presented children with perceptual questions and practical tasks; they were not designed to measure learned skills, such as reading, writing, or other aspects of "rote learning."[76] The line between practical and learned skills is, however, imprecise. One task involved counting coins, which could of course be characterized as "rote learning" as much as a practical skill.

Other typical tasks require the child to make analogies, such as "speedometer is to a car as thermometer is to a (rose, sun, turnip, or airplane)."[77] One question even had the child assess which face was "prettier" than the others, with the different choices presented suggesting different racial attributes. These and other tasks "supposedly involv[ed] such basic processes of reasoning as 'direction (ordering), comprehension, invention and censure (correction).'"[78] Perhaps the prettiness question was supposed to measure judgment, but the "right" answer to this question demonstrated clear cultural and racial bias, and the question was a favorite target of those alleging bias in the tests. Most so obviously culturally and racially slanted questions have since been removed, but many more subtle ones persist.[79]

Binet and Simon believed that the array of "short tasks" they had devised "related to everyday problems of life,"[80] and that a child's ability to reason could be measured by the child's response to the tasks. They assigned to each task a mental age that denoted "the youngest age at which a child of normal intelligence should be able to complete the task successfully." They then associated with the child the mental age of the last successfully completed task and "hoped that by mixing together enough tests of different abilities [they] would be able to abstract a child's general potential with a single score."[81]

Originally Binet and Simon *subtracted* the child's mental age from his or her chronological age to calculate general intellectual level. In 1912, however, the German psychologist Wilhelm Stern proposed instead that a person's score on the Binet-Simon test be calculated by *dividing* mental age by chronological age. It is this score that came to be known as the intelligence quotient, although the means of calculating it is different today.[82] Neither Binet nor Simon presumed that the tests provided exact measures of a child's intelligence, recognizing that the phenomenon of human intelligence was too varied and complex for any test score "to capture with a single number."[83] They simply viewed their tests as "rough, empirical" guides of a child's present intellectual ability.

Most interesting, perhaps, Binet and Simon disclaimed that the empirical validity of their intelligence tests depended on the kinds of tasks used to measure intelligence. Rather, they believed that it arose from the quantity of tasks posed. As Binet remarked, "One might almost say, 'It matters very little what the tests are so long as they are numerous.'"[84]

Binet and Simon "declined to define and speculate upon the meaning of the score . . . assigned to each child"[85] because they understood the tendency of people, as expressed by John Stuart Mill, "to believe that whatever received a name must be an entity or being, having an independent existence of its own."[86] Because they were averse to any potential use of their tests to limit a child's intellectual possibilities or sense of personal worth, they attached no labels to the ranges of test scores. Nevertheless, they were concerned that the test scores themselves would become labels if schoolmasters used the scores to "[get] rid of all the children who trouble [them]" because they were either "unruly or disinterested in school."[87] They therefore took pains to emphasize that "children with defective comprehension are legion" and that helping "retarded" children to realize their full potential by "interven[ing] actively and usefully" is important for all of society, because "[t]he child who loses the taste for work in class strongly risks being unable to acquire it after he leaves school."[88]

Binet and Simon also worried that the scores might be misperceived by the child and the teachers as a fixed prediction of the child's future abilities and inabilities and that the scores might become self-fulfilling prophesies.[89]

> Our purpose is to be able to measure the intellectual capacity of a child who is brought to us in order to know whether he is normal or retarded. We should therefore study his condition at the time and that only. We have nothing to do either with his past history or with his future; . . . we do not attempt to establish or prepare a prognosis, and we leave unanswered the question of whether this retardation is curable, or even improvable. We shall limit ourselves to ascertaining the truth in regard to his present mental state.[90]

Their fears materialized. As H. H. Goddard popularized the Binet-Simon IQ tests in the United States during the early 1900s, the tests became the tools of the eugenics movement. It was Goddard who attached terms like "idiot," "imbecile," "moron," and "dull normal" to the ranges of deficient scores and thus "indelibly labeled" the adults and children who fell within those ranges.[91] He spearheaded a campaign of mental testing at ports of immigration[92] and throughout the general U.S. population:

> With Goddard's encouragement, psychologists and others applied the tests outside of institutions for the feeble-minded, in schools, prisons, and almshouses. It was distressing to find, according to the tests, that many children considered slow learners were really morons, and that many dependents, delinquents, and criminals were mentally retarded . . . The climax of the rage for mental testing occurred during World War I when statistics demonstrated that 47.3 percent of white men drafted were "feeble-minded."[93]

The intelligence test, as used in the United States, had become a negative instrument of social control. It had been transformed from a tool for identifying children with disabilities in order to educate them properly into an instrument for labeling—and disabling—countless "normal" children and for disparaging the underclasses.

Moreover, the test was used in support of other campaigns, such as the campaign against prostitution: "Social workers and social minded physicians . . . soon realized the implications of mental defect for casework. [One prominent physician] suggested that 'probably many of the prostitute class are feeble-minded and should, therefore, be taken out of the community and put under permanent custodial care.'"[94] Testing was also used to "weed out" certain "abnormal" persons—children and adults—who were increasingly feared. Social myth translated their "mental defect" into an innate moral defect as well, one whose pathology was manifested by sexual promiscuity and criminal behavior. Social workers called for detection and segregation of "defectives" and declared that "[t]he community had to comprehend the danger involved in leaving a child with 'no moral sense' in the midst of normal children."[95]

Armed with the IQ test, social workers engaged in a concerted "drive to expose and repress the feeble-minded . . . For [that group] alone, psychiatrists and social workers reserved a pessimistic, biological determinism."[96]

Evolving Definitions of IQ

The 1912 change in the means of calculating IQ (from subtraction of mental age from chronological age to division of mental age by chronological age) was not the last. The technical definition of IQ that Binet and Simon used after 1912, a ratio of tested "mental age" (MA) to "chronological age" (CA), was usually expressed as a quotient multiplied by 100: $IQ = MA/CA \times 100$. The mental age number was derived from test performance as described above, and the chronological age factor was the actual age of the person being tested. For example, a seventeen-year-old person whose IQ test score is comparable to that of the average seven-year-old will be deemed to have the mental age of a seven-year-old and an IQ of 41 ($7/17 \times 100 = 41$).

That definition attests to Binet and Simon's use of young children as test subjects, for the formula works only for children, and especially for young children. A moment's reflection reveals obvious defects in a chronological age-based comparison when applied to adult populations, where intellectual growth is both slower and more uniform. For example, it is more sensible to say that an eight-year-old with an IQ of 50 has a mental age of four than it is to say that a forty-year-old with an IQ of 50 has a mental age of twenty. As the denominator of Binet's formula is merely the patient's age, and intellectual growth flattens, the application of a chronological age-based comparison to an older population would yield misleading results.

An alternative test was thus proposed for adult intellectual assessment. The Wechsler test is not a chronological-age-based comparison, but rather a compendium of absolute raw scores on various subtests, which are eventually converted to a scaled score with a common mean and standard deviations.[97] The standard deviations mark the proximity between any test result and the test's mean score.[98] These standards are computed by means of a statistical model, in which the results of tested individuals are defined in terms of their position within a somewhat bell-shaped curve. The test results dubbed "normal" are those that fall within a predetermined percentage of the population.[99]

It is recognized that statistical parameters like standard deviation draw arbitrary lines in defining both mental retardation and its degree of severity.[100] Of course, as a statistical device, the distribution itself makes no value judgments; there is no inherent importance in falling two, three, or four standard deviations above or below the mean. As a community attaches labels to results above or below a certain number of standard deviations from the mean, however, the position of one's results takes on the freight of social significance. Just as an arbitrary number of standard deviations from a mean height eventually results in the description "dwarf," so does a number of standard deviations eventually result in the description "retarded."[101]

Today IQ is generally defined in terms of standard deviation, and that approach describes most tests currently used. Figure 3.1 illustrates the theoret-

Figure 3.1 The theoretically normal distribution of the Stanford-Binet IQ (from Baroff 1986)

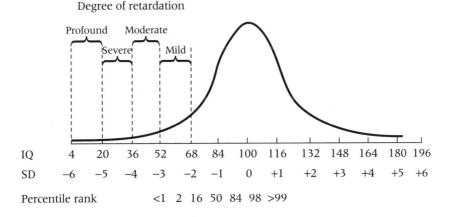

Degree of retardation												
IQ	4	20	36	52	68	84	100	116	132	148	164	180	196
SD	−6	−5	−4	−3	−2	−1	0	+1	+2	+3	+4	+5	+6
Percentile rank				<1	2	16	50	84	98	>99			

ically symmetrical distribution of the Stanford-Binet IQ test, with a score of 100 considered to be the mean. In reality, however, "the actual bell curve is skewed by a raised tail to the left, representing neuromedical disorders and socioenvironmental barriers."[102] As is characteristic of results based on standard deviations and a bell curve, IQ test results are particularly arbitrary for persons clearly in the subnormal or above normal ranges. The system was not designed to find Einsteins or to distinguish between IQs of 12 and 20, and it does not make those measurements with any accuracy.

IQ Testing Today

Testing is still defended primarily as an efficient means of detecting children who will have trouble in academic settings, and there is some utility in testing early, because early education is a proven effective means of ameliorating deficits. Of course, the positive effect that this testing can have for children helped by specialized early education can be achieved only if such education is actually provided. Even then, positive effects on those children must be balanced against negative effects that testing can have, both on those misdiagnosed and on those correctly diagnosed as having retardation. Despite potential legitimate uses, the same two problems that plagued intelligence testing in the past persist today: IQ tests mislabel people to their detriment; and even when apparently accurate, IQ test scores are taken to reflect more than the limited factors they measure.

IQ tests can be criticized as an inadequate means of defining and measuring intelligence partly because of the inherent arbitrariness that is apparent in the definitions and scoring of the tests. In addition, the tests contain inherent socioeconomic and cultural biases, including biases based on race. Children from middle-class families tend to test significantly higher on average than children of low-income families. Moreover, due to a child's different cultural exposure, IQ test scores may not accurately reflect a child's native intelligence if he or she does not relate to or understand the fundamental cultural premises of some of the questions. Although cultural bias has long been obvious, it is not repaired in most tests still commonly used. Questions such as "Why is it good to put money in the bank?" and "Why is it generally better to give money to an organized charity than to a street beggar?" with their preferred responses plainly reflect the cultural norms of some social classes rather than others.[103]

Nor do the Wechsler adult assessments escape these biases. With vocabulary subtests that ask the meaning of such words as *vesper, catacomb, traduce, casuistry,* and *chattel* and an information subtest that asks who discovered the South Pole, the Wechsler knowledge-based answers also are susceptible to unfairness across social classes.[104]

If answers to such questions are taken as a measure of a person's native intelligence, and a poor score is the result of a lack of exposure to a particular culture, the resulting mislabel can handicap a child throughout life. A problem as serious as misdiagnosis, however, is the assumption that IQ is a measure of native intelligence. That problem is independent of cultural and other biases, although it often interacts with them. IQ tests were designed to predict how well a person will do in academic settings, and that is what they predict well. A poor score that may result from differing cultural backgrounds may in fact reflect the child's inability to do well in school, if schools embody the same biases as the tests do. But a student may also adapt, given exposure to a new environment.

In any event, the types of intelligence tested by IQ tests are very limited indeed. In attempting to combat that and to obtain a more complete picture of the child, some tests have added more categories of testing. The effort is to avoid misdiagnoses and to benefit all test subjects by exposing areas of strength and weakness. The concept is not a new one; efforts have been made over the years to move in that direction. In 1986, for example, the Stanford-Binet Scale that was used to test children over the age of two was changed in response to criticism that it yielded "a single mental age rather than providing a profile [of the child's] strengths and weaknesses." The shortcoming was to be remedied "by using fifteen tests to assess four areas of intelligence: verbal abilities, abstract/visual thinking, quantitative reasoning, and short-term memory." The changes aimed at permitting "the evaluator to determine, using some caution, areas of relative strengths and weaknesses." Similarly, the 1989 versions of the Wechsler Preschool and Primary Scale of Intelligence for children between three and seven years of age and the Wechsler Scale for Children (over six) contain numerous subtests of verbal and performance skills, "allowing the examiner to determine a series of I.Q.s in different areas, thereby obtaining a more accurate picture of a child's strengths and weaknesses." One result has been that children with retardation occasionally score within the normal range in one or more performance areas.[105]

Even with such improvements in testing, however, substantial mislabeling exists. As well as causing injustice to affected individuals, mislabeling both reflects and reinforces racial and class biases. The 1996 amendment to the federal Individuals with Disabilities Education Act (IDEA) concluded:

   i. Greater efforts are needed to prevent the intensification of problems connected with mislabeling and high dropout rates among minority children with disabilities.
  ii. More minority children continue to be served in special education than would be expected from the percentage of minority students in the general school population.
 iii. Poor African-American children are 3.5 times more likely to be identified by their teacher as mentally retarded than their white counterparts.
  iv. Although African-Americans represent 12 percent of elementary and secondary enrollments, they constitute 28 percent of total enrollments in special education.[106]

Current medical literature warns physicians and psychologists examining children for signs of mental retardation that "[i]ntelligence tests are subject to error and should be questioned when they do not support clinical findings. Illness, language barriers, or cultural differences may hamper a youngster's test performance."[107] Furthermore, "deficits in language and personal-social skills may be caused by emotional problems, environmental deprivation, learning disorders, or sensory defects without" any mental retardation.[108] Although this advice is now available, it is not consistently followed.

It is difficult to imagine the pro-establishment biases in the IQ tests themselves being fixed. Few would argue that there are not political questions lurking in decisions that must be made about how much of which kind of question to include—questions that self-evidently favor persons of one gender over another, for one example, such as questions about sewing and about tools, both of which appear on a typical test. Perhaps the bias would be mitigated by allowing persons of different cultures full representation in decisionmaking circles—a change that predictably will be long in coming.

Undoubtedly, some children who are typed by the current system would function better and develop more fully if they were not labeled so early in their lives. But while the problem is easy to detect, it is more difficult to cure, and our history has shown that the cure may be as harmful as the disease.[109] In the United States, the ever-present issue of cultural and social bias in intelligence testing has been linked with another phenomenon: the shift of emphasis in IQ tests away from practical, everyday skills to more academic and abstract ones. This movement from everyday living skills to greater abstraction began early; the Binet of 1937 was already much more academic in his orientation than he was prior to World War I, when he focused on everyday living skills.

It is partly a concern with social bias that is responsible for the shift from practical to more and more abstract IQ testing. The problem is that asking children practical problems ("What would you do if . . .?") necessarily favors children with one kind of experience rather than another. In trying to get away from questions which by their fact-specific context are easier for some social or cultural groups than others, the examiners have moved to questions that have little to do with anyone's life—that is, abstract questions and puzzles with right or wrong answers. Indeed the very point is to give questions that *no one* would have encountered in life (except of course in IQ prep courses, which some parents use today to produce a superior IQ test score in their children). Although less biased, these more abstract questions present different problems, such as concerns about the utility of a score that measures only intelligence at that level of abstraction.

The biggest problem for both correctly and incorrectly labeled children is that the state and society still give weight to the labels and to the IQ scores associated with them in many settings, including settings in which they are not relevant. After all, if the purpose of the test is to predict academic performance, it should have no relevance when the subject has completed school.[110] But instead, IQ numbers are often used to define a person generally throughout his or her life—especially if the person's number falls within the subnormal range. The mystique that has attached to the shorthand label of the IQ number, although it is based on ignorance of what the test actually represents, has meant that a low test number can itself become a permanent handicap.

Part of the mystique of IQ number may result from the name, but as Christopher Jencks has explained, IQ itself is a misnomer:

> whether we should call [the IQ test] an intelligence test is a political question . . . My own preference would be to abandon the term [intelligence], since IQ tests seem to me to define intelligence far more narrowly than adult society does. But whatever we call the test, we need to recognize that it has no magical significance. IQ scores provide essentially the same information as a battery of conventional achievement tests covering vocabulary, reading comprehension, arithmetic reasoning, and general information.[111]

Similarly, the term "mental age" is misleading, suggesting perhaps that the evaluation concerns everything that goes on in the mind. "Academic age," or, as today's tests would have it, "abstract reasoning age," would be more accurate, if it is necessary to state results in terms of age at all.[112] The IQ could then become the ARQ, or "Abstract Reasoning Quotient." The labels affect the way society thinks about the tests and about retardation. But with or without relabeling, society should be made to recognize the gross overuse of the test results as a measure of persons, including in settings to which they lack relevance.

In recent years physicians and psychologists have reaffirmed Binet's and Simon's conviction that intelligence is not a "single, innate entity."[113] Within the last decade, a growing number of physicians and psychologists are internalizing the arbitrariness of the statistical demarcation between "the retarded" and "the nonretarded" and are attempting to return IQ testing to its original purposes of diagnosing mental retardation and identifying "areas of deficit" that can be helped with appropriate special education.[114]

It is also now increasingly recognized that it is not possible clearly to draw lines between "the retarded" and "the nonretarded" based on IQ scores or any other standard for measuring human intelligence. Not only is IQ a political question, but the definition of intelligence is itself up for grabs. Similarly psychiatrist Stanley Greenspan says that IQ tests' "measure of intelligence has 'not been terribly good . . . Many areas of intelligent activity are not represented' . . . Traditional tests of 'intelligence quotient,' or IQ, date back to the turn of the century. They equate high intelligence with 'the ability to do well at manipulating words, numbers or shapes.'"[115]

Greenspan is joined by psychiatrist Daniel Goleman and Yale psychology professor Robert Sternberg in espousing a new definition of intelligence. Goleman's 1995 book, *Emotional Intelligence: Why It Can Matter More Than I.Q.*, stressed that emotional intelligence is as important, if not more so, than the limited kinds of intelligence measured on IQ tests. Emotional intelligence includes the ability to rein in emotional impulses, to read another's innermost feelings, to handle relationships smoothly, and to motivate oneself.[116] It was Sternberg's own experience with intelligence tests that fueled his resolve to challenge the definitions of intelligence that most IQ tests value.[117] As a child, Sternberg says he "blew the IQ tests [he] had to take." As a result, his elementary school labeled him a "dum-dum." Now the author of forty books, Sternberg seeks "to broaden what it means to be smart." Like his colleagues in the field, he warns that "childhood reading and IQ tests measure only a small part of the intellect and don't predict success in later life."[118]

A survey of experts in the field of intelligence testing conducted in the

Table 3.5 Survey of test experts on importance of types of intelligence

Type of intelligence	% who consider it "important"	% who consider it "not adequately measured"
Abstract thinking or reasoning	99.3	19.9
Problem-solving ability	97.7	27.3
Capacity to acquire knowledge	96.0	42.2
Memory	80.5	12.7
Adaptation to one's environment	77.2	75.3
Mental speed	71.7	12.8
Linguistic competence	71.0	14.0
General knowledge	62.4	10.7
Creativity	59.6	88.3
Sensory acuity	24.4	57.7
Goal-directedness	24.0	64.1
Achievement motivation	18.9	71.7

Source: Compiled from Snyderman and Rothman (1986), 79–97.

mid-1980s compiled data about the types of intelligence considered to be "important" and the extent to which these forms of intelligence were inadequately measured by the most commonly used intelligence tests (see Table 3.5).[119] Among the forms of intelligence that many thought important but inadequately tested were capacity to acquire knowledge, adaptation to one's environment, and creativity. Other factors deemed inadequately tested but less important to "intelligence" were sensory acuity, goal-directedness, and achievement motivation.

Among the kinds of intelligence not measured in IQ tests that Sternberg and others seek to promote are emotional, practical, creative, and moral. Howard Gardiner's *Frames of Mind: The Theory of Multiple Intelligence* is credited with bringing "new definitions of intelligence" to public attention. Celebrating the tenth-anniversary edition of the book, published in 1993, Gardiner listed variable types of intelligence: "linguistic, used in reading and writing; logical-mathematical, used in logical reasoning; spatial, used in reading a map; musical, used in singing songs or playing an instrument;

bodily kinesthetic, used in dancing and sports; interpersonal, used in relating to others; intrapersonal, used in understanding ourselves."[120] Some of these kinds of intelligence (the first three) are likely to be lower than average in a person labeled "retarded." The other forms listed may or may not be lower. Even more noteworthy, a person's IQ reveals little about how well he or she can cope. A subnormal score may suggest that a person would not make a winning chess or bridge partner and is unlikely to be particularly adept at crossword puzzles; but it says little about understanding human emotions or the ability to wash dishes, hold down a job, keep an orderly house, dance the Macarena, or be a loving friend or mother.

PART **II**

Procreation

Although parenting by persons with retardation and policies concerning procreation by them are often discussed as two separate and unrelated topics, it should not be difficult to see the connections between them. Protecting a person's choice to procreate carries a very different meaning in a society that removes her children at birth than in a society that allows her to parent and even assists her efforts to do so. Similarly, a society that protects the ability of persons with retardation to parent once they have given birth, but forces sterilization, abortion, and contraception upon them whenever it can, is not truly favorable to parenting by persons who have retardation, although such a society may be reconciling conflicting policies in the way it deems most appropriate.

Part II surveys and evaluates existing practices concerning sterilization, contraception, and abortion and the particular ways they have been applied to persons diagnosed as retarded. It also considers the role of guardianship in decisions of a "ward." Part III then proposes changing the legal rules.

CHAPTER 4

Procreative Choice—But Whose?

LaVista Earline Romero now has mental disabilities, but until she was thirty-three years old she was considered a "normal" mother of two children. She then suffered from acute diabetes, acquired brain damage, and was left with an IQ of 74.[1] At that point, her children were removed from her custody, and Ms. Romero was confined to a nursing home, declared legally incompetent, and placed under the guardianship of her mother.[2] Nevertheless, Ms. Romero hoped that before her childbearing years were over she would be able to live independently and have the opportunity to conceive and bear another child. When she was thirty-seven, however, her legal capacity to make her own procreative choices was challenged when her mother-guardian petitioned the district court of Delta County, Colorado, to have Ms. Romero sterilized.[3]

Ms. Romero did not want to be sterilized, but her mother-guardian, three physicians, and a social worker on the staff of her nursing home told the court that she was incapable of either granting or withholding consent to sterilization "knowingly." They also said that it was in her best interests to be sterilized, even though it was against her wishes. The mother-guardian asked the court to allow her to make the sterilization decision for her daughter.

Before deciding whether to grant or deny the petition for sterilization, the court considered whether Ms. Romero had the legal capacity to decide for herself, even though she was under guardianship. If she could decide, the court would deny the petition. But if the court found that she could not decide for herself, it would rule on whether sterilization was in her best interests and, if so, it would issue an order permitting the mother-guardian to consent to sterilization.

A dramatic moment in the trial came after the court had heard all of the expert testimony about Ms. Romero's medical and mental condition. Ms.

Romero was in the courtroom during this testimony. When it was over, the judge placed her on the witness stand and questioned her to determine whether she had the legal capacity to decide for herself:

Q. Do you understand if you got pregnant that it might be risky for your health?

A. No.

Q. Because you've got diabetes it might make it unsafe for you to be pregnant?

A. It didn't hurt me the first time. I mean the second time is what I should say.

Q. Even if there was a risk would you want to get pregnant and have another baby?

A. Not at the nursing home, no.

Q. What about if you are out of the nursing home? What if you were married to Dean? [the man with whom Romero was in love]

A. Yes, I would want a baby then.

Q. Even though it would be risky for you?

A. Yes.

Q. And the doctors have been telling me here today in the hearing that that would be very dangerous for you to do. In fact, it could be threatening to your health, or even to your life. Did you hear that testimony?

A. Yes.

Q. Does that make you feel maybe you should be more cautious or maybe you shouldn't have a baby because of what they have said?

A. No.

Q. Why is that?

A. Because I want one bad enough.

Q. Realizing that it could even kill you?

A. Yes, sir.[4]

Ms. Romero clearly stated that she did not want to be sterilized, but the judge, believing that her wishes were irrational and wrong, followed the medical experts and granted the petition for sterilization. He did this even though Ms. Romero's guardian *ad litem* (a court-appointed guardian to assist an "incompetent" in litigation)[5] joined her in opposing the procedure. The court took the decision upon itself because Ms. Romero lacked "the capacity to understand the risks involved in pregnancy."[6]

A more plausible interpretation is that Ms. Romero did understand the risks of pregnancy but was willing to assume them. The Supreme Court of

Colorado so found when it reversed the sterilization order.[7] Ms. Romero was entitled to value the possibility of having another child more than her own life and to act on that priority. It was only because the trial judge had a different set of values that the judge decided that Ms. Romero lacked legal power to decide for herself. He thought it necessary to protect her from exposing herself to the risks of pregnancy, partly because he could not understand risking one's life to create a child.

Before considering any kind of decisionmaking by third parties (such as parents or guardians), courts and physicians must usually make fundamental decisions about whether a person is herself capable of making the particular procreative choice. Legal and medical practice vary depending on the procreative choice involved; sterilization, abortion, and contraception will not necessarily be treated in the same manner. Even more markedly, application of the rules varies with each individual decisionmaker.

Decisions about capacity to consent are often subjective in nature and are affected by the values and biases of the person making the decision. It is not unusual for judges simply to dismiss a woman's reproductive autonomy as illusory.[8] In addition they frequently do not understand that her bodily integrity may have importance to her even apart from any likelihood of having children. Their attitude is reminiscent of Holmes's in Buck v. Bell when he referred to coerced sterilizations as "these lesser sacrifices, often not felt to be such by those concerned."[9] Moreover, LaVista Earline Romero's case illustrates vividly another problem: pronouncements about a person's mental capacity to consent often confuse the concept of mental ability to consent with a different inquiry—whether the person's proposed procreative choice appears "rational" or "right." Both judges and doctors tend to require persons who have mental retardation to make "rational" and "right" decisions about family matters if their decision is to control. Other persons are permitted to make a much broader range of decisions.

The case of LaVista Earline Romero demonstrates these points and raises a question whether the law should require that the wishes of the patient with mental retardation be respected when those wishes are known. In that case, the Colorado Supreme Court ultimately held that the patient's wishes should be respected; but not all courts would agree with the result.

Different Legal Approaches

Under established constitutional law, competent adults—virtually all persons over eighteen who are not called "retarded"—have a constitutional right to make their own procreative choices. The constitutional right to privacy, derived from the Due Process clause of the U.S. Constitution and developed by the U.S. Supreme Court, does not dictate any particular decision (concerning marriage, contraception, abortion, and so on) but instead makes the individual her or his own decisionmaker. It prevents the state from imposing unnecessary regulation on subjects like having children. Instead of emphasizing that the individual patient is the appropriate decisonmaker, as the U.S. Supreme Court has done, it could have allowed governments to require or favor particular outcomes. For example, government might decide as a matter of law to encourage persons to have children, or it might instead adopt rules cutting off or regulating their reproductive capacity. Possible examples are state statutes prohibiting abortion, sterilization, vasectomy, even life-threatening medical procedures, unless both husband and wife consent. Such a result, not possible under current interpretations of the U.S. Constitution, at least with respect to abortion[10] (and presumably by analogy to other subjects as well), would promote particular results (weighting the scales in favor of childbirth and against life-threatening procedures) rather than promoting an individual's choice above all other goals.

Rules for persons with retardation might or might not follow the same pattern as rules for other persons. In the context of mental retardation, one possible legislative course is to set out special rules governing procreation for persons it considers incompetent. Instead of focusing on who will decide, it could provide, for example, that particular procedures like sterilization or hysterectomy, when they are nontherapeutic, will not be available to persons unable (legally or in actuality) to consent for themselves. In effect, the state legislature would become the decisionmaker and would decide by category (persons unable to consent for themselves) rather than anyone weighing the merits of sterilization in each particular case. It may be the absence of any decisionmaker able to make such an individualized inquiry that presents the strongest case against such an outcome-oriented, rather than decisionmaker-oriented, approach.

For whatever reason and despite other possibilities, the preoccupation with determining who is the appropriate private decisionmaker in the constitutional law of reproductive rights has carried over to issues concerning reproduction for people with mental retardation. The most perplexing question is whether a woman who has mental retardation should make her own procreative choices or whether some other person's decision should substitute for hers. If there is to be a substitute, who should that be and what should be the standard for decisionmaking?

If a person is not legally competent, an obvious substitute decisionmaker is her parent or guardian. Persons who are not legally competent include adults who have been ruled incompetent in a legal proceeding, as well as minors.[11] If there has been a legal proceeding adjudicating her incompetent, a guardian will usually have been appointed.

If an adult with retardation has no legal guardian, or if she has a "limited guardian" whose authority does not cover questions concerning procreative rights,[12] parents might be looked to as substitute decisionmakers. Other family members, or conceivably friends standing *in loco parentis,* are also possibilities. Caretakers at institutions or community residences for persons with retardation might also be consulted. Another approach would reserve decisionmaking power to the judiciary, advised by any of the possible decisionmakers above or perhaps instead by a team of experts or a disinterested guardian *ad litem.* Most jurisdictions in fact allow some combination of these persons to make decisions concerning at least some procreative choices for people with retardation.

Discrimination against Persons Who Have Retardation

Both judges and physicians, when called upon to evaluate a particular woman's capacity to consent, if they consider her "retarded" tend merely to repeat impersonal textbook descriptions about the inabilities of persons with retardation. In practice, they also often hold persons with retardation to higher standards of legal capacity than are required for other persons.

Often the evaluations give the impression that the decisionmakers never considered the subject as a real or whole person capable of feeling, understanding, or doing anything "normal." Such an approach to persons with retardation has long been standard, in the legal as well as the medical community. Judges, like physicians, are accustomed to seeing persons with retardation as different and as appropriately conceived of as "other." Accordingly, they subject them to different rules.

Of course, there are occasions when mental capacity can make a difference and when the same opportunities and treatment cannot be afforded to persons without the mental capability to handle them. But it is critical to start with a presumption of the sameness—and the full humanity—of the person with retardation, rather than with presumptions of difference and of incapacity.

The Patient as the Appropriate Decisionmaker

In keeping with the principle that persons with retardation should be treated more like other persons, the preferable decisionmaker concerning issues of procreative choice is not some third person but the woman herself. Procreation is not an area where decisions are made according to some "right" answer, arrived at through sophisticated intellectual processes. Moreover, childbirth decisions reached on bases other than rational ones often prove as satisfactory as those that have been more intellectually weighed. There is no reason why the "right" answer should be required just for the person with retardation, especially when such an answer would have to be devised by third persons whose interests are potentially in conflict with her own. Individuals with retardation should be allowed and encouraged to take responsibility for consenting to procreation or to measures designed to interfere with procreation, just as other people are. It discriminates against them for some third person to have legal authority to foist the "right" answer upon them.

This approach would alter the law in every U.S. jurisdiction. Most states recognize (at least in theory) that retardation need not preclude consent in this and other areas of decisionmaking. But in the context of medical, including reproductive, decisionmaking, application of "informed consent" requirements preclude persons who have retardation from making many of their own choices.

Informed consent doctrines require physicians to ascertain that a patient, before consenting to a medical procedure, has been informed and understands what will be done, including the risks and benefits of the procedure and the alternative courses of action. A physician who fails to comply may be guilty of malpractice and liable for that or for a violation of the duty to obtain informed consent, depending on the particular state's law.

In addition, if a physician touches a patient without obtaining her consent,[13] a state could charge the physician with the crime of battery, or a patient could sue for damages, because battery is also an intentional tort. The meaning of "consent" under the laws of battery is less strict than under informed consent doctrines. The same imparting of information and understanding is not required. Nonetheless consent will not be a successful defense to battery if the physician has obtained it through coercion, fraud, or deceit, or if the patient lacks the legal capacity to consent.

The problem for persons with retardation who want to make their own decisions is that physicians often are unable to ascertain whether such patients are legally competent to consent. Moreover, the physician may have a very low estimation of the would-be patient's degree of understanding of the medical procedure, let alone her comprehension of the risks, benefits, and alternatives, as required by informed consent doctrines. Cautious physicians may thus presume legal incapacity when a patient has mental retardation rather than risking the specter of legal sanctions that might follow acceptance of her consent to a procedure.

The suggested approach would expand the situations in which it is the consent of the person called retarded that is relevant, even if that person does not have the capacity to give the informed consent that law currently requires. Physicians would still have to convey relevant information to the patient and do so in a manner designed to maximize the patient's understanding and participation in the decision. But the physician would not be required to certify to the patient's full understanding as a precondition to providing a medical service. In other words, physicians would be encouraged to respect the procreative decisions of their patients, despite any mental retardation, without requiring consent from third-party decision-makers—guardians, parents, institutional caretakers, or courts.

Benefits and Costs of Protective Measures

The most difficult issue is whether to adopt measures to protect persons with retardation from undue influence by others. Physicians, for instance, can easily influence a patient's decision out of their own motives or because of perspectives the person with retardation might not share. Certainly it is not difficult to imagine situations where protection seems warranted. Betty R., for example, is a twenty-eight-year-old woman with retardation classified as mild. She lives with her husband, who is visually impaired and considered to have low-normal intelligence. Betty was very pleased when she learned she was pregnant, but when she visited her physician he persuaded her that it would not be safe for her to have the child and that she should undergo abortion, which the physician scheduled for the next day. The physician did not make clear to her whether it was her safety or the child's that was his concern, but his position was cloaked in the language of medical judgment. Accordingly, Betty consented to the operation.

In fact, further discussion with the physician, by other members of Betty's family, revealed that the physician, like many other persons, just did not think it was a good idea for persons with retardation to be parents; he was skeptical that Betty and her husband (whom he had never met) could do an adequate job. In this case, the abortion was not performed, because Betty consulted that evening with her husband and other friends who were supportive of her desire to parent and who inquired further about the doctor's diagnosis. But the outcome could easily have been different; recognizing Betty's ability to consent could have resulted in a procedure she did not at all desire.

In other cases, however, protective legislation can be restrictive and harmful to persons intended as its beneficiaries. The women's movement fought hard and successfully to get rid of protective legislation, such as laws limiting women's but not men's hours of work or working conditions, recognizing that such laws ultimately did not redound to the benefit of women.[14] The way in which the same phenomenon occurs for persons with disabilities is illustrated by the story of LaVista Earline Romero. It also is illustrated by Norma Jean W.

Norma Jean is a twenty-six-year-old woman who has Down's syndrome and who is sexually active. She is "high-functioning" compared to many persons who have Down's syndrome, having completed the eighth grade in school, and she lives in a home with two other young women and a caretaker-companion who is available to help them with any problems that arise but who otherwise encourages them to live as independent and competent young women. Norma Jean's parents pay for her apartment and a third of her caretaker's salary; otherwise she lives on her own earnings. She works in the kitchen of a fast-food restaurant.

Norma Jean is proud of her reading ability, her "normal" life style, and her independence. She hates being identified as or called "retarded," but despite her successful assimilation that does sometimes occur, usually because it is apparent from her physical features that she has Down's syndrome. Accordingly her visit to the clinic to obtain birth control pills was an extremely humiliating and painful experience.

When Norma Jean and her boyfriend decided that she should procure birth control pills, she made an appointment at a clinic for her day off. When she had her physical and told the physician that she wanted the pills, however, he asked her if she had a guardian. Norma Jean assured him that she did not and that she took charge of her own affairs. The physician then asked her how he could get in touch with her parents. "But I'm twenty-six years old!" she cried. "I'm sorry," said the physician, "but you're retarded. I risk liability if I prescribe medicine to persons who are obviously incompetent."

This physician's attitude is not atypical. Indeed, it is almost inevitable if the legal system causes physicians to fear liability when they act at the behest of a person who might be considered incompetent. The standard is an inherently amorphous one: How much understanding is sufficient? The law gives physicians initial responsibility for determining whether that standard is met. If the physician believes that the patient does not have the mental capacity to understand enough to satisfy the informed consent rules, then current law requires the prudent and self-protective physician to refuse to administer the treatment. Note that the physician may so act, perhaps must so act, despite the absence of any guardian or incompetency adjudication.

Physicians may vary the degree of mental competency or understanding they require according to whether they agree with the need for the proposed procedure and also according to how drastic the procedure appears. Even physicians who would not have second-guessed Norma Jean's request for birth control might have called for the consent of a guardian or parent before they would be willing to perform an elective abortion or sterilization.

So when *should* third-party consent be required? On the one hand, without it there is the specter of overzealous physicians (or parents or social workers) persuading women with retardation to submit to procedures like sterilization or abortion—or even insertion of an intrauterine contraceptive device (IUD)—when the patient does not really desire or even understand the procedure. Surely that is a situation worth protecting against. One possible strategy when a patient who seems incompetent comes alone to ask for a procedure would be to inform a family member or guardian of the proposed procedure and encourage that person to consult with the patient.[15]

On the other hand, the existence of a different procedure to be followed if the patient is considered "retarded" requires that every patient be labeled—as either competent and able to make her own choices, or retarded and requiring consultation with a parent or guardian. This sorting out means that persons like Norma Jean, who should be encouraged in their desire to function "like everyone else," will be labeled and considered incapable of acting alone even though they are actually and legally capable of making their own reproductive decisions. Unfortunately, there does not seem to be any way of sorting persons into those who need a special procedure and those who do not *without* this kind of disparagement of some persons' decisionmaking ability. Such disparagement not only serves to dampen the self-image of persons like Norma Jean; it can also chase from the health care system those who care deeply about not being treated disrespectfully.

Resolving the Problem

There is no apparent way both to respect decisions of persons who, though "retarded," are competent to decide, without subjecting them to a special procedure because of their retardation, and also to protect persons whose retardation makes them particularly vulnerable to abuse. Perhaps either goal could reasonably be chosen over the other, but this book opts in favor of permitting persons with retardation to decide these questions for themselves. It opts against any special procedures being invoked because the decisionmaker is deemed to have mental retardation. This choice fits in with the book's general theme that persons with retardation should be treated more like other persons and should usually not be subjected to special inquiries and procedures.

This book takes this position even while recognizing that persons deemed retarded who are exercising "their own" choices will often have been heavily influenced by their helpers[16] or others. Nonetheless, as long as the decision represents the choice of the patient, insofar as that choice is discernible, the patient's choice should be recognized as legally valid.

There are some variables, however. In some respects (although fewer than might be supposed) the rules vary according to whether the individual with retardation is legally competent (meaning whether she is her own guardian). Moreover, current rules differ according to whether the method of procreative control under consideration is sterilization, contraception, or abortion.

Finally, with respect to all reproductive issues, there is a class of persons (although a small one) who literally cannot make choices for themselves because they cannot communicate. This group will be called "nonexpressive persons," a category limited to people who simply cannot convey a preference. It includes some persons with retardation as well as others who cannot communicate (such as newborns, or persons who are comatose). For those persons' reproductive choices, there has to be either a substitute decision-maker or a state rule that dictates what outcome will prevail.

This proposed course of treating persons with retardation like others by extending to them the legal authority to make their own decisions is defended and developed in Part III. First, we must further explore the impact of existing practices.

CHAPTER 5

Evolution of Policies
toward Sterilization

Sterilization is the one subject related to procreation and parenting in which there are clearly articulated positions and policies.[1] Moreover, those positions have been debated extensively, and the dominant thinking has changed considerably over time.

The history of sterilization is inextricably linked to the history and practices of institutions for persons with retardation. Institutionalization of persons considered "feebleminded" began in Europe and the United States toward the end of the eighteenth century. The first institutions (called Public Residential Facilities) were a response, in part, to the rise of humanism, and their purpose was to habilitate and train. The first residential facility exclusively for persons with mental retardation, Abendberg, was built in 1841 in Berne, Switzerland, and covered forty acres. It consisted of a large central structure with an assembly hall, playrooms, bathing facilities, and classrooms. Training and rehabilitative programs stressed a range of sensory motor training methods and gymnastic techniques. Clients had daily exposure to pure mountain air, the beauty of nature, a simple diet, massage, and warm baths. This treatment in the spirit of neo-romanticism was intended to "awaken the souls" of the "unfortunate" children.[2] In 1848 Samuel Howe visited Abendberg and returned to the United States to lobby for funds to train children with retardation in Massachusetts, New York, and Pennsylvania.

Training schools established in the United States during the 1840s and 1850s were modeled on the Abendberg ideal. By 1900, however, the original humanistic intent behind institutionalization was being lost, as growing pressure from parents, professionals, and the public to prevent reentry into the mainstream of society altered the institutions' purpose from rehabilitation of persons with retardation to segregation of them.[3] The high point of the craze for institutions spanned the years from 1950 to 1970. More institutions were built, refurbished, and expanded in those two decades than during any other time in U.S. history. The population who lived in institutions increased from 116,888 to 193,188 between 1946 and 1967, a 65 percent increase, nearly twice the rate of increase for the population at large. The increase in the number of institutions was accompanied by a decrease in levels of care, and conditions were deplorable. Federal money was available for building institutions but not to pay for operating expenses, staff, or maintenance.[4] This situation persisted on a broad scale until the early 1970s, when deinstitutionalization and movement into the community began to take hold.

During the first half of the twentieth century, a majority of states had an active and explicit policy of sterilizing people diagnosed as retarded. The advent of the eugenics movement and the development of relatively simple surgical techniques for sterilization gave impetus to compulsory sterilization in the late nineteenth century.[5] While much of the eugenics movement was directed toward "positive eugenics," which sought to propagate qualities deemed desirable for human beings, it is "negative eugenics" that supported sterilization of "the feebleminded."[6] According to this theory, conditions such as mental retardation, mental illness, epilepsy, and criminality, as well as other social defects, were inherited. As such they could and should be bred out of the gene pool in order to ensure the progress of the human species.[7] Walter Fernald described a key rationale in 1912: "Feebleminded women are almost invariably immoral and, if at large, usually give birth to children who are as defective as themselves."

In 1897 Michigan introduced the first compulsory sterilization legislation, but the bill was defeated.[8] In 1905 the Pennsylvania legislature passed "an Act for the Prevention of Idiocy," but it was vetoed by the governor.[9] The first compulsory sterilization law to take effect was enacted in 1907 in Indiana. That statute remained in effect for fourteen years before it was held unconstitutional.[10] Other jurisdictions enacted similar statutes during the same period, and some of them as well were held unconstitutional.[11]

Nonetheless, after 1907 a large number of compulsory sterilizations were performed in this country, especially in California.[12] By 1925 state courts had held four state sterilization statutes unconstitutional, but two had withstood constitutional attack.[13] Two years later the Supreme Court of the United States entered the arena with its landmark decision in Buck v. Bell, affirming the Virginia Supreme Court's decision to uphold Virginia's compulsory sterilization law.

The Buck v. Bell decision both legitimated and gave impetus to the sterilization movement. In a famous opinion written by Justice Oliver Wendell Holmes, the Supreme Court upheld the constitutionality of a Virginia statute that provided for the sterilization of persons with mental handicaps who had conditions thought to be inherited. Justice Holmes determined that sterilization of "the feebleminded" was a valid exercise of the state's police power "to prevent our being swamped with incompetence."[14]

In fact, it appears that the woman forcibly sterilized in that case did not have retardation.[15] Like many persons placed in institutions for "the feebleminded" at that time, she was an unwed mother.[16] But her pregnancy did not even show she was "promiscuous," a characteristic then frequently associated with retardation; it was the result of rape. Moreover, Carrie Buck had been raped by a relative of the same woman who had her committed to the state institution. These facts were not developed in her case, because her lawyer was apparently acting in collusion with the defenders of the sterilization law, who wished to use the case as a "friendly lawsuit" to encourage the movement toward eugenic sterilization.[17]

The creators of Buck v. Bell accomplished their aim of promoting forced sterilization. During the decade after that decision, twenty states passed compulsory sterilization statutes that resembled the Virginia law.[18] A total of thirty-one states and the Commonwealth of Puerto Rico enacted sterilization statutes.[19] Even Margaret Sanger, the liberal advocate of women's rights and leader of the birth control movement in the United States,[20] argued that "morons, mental defectives, epileptics, illiterates, paupers, unemployables, criminals, prostitutes, and dope fiends" ought either to undergo surgical sterilization or to live a segregated existence in labor camps.[21] Over seventy thousand persons were sterilized without their consent in this country.[22]

Many in our society feel great shame about the era of forced sterilization of persons with retardation. But even those agreeing that eugenic sterilization was immoral disagree sharply concerning the appropriate policy with which to replace it.

Procedural Protections

The initial response of persons wishing to protect against unwarranted sterilizations took the form of solely procedural protections. The first compulsory sterilization laws were often successfully challenged as violations of procedural Due Process, because they permitted guardians or superintendents at state institutions to obtain sterilization of patients without hearings and without judicial approval. (The statutes were also sometimes held to violate Equal Protection when they applied to persons within institutions and not to all those with similar disabilities remaining in society at large.)[23]

States soon learned how to comply with required procedural protections while maintaining an active sterilization program. The Virginia statute challenged in Buck v. Bell, for example, met the minimal requirements of procedural Due Process. The institution's sterilization board had to give the patient and her guardian notice of the petition for sterilization and provide a quasi-judicial hearing at the institution. If the person to be sterilized did not have a guardian, the superintendent of the institution would apply to the county court for appointment of a guardian *ad litem*.

The statute required the board to permit the patient and her guardian to attend the hearing, if they wished. Moreover, the board was to put in writing its evidentiary findings, along with its order. The patient, guardian, or superintendent could appeal the board's order, first to the county court and then to the state's Supreme Court of Appeals.[24]

More recent procedural protections are more developed and sophisticated. For example, the Washington Supreme Court has set out the procedures it would require for granting sterilization petitions: the petition must be reviewed in an official court proceeding; the patient must be represented by a disinterested guardian *ad litem*; to the greatest extent possible the court must receive independent and comprehensive medical, psychological, and social evaluations of the patient; and, finally, the court must elicit and take into account the patient's views about being sterilized.[25]

In some other states, the legislature has spelled out required procedures in statutes. Most current statutes governing sterilization require that notice be given to the subject of the petition and that he or she be given an opportunity to testify, cross-examine witnesses, and appeal the court's order.[26] They also require the appointment of a guardian *ad litem* and sometimes legal counsel. Most require expert evaluations by disinterested medical professionals as well. These evaluations are an essential part of the initial competency determination that most statutes require. If a patient is found to be legally capable of consenting, the inquiry should promptly end, as a few statutes explicitly require.[27]

The Need for Substantive Reforms

Even if there are to be procedural protections—as is the norm today in the United States—the question remains whether the choice of sterilization should be taken from persons with mental retardation. Who is to make the decision, and what is the standard to be?

Buck v. Bell held that procedural norms must be followed but showed no respect for any substantive right to resist sterilization on the part of persons considered feebleminded. The Virginia statute upheld in that case allowed superintendents of state institutions to petition a special board to order the sterilization of their patients when it was deemed to be in the "best interest of the patients and of society."[28] Under that substantive standard, the public interest in sterilizing persons who were "the probable parent of socially inadequate offspring" was determinative, unless sterilization threatened the patient's "general health."

Any interest the patient might have in retaining her ability to have children was not taken into account or even recognized. Justice Holmes's famous words make clear that society's interest was the focus and, further, that the jurisprudence was not characterized by compassion for the patient:

> We have seen more than once that the public welfare may call upon the best citizens for their lives. It would be strange if it could not call upon those who already sap the strength of the State for these lesser sacrifices, often not felt to be such by those concerned, in order to prevent our being swamped with incompetence. It is better for all the world, if instead of waiting to execute degenerate offspring for crime, or to let them starve for their imbecility, society can prevent those who are manifestly unfit from continuing their kind. The principle that sustains compulsory vaccination is broad enough to cover cutting the Fallopian tubes . . . Three generations of imbeciles are enough.[29]

This notorious pronouncement—delivered by the U.S. Supreme Court in a feigned case—makes Buck v. Bell, to persons with retardation, the equivalent of the *Dred Scott* decision to African Americans.[30]

During the civil rights movement of the 1960s, social reformers championed reproductive rights of persons with disabilities and advocated repeal of compulsory eugenic sterilization laws. Numerous state legislatures did in fact repeal these statutes. Some left in their wake a statutory void, while others enacted reformed laws.

Some of the "reformed" statutes still allow sterilization without the patient's consent, but only in carefully limited circumstances. Many follow the approach that the Supreme Court of Washington adopted in 1980, allowing courts to exercise *parens patriae* authority over petitions to sterilize persons who are unable to consent to the procedure themselves[31] but requiring "clear and convincing evidence" both that the patient is incapable of consent and that the sterilization is in her best interests.[32] In addition, the statutes establish a host of substantive requirements or variables to be taken into consideration, for example that all less drastic means of contraception have proven unworkable[33] and that the person to be sterilized would likely be incapable of caring for a child.[34] Some state legislatures thus endorsed limited nonconsensual sterilization, but other states' statutes have forbidden nonconsensual sterilization altogether. Both the California and the Colorado legislatures attempted such prohibitions, as we shall see in the next chapter, although both states have moved away from that position today.[35]

In those jurisdictions where old statutes were repealed and not replaced by new legislation, or in states that had never legislated concerning forced sterilization, the void in statutory law was sometimes filled by judicial decision. But other times it was not filled at all, as courts ruled that they should not intervene absent legislative guidance. Many states still have neither statutory nor case law answering fundamental questions about whether sterilization is available.[36]

When courts did take on the policymaking role, they, like legislators, differed concerning whether nonconsensual sterilization should ever be allowed. The Washington and New Jersey Supreme Courts[37] were among those ruling that sterilization should be available to people who have retardation under the strictly limited circumstances that the courts spelled out. Other courts, by contrast, have said that, particularly in view of this country's shameful history of sterilizing those called "retarded," courts should never allow sterilization absent explicit authorization by the legislature.[38]

Judicial Decisionmaking in a Legislative Void

Courts also disagreed about whether judges had power to sanction nonconsensual sterilization in the absence of legislative guidance. States might not have any law about coerced sterilization, either because prior legislation had been repealed and not replaced or because they had never had any statutory law on the subject. In those states, judges were sometimes asked to endorse sterilization of a particular person deemed incapable of consenting. Without legislative guidance, many judges were reluctant to grant petitions to sterilize persons alleged to be retarded, even petitions filed by parents or guardians rather than the state.

Some judges went so far as to say that they lacked jurisdiction, or judicial power, to approve sterilization petitions absent explicit legislative authorization. A prominent, rather legalistic battle has been waged in many state courts about whether judges have power to support sterilization without a legislative mandate to do so. Much discussion in a good many cases is devoted to this somewhat technical issue. This section sets out the main themes in this debate.

Many judges and advocates for persons with retardation consider it inappropriate for third-party decisionmakers (courts or others) to apply their own best interests standards instead of standards created by a legislature. The issue was raised in 1988 in Iowa, when the parent-guardians of Helen Matejski, a thirty-three-year-old woman with mental retardation, petitioned an Iowa court for permission to have her sterilized. In Guardianship of Matejski, Helen's court-appointed counsel succeeded in persuading the trial court to dismiss the petition for lack of subject matter jurisdiction, because Iowa had no statute governing the sterilization of incompetent persons.[39] The Supreme Court of Iowa reversed, holding that the court should have assumed *parens patriae* jurisdiction over the petition.

An argument sometimes used against judicial allowance of sterilization is that legislative silence on the question reflects a legislative judgment that no nonconsensual sterilization should be tolerated. This argument may be most forceful in jurisdictions that repealed preexisting sterilization statutes on the basis of a disagreement with their philosophy. Arguments from legislative silence are suspect, however: in many contexts, it could be argued equally plausibly that the reason the legislature did not enact any regulations is that it did not want any restrictions to apply. Moreover, a legislature may be uncertain of the appropriate rules to govern a particular subject. It may think that the rules will be better developed by courts, on a case-by-case basis. Or the subject may simply not have commanded the legislature's attention. At any rate, if the legislature affirmatively did not want any forced sterilization to exist, it could have enacted a statute forbidding it instead of simply remaining silent. Indeed, that is what the California and Colorado legislatures once did.[40]

A different argument against courts' taking over sterilization decisions is that the absence of legislation means the absence of standards to guide judicial decisionmaking. But standards could be developed by judges instead. If the deciding courts early set out rules about who could be sterilized without personal consent, under what procedures, and in what circumstances, then decisionmaking would not be ad hoc and could be governed by the judge-made law. Such judicially formulated law is familiar in the Anglo-American legal system and is accepted as legitimate. Court decisions involving mental retardation that set out standards as precise as one would expect to find in legislation include Guardianship of Hayes (decided by the Washington Supreme Court); *In re* Grady (decided by the New Jersey Supreme Court); and *In re* Moe (decided by the Massachusetts Supreme Judicial Court).

The surprising feature of the *Matejski* decision is that the Supreme Court of Iowa, while holding that courts *can* decide on sterilization despite a legislative void, refused to create any standards to guide lower courts' judgments. Both parties had proposed that if the court assumed jurisdiction it should "outline a series of procedural protections and substantive criteria to guide the lower courts in adjudicating these applications."[41] The court's failure to establish procedural and substantive rules effectively left it to the discretion of lower courts in Iowa to develop their own standards for granting sterilization petitions.

Thus lack of standards became intertwined with the arguments against judges acting in the absence of legislation. The dissenter in *Matejski*, Justice Harris, spoke forcefully of the need for courts to stay out of these controversies. He stressed particularly the standardless posture in which the decision left sterilization questions, even though sterilization is of potentially great importance to the parties involved. "We should not," the dissent suggested, "claim authority in an area which should be and has long been within the exclusive province of the legislature":[42]

> Reproductive rights for retarded persons make up a subject which is, to put it mildly, shot through with searching social and ethical questions which are as controversial as they are complex. In taking this first wide leap the majority commits itself to the eventual resolution of a twisted conglomeration of attendant social and ethical issues. Future litigants, faced with unanswered questions of great social and ethical dimensions, or with missing ingredients of a vague application process, will continue to press us for determinations which we are singularly unfit to reach.[43]

The dissent went on to describe the substantive and procedural conundrums created by the majority's open-ended ruling:

> [At] what level of mental retardation can sterilization be compelled? Will other mental abnormalities subject a person to sterilization? Will any other afflictions? Will a decision to compel sterilization be a matter of the probate

court's discretion? What board or body, if any, will suggest statewide standards? Can any branch of district court, other than probate, entertain applications? If so, does that change our scope of review on appeal? Will an attorney be required to represent the person to be sterilized? Who will pay attorney fees and by what authority? Who will pay other court costs? To whom will the sterilization order be directed? What voice does the person being sterilized have in selection of a physician? How will the court order be structured as to the manner of the sterilization, time, and place? If there is resistance how will the order be enforced?[44]

The dissenters in the Supreme Court of Washington, which had decided similar issues in Guardianship of Hayes, agreed with Justice Harris in *Matejski,* saying judges should not act in the absence of legislative authorization. In this case (discussed in detail in the next chapter) a mother petitioned to sterilize her sixteen-year-old daughter. The Washington Supreme Court majority denied the petition, but it held that courts *could* exercise jurisdiction over sterilization petitions by parents or guardians, even though no statute addressed the matter. The *Hayes* dissenters objected not only that standards were needed, but also that the legislature, rather than judges, must provide these standards. They stressed that the issues raise fundamental questions of public policy: "what personal rights should be protected from society; to what extent should they be protected; and in what manner."[45] Because the answers to those questions strike "so near the underpinnings of the right to privacy" and may result in "the permanent and irreversible loss of a fundamental personal right," according to the dissenters, they ought to be provided by the legislature, instead of the judiciary:[46] "Not only because the courts lack inherent power to order such invasions of human privacy, but because the undertaking is of such grave consequence and error so irreversible, wise courts have acknowledged that only the people's representatives can rightly determine whether and under what circumstances such measures are desirable and necessary."[47]

So, the argument goes, only after state legislatures resolve these policy questions should courts assume the limited role of determining "whether the declaration and implementation of that policy has been accomplished in a constitutional manner."[48] This must necessarily be the case, according to Justice Harris in *Matejski,* because "[o]nly fragments of a social problem are seen through the narrow windows of a litigation" and should not be consigned to "individual trial judges for *ad hoc* determinations."[49] Many judges support this position on court-ordered sterilization, although theirs is a minority view.

Ambivalence toward Eugenics

Today, the underlying theory of negative eugenics is considered invalid;[50] medical science has discredited the strong causal link between hereditary genetics and mental retardation that eugenicists had posited as the central justification for compulsory sterilization. It is known that most forms of even genetic mental retardation are not passed from parent to child but result from gene changes caused while the fetus is developing. Any many important causes of retardation have no genetic link, such as fetal alcohol syndrome, oxygen deprivation, head trauma, and fevers from childhood diseases.

As a consequence of changing views about heretability, medical research has also come to challenge "the ancient notion of untreatability" of mental retardation.[51] Public and medical interest in mental retardation is often viewed as "unfashionable in an age oriented toward productivity and efficiency," but nonetheless advances have taken place in our understanding of its causes and consequences.[52]

Even though there are links between some hereditary conditions (like the fragile X syndrome) and mental retardation, offspring of persons with mental retardation are usually born with the capacity for normal intellectual development. Moreover, the vast majority of children with retardation are not born to parents who have it; they are born to parents "of normal intelligence."[53]

In addition to the debate about whether mental retardation is hereditary, a distinct debate has raged over time about whether "intelligence" is inherited. Central to the debate is the distinction between characteristics *associated* with family and those *inherited* from family. A widely used textbook on human genetics explains,

> The highest correlation between parents and offspring for any social traits in the United States are those for political party and religious sect. But they are not heritable. The distinction between familiality and heredity is not always so obvious. The Public Health Commission that originally studied the vitamin-deficiency disease pellagra in the southern United States came to the conclusion that it was genetic because it ran in families!

To determine whether a trait is heritable in human populations, we must use adoption studies to avoid the usual environmental similarity between biological relatives. The ideal experimental subject is the case of identical twins raised apart, because they are genetically identical but environmentally different. Such adoption studies must be so contrived that there is no correlation between the social environment of the adopting family and that of the biological family. These requirements are exceedingly difficult to meet, so that in practice we know very little about whether human quantitative traits that are familial are also heritable . . .

Personality traits, temperament, and cognitive performance (such as IQ scores) are all familial, but there are no well-designed adoption studies to show whether they are heritable. The only large-sample studies of human IQ performance that claimed to involve randomized environments (Cyril Burt's reports on identical twins raised apart) have recently been shown to be completely fraudulent.[54]

Nevertheless, the important distinction between whether a personality trait such as intelligence is heritable or familial is rarely made with clarity, even in the most respected medical texts. For example, the Merck Manual states: "Intelligence is polygenetically and environmentally determined. [Polygenetically means the result is caused by a set of cooperating genes, each of which produces a small quantitative effect.] The genetic and environmentally caused predispositions to [mental retardation] may be indistinguishable. The incidence of familial retardation in offspring of 2 retarded persons is 40%; for one, it is 20%. In 80% of cases, the cause of MR is unknown. The etiology is more likely to be identified in the more severely retarded child."[55] Similarly, the American Psychiatric Society's Textbook on Psychiatry contains a table entitled "Selected biological mechanisms causing mental retardation and pervasive developmental disorders" that lists as "hereditary" those cases of mental retardation "postulated for familial retardation associated with sociocultural or psychosocial disadvantage."[56] The text associated with the table explains:

The most common form, idiopathic mental retardation "associated with sociocultural or psychosocial disadvantage," is typically seen in the offspring of retarded parents ("familial"). [Idiopathic means of unknown origin.] Degree of retardation is generally mild (or moderate). Intellectual and adaptive deficits are presumed to be determined by a "polygenic" mechanism, though, currently, emphasis is placed on the intervening social factors. These individuals live in low socioeconomic circumstances, and their functioning is influenced by poverty, disease, deficiencies in health care, and impaired help seeking. Family size may exceed parental capacities for attention and positive stimulation of the children. Social disadvantage contributes heavily to the [causes] of some forms of mild mental retardation. Nonetheless, the overrepresentation of various genetic, physical, and neurological abnormalities in persons with mild mental retardation is a reminder that social forces may not be the predominant [causal] factors.[57]

Despite this possibility of there being unknown genetic variables at play in cases of mental retardation attributed to psychosocial causes, the textbook makes clear that the cases of severe to profound mental retardation—for which the biological causes are largely known—are evenly distributed between parents of low and high socioeconomic status. In contrast, the vast majority of cases of mild retardation are found in families with low socioeconomic status.[58]

Moreover, even when it is known that a condition "is hereditary," that fact is of much less significance than it might appear.[59] Finding a condition is hereditary, absent further information about the precise causal link, establishes an *upper* limit on the influence of heredity, but does not mean that the condition is not environmentally caused. Or looked at from the other end, hereditary estimates establish a *lower* limit on environmental influences but not an upper limit.

The reason heredity estimates cannot say more is that they do not purport to sort out whether the hereditary factor itself causes the condition or is merely associated with it. If there is an association, it may be the social response to the hereditary condition that is determinative, rather than the condition itself. As Christopher Jencks explains, if blond hair in children is entirely genetically determined, and if blonds are given more attention and treated better, resulting in higher IQ scores on the average, there then is a correlation between heredity (blondness) and IQ, but that connection does not prove in any way that the blond person's higher IQ is genetically rather than socially (environmentally) caused. Similarly, if it were found that children of persons with retardation had lower IQs than other persons on average, that could be because fewer opportunities were made available to these children than other children on average, rather than because of genetic difference between them.[60]

Even though today it appears that the vast majority of retardation is not inherited, there are forms of retardation that are known to be hereditary, such as the fragile X.[61] Even with hereditary conditions, environment does still affect the degree of development that will take place and may have a very large effect. It also will affect whether mental retardation is a huge problem for those who have it or whether instead it is consistent with a full and happy life.[62]

Appreciation of the tenuousness of the connection between retardation and heredity has led to a reaction against Buck v. Bell. Today, negative eugenics theories are considered "politically incorrect" in the United States (though not in all other countries), and society takes more seriously a moral obligation toward persons with retardation.

But traces of eugenics views linger. Persons labeled "retarded" are almost invariably still vulnerable to involuntary sterilization,[63] albeit usually with procedural safeguards. The explanation now more frequently is that it benefits them; but occasionally society's interest explicitly rears its head. Mississippi, for example, still allows the directors of certain state institutions acting in "the best interests of the patients and of society" to sterilize inmates with "hereditary forms of . . . feeble-mindedness."[64] Moreover, court decisions allowing sterilization sometimes rely on eugenics concerns (such as the need to prevent the birth of "defective" offspring) as a supporting reason. Many courts believe it would be unconstitutional to sterilize as a punishment for crime,[65] but nonetheless hold the state has a valid interest in sterilizing those thought to have retardation.[66]

In addition, eugenics is becoming more fashionable in other arenas—a development that may adversely impact society's treatment of those it labels "retarded." For example, eugenics considerations are increasingly becoming a basis for private procreative choice. Many individual mothers-to-be find out through tests like amniocentesis or *chorionic villius* what the genetic attributes of their offspring will be and use that information to make a decision whether to continue the pregnancy. And medical technology is advancing rapidly in its ability to detect defects and differences before birth and sometimes prevent them before conception. More and more conditions may therefore be detected and, through contraception, abortion, or medical treatment, be eradicated or sharply reduced.[67]

Both legislatures and courts have therefore endorsed involuntary sterilization, although there is no unanimity of view or approach. But even when such sterilization is allowed, today's rationale is usually not the coercive, police power rationale with its emphasis on protecting the community from "incompetence" that was found in Buck v. Bell. Instead modern cases frequently stress the *parens patriae* protective role of the judiciary to exercise its power "for the good of" the person who has retardation.

In Guardianship of Hayes, for example, the court's approach differed dramatically from that in Buck v. Bell. Most important, its focus was the patient's best interests. The court took pains to distance itself from the history of eugenic sterilization. Instead, it tried to strike an acceptable balance between protecting her right to procreate and protecting her access to sterilization. The court held that more weight should be given to the right to procreate, because sterilization is usually irreversible and can have "longlasting detrimental emotional effects."[68]

CHAPTER 6

Current Policy Issues
concerning Sterilization

Today it is agreed that procedural protections, while necessary, are in no way sufficient to protect against sterilization, but that is
where agreement ends. Opinions differ about whether persons with retardation should be afforded Equal Protection with other persons. But even
those who do champion equal treatment for persons with retardation cannot agree about what freedom and equality and lack of prejudice *mean* in the
context of sterilization. In attempting to devise a proper and egalitarian response, they cannot agree on whether to protect persons with retardation
from sterilization, or instead to provide them with access to sterilization, like
everybody else.

Most people consider access to sterilization an important right, and one
that should be preserved for individuals who have retardation—even those
deemed incapable of giving informed consent—along with the freedom to
preserve one's reproductive capacity. In support of their position, they can
point to statistics showing that sterilization is the birth control method of
choice in the United States today.[1]

There was a period when elective sterilization was denied to all women.
Earlier in this century, the medical establishment followed "the 120 rule,"
allowing the option of sterilization only to women whose age multiplied by
the number of children they had was 120 or more.[2] For example, the sterilization choice of a forty-year-old woman with three children would be respected, as would the choice of a thirty-year-old woman with four children—but not that of a twenty-year-old with five children or a thirty-five-
year-old with three. This restriction of women's reproductive choices was
imposed not by the state but by the medical establishment with the tolerance of the state. Many consider this era a shameful example of disrespect

for women and their ability to be their own medical decisionmakers. When women with retardation today are considered ineligible for sterilization, that same perspective would suggest that they are being belittled, rather than appropriately protected.

That perspective is not, however, unanimously accepted. A minority believes that proper protection for individuals with retardation requires prohibiting nontherapeutic sterilization of individuals whom the law does not allow to consent for themselves. The aspect of historical practice this group stresses is not the era when women in general were denied access to elective sterilization but instead the forced sterilization abuses that the population identified as retarded has historically suffered. There is much to be said for this minority perspective, especially given that the majority is not advocating choice by the patient herself.

Those who would take the course of preserving access to sterilization for persons with retardation are essentially arguing for a right to choose. Insofar as they do not urge that the patient herself make the choice, the real question becomes how the choice is to be made and who, under what conditions, is to make the choice for her. Jurisdictions differ concerning how seriously they regard the wishes of the individual patient, despite her retardation, and on whether guardians and courts can decide the issue for her.[3] They also differ on what the standard for any decision should be.

The minority position, advocating prohibition of sterilization at least to some classes of persons who have retardation, avoids this problem of choice. Its adherents point out that the right the majority would preserve for persons with retardation is not the same right as that shared by the rest of the population. The right that others have is a right to *choose,* and a young woman with retardation is not gaining the right by having someone other than herself make the choice. Neither side, therefore, can make the claim that it is treating persons with retardation the same way as everybody else. Nor is either side affording them the same "rights" as other persons.

In one sense the main differences between the two positions concern (1) who should decide, private individuals or the state itself; and (2) whether the choice must be made on the basis of facts concerning the particular individual or whether a general prohibition is permissible. Indeed, some consider a general prohibition necessary, because of the potential for abuse inherent in decisionmaking on this subject by individuals other than the patient herself.[4] The next two cases demonstrate this clash in views.

Strict Prohibition of Nonconsensual Sterilization

Valerie N. was twenty-nine when her "conservators" (the name California law uses for guardians) requested her sterilization. Their request became the subject of an important and interesting decision by the Supreme Court of California in 1985. In *In re* Valerie N., that court struck down California's statute prohibiting nontherapeutic[5] sterilization of persons with retardation who could not personally consent to the procedure.[6] It held that the statutory scheme violated both the U.S. and the California Constitutions because it denied to persons with retardation the right of reproductive choice:[7] "True protection of procreative choice can be accomplished only if the state permits the court-supervised substituted judgment of the conservator to be exercised on behalf of a conservatee who is unable to personally exercise this right."[8]

The court reasoned that "[a]n incompetent developmentally disabled woman has no less interest in a satisfying or fulfilling life free from the burdens of an unwanted pregnancy than does her competent sister."[9] Emphasizing that sterilization might "protect her interests in living the fullest and most rewarding life of which she is capable," the court held it illegitimate to deny to her conservators one of the choices that is available to everyone else and "the one choice that may be best for her."[10]

The court pointed out that Valerie's conservators in any event had a great deal of control over her life; that if sterilization were unavailable they might well limit her freedom to socialize out of fear that she would become pregnant; and that there was no way to prevent them from so restricting her. Moreover, the court took it as a given that conservators do have the right to impose abortion in the case of pregnancy.[11] Accordingly, it reasoned that any interest Valerie might have in being able to procreate over the wishes of her conservators was not in any event being protected.

One might reasonably argue from the extent of the guardians' control over the ward's life in cases like *Valerie N.* that it does not make sense to deny guardians the one particular choice of sterilization. The individual who has retardation is not effectively protected against her guardians anyway, nor could she be; she must rely ultimately on their good faith and sense of responsibility toward her and their love for her.

Although the arguments mentioned above do suggest the appropriateness of ceding power to the guardians, the court in *Valerie N.* did not endorse the implications of that position; instead it placed strict limits on guardians' exercise of discretion. The court indicated that it would not permit them to opt for sterilization without demonstrating to a court that the sterilization is necessary to the individual's habilitation and that less intrusive means of contraception are not available.[12] It found that on the record developed in the case these standards had not been met, but it remanded to allow another hearing at which the void in the record might be filled.

The California legislature's ban of nonconsensual sterilization was unusual but not unique. In 1975 Colorado also passed a statute prohibiting sterilization of adult persons with retardation who either failed to consent to their sterilization or who were incapable of consenting to the procedure.[13] The statute appears to state a clear legislative position: that no one with retardation is subject to sterilization by third-party consent. Ironically, however, the statute was interpreted not to apply to persons under eighteen years of age. For minors, sterilization was wholly unregulated because Colorado law neither barred their sterilization nor provided any standards: therefore, the Colorado Supreme Court said, judges have authority to allow sterilization of minors and to devise standards for it.

In *In re* A. W., a 1981 Colorado Supreme Court case involving a girl with retardation, the guardian *ad litem* tried but failed to bar her sterilization and hysterectomy, which her parents had requested. Instead the Colorado Supreme Court viewed minors as having a constitutional right of access to sterilization—a position hardly in keeping with the legislative ban on nonconsensual sterilization of adults (and suggesting that Colorado's Supreme Court would agree with California's). The court read the legislative silence concerning minors as a void that the court itself should fill by promulgating judicial standards for reviewing parental petitions to have a child with retardation sterilized.

A. W. was twelve years old when her parents decided to have her sterilized. She had been born oxygen-deprived and was characterized by the trial court as "severely retarded," a term that, "accurately used," refers to persons with IQs in the 20–40 range. A. W. attended a special school for children with IQs below 50. She was able to dress herself, feed herself, and bathe herself, as well as brush her teeth and comb her hair. (That description seems inconsistent with severe retardation, as the state supreme court also noted.)

At the age of twelve A. W. began to menstruate. According to her parents, she was unable "to cope adequately with her monthly periods, which caused A. W. 'a considerable degree of fright, fear, and a general feeling of

unrest."[14] She did not understand menstruation or "the relationship between intercourse and conception," and though A. W.'s parents believed she
had never been sexually active, they feared that the overnight trips she took
with her school "afforded some opportunity for sexual activity."[15] Their primary worry was that A. W. would become pregnant. They wanted her to
undergo a hysterectomy, to both sterilize her and end her menstrual periods. A. W.'s parents had never attempted to interfere with conception by
birth control pills or other reversible means.

The trial court ordered A. W.'s sterilization, after a hearing at which only
A. W.'s parents and her obstetrician testified. It found authority for its decision in Colorado's statute providing parents with the power to consent to
the health care of their minor children.[16] A. W.'s guardian *ad litem* appealed.
The Colorado Supreme Court reversed the order, ruling that the general parental consent statute did not govern the "special case" of sterilization of a
minor who has mental retardation. But in that opinion, the court also rejected the guardian *ad litem*'s argument that the 1975 sterilization statute described above limited the right of persons with retardation to be sterilized
"to cases in which the person is over eighteen years of age, has given consent, and has been deemed competent to consent."[17]

The court's holding is bizarre at best. The upshot of its interpretation of
Colorado law is that it protects an adult's right to be free from involuntary
nontherapeutic sterilization but does not protect a child in the same way.
For some reason the court thought that a legislature that concededly wanted
to preclude involuntary sterilizations of adults nonetheless did not want that
"option" "completely foreclosed" for minors.

The court then proceeded to set forth standards by which courts, acting
within their power, could grant petitions to sterilize minors with retardation. The deciding court (1) should, but need not, "talk with the person
and observe the person's physical and mental condition," weighing heavily,
though not conclusively, the person's wish not to be sterilized; (2) "must determine that the person's capacity to make the sterilization decision will not
likely improve in the future"; (3) must determine that the person is capable
of reproducing; (4) "must find by clear and convincing evidence that sterilization is medically essential."[18]

This last requirement—medical necessity—would seem to separate A. W.
from other cases, where nontherapeutic, elective sterilizations are at issue.
After all, a strict prerequisite of medical necessity, limited to protection of life
or physical health, essentially allows *no* elective sterilization. Many of the

court's statements indeed are more convincing if medically required sterilizations are involved—for example, the statement that minors have a constitutional right of access.

The court blurs the issue by using the "medical necessity" terminology, but in fact it defines "medically essential" so as to allow elective sterilization under that rubric. The first step is its broad definition of medical necessity: "A sterilization is medically essential if clearly necessary, in the opinion of experts, to preserve the life or physical or mental health of the mentally retarded person." This inclusion of mental as well as physical health has, in other contexts like abortion, been a way of broadening a medical necessity requirement to include things that the patient strongly wants. Second, the *A. W.* court included "the possibility of pregnancy" as among the medical necessities "if supported by sufficient evidence that it would threaten the physical or mental health of the person and that no less intrusive means of birth control would prove safe and effective."[19]

Two Justices wrote separately, each stressing that Colorado's sterilization statute should be read to prohibit sterilization of minors. The statute was designed to protect procreative choice when and only when subjects are of legal age to make the choice for themselves and when, whether or not they have mental disability, they are capable of expressing their choice and are deemed legally capable of making it.[20]

Retreat from Strict Prohibitions

The legislatures of both California and Colorado distrusted nonconsensual sterilization more than the courts did. But the Colorado legislature has since retreated from its apparent prohibition of nonconsensual sterilization. In 1992, the statute was repealed and reenacted to include a provision explicitly allowing court-ordered sterilization of incompetent persons who have retardation, whether they are adults or minors. The statute requires the court to follow the usual procedures and attest to strict conditions, such as that sterilization is the least intrusive means available; and, like the *A. W.* majority, it also requires that the sterilization be "medically necessary to preserve the life or physical or mental health of the person."[21] Presumably the medical necessity thus required will continue to be interpreted very loosely, as in *A. W.* If read strictly, it could eliminate elective sterilization by third-party consent, and the Colorado legislature would not have retreated at all.

California's new statute is less ambiguous. Its legislature has stuck to its antisterilization stance, to the extent that its highest court has permitted. Effective in 1991, six years after *Valerie N.*, the legislature replaced the absolute prohibition that its Supreme Court had struck down with a statute that does not allow nontherapeutic sterilization of minors at all and that is the strictest legislation in any state concerning nonconsensual, nontherapeutic sterilization of adults with mental retardation.[22]

The pertinent part of the statute says:

The court may authorize the conservator of a person proposed to be sterilized to consent to the sterilization of that person only if the court finds that the petitioner has established *all* of the following *beyond a reasonable doubt*:

(a) The person . . . is incapable of giving consent to sterilization . . . and the incapacity is in all likelihood permanent.

(b) . . . [T]he individual is fertile and capable of procreation.

(c) The individual is capable of engaging in, and is likely to engage in sexual activity at the present or in the near future under circumstances likely to result in pregnancy.

(d) Either of the following:

  (1) The nature and extent of the individual's disability as determined by empirical evidence and not solely on the basis of any standardized test, renders him or her permanently incapable of caring for a child, even with appropriate training and reasonable assistance.

  (2) Due to a medical condition, pregnancy or childbirth would pose a substantially elevated risk to the life of the individual to such a degree that, in the absence of other appropriate methods of contraception, sterilization would be deemed medically necessary for an otherwise nondisabled woman under similar circumstances.

(e) All less invasive contraceptive methods including supervision are unworkable even with training and assistance, inapplicable, or medically contraindicated. Isolation and segregation shall not be considered as less invasive means of contraception.

(f) The proposed method of sterilization entails the least invasion of the body of the individual.

(g) The current state of scientific and medical knowledge does not suggest either

  (1) that a reversible sterilization procedure or other less drastic contraceptive method will shortly be available, or

(2) that science is on the threshold of an advance in the treatment of the individual's disability.

(h) The person . . . *has not made a knowing objection to* his or her sterilization. For purposes of this subdivision, an individual may be found to have knowingly objected to his or her sterilization notwithstanding his or her inability to give consent to sterilization . . . In the case of persons who are nonverbal, have limited verbal ability to communicate, or who rely on alternative modes of communication, the court shall ensure that adequate effort has been made to elicit the actual views of the individual by the facilitator appointed [to do so] . . . or by any other person with experience in communicating with developmentally disabled persons who communicate using similar means.[23]

Even though Colorado's and California's legislatures have stepped back some from their prohibitions, other states still apparently support the position that sterilization is available only to adults who can give informed consent.[24] Moreover, states without statutes whose judges claim to lack power without legislation[25] achieve precisely the same result: sterilization is available only to those who can give informed consent. The vast majority of states nonetheless allow third-party consent, following the route of the *Valerie N.* majority.

Judicial Supervision of Third-Party Consent to Sterilization

Much of the *Valerie N.* opinion is devoted to discussing why the best policy is to make sterilization available to persons with retardation who are under guardianship and who are considered legally incapable of deciding for themselves. It quotes from other jurisdictions that have articulated standards courts should use to decide whether to allow third-party consent to sterilization in a particular case. Several states besides California had already adopted the view that sterilization should be available to persons with retardation, even to those who could not themselves effectively consent.

The Judge as the Appropriate Decisionmaker

Most states that have adopted a position do allow nontherapeutic nonconsensual sterilization of persons who cannot consent for themselves, but most also require that courts oversee nonconsensual sterilization. Judicial permission to sterilize has been required precisely because of the inherent conflict of interest of private substitute decisionmakers and because of our society's historic abuses regarding sterilization. Because law does not give one individual the power to consent to nontherapeutic sterilization of another without judicial approval, when sterilization is requested the judge becomes substitute decisionmaker along with the relative, caretaker, or guardian who instituted the proceeding.

Similarly, in *A. W.*, when the Colorado Supreme Court decided to allow the sterilization of minors with retardation, it also required judicial oversight of any such sterilization decision. Moreover, it ruled, a court's sterilization decision has to be based on the court's own informed estimation of the patient's best interests, not just judicial deference to the opinions of well-meaning parents.[26]

The New Jersey Supreme Court had ruled similarly in the context of adults. In the 1981 case *In re* Grady, it established that the judge was the appropriate decisionmaker concerning sterilization, not Lee Ann Grady's parents. Lee Ann was born with Down's syndrome in 1961. She was brought up at home by her parents with a younger brother and sister, neither of whom had disabilities. During her childhood and adolescence, Lee Ann attended a special education program provided by the state. She learned to write her name and developed a limited ability to count, but she did not learn to read. She was also moderately self-sufficient. She could dress herself but sometimes selected clothes that did not match or were inappropriate for the season. She could bathe herself but sometimes needed help in regulating the temperature of the water. She could feed herself, warming canned soups with some help in selecting the proper heat level on the stove. Lee Ann also was successful at simple household chores, like folding laundry and dusting. Her leisure activities included playing simple games, watching television, taking walks, swimming, and bowling.

At the age of nineteen, Lee Ann's parents described her as "an attractive young woman" whose mood was "often jovial and friendly."[27] But they were afraid that, when the time came for her to leave home, she would become involved in sexual relationships that could lead to pregnancy.

From her parents' perspective, a pregnancy for Lee Ann would always be unwanted regardless of her age or the extent to which she might mature. In fact, the Grady parents had feared pregnancy ever since Lee Ann had begun to menstruate, and they had regularly provided her with birth control pills from the age of fifteen. They also had sheltered her socially and had not taught her the facts of life. At age nineteen, Lee Ann had never been sexually active and had "no significant understanding of sexual relationships or marriage."[28]

The parents' plan was that at age twenty, when she finished her course of public special education, Lee Ann would move from home into a residence providing assisted living for persons with retardation. They were afraid that her life there would not be as strictly supervised as in their home and that she might become intimate with men. Accordingly, when Lee Ann was eighteen years old her parents, with the advice of their doctor, tried to have their daughter surgically sterilized at a local hospital. The hospital refused, saying that it "could not legally permit the operation without judicially authorized consent for Lee Ann."[29]

Lee Ann's parents thought that they, and not the court, should have the right to be the substantive decisionmakers for their daughter and that the issue was whether they in good faith believed sterilization was in her best interests. The trial court essentially agreed, although it also imposed standard procedural safeguards and substantive requirements that Lee Ann be found incompetent. The upshot was that Lee Ann's parents were granted the power they sought—to consent to their daughter's sterilization.

The guardian *ad litem* supported this result, but the public advocate and the attorney general disagreed, saying it inadequately protected Lee Ann's interests. The Supreme Court of New Jersey reversed, saying "[i]t must be the court's judgment, and not just the parents' good faith decision, that substitutes for the incompetent's consent."[30] It reasoned that "[i]ndependent judicial decision making is the best way to protect the rights and interests of the incompetent and to avoid abuses of the decision to sterilize."[31]

It concluded that a court must not authorize sterilization unless it is persuaded, by clear and convincing evidence, that the sterilization is "in the best interests of the incompetent person."[32] At the same time, the court rejected the public advocate's attempt to limit sterilization by substituted consent to cases where sterilization is absolutely necessary and not, for example, just one of an array of workable birth control options;[33] the court did not want to undercut Lee Ann's constitutional right of access to sterilization. Although it tightened the rules, the New Jersey Supreme Court, like the trial court and the parents, was clearly supportive of sterilization for Lee Ann—leaving open mainly the question whether it should occur now or in the future.[34] It accepted the finding that Lee Ann was permanently incapable of deciding for herself (which had been stipulated by all of the parties as well as supported by independent reports).

Today much of the *Grady* approach is commonly accepted. Certainly it is accepted that parents, guardians, and caretakers cannot decide on sterilization themselves, without obtaining judicial approval. This might be considered the most fundamental procedural protection prerequisite to forced sterilization today.

There is reason for requiring judicial involvement. Without it, standards and limitations on nonconsensual sterilization might be enunciated, but no disinterested decisionmaker could determine whether or not they were actually satisfied. Judges usually are without direct interest in the particular controversy and can supervise the decisions of parents, guardians, or caretakers to assure that they follow the rules.

But judges also have their prejudices and their shortcomings, and judicial discretion also can be abused. When it is, the person wrongly sterilized is without remedy because judges are protected from liability under doctrines of judicial immunity.[35] It is this reality that has made many states stress the need for legislative standards to guide and limit judges' discretion.

The Need for Standards

One case in which such standards were developed is Guardianship of Hayes, which involved a mother's petition to sterilize her sixteen-year-old daughter, Edith Hayes. The case followed the now familiar approach of having courts assess the patient's "best interests." Recognizing the substantial discretion such a standard leaves the fact finder, the Washington Supreme Court established firmer standards for sterilization. The case is unusual because the court found that the evidence failed to establish that sterilization was in the patient's best interests; moreover it said that the best interests requirement will be satisfied only in "a rare and unusual case."[36] It also stated, "There is a heavy presumption against sterilization of an individual incapable of informed consent."[37]

The court required procedural protections, like effective representation for Edith, but in addition it placed strict substantive limitations on when sterilization could be ordered. The threshold requirement was a finding of incapacity, and the court found that requirement unmet in Edith's case. The court said that the sterilization petition should not be granted unless there was "clear, cogent and convincing" evidence that Edith was presently incapable of making the sterilization decision for herself and unlikely to "develop sufficiently" to make "an informed judgment about sterilization in the foreseeable future."[38] Edith's mother asserted that she had severe retardation, functioned "at the level of a four to five-year-old," and did not "understand her own reproductive functions or exercise independent judgment in her relationship with males."[39] Edith was sexually active (and the level of independence she apparently had does not match the "severely retarded" label). Nonetheless, according to the Washington Supreme Court, "[i]t cannot be said that Edith Hayes will be unable to understand sexual activity or control her behavior in the future."[40] Other requirements the court imposed were also not proven: that no suitable alternative contraception existed; that pregnancy would be hazardous; and that Edith "would never be capable of being a good parent."[41]

Not only the court's attitude toward third-party sterilization but also some conditions *Hayes* imposed were substantially stricter than those in *Grady*. For example, "all less drastic contraceptive methods, including supervision, education and training, have been proved unworkable or inapplicable"; second, "the proposed method of sterilization entails the least invasion" of the patient's body; and, finally, "the current state of scientific and medical knowledge does not suggest either (a) that a reversible sterilization procedure or other less drastic contraceptive method will shortly be available," or (b) that science is on the threshold of an advance in the treatment of the individual's disability."[42] Moreover, the *Hayes* court presumed that sterilization would have detrimental effects on the physical or emotional health of the patient, a consideration most courts have ignored; it required the proponent of the sterilization to show that such adverse effects would not result. Requiring such specific findings was designed to limit judicial discretion and to weight the scales against sterilization. The court specified that even after all the above findings of facts have been made, the judge can order sterilization only if he or she finds *in addition* that the sterilization is in the patient's best interests.

Different Approaches to Regulating Judicial Discretion

State rules vary on whether and how sterilization can be approved, and they will continue to vary unless the U.S. Supreme Court spells out a constitutional rule that must be followed. It is not only in the substance of the factors that the *Hayes* court is stricter than *Grady*. They also differ concerning what role those factors play in the ultimate determination. In *Grady,* the New Jersey Supreme court created a nonexhaustive list of factors it considered *relevant* to the court's decision that sterilization was in Lee Ann's best interests. The factors were not requirements, however, unlike the *necessary* factual findings in *Hayes.*

The New Jersey factors, articulated in *Grady,* were that the patient is fertile (even though she may not be likely to become pregnant); that pregnancy and childbirth would cause her trauma or psychological damage; that she will likely engage in voluntary sexual intercourse or be raped in the future; that she is unable now or in the future to understand human reproduction or conception; that other less drastic birth control measures are less feasible or medically inadvisable as compared to sterilization; that sterilization is advisable at the present time; that the patient would likely be unable to care for a child and unlikely to marry and, with a spouse, care for a child; and that proponents of sterilization appear to be seeking it in good faith, with a primary concern for the best interests of the patient rather than their own or the public's convenience.

There are some differences between these factors and the factual findings required in *Hayes,* but the most important difference is that the New Jersey court avoided per se requirements (except for procedural requirements and the threshold requirement of incapacity to decide for oneself). Instead, the New Jersey court ruled that courts should balance the young woman's more heavily weighted right to procreate against her right of access to sterilization. This balancing process requires all variables to be considered, but none plays a predetermined role. Such a balancing test to guide court decisions is usually easier to satisfy than a test like the one in *Hayes,* listing per se requirements all of which must be met.

Moreover the *Grady* approach shares the vice of most balancing tests: decisionmakers can "balance" to produce any result they want. Chief Justice Traynor captured the central shortcoming of balancing tests when he asked how "[c]an you weigh a bushel of horsefeathers against next Thursday?"[43]

CHAPTER 7

What Should the Standards
for Sterilization Be?

When sterilization has been authorized, the lawmakers—whether courts or legislatures—have had to decide what the standards for sterilization will be. As we have seen, an array of both procedural requirements for nonconsensual sterilization and substantive limitations on when it can occur have developed in this country. There exists today a wide assortment of judicial and legislative standards for sterilizing persons whom the law does not allow to consent for themselves. Often, but not consistently, the recipients of such sterilizations "by substitute consent" have been persons with extreme mental retardation. As a practical matter, they are almost exclusively women, although in form statutes are often gender-neutral.

Substituted Judgment or Best Interests?

There are two principal competing modes of analysis for the decisionmakers, commonly dubbed the best interests approach and the substituted judgment approach.[1] Once society's perceived interests were discarded as the paramount consideration, the subject's best interests were used both to justify courts' results and to direct them. Many courts continue to use best interests terminology, while differing in the extent and the manner in which they attempt to confine the fact finder's discretion. As we have seen, reported cases offer generally similar standards for determining the ward's best interests.[2] The opinion of the ward must usually be elucidated somehow, whether through a guardian *ad litem* or through her actual appearance and testimony in court. The court will also hear expert testimony on whether she is competent to make the sterilization decision and, if not, whether sterilization is in the ward's best interests. On this question it will consider, among other things, testimony relevant to her capacity to parent; whether she is sexually active; and whether sterilization is the "least restrictive alternative" form of birth control for her.

The purpose of such best interests analysis is to protect legally incompetent people from exploitation, but in doing so it does not provide equality. It does not give people labeled "incompetent" the same right of choice that other people have. Not only can they not make their own choice, but also the person deciding for them must always choose "in their best interests," a formulation that limits their options in comparison to other people. Procreative choice is not a subject of decisionmaking on which persons are particularly prone to act in their best interests, as rationally calculated. Emotional and nonrational considerations on the part of the person deciding whether to parent often play a large role, perhaps appropriately. A choice that is made *for* a person differs inherently from a decision by the person herself, and a wholly rational decision also differs from other people's decisions.

Some courts have challenged the assumption that best interests is the appropriate test for persons who cannot decide for themselves and have put forth instead a "substituted judgment" test. Recognizing that all people make decisions that could be regarded as foolish, proponents of this doctrine would in theory entitle those labeled "incompetent" to make their own share of bad choices—to do what they want to do instead of what might be considered best for them. This somewhat extreme explanation of the doctrine of substituted judgment was among the rationales of the Massachusetts Supreme Judicial Court in *In re* Moe, one of several cases forsaking the "best interests" terminology altogether in favor of "substituted judgment."[3]

In *In re* Moe, a mother sought a tubal ligation for her twenty-three-year-old daughter, a woman with mental retardation. The *Moe* court, like most others, held that it was within judicial power to grant a sterilization petition and also that third parties cannot consent to sterilization without judicial backing. Indeed, Massachusetts law gave some basis for arguing that third parties could not consent at all because its statutes forbid sterilization of any person, absent that person's "knowledgeable consent."[4]

A possible argument that the knowledgeable consent provision did not apply to "incompetents" stemmed from provisions conferring the "care and custody"[5] of a ward upon the guardian. Yet no Massachusetts statute explicitly grants a guardian the power to authorize sterilization, and Massachusetts courts have required prior judicial approval before a guardian can consent to "extraordinary medical treatment."[6] The *Moe* court held that sterilization falls within that rule, because sterilization is "an extraordinary and highly intrusive form of medical treatment that irreversibly extinguishes the ward's fundamental right of procreative choice."[7] On this basis, it decided that guardians can initiate sterilization petitions but cannot consent to sterilization without court approval.

The court next reviewed "the sordid history of compulsory eugenic sterilization laws in the United States," pointing out that Massachusetts had never had such laws. It endeavored to separate the court-approved sterilization it allowed from the prior abuses, saying the issue it must decide was whether "an incompetent person is to be given the same rights as those vested in a competent person, and, if so, how and by what means." It assumed that "incompetent persons need some forum in which to exercise their statutory and constitutional rights, the same as competent persons," and explained that it could accomplish that "through the doctrine of substituted judgment determined by proceedings in a court of competent jurisdiction."[8] It went on to discuss and develop the substituted judgment doctrine.

The court described the goal of substituted judgment: "to maintain the integrity of the incompetent person by giving the individual a forum in which his or her rights may be exercised." The method by which the court is to achieve this aim is to

don "the mental mantle of the incompetent" and substitute . . . itself as nearly as possible for the individual in the decisionmaking process . . . [T]he court does not decide what is necessarily the best decision but rather what decision would be made by the incompetent person if he or she were competent. "In short, if an individual would, if competent, make an unwise or foolish decision, the judge must respect that decision as long as he would accept (or be bound to accept) the same decision if made by a competent individual in the same circumstances.[9]

The court anticipated criticism of the substituted judgment approach but thought it an improvement on the best interests alternative because it better respects the "personal rights and integrity" of the subject of the decision:

To speak solely in terms of the "best interests" of the ward, or of the State's interest, is to obscure the fundamental issue: Is the State to impose a solution on an incompetent based on external criteria, or is it to seek to protect and implement the individual's personal rights and integrity? We reject the former possibility. Each approach has its own difficulties, but the use of the doctrine of substituted judgment promotes best the interests of the individual, no matter how difficult the task involved may be.[10]

Through the substituted judgment doctrine, then, a court attempts to recreate the subjective decisionmaking of the person at issue and exclude consideration of interests other than hers. By viewing the issue from the patient's own perspective, it seeks best to approximate freedom of choice for the patient.

While these aspirations of approximating equality lie behind the substituted judgment approach, and it seeks to distinguish itself from prior best interests doctrine, in fact the tests bear many similarities. Substituted judgment does not prevent the judge's own value system from playing a prominent role in any decision. Even the most sensitive and empathetic of judges has deeply ingrained ideas and values that are extremely difficult to put aside. The inherent flexibility of the "don the mental mantle" process makes judges' own ideas and values prominent determinants of any result.

Consequently, despite the difference in the theory of the best interests and substituted judgment approaches, in practical terms they often merge. Substituted judgment may be particularly likely to amount to best interests by another name when applied to persons, like most of those with mental retardation, who have never been considered capable of making decisions for themselves. For such persons there are no past statements uttered while the person was legally competent that the judge can follow. In those circumstances many judges following substituted judgment would decide to do whatever they believed to be in the patient's best interests.

One could, of course, interpret and apply the substituted judgment test to differ from the best interests standard. For example, one could read it to require that the patient's actual wishes be followed if they are known, without regard to whether the patient is considered "retarded." Only when her own wishes were unknown or unknowable would others' judgments come into play. Indeed, that is the way this book suggests that substituted judgment *should* be interpreted, so that the substitute applies his or her own answer only when the subject's wishes cannot be ascertained.[11] This interpretation of substituted judgment would clearly distinguish it from a best interests formulation and would be a courageous and appropriate resolution of the issue.

The *Moe* court, however, did not consider the patient's own wishes dispositive, even when they could be ascertained. It did consider the patient's wishes important: "The courts . . . must endeavor, as accurately as possible, to determine the wants and needs of this ward as they relate to the sterilization procedure."[12] Moreover, later in the opinion, when the court was discussing how the hearing should be conducted, it said:

> The court, to the extent possible, must also "elicit testimony from the incompetent concerning (his or) her understanding and desire for the proposed operation and its consequences" . . . The judge, in his discretion, and the guardian *ad litem* in his recommendation, should attempt to ascertain the ward's actual preference for sterilization, parenthood, or other means of contraception. This inquiry is an important part of the substituted judgment determination.[13]

But while the effort was to "bring the substituted judgment into step with the values and desires of the affected individual,"[14] the patient's wishes were not necessarily determinative, according to the Massachusetts court.

Moreover, the *Moe* court came up with a peculiar and much criticized approach to giving content to the substituted-judgment formulation: The court was to follow the wishes the patient *would have had if she were competent.* Read for all it is worth, this formulation calls for total speculation in the case of most persons with retardation. While using substituted judgment language, it would in fact invite the judge to make any decision the judge deemed best.

It is not entirely clear from the *Moe* opinion that the court intended this statement of its test to result in such a speculative inquiry. "What she would have wanted if competent" could mean simply "what she would have wanted if she were legally permitted to decide for herself." The latter formulation would require (as this book suggests) that her actual known wishes be followed.

Some of the court's statements of its test in *Moe* are consistent with this narrow reading. For example: "[T]he court is to determine whether to authorize sterilization when requested by the parents or guardian by finding the incompetent would so choose if competent. No sterilization is to be compelled on the basis of any State or parental interest."[15]

Later in the opinion, however, the court describes the decision the judge is to make in a way that shows the judge is not necessarily to follow the incompetent's known wishes: "The result of the judge's exercise of discretion should be the same decision which would be made by the incompetent person, 'but taking into account the present and future incompetency of the individual as one of the factors which would necessarily enter into the decision-making process of the competent person.'"[16]

It appears, then, that *Moe* requires the judge him- or herself to assess and evaluate the impact of the mental retardation, both on what the woman now wants to do and on her capability to do it. The rationale is that if she were competent she would take this factor into account. While on one level this seems to make sense, it is also noteworthy that the "if competent" part of the test allows the judge to dismiss the perspective of the person who will be subject to the operation, departing from the fundamental purpose of the substituted judgment formulation. The perspectives of the competent population concerning disability intervene through this "if competent" facet of the test, empowering them to decide whether to allow her wishes.

One interesting point the *Moe* court made was that it could and indeed must still be guided by the young woman's values. Specifically, "the court must consider the ward's religious beliefs, if any."[17] Undoubtedly the court should, and that is one factor that might pose some constraint on a judge's total discretion. But even this respect for the patient's religion poses conundrums of its own. For example, to what extent should it apply when the patient's religion is simply a choice imposed by her parents and when there has been comparatively little participation and involvement by the patient herself? Moreover, it may not be appropriate for courts to have to wrestle with questions such as whether the tenets of the Catholic faith, involving sterilization or abortion perhaps, should be imposed upon a young woman because she has been baptized in the Catholic church. The First Amendment to the U.S. Constitution counsels against government entanglement with religion, and judicial involvement in questions of religious doctrine lies within its ban.

The *Moe* court's criticism of the best interests standard is more convincing than its positive case for the substituted judgment test, as it interprets that test. Such a subjective, hypothetical, and creative judicial approach obviously carries potential for abuse. Moreover allowing judges to discount even expressed preferences departs from the core rationale of the test. Finally, a judge's success in ascertaining an individual's actual preference may often depend on the sensitivity and empathy of the judge—a person whose situation, usually including gender, will differ markedly from that of the woman whose fate is at issue. Obviously not all judges have the capacity for compassionate identification with a powerless woman who has retardation and who may want someday to have a baby.

The substituted judgment test, if it is to improve on the best interests approach, will do so primarily in cases in which the wishes of the patient have been expressed while the patient was competent and the test directs the court to follow them. It is less of an improvement when the wishes of the subject of the decision have never been known and the judge is "unable to draw upon prior stated preferences the individual may have expressed."[18] Nor can it be successful when the law directs that her actual wishes must be discounted because of her "incompetence." The judge, guardian *ad litem*, parent, or guardian, hypothesizing what the patient "would have wanted" had she been competent, will arrive at the same answer if contemplating what is in the patient's best interests.[19]

In those cases, the advantage of the substituted judgment test, if there is one, is in encouraging substitute decisionmakers to look at the problem from the perspective of the subject of the decision. To the extent that they decline to look from her perspective because she is "incompetent," that advantage is obviously lost. Moreover, many family members of persons with retardation find the substituted judgment formulation particularly offensive because it uses wholly fictional preferences of the patient to justify an outcome that is in fact imposed. Similarly a dissenter in *Moe* described it as "a cruel charade."[20]

Even when the substituted judgment test is applied to take *some* account of the actual preferences of the patient, it does not distinguish itself from many best interests tests in that respect, *unless* it makes the patient's preferences determinative. For the best interests test can take account of the patient's own wishes just as the substituted judgment approach can. In *A. W.*, for example, the Colorado court applied a discretionary best interests test but suggested that best interests and the actual wishes of the patient will often coincide. Like the Massachusetts court in *Moe*, it said that "[t]he wishes of the person, although not conclusive, are relevant, and a strong indication that the person does not wish to be sterilized must weigh heavily against authorizing the procedures."[21]

Standards for Who Can Be Sterilized and When

As soon as it is accepted that others can decide whether sterilization will be administered to a woman with retardation, it becomes necessary to decide when sterilization will be permitted and whose sterilization will be permitted. It is now accepted in this country that a judge must give final approval before an elective sterilization can be performed without informed consent from the patient. Accordingly, law must determine when such sterilizations are available, and the reasoning must be spelled out in ways that would not be required if a parent or an institutional caretaker were permitted to make the decision without judicial review.

One reason for having judges decide when sterilization will be available is to enforce existing rules designed to limit the discretion of others—guardians, parents, institutional caretakers. But as soon as the law embarks upon this course, difficult questions present themselves about what the rules ought to be. Even though the basic factors relevant to third-party sterilization are fairly similar from state to state,[22] there are significant differences, and many questions are unsettled. This section focuses on a few of the open issues. The examples show not only the difficulty of the issues that exist but also the awkwardness of involving the judiciary—the government—in their resolution.

If sterilizing a legally incompetent daughter were considered part of "private choice," as the parents sought in *Grady,* then many questions about the propriety and rationale of sterilization would be resolved on a case-by-case basis, without their ever being exposed to public view. A "government position" on the issue would be avoided, but gross inconsistency in outcomes would be the price. If parents or physicians—or even caretakers at institutions or group homes—were permitted final decisonmaking authority over sterilization decisions, there would be no scrutiny of whose interests they were protecting or of the legitimacy of their reasons for acting.

Despite its limitations, the advantages of judicial decisionmaking as opposed to the alternatives may be worth the costs. That issue in any event has been resolved in favor of judicial review. But that review will entail resolving many difficult and awkward legal issues. Some will be decided by legislatures and some by courts. There is no particular reason to believe that all will arrive at the same resolution.

Relevance of Interests Other Than the Patient's

It is generally conceded today that the interests or desires of the patient are central. But should they be the sole determinants of the sterilization decision, or should the interests of other persons also weigh in the balance? If others' interests can be relevant, there are many that might contend for recognition. Common examples include the parents' interest in reducing their own caretaking responsibilities, or the caretakers' interest in saving themselves from the inconvenience associated with maintaining a patient's hygiene during menstruation.[23] The state also has an interest in avoiding an array of financial burdens, including providing parental training; family support if the mother keeps her child; and foster care if the child is removed from home.

Most courts today state that only the needs of the patient can be considered.[24] Equal treatment requires that approach. Family interests and societal interests could defensibly play a role in procreative decisonmaking for *all* persons, but our lawmakers have not pursued that policy. Perhaps a first wife with two children to support should be able to object before her ex-husband brings more children into the world;[25] perhaps a look at the whole family would dictate that his sterilization was in the family's and society's interest. But that approach has been definitively rejected, as it has consistently been held that procreative decisionmaking is a matter of individual choice. Indeed, the doctrine extends so far that a husband does not have any say in his wife's abortion decision; the state cannot even impose a requirement that he be notified. The choice whether to abort belongs to the individual woman whose body is involved.[26]

Because this is the clearly adopted policy for procreative decisionmaking by other people, there is no room for argument that persons with retardation should be subject to decisions made for the family's or the public's good. On this question, at least in theory, the law has recognized that persons with retardation should not be treated differently from all other persons. To do so would reflect our tradition of eugenic sterilization for the public good, and it would be inconsistent with our Constitution's guarantees of equal treatment.

Accordingly, courts eschew considering the perspectives of the parents, the government, and the taxpayer, even though as a practical matter those perspectives might warrant some weight.[27]

But even if one decides that the patient herself is the sole concern, it is not always easy to decide what her best interests are or to distinguish her interests from those of her caretaker. This difficulty of distinguishing between the patient's and other persons' wishes and interests allows courts to sacrifice her interests to others', while disguising that fact.

Consider Judith B., an eighteen-year-old woman who lives with foster caretakers, Mr. and Mrs. K. Judith obtained this placement in the community after many years in institutional care. She is diagnosed as having mental retardation, has an IQ of 55, and is confined to a wheelchair.

It was difficult to find a placement in the community for Judith, but this one is going quite well. The Ks are kind and pleasant, and Judith has become more outgoing and alert since she was moved into their home from the institution. There is one problem, however: Although the Ks enjoy having Judith with them and are generally happy with the arrangement, they cannot tolerate Judith's inability to maintain personal hygiene during her menstrual periods. Accordingly, they have informed the Department of Mental Retardation (which arranged the foster placement) that they want Judith to have a hysterectomy. Otherwise they seriously doubt they can keep her.

In one sense, obviously, the hysterectomy can be said to be in Judith's interests. There is a good chance that if the Ks cannot keep her, she will have to return to the institution, or in any event to a placement less satisfactory than the present one. On the other hand, is it appropriate to let the Ks foist this decision on Judith? It clearly is their needs and interests that the operation would address, and the operation can be said to be in her interest, if at all, only because it is in her interest to succumb to their desires.

This somewhat unusual case presents a dilemma that also arises in more common circumstances. For example, it may be in the best interests of many young women to be sterilized because otherwise their parents or their community home will not allow them to socialize with men. If one uses the best interests test in this way to encompass what is in the patient's best interests *only because of what others require of her,* then in reality the best interests test encompasses others' concerns and needs as well.

This question of whether interests other than the patient's can legitimately be weighed in the balance is distinct from the question discussed earlier of whether best interests or substituted judgment is the preferable formulation. Whose interests are relevant must be resolved, whether one employs a best interests or a substituted judgment standard. Under either formulation, a case can be made for taking into account the interests of other parties, and even the public interest. In Judith's case, for example, it can be said to be in her best interests to undergo the hysterectomy if her staying in her foster home is contingent upon it. Similarly, under the substituted judgment test, the argument can be and is made that, if she were making the decision, a person with disabilities would not want to impose undue burdens on her family; thus, undue burdens on the family become part of the substituted judgment calculus.

Such arguments could, of course, lead to endorsing anything a loving caretaker wants to do. The apparent alternative is to treat persons with retardation like others and, if imposing a decision at all, to rest it only on their actual needs and wishes. Families like the Ks have to be counseled and taught to accept Judith as she is and to deal with her hygiene problems in some less drastic way. Foster families, biological families, and other caretakers in the Ks' position must be taught to allow their charge to grow without requiring of her things that otherwise would not be in her interest. Concerning procreative decisionmaking, many families with all kinds of children have to learn to accept and allow their children's growth without imposing on them requirements that interfere with their self-determination.

Is Heritability a Legitimate Consideration?

One issue that many persons would prefer remain out of view but that occasionally comes to the fore in judicial decisions is the legitimacy of interfering with reproduction because the patient has a disability that might be inherited. There are obvious problems with acknowledging such a factor in decisionmaking. One is deciding which heritable disabilities will justify a substitute decision to interfere with a person's procreation.[28] Still more difficult is whether the government should be permitted to take the position—through legislation, regulation, or judicial decisions—that human beings with retardation or other handicaps are less worthy than others and should be eradicated, or at least prevented from coming into being, wherever possible.[29] Justice Holmes was willing to take such a position in Buck v. Bell. That case has not been formally overturned, but it is discredited now, as a matter of constitutional law.[30] Moreover, the opinion's supposed scientific foundations (that retardation in general is likely to be inherited) are now known to be erroneous.[31]

Nonetheless, many advances in the science of genetics can be used to serve the purposes of negative eugenics, which are the identification and eradication of "abnormal" genes or chromosomes in human beings. A central issue, of course, is which disabilities are serious enough to warrant eradication.[32] Some would eradicate any "disability" (raising important and interesting definitional problems), while others focus especially on mental disability and look upon mental handicap as what makes some people most different from others.

In *In re* Grady, the public advocate contended that "the State's interest in authorizing sterilization is limited to preventing the birth of genetically defective children and children whose parents are unable to provide adequate care."[33] The New Jersey Supreme Court rejected the "suggestion that the

State's interest in preventing the birth of genetically defective or uncared for children is sufficient to necessitate the sterilization of anyone who does not want to be sterilized. In determining whether to authorize sterilization, a court should consider only the best interest of the incompetent person, not the interests or convenience of society in having the incompetent person sterilized."[34] Early cases, however, had relied expressly upon public or family interests in support of sterilization.[35]

Just as consideration of heritability of retardation did not altogether disappear from litigation when the eugenics era ended, so did it persist in some legislation.[36] For example, a North Carolina statute used as the basis for sterilizing Tempie Johnson in 1980 provided two substantive bases for sterilization: first, that because of her retardation, the woman would "probably be unfit to care for a child or children";[37] and, second, that she "would be likely to procreate a child or children who would probably have serious mental deficiencies."[38]

In other contexts, however, even when a serious hereditary condition exists, sterilization is not the remedy of choice, especially if the gene carrier has any interest in having a child. Instead genetic counseling is encouraged, in which prospective parents will be advised about the likelihood of transmitting their condition to offspring.

The Ad Hoc Committee of the American Society of Human Genetics recommends genetic counseling as a self-consciously ethical process:

> Genetic counseling is a communication process that deals with the human problems associated with the occurrence, or the risk of occurrence, of a genetic disorder in a family. This process involves an attempt by one or more appropriately trained persons to help the individual or family (1) comprehend the medical facts, including the diagnosis, the probable course of the disorder, and the available management; (2) appreciate the way heredity contributes to the disorder and the risk of recurrence in specified relatives; (3) understand the options for dealing with the risk of resurgence; (4) choose the course of action that seems appropriate to them in view of their risk and the family goals, and act in accordance with that decision; and (5) make the best possible adjustment to the disorder in an affected family member and/or to the risk of recurrence of that disorder.[39]

The dominant fact is that the decision whether to reproduce is left to the parents, not assumed by society.

That approach is used even when dealing with serious illnesses that could be eradicated through a program of forced sterilization. Huntington's disease, for example, could disappear in a generation if persons with the condition were identified through testing and prevented from having children. The reason Huntington's disease lends itself to such simple eradication is that it has been identified with a dominant gene, making all carriers detectable. Yet even with that available option, decisionmaking is left to the carriers and potential carriers. Their self-determination in reproductive matters takes priority over any societal concerns or interests.

The most prevalent hereditary form of mental retardation, the fragile x syndrome described in Chapter 3, unlike Huntington's, does not lend itself to effective genetic counseling. There are three reasons. First, many carriers who transmit the gene for the fragile X syndrome are asymptomatic. About 20 percent of males who carry the fragile X chromosome are not clinically affected, as are up to 50 percent of female carriers. Second, although there is a particularly high incidence of mental subnormality among female carriers who inherited the fragile X gene from their mothers,[40] prenatal diagnosis of the extent of intellectual impairment among affected carriers is otherwise unpredictable. Third, current genetic testing to detect the fragile X syndrome among female carriers is inconsistent because there are technical difficulties in locating the X chromosome's fragile site in the culture conditions in which the genetic testing occurs.[41] The pitfalls of these genetic tests have compelled fragile X screening programs also to pay attention to more discrete clinical signs of the syndrome's physical stigmata, such as an unusually long face; large, protuberant ears; large testicular size; and hyper-extensible joints.[42]

Must Sterilization Be the Least Restrictive Alternative?

Many courts that have approved of allowing "incompetent" persons to be sterilized nonetheless have held that sterilization is permissible only when a court finds it is "the least restrictive alternative" for the subject of the sterilization.[43] But it is not self-evident how that standard should apply to the issues that arise in practice. Least restrictive alternative is sometimes (but not consistently) thought to require, for example, that the young woman be sexually active; or that she be found incapable of ever parenting; or that no alternative birth control be available. Consideration of those examples illustrates again that even when all agree that only the patient's own interests can appropriately be considered, there are many variations in how to assess those interests. Which approach is adopted on those and similar issues can determine whether least restrictive alternative and all the strict-sounding rules really do serve to protect the subject of the sterilization petition.

In spelling out prerequisites for sterilization many courts require a showing that the girl or woman is likely to engage in sexual activity. For example, to satisfy the burden of proving that there is a need for contraception, the *Hayes* court required the judge to find that the individual was "likely to engage in sexual activity at the present or in the near future under circumstances likely to result in pregnancy."[44] Similarly, the *Grady* court set forth as a factor for consideration "[t]he likelihood that the individual will voluntarily engage in sexual activity or be exposed to situations where sexual intercourse is imposed upon her."[45]

In Guardianship of K. M., the fifteen-year-old subject was not sexually active: her mother merely testified that "K. M.'s compliancy and naivety cause [the mother] concern that K. M. may engage in sexual activity without the ability to make judgments regarding the consequences."[46] Similarly, there was no evidence of ongoing sexual activity or any interest in sexual activity in *Grady*. In *Moe, Hayes*, and *Johnson*, however, sexual activity had already occurred.

Does it make sense to prohibit parents from protecting against the possibility of pregnancy before sex occurs? Some parents would like to have their child sterilized before they know that she is sexually active, and most courts will allow that if they consider imminent sexual activity to be likely.

Some advocates of sterilization would go further still, encouraging it even when the subject does not and is not expected to have a sex life. The justification put forward (as in the quotation from *Grady* above) is "to protect the subject from exploitation." That protective rationale can be used expansively. In reality, of course, sterilization would not protect her from sexual exploitation but would simply cover up the evidence that exploitation had occurred.[47]

A second common component of the general requirement that sterilization must be necessary is a requirement that the judge find the subject permanently incapable of parenting. After all, if the woman truly can never parent, it probably is in her interest not to give birth to a child who will have to be removed. Another justification for requiring permanent inability to parent is that, in that case, the grandmother may well have actual responsibility for the child after birth, so her opinion should carry more weight than in the typical case.

In many states judges are required to make findings that women are permanently incapable of parenting whenever they approve sterilizations, and they do make such findings. These findings are profoundly disturbing, given that our society does not judge the parenting skills of any other group before its members are allowed to parent. Moreover, the issues are often decided on the basis of nothing more than conclusory statements by the subject's parents and doctors. It always is difficult, if not impossible, to make confident judgments that will remain accurate regardless of any changes in the subject's circumstances. Requiring a finding that a person is permanently incapable, regardless of what circumstances might develop, seems contradictory to considering her independent enough to be consensually sexually active.

More fundamental, retardation alone does not suggest permanent incapacity to parent, and to presume that it does constitutes illegal discrimination. The generalization that persons with retardation cannot responsibly parent may well be true of many persons labeled "retarded." (Of course, it is true of many other people as well.) But it certainly is not true of all persons with retardation and may not even be true of as many as we are accustomed to believing cannot parent. Because society has not let parenting occur on a broad scale among those with retardation, it is difficult to assess reliably whether widespread parenting would be successful.[48]

A judgment approving sterilization after finding that a woman will be sexually active but will never be fit as a parent is particularly disturbing when made concerning a very young woman. Nonetheless, courts frequently approve sterilizations of minors and even twelve-year-olds.[49]

A third common prerequisite for court-ordered sterilization is that other, more reversible forms of birth control not be available alternatives. For example, the *Hayes* court explicitly said,

> there must be no alternatives to sterilization. The judge must find that by clear, cogent and convincing evidence (1) all less drastic contraceptive methods, including supervision, education and training, have been proved unworkable or inapplicable, and (2) the proposed method of sterilization entails the least invasion of the body of the individual. In addition, it must be shown by clear, cogent and convincing evidence that (3) the current state of scientific and medical knowledge does not suggest either (a) that a

reversible sterilization procedure or other less drastic contraceptive method will shortly be available, or (b) that science is on the threshold of an advance in the treatment of the individual's disability.[50]

Since 1980, when that court spoke, Norplant has become an available and popular alternative. Many women have opted to use it (although there also have been government attempts to coerce or heavily encourage that choice, especially with regard to women on welfare or teenagers labeled "at risk" of pregnancy).[51]

One would expect the existence of a reversible procedure like Norplant to cut down considerably on any need for sterilization—at least if medicine continues its current optimism about absence of long-term risk. There are some for whom Norplant is clearly not an alternative; it is contraindicated for women who are over thirty-five years old and who smoke more than fifteen cigarettes per day because it results in an increased risk of blood clots, heart attack, and stroke. For most younger women who do not smoke, however, Norplant would seem to be a less restrictive but adequately effective alternative to sterilization.

Accordingly, if the declared limitations on sterilization are actually followed, sterilization should be ruled out in many cases. And even if Norplant were not an option, the result might be the same. For most women, an IUD or a contraceptive pill is an available alternative, even if some caretakers would prefer that they be sterilized. In short, the requirement of the least restrictive alternative would seem to preclude many sterilizations, but all evidence suggests that this part of the articulated test is not followed in practice. Instead, parental requests for sterilization are usually granted with little ado.

Disagreement about the Reasons for Sterilization

It is not surprising that people cannot agree on what the requirements for nonconsensual sterilization should be, given that there is no agreement on the underlying issue of what the sterilization is supposed to protect against. The problem is more than academic, for different possible purposes suggest different permissible scopes for sterilization. One possibility discussed above—protecting against hereditary conditions—would lead to a different set of restrictions on procreation than some of the other concerns. For example, a person whose retardation stemmed from oxygen deprivation would not be sterilized, even if it did not appear that she could handle parenting. If protection against inadequate parenting were the issue, sterilization might be allowed more broadly (but it would be difficult to explain limiting it to persons with retardation and not other predictively inadequate parents.) And if protection of the interests and convenience of persons other than the person to be sterilized were legitimate, that approach could permit sterilizations not held to be in the subject's own best interests. It also might affect the type of sterilization that would be permitted—for instance, by allowing hysterectomy so that caretakers would not have to deal with menstruation, as well as to prevent pregnancy.

Sometimes it appears that the decisionmakers aim to protect people identified as "retarded" against "adult experiences" that are deemed inappropriate for them. The person called "retarded" is considered to be childlike, an approach encouraged by that favorite datum in many opinions, the patient's so-called mental age.[52] If an adult with retardation is viewed as equivalent to a child (sixteen being the "mental age" of persons of average intelligence), sex, as well as parenting, seems inappropriate. Similarly, opinions frequently contain the statement that the subject to be sterilized would not understand the pain of childbirth and so should not experience it.[53] If that reasoning were applied to all women, there would be very few mothers indeed.

Other times decisionmakers seek to protect the person called "retarded" from "adult responsibilities," on the assumption that she will be unable to fulfill those responsibilities. The protection is not only for her but even more for the child who would otherwise be born to her. (Of course, there is a difficulty in justifying the policy from the child's point of view, for the "protection" consists in not having the child born at all.) Here again the assumption is that the person with cognitive disabilities is irresponsible like a child and also that her capabilities are very limited. The assumption may be true for many persons labeled "retarded"—how many we do not know. But it surely is not true for all.

CHAPTER 8

Sex and Contraception

Many courts, such as the Massachusetts Supreme Judicial Court in *In re* Moe, refer to supervision as a "less drastic contraceptive method . . . [t]he possibility and effectiveness" of which must be considered by a court before it approves a petition for sterilization.[1] The object of supervision, of course, is to ensure that the adult or minor remain celibate. Indeed, many parents of children with retardation have relied on supervision to prevent their daughters from having a sex life that might lead to pregnancy. Often they seek sterilization because of fear that when their daughters move away from the sheltered environs of the parents' home into community-living contexts, supervision will not be sufficient to prevent sex and pregnancy. This was the acknowledged fear of the parents in *Grady*, for example.[2]

But supervision to prevent sex is not necessarily "least intrusive" for the young woman. Nor is it necessarily in her best interests to be prevented from having a sex life if she wants one. Clearly the Grady parents envisioned that Lee Ann might have sexual relationships when she left home. But many persons still question the desirability of enabling persons with retardation to have sexual freedom.

A fundamental issue is whether the women whose fates are being decided have a "right" to a sex life. Many judicial opinions and other statements about appropriate policy for people with retardation reflect assumptions about this issue without resolving it or even explicitly addressing it. In the course of our history, popular attitudes toward sex for persons who have retardation have changed considerably. The traditional horror at the thought that "mental deficients" might reproduce was accompanied by the myth of the oversexed and potentially dangerous man with retardation. Moreover, promiscuousness and illegitimacy were among the characteristics that contributed to a diagnosis of mental retardation in women, before IQ tests were routinely used to provide a numerical formula purporting to measure intelligence.

Today the myths have been exploded, and persons with retardation are not thought to have any greater or lesser sex drive than anyone else. It is also clear that most people with retardation (like most other people) are capable of being taught to control their impulses appropriately and that persons with retardation are as prepared to face a sex life as anyone else. Allowing persons to develop close human relationships, including sexual relationships, without regard to their IQ is required by the current policy of normalization. It is an essential part of accepting persons with retardation as full persons and as members of our community.

In 1996 The Arc issued the following policy statement concerning the sexuality of persons with retardation and procreation and parenting by them:

Sexuality is a natural part of every person's life. Sexuality includes gender identity, friendships, self-esteem, body image and awareness, emotional development and social behavior, as well as involvement in physical expressions of love, affection and desires. This issue requires respect and understanding.

Position

The Arc recognizes and affirms that individuals with mental retardation are people with sexual feelings, needs and identities, and believes that sexuality should always be seen in the total context of human relationships.

The Arc believes that people with mental retardation have fundamental rights as individuals to: have privacy; love and be loved; develop friendships and emotional relationships; learn about sex, sexual exploitation, sexual abuse, safe sex and other issues regarding sexuality; exercise their rights and responsibilities in regard to privacy and sexual expression and the rights of others; marry and make informed decisions concerning having children; and develop expressions of sexuality reflective of age, social development, cultural values and social responsibility.

The Arc further advocates that on an individual basis people with mental retardation who have children receive proper supports to assist them in rearing their children.

The Arc also believes that the presence of mental retardation regardless of severity must not, in itself, justify either involuntary sterilization or denial of sterilization to those who choose it for themselves.[3]

Constitutional Law concerning Minors' Access to Sex

It may be appropriate for a child, regardless of IQ level, that caretakers attempt to prevent sexual activity, through supervision or other rule setting. It is not at all clear that a minor has a "right" to a sex life. In Carey v. Population Services, the Supreme Court Justices discussed but did not decide whether minors have a constitutionally protected right to engage in sex. The Court majority did hold, by a 7–2 vote, that the U.S. Constitution forbids denying minors access to birth control. Arguably, that holding necessarily encompasses a right to engage in sex. After all, if minors are not going to have sex, why do they need birth control?[4] Four of the Justices, however, did not believe they had answered the question of minors' rights to a sex life (even though three of those Justices protected access to contraception), and others denied that minors' sexual privacy could be constitutionally protected.

On the issue of contraception for minors, there was no opinion for a majority of the Court, even though seven of the Justices decided that contraception must be available. Justice Brennan's opinion for a plurality of four said that "the right to privacy in connection with decisions affecting procreation extends to minors as well as to adults,"[5] but that it was unnecessary to pass upon the argument "that the State's policy to discourage sexual activity of minors is itself unconstitutional, for the reason that the right to privacy comprehends a right of minors as well as adults to engage in private consensual behavior." He also said that "in the area of sexual mores, as in other areas, the scope of permissible state regulation is broader as to minors than as to adults."[6]

Other Justices were more unequivocal in dismissing the possibility of a constitutionally protected right of access to sex, as opposed to contraception. Justice Stevens described "as frivolous [the] argument that a minor has a constitutionally protected right to put contraceptives to their intended use, notwithstanding the combined objections of both parents and the state,"[7] a statement with which Justice White, concurring separately, explicitly agreed. Justice Powell, concurring separately, opined, "the extraordinary protection the Court would give to all personal decisions in matters of sex is neither required by the Constitution nor supported by our prior decisions."

Finally, Justice Rehnquist, the sole dissenter other than Chief Justice Burger (who did not write or join in any opinion), pointed out that those who fought the Revolution and framed our Constitution and its Amendments would be most surprised that their efforts led to unmarried minors' rights to buy contraception.

Constitutional Law concerning Adults' Access to Sex

Even if it is appropriate to use supervision to deny a sex life to minors, including minors with mental retardation, the analysis differs for adults. Surely adults have a right to pursue consensual sexual relationships—at least a right to have government not interfere with most consensual sexual activities. Popular opinion would suppose that was the law in the United States, partly because it reflects current practices. Of course, the state is not obliged to provide everyone or anyone with a sex life, but only to avoid interfering with what individuals can come up with on their own.

In fact, however, there is extreme ambiguity in current constitutional law concerning the bounds of even adults' right to choose. It clearly exists within marriage,[8] but arguably states can interfere even with adult persons' consensual sex lives, as long as they do so evenhandedly, through laws proscribing fornication or adultery. Despite considerable opinion that such laws would no longer pass constitutional scrutiny, the Supreme Court has studiously avoided ruling on the issue, while enforcing and developing a constitutional right of access to birth control even for unmarried adults and minors.

In Eisenstadt v. Baird, for example, the Court found that unmarried persons have a constitutional right of access to contraceptives, but at the same time assumed that the state could constitutionally criminalize sex outside marriage. And even in Carey v. Population Services, decided when the constitutionalization of reproductive rights was in its heydey, the Court pointed out not only that a right to contraception does not include a right to sex but also (according to Justice Brennan) "that the Court has not definitively answered the difficult question whether and to what extent the Constitution prohibits state statutes regulating such behavior among adults." Justice White argued that it was unclear that adults have constitutional rights to noninterference in their extramarital consensual sex lives, and he joined in the *Carey* opinion, as he had in others, only on the assumption that it did not declare unconstitutional any state law forbidding extramarital sexual relations.[9] Justices Powell and Rehnquist also expressed skepticism.

More recently, in a civil suit against a man for knowingly and fraudulently transmitting the herpes virus, the consensual sex partner who sued was not permitted to recover. The court's theory was that she was a partner in the crime of fornication, which is still illegal in Virginia, and because of her own involvement in illegal sex, she could not sue for fraud.[10] That case amounts to a holding, albeit not by the U.S. Supreme Court, that a state can constitutionally punish consensual extramarital heterosexual sex. Accordingly, even when adults are involved, it is not clear that their right of access to contraception includes rights to engage in sex outside of marriage.

In short, the precise contours of the right to choose to engage in sexual relationships have not been established for minors or even adults, but whatever the boundary line of constitutionally protected activity is, it should be the same whether or not persons are labeled "retarded."

Access to Sex for Persons with Retardation

Even though sex should not be illegal for anyone on the basis of her or his IQ, difficult issues remain: for example, how to regard consent by persons with retardation and how to protect against exploitation while preserving the right of vulnerable people to experience a full life.[11] Nevertheless, persons with retardation should no more be denied a sex life because of fears of exploitation than they should be denied the opportunity to live in the community because of the possibilities of exploitation, or denied the right to attend school because they may be teased or have other painful experiences there. Society's obligation is to work to reduce or eliminate the exploitation and other shameful treatment, not to "protect" persons by denying them access to a full life.

Despite public disapproval of sex lives for persons with retardation, the population with disabilities disagrees. If substituted judgment were defined to reflect the actual wishes of the subject, access to sexual relationships would be permitted them on the same basis as it is for others.

The interest of this population in having normal sexual relationships is illustrated by the experiences that the producers and directors of Warner Brothers' *Life Goes On* had when they met with five young persons with Down's syndrome to get advice about plotting that prime-time television series. One of the show's primary characters, Corky, was a twenty-year-old man with Down's syndrome. When the consultants were asked what they wanted to see happen in the show, the five unanimously agreed that "what they wanted most was not on the story list." They wanted "Corky to have a girlfriend, or at least a date. Either would be good." One of the men who had seemed inattentive before this suggestion suddenly looked up and asked, "Could we have a love triangle? . . . One girl could be normal. One could have [Down's] . . . Or one could just be disabled. Maybe in a wheelchair."[12]

The show's directors responded, "We love it. Corky would be put in a position of having to hurt someone, reject someone. That hasn't happened before."[13]

It was important to the consultants that the story line characterize them as whole human beings with normal human feelings of love and sexuality. One young man, aged sixteen, said that he did not have a girlfriend but then added, "I wish." In response, a twenty-two-year-old woman with Down's syndrome said, "I don't know . . . I'd just like to have myself a boyfriend. We'd talk, hold hands, things like that. We could got to movies, restaurants. I could see what his hobbies are. Is he talented?"[14]

The Down's syndrome consultants and actors in *Life Goes On* were varied in their abilities and also were aware of and open about their limitations.[15] Chris Clubb, the originator of the love-triangle story line, has a maintenance job at a record store and, though he has difficulty in managing the money he earns, he is improving with the help of an independence trainer; another consultant said that he used to feel scared when he was left home alone but now feels that he can handle it and even orders pizzas on his own and pays the delivery person.

Clearly societal views are moving in the direction of accepting a sex life for persons with retardation on the same basis as everyone else, although they have not yet fully embraced that position. Part of the difficulty in reporting any consensus on this subject is that people differ so radically and so feverishly about what kind of sex life should be seen as acceptable behavior for people in general. This fundamental and hard-fought dispute spills over to other issues. For example, many who disfavor sexual relationships outside marriage also disfavor sex education. Others believe that today it is more realistic to provide sex education, and possibly even access to condoms, even in settings like high schools, where the preferred course is undoubtedly abstinence.[16]

The Importance of Sex Education

If the possibility of a sex life for persons with retardation is recognized, meaningful sex education must be provided. Persons with retardation, even more than other people, may need to be taught how to act safely and responsibly and to understand what feelings are normal and what actions are socially acceptable. They may need education more than people with higher IQs do, because it is more difficult for them to pick up knowledge in other ways—through reading or casual conversation. Under the traditional approach of simply not talking to persons with retardation about these matters, imagine how difficult it was for young persons without any information to experience the changes of puberty. Especially for someone who has been dubbed "abnormal" all of his or her life, these changes, without any outside acknowledgment or information, could be very frightening indeed.

Sex education for persons who have retardation may cover a broad range of activities. It may, for example, include instruction in the social norms of dating and how to progress in a dating relationship—subjects not necessary to teach most teenagers but which persons with retardation often need to be taught in order to function well in the community and adapt to the mainstream. Sex education is increasingly becoming an important program in special needs and other schools; at institutions, sometimes under court-supervised consent decrees; and also in community-based homes.[17] Nonetheless more remains to be done. As the Arc's 1996 policy statement pointed out: "The commitment to full inclusion into the community has given people with mental retardation new experiences, different risks, and more opportunities to make choices. Currently, many people with mental retardation are not receiving education and support to protect them from abuse, exploitation, unwanted pregnancy, and sexually transmitted diseases, while safeguarding their dignity and rights."

When persons with retardation are taught to act responsibly, they are made more competent—more like everyone else. They are also treated with dignity when they are provided with meaningful sex education and taught to make their own decisions, instead of being controlled.

Today providing persons who have retardation with information about biology and sex is considered part of normalization, but only relatively recently have institutions and community-living facilities begun providing sex education to adults with retardation. For persons with retardation who were institutionalized as late as the 1960s and 1970s, sex education was unknown. Consequently, many of these people, now middle-aged, have little or no understanding of basic facts about human sexuality.[18]

The central goal of the "no sex" policies in institutions was to keep persons with retardation from having children. If they were kept ignorant of their sexuality, so the theory went, they would be less likely to engage in sex. But by not teaching persons with retardation, or even engaging in discussion with them about how their bodies were developing and why the changes were normal, educators created more confusion about sex then was necessary. They also missed an opportunity to teach people with marginal IQs how to express, control, and act upon their sexual desires appropriately. In fact, a person's ability to learn and to understand in this area is much more likely to correlate with whether she is interested in having sexual relationships than with her IQ number.

There have always been substantial reasons for providing sex education to persons with retardation, but the HIV/AIDS epidemic has created yet another. In 1991 the Arc's HIV Prevention Project published a statement suggesting that AIDS can have a particularly strong impact on persons with retardation because "adults with mental retardation may be the victims of sexual abuse and sexual exploitation. In the age of safer sex, some people refuse to take precautions. Sometimes, their sexual partners are adults with mental retardation."[19] The project reported that sex education is a proven preventative measure when teaching methods are specifically tailored to persons with retardation. Finally, the project's statement included a detailed list of sexual activities that it rates in categories ranging from "unsafe" (such as unprotected intercourse); to "safer," including protected intercourse and forms of sexual expression short of intercourse. "Safer sex," it explains, lowers "the risk of infection with the AIDS virus and other diseases . . . [and] also reduces the risk of unwanted pregnancy." The statement underscores, however, that the "only fully 'safe sex' is no sex." It thus proposes celibacy as a valid personal choice for people—a significantly different stance from touting the need for supervision to enforce celibacy.[20]

Unless sex education is provided tactfully and with sensitivity, it should not be provided at all. Some programs report that they have offered sex education but have had little success in getting clients to discuss sex. And success in teaching anything to persons with retardation requires care in explaining things simply, in ways that will be understood.

Moreover, the distinction between sex education and indoctrination is an important, though difficult, one. Views about appropriate sexual activity differ radically, and it is not appropriate simply to indoctrinate residents, clients, or students with the instructor's own or the institution's views and values. Yet it is often unclear how to draw the line. If a client expresses a desire to have a child, most educators or social workers would see it as their role to discourage the client, or even to change the client's mind. They would do so believing it impossible for the client to raise a child. But whether it is appropriate for caregivers or supervisors so to counsel their charges is debatable (and will be addressed in Part Four).

Even though sex education cannot solve all problems, most institutions and residences that have adopted it express satisfaction with the results. This is true even though it makes people more aware of sexual issues and practices and makes it more difficult to follow practices like feeding a woman birth control pills without her consent. As a general matter, through sex education (like other education) persons with retardation do grow in sophistication. From their point of view, it is clearly preferable for others to talk to them about social and sexual relationships than it is for others simply to make the decisions.

Sex education thus facilitates normalization and promotes informed sexual choices. As the court in *Moe* suggested, it can make workable the alternatives to sterilization.[21] It does that by giving persons with retardation what is most in their interest to have: knowledge about how to make informed and responsible sexual choices for themselves.

Preferring Contraception over Sterilization

Other methods of contraception are far preferable to sterilization—at least for those who are not making their own decisions. Indeed, most states' laws provide that sterilization is available for "incompetent" persons only when no alternative contraception is possible. Although that limitation exists in the law and in theory, it often is not followed in practice.

The chief reason contraception is preferable is that it is reversible, whereas sterilization generally is not.[22] Most contraception preserves options for the future, as the young woman's circumstances change. Moreover, sterilization is a more intrusive medical procedure than most contraceptive alternatives. It also, to many persons with retardation, is regarded as a badge of inferiority, as evidence of being considered "a retard." That perception is particularly common in persons previously institutionalized. It may change with changing social attitudes, as there come to be fewer persons with retardation who have had experience in state facilities.

It must nonetheless be acknowledged that sterilization is the procedure of choice for a significant percentage of women in the United States.[23] This fact could be and is used to support the argument that persons who cannot make their own choices should have access to sterilization, as others do. Nonetheless the law's articulated preference for other means of contraception for persons who are not making the decision for themselves is defensible. Sterilization is a more drastic alternative; is comparatively more permanent; and has a history of extreme abuse.

Even accepting contraception as preferable to sterilization leaves open the problem of what the rules should be for administering contraception to nonconsenting persons. Should it be limited to persons who are sexually active? Should forgoing contraception also be considered an option? Who is to be the decisionmaker? And, most important, who are the persons who will not be permitted to consent or refuse consent themselves but will be subject to the decision of somebody else?

In short, the questions are the same as those posed with regard to sterilization. Are the answers the same as well? First let us survey what occurs in practice; then we will examine the governing law.

Contraception: Practice and Law

Different methods of administering contraceptives to women with retardation occur, whether at state schools or other institutions, community residences, or family homes. Interviews with parents, the young women themselves, and a range of workers in these settings and in sheltered workshops suggest that a great many persons who have developmental disabilities—including persons who have not been declared legally incompetent—are receiving contraception at the behest of their caretakers, although these people with disabilities have limited knowledge and an extremely limited ability to refuse. At the same time a duty to keep the patient informed is increasingly acknowledged, at least in principle. And in many homes and other residences, persons with retardation are being brought into decisions about their own well-being more than ever before.

Past practice was to exclude them.

Even within a state, practices at state facilities have varied over time and also between facilities, depending in part on the population the facility has served. What follows is a description of one model that was typical in the 1960s—a model that describes past practice at one Massachusetts state school. (In Massachusetts today, parents of persons who are still living in state facilities prefer the term "state schools" or "state facilities" to "institutions.")[24]

Every woman who was diagnosed "retarded," who appeared capable of reproducing, and who had even the slightest independence was placed on birth control pills without discussion. Nurses handed out pills and clients took what they were given, so the norm was that the client was not even informed that she was on contraception. At this facility there was no rule requiring family members' consent, unless they had become the client's legal guardian. At some other facilities, however, parents or other close relatives were always informed when the client was deemed "incompetent," even if there was no guardian.

Parents did not typically resist the imposition of birth control when the decision to administer it was communicated. They often feared pregnancy as much as the school did. Part of the fear was the prevalent myth that parents with retardation would have children with retardation. Even parents whose religious beliefs led them to oppose contraception as a general matter did not raise objections.

Most institutionalized women with retardation and many others were fed birth control pills over a period of years, often without their personal knowledge. For many of the women the contraception was utterly unnecessary, because they were not sexually active.

Current practice is often more enlightened. But it typically does not go so far as to require consent from the client herself. The law might suggest that relying on her consent would be most appropriate, unless there is a guardian with power over contraception. The failure to rely on the client (and sometimes even to involve her) reflects an assumption that the client herself would be incapable of giving meaningful informed consent, even though no guardianship proceeding has been undertaken.

The debate continues about whether parents should be involved in decisions made in state and other facilities, when the parents are not legal guardians and their children are over the age of majority. Some schools and other facilities do attempt to involve the family in decisonmaking and to achieve consensus with them, even if family members are not guardians and there is thus no legal requirement that they be involved. But practices are inconsistent, and the issue is a sensitive one.

At some state facilities and private and community homes, caretakers said that their charges do formally make their own decisions despite retardation. They are, however, "encouraged," "pressured," or "persuaded" to take birth control pills.

The same range of practices that exists in state and community facilities also exists for women who live in their family homes.[25] Some parents inform and involve the young woman in the decision to take birth control pills, and some do not. Some of those who do inform their daughters exert considerable pressure to use birth control, and some do not. Some take care that contraception is limited to circumstances and times it is necessary, but some do not. Even if the state were to attempt to enforce rules about involving the young woman, or even making her decision determinative, they would be difficult or impossible to enforce in the context of a young woman living with her family.

At the same time, having such rules can help create a norm. In any event, progressive trends are noticeable. There is definitely a trend toward recognizing self-determination by persons with retardation and increasingly involving them in their own life decisions. The attitudes of social workers, directors, and staff at community residences in many parts of the country reflect these attitudes. They also are reflected in what is taught young women with retardation who attend specialized classrooms or schools.

The emphasis on self-determination often does not extend, however, to issues concerning procreation. Some of the schools most protective of students' right to make their own life decisions also teach young women with disabilities that they will not be able to have children. They are not trying to do the students any harm. Administrators simply presume that the students would not be able to raise a child. Accordingly, they conclude, allowing the students to get pregnant and have babies they would have to give up would not be in the students' best interests.

Different Legal Treatment of Sterilization and Other Contraceptive Measures

In some ways it seems hypocritical to prohibit sterilization by substituted consent but still allow third persons to consent to contraception. After all, both procedures interfere with procreation and, if not personally selected, with procreative choice. Effective contraception, if administered continuously, interferes with pregnancy and parenting as effectively as sterilization does.[26] Moreover, the possible substitute decisionmakers—caretakers, guardians, parents, judges—have the same conflicts of interest.

Relevant to both procedures is the tendency of third-party decisionmakers to disfavor childbirth by persons who legally cannot make decisions for themselves. The common attitude that parenting is not a serious option no doubt reflects the decisionmakers' perception of the young woman's own interests. But it also usually accords with their perception of their own interests, in the case of parents, caretakers, and guardians, for the young woman to avoid pregnancy. And it certainly accords with common conceptions of societal interests.

Even though other contraception, administered continuously, has the same effect as sterilization and is also subject to the risks, as well as benefits, of third-party decisions, third-party contraceptive decisions are treated in the law very differently from third-party sterilization requests: Modern procedural reforms require judicial decisionmaking in the case of sterilization but not for contraceptive decisions. This difference in judicial supervision is critical, even though the other "rules" for sterilization and contraception seem similar.

There are no reported cases where a parent or guardian was required to come to court in order to obtain permission to administer contraception. Similarly, there are no statutory laws governing contraceptive issues as such for persons deemed incapable of giving informed consent. Instead, the norm with contraceptives—as with other medications, whether over-the-counter or prescription—is to administer them to persons who cannot consent for themselves without seeking judicial approval. A substitute decisionmaker, in consultation with a physician if a prescription is needed, simply decides.

This different approach does seem justified. A moment's reflection makes clear why judicial oversight of contraceptive decisions would not be administrable, and in any event would not be desirable.

There are many opportunities in life for parents or guardians to act in ways that are arguably affected by their own interests and that arguably may not be in the interests of their child or ward. When a mother decides not to allow her daughter to attend a coed dance because she fears her daughter may form relationships with men, she may not be acting in the best interests of her daughter, and part of her motivation may in fact be selfish. (She may not want to share her daughter's company with young men; or she may wish to avert the possibility of having to care for her daughter's child, for example.)

But does this mean that the decision should be transferred to a judge? Can the daughter bring a lawsuit to force her mother to let her know the world? Can a guardian *ad litem* make the objection for her? Many of us, even if we think the decision confining the daughter is manifestly wrong, would not expect or want the propriety of such decisions to be reevaluated by a judge for somewhat obvious reasons: Judges can't do everything. Many believe that in the United States they do too much already, even without jurisdiction over these types of domestic disputes. Moreover, judicial expertise may be singularly lacking with respect to many of the decisions that would arise. Finally, formulating a "law" over the right way to act in such situations would diminish the diversity in ideas and practices that today characterizes American society and is part of our protected "right to privacy."

Parents or guardians, usually in consultation with a physician, routinely decide whether to administer contraception, how to administer it, and what method to use. They also decide whether to inform the patient that she is being fed birth control pills or whether simply to administer contraception without any discussion. Sometimes instead of contraception, third-party decisionmakers will opt for abstinence, with or without the assent of the subject, by providing continuous supervision, for example. Rarely will third-party decisionmakers encourage pregnancy or choose birth.

Distinguishing Sterilization from Other Contraception

Another reason it may seem absurd to have sharply different rules for sterilization and other contraception is that it is increasingly difficult to distinguish between the two categories. Today there exist both relatively permanent contraception and reversible sterilization. What rules should apply to them? How, in general, should judges draw a line on the slippery slope between sterilization and contraception, as they must if sharply different rules come to apply? If there are to be different rules there will be difficult issues about where to draw the line, issues that in the end will probably be resolved by a series of arbitrary judgments.[27]

Norplant, for example, is increasingly popular and increasingly available; it is generally considered a form of birth control—contraception—but it is rather long-lasting; its insertion protects against pregnancy typically for five years. The device can be removed before it has expired, but the removal procedure is both more expensive and more intrusive than is the insertion; and indeed in some government programs insertion has been funded for teenage mothers and others, but the mother herself must pay if she desires removal—usually a few hundred dollars.[28] The IUD is also permanent in comparison to birth control pills, which must be taken daily to be effective, or condoms and diaphragms, which must be used every time.

Indeed, the permanence of Norplant raises the question why today sterilization would ever be necessary (except in those cases where there are real, not fabricated, counterindications). Surely Norplant provides sufficient protection, and it also leaves open the opportunity for change, if circumstances ever allow that. Moreover, as a new procedure that many persons are using by choice, it does not carry the stigma for persons with retardation that sterilization does. Still, the comparative permanence of Norplant makes it a more intrusive alternative than other forms of birth control, and they should be preferred if adequate.

Not only is there relatively permanent contraception, but also there is reversible sterilization; that phenomenon probably influenced the U.S. Supreme Court's declining to review one of the most egregious sterilization cases of the past decade. Estate of C. W., which will be discussed in detail in Chapter 11, involved sterilization of a twenty-year-old woman on the petition of her mother and over the vehement objections of the guardian *ad litem*. During the trial it evolved that the sterilization could be performed by laparoscopic tubal ligation with high frequency current. An obstetrician at the University of Pennsylvania Hospital testified, as an expert for the mother seeking sterilization, that "one of the important things about [this type of sterilization] is, although it is considered to be a permanent sterilization, it really is not. The rate of reversibility is upwards of 80%." As he explained, "laparoscopic electrocoagulation involves the insertion of [a] telescope into the belly button with [a] distal light source, identifying and burning a segment of the Fallopian tubes so that they are closed. Should the patient decide to reopen the tubes, the surgeon can often cut out the obstruction and successfully bring the two open ends together again." The outrageousness of the C. W. case[29] made it an ideal candidate for Supreme Court intervention to resolve continuing disputes about sterilization by third-party consent. But the alleged reversibility of the new laparoscopic methods made the case arguably not about sterilization at all, as opposed to other contraception. Whether for this reason or another, the U.S. Supreme Court declined to review the case.

Norplant, laparoscopic tubal ligation, and other procedures already in use or yet to come show that sterilization and other birth control occupy a spectrum and are not two clearly defined and different categories. Just as Norplant should be considered more intrusive than other contraception (though the ranking on this spectrum need not alone determine results), so perhaps should laparoscopic tubal ligation be considered less intrusive than the more traditional and more permanent methods. Because it is less invasive, it should be preferred, especially when third-party decisionmaking controls.

Nonetheless the Court in *C. W.* should not have been dissuaded by the apparent reversibility of the sterilization procedure—that is, the apparent good chance of reversibility.[30] Even if C. W. were one of the 80 percent for whom reversal could work, who is ever going to get the tubal ligation reversed for her? As a practical matter, the tubal ligation is the end of C. W.'s childbearing potential. It is more final than Norplant, which would have to be renewed each five years, or than an IUD, which would have to be checked annually.

In addition, one of the judges involved in the case made the point that the sterilization of old, which had existed when the sterilization rules were crafted, has been replaced in many areas by this "highly reversible" procedure. The implication is that all sterilization should now perhaps be treated as mere contraception. In addition, the judge added that even without rejoining the fallopian tubes, the recipient of a tubal ligation can now become pregnant through in vitro fertilization (IVF). That may be a significant point to be considered by those deciding for themselves, but IVF is hardly likely to be available to the young woman with mental retardation having sterilization imposed on her.

Although Norplant especially threatens any dichotomy between sterilization and other contraception, for the time being at least the conventional line is as good as any: judicial oversight should extend to all those procedures commonly dubbed sterilization, while allowing other birth control to escape judicial scrutiny. In the future, sterilization and contraception categories may merge even more, calling for reformulation of which cases require judicial review. For the moment, it is worthwhile to draw a line on the slippery slope separating sterilization from other contraception and to maintain distinct treatment of the two subjects for purposes of third-party consent.

Although contraceptive decisions probably cannot and should not be made by judges, the almost total lack of supervision that exists today seems dangerous. A central problem is that any limits one would impose—such as a requirement that the young woman be sexually active, or at least that there be some likelihood of sexual activity—cannot be regulated at all. But allowing parents and guardians to exercise their own good faith judgments, as current practice does, is still preferable to judicial decisionmaking. After all, parents and guardians make many decisions for their charges—sometimes virtually all of their decisions—without legal supervision. What medications to provide a woman, whether to take her to a physician, and other important decisions can be every bit as important as whether to administer contraception, yet legal oversight is not deemed necessary or desirable.

Some safeguard to parental abuse lies in the necessity of physician consent and participation in obtaining prescription-only medications and in administering many forms of birth control (for example, the IUD). One appropriate (though slow and indirect) means of improving decisionmaking in this context lies in medical school education. Physicians in training should be acquainted with the ethical dilemmas inherent in dealing with vulnerable persons. Medical students and doctors also need to learn about the value of human beings with different capabilities and conditions, and they need to be acquainted with the perspectives of persons who have socioeconomic circumstances and levels of opportunity that are drastically different from the physicians' own.

Even accepting that judicial oversight of contraception decisions should not exist (at least where the government itself is not guardian or caretaker), issues remain about the propriety of the individual's taking control of her own decisions, and if she cannot, about what the alternative decisionmaker should decide and on what basis. Although a court will not be deciding those issues, they remain with the guardian, or parent, or other persons influencing the choice.

Even without judicial oversight, a third-party decisionmaker should be guided by the same considerations of respecting the personal integrity and the dignity of the subject of their decision. In the context of contraception, the decisions will often be made by parents and caretakers; in the context of sterilization, legislators, judges, and other policymakers will control. The same considerations that guide decisionmaking by judges should be norms for private third-party decisionmakers.

The Legal Status of Persons with Mental Retardation Compared with That of Children

With children, the third-party decisionmaker's role is more clear-cut than with other "incompetents": The caretaker's substitute decisionmaking automatically ends as the child passes the magic line of majority, usually eighteen years of age.[31] At majority, children obtain the *legal right* to make their own decisions. (In practice, however, they may have already assumed control of their decisions; or *per contra*, they may remain in fact dependent for a few more years.) Whether or not the legal age of majority causes a child actually to assume control at that moment, the child is likely to know that she now has that legal right. And she is likely, to some extent at least, to have the wherewithal to assert it, if asserting it is important to her.

For persons with mental retardation, there is no such clear moment of transition from legal incompetence to legal competence. Moreover, many in that group, of whatever age, may be unable to resist dominating caretakers, even when they know that they want to. Neither in law nor in practice is there a clear line as to when persons with retardation should begin to speak for themselves or should be recognized as having authority to do so.

Some may object that there is a clear line, at least for legal purposes, and that it turns on guardianship: In the spirit of treating persons with mental retardation like all other people, persons over eighteen years of age should be presumed their own decisionmaker, unless they have a guardian. This is probably "the law" and probably the best policy, yet this approach creates certain serious dilemmas. For example, when a person is not under guardianship but does not in fact seem capable of giving informed consent to a medical procedure, what is a physician to do? Moreover, even if there were a clear presumption of competence to decide absent guardianship, that seemingly clear rule does not impart much information about who is permitted to make their own decisions, because it does not reveal when a guardian will be deemed appropriate and when one will not.

CHAPTER 9

The Limited Impact
of Guardianship

Thus far we have considered sterilization and other contraceptive decisionmaking without distinguishing sharply between adults who have been placed under guardianship and those who have not. Is guardianship an important variable affecting reproductive decisionmaking?

Guardianship deprives the ward of her civil rights and takes away her legal ability to make her own decisions. It makes her an incompetent person in the eyes of the law. That is the theory of guardianship, and it is reserved for those in some sense deemed unable to decide for themselves. Some persons are obviously in that category, such as persons who are comatose and young children. But guardianship has also been traditional with respect to both persons with retardation and persons with mental illness.

For both those groups, however, guardians and guardianship are becoming less important than they once were. Instead of the "general guardianship" that once prevailed, guardianships are commonly limited now, perhaps to financial matters or to therapeutic medical decisionmaking, on the assumption that subjects can make other decisions for themselves. Limiting the scope of decisions a guardian is to make fits well with current trends toward normalization of persons who have retardation, and increased respect and encouragement for what people can do despite retardation. At least in theory, the limitations on a guardianship should protect the individual's right to make her own decisions when she can.

Moreover, many persons who have retardation do not have guardians at all. Perhaps surprisingly, whether they do have a guardian does *not* reflect their relative competence. Instead it reflects only whether someone has brought the required legal proceeding. Many of the people who are the least competent in fact will not have guardians simply because no one has instituted the procedure for them. But simply lacking a family does not prevent guardianship; the state can become guardian of persons without family or friends to assume that role, and it was traditional in institutions and state schools for the state to have guardianship of some of the clients.

Failure to institute guardianship proceedings can occur because no one takes any interest or because of simple inertia. Or it can result from a caretaker's desire to treat her charge with respect, because to impose guardianship is to take away another's civil rights. Guardianship transfers the ward's legal rights, in a sense, to the guardian, although its purpose is beneficent, "for the ward's protection."

It is often assumed that central to the issue of procreative (and many other) choices is whether a person is "legally competent" or instead has a guardian. If so, cases like *Valerie N.*, in which parents had been named conservators or guardians, would have little bearing on others involving adults who might have retardation but who had not been placed under guardianship.

Indeed it is common to propose sorting persons with retardation into two groups, according to the presence or absence of a guardian, and following different approaches for each. For example, one author, stating what policy should be adopted to protect the rights of persons with retardation, opines that a "good community-based system should, in effecting normalization, treat . . . its clients as competent and should insist that the community do likewise, excepting only those persons who have court-appointed guardians and those declared incompetent in a court of law."[1]

Such a separation in empowerment between those who are legally competent and those who are under guardianship seems perhaps obvious, but it also is extremely unhelpful and even misleading. There are two separate reasons: persons who *have* guardians still may have authority to make the particular decision at issue; and persons who *lack* guardians do not always in fact have authority to make the decisions. Consequently, guardianship is less significant than it appears, and its existence or nonexistence cannot be used to identify whether substitute decisionmaking is appropriate.

Four Scenarios

To examine whether guardianship has significant effects, it is necessary to separate decisions for which judicial review is required, like sterilization, from other, unsupervised decisions a guardian might make, because the effect of guardianship differs in these two kinds of decisions. Accordingly, we

Table 9.1   The impact of guardianship on reproductive matters

Subject under guardianship	No guardianship
Sterilization	
Judicial supervision required.	Remains vulnerable to guardianship in two ways:
Guardian's decision to sterilize must be approved by court.	May need to obtain a guardian as prerequisite to sterilization.
Court will examine ward's ability to decide; even without that ability, her wishes will be consulted.	Third party who wants her sterilized can institute proceeding to become guardian and petition for sterilization.
Contraception (and other situations without official supervision)	
Guardian stands between ward and third parties. (This is the most significant effect of guardianship.)	Third parties may or may not accept a woman's own decision as controlling; they may require another's consent.
Guardian may or may not dominate ward's decisionmaking, depending on their relationship.	Caretaker may or may not dominate woman's decision-making, depending on their relationship.

will explore the effect of guardianship in each of the following four situations: sterilization decisions in cases where there is a guardian; sterilization decisions when there is no guardian; other contraceptive decisions when there is a guardian; and other contraceptive decisions with no guardian. The object is to demonstrate the limited relevance of guardianship to reproductive and other elective matters.

Table 9.1 incorporates the conclusions of this exploration and shows that in the spectrum of situations that can occur, the impact of guardianship on the ward's own ability to decide is less than is commonly supposed.

Does the guardian, at least the general guardian, have authority to make decisions concerning reproductive choices? The sterilization cases show, in that context anyway, that a guardian's authority is limited by two other possible decisionmakers: the patient herself and the court.

If a woman is under general guardianship, it has already been adjudicated that many decisions are not for the ward to make. But even in that situation, modern sterilization cases require an inquiry into her own ability to understand and make the sterilization decision, rather than simple reliance on the prior appointment of even a general guardian.[2] So in that sense, the status of being under guardianship is not determinative: The ward's wishes may be relevant or controlling. If abortion needs judicial approval, the same approach would presumably follow for abortion.

In another sense as well, the guardian lacks power over sterilization. Modern sterilization cases suggest that whether or not a guardian has already been appointed, sterilization of anyone based on third-party consent must be approved in a judicial hearing.

Although persons under even general guardianship sometimes get to make their own decisions, those who do not have guardians may still be vulnerable to third-party decisionmaking. The most important reason is that a third person who wants to make a decision for them can petition to become their guardian; they are vulnerable to guardianship if their incapacity could be shown to the judge's satisfaction in a court proceeding. Moreover, they themselves may be driven to seek a guardian, even though they feel capable of making decisions without one, because third parties will not accept their personal consent as sufficient.[3]

Jane R., for example, who is twenty-five years old and has moderate retardation, has no guardian. But if her mother wants to get her sterilized, she might accomplish that by going to court and asking to be made Jane's guardian so that she (Jane's mother) can consent to sterilization. Indeed, Jane's mother might have to take those steps to have her daughter sterilized, even if Jane wants the sterilization procedure—even if Jane was the initiator—if a physician refused to accept Jane's consent to her own operation because of her retardation.

In the case of sterilization particularly, it makes little difference whether one already has a guardian before the sterilization petition, because it is necessary to obtain the court's consent for sterilization anyway. If a petition for guardianship must also be filed, that may not even add an extra judicial proceeding.

Clearly then, with respect to sterilization, there is not a huge difference between those who have a guardian already before anyone attempts to have them sterilized and those who do not. But most decisions made by general guardians for their wards, unlike sterilization, do not require judicial approval. How relevant is guardianship in those circumstances?

When decisionmaking operates outside the legal-judicial process, it may be more important whether a person already has a guardian. On the one hand, guardianship would seem critical, because legally the guardian is the final decisionmaker. On the other hand, closer analysis shows that guardianship may not have much to do with the individual's actual authority.

Guardianship does create legal authority in the guardian to make decisions, within the scope of the guardianship. That can make a substantial difference in control of the ward in her relations with outsiders. The guardian in a sense becomes an intermediary who is put in a position to protect the ward in her relations with others. The guardian's dealings with the ward herself concerning personal matters may not, however, be any different from those of a parent or caretaker who is not a guardian. The guardian and the caretakers can persuade and control up to a point, but ultimately their decisionmaking will usually depend on the patient's cooperation.

Probably the most important area of control for guardians is in the ward's dealings and relationships with third persons. If a patient has a general guardian (or a medical guardian), a physician will involve that person in any medical decisionmaking. Similarly, if there is a caretaker other than the guardian, that person will consult with the guardian before making significant decisions. As long as third persons know about the guardianship, they know that the law does not protect them in their dealings with the ward, so it is in their self-interest to comply with the law and involve the guardian in decisionmaking.

Especially if the guardian is *not* the direct caretaker, the likelihood that the guardian will be brought in on significant decisions may be reason for a parent to obtain guardianship even if the parent firmly respects the offspring's right to decide for herself. For a guardian can serve to protect the ward against third persons' imposing their wishes on her. The guardian can substitute his or her assessment of best interests for that of other third parties. If the guardian is a believer in self-determination, he or she may choose to involve the ward to the maximum extent possible and, indeed, to defer to the ward's wishes.

An adult person who is not under guardianship has a legal right to make her own decisions. If she has apparent retardation, however, it is unpredictable whether third persons will accept her own decision as controlling. If, for example, a woman with retardation goes to a physician for a prescription or a medical procedure, the physician may deal with her directly as with any other patient. But the physician may worry about accepting her as her own decisionmaker.

Whether the physician accepts the patient's ability to consent for herself should in theory, under accepted doctrine, turn upon her ability to give informed consent, but informed consent itself is an amorphous and flexible concept. In practice, whether the physician will accept her ability to deal for herself will turn both on the physician's conception of informed consent and also on whether he or she feels vulnerable to suit in proceeding without consent from third parties.

If the patient can give informed consent to the satisfaction of the physician, obviously there is no problem, and she will, if she wishes, represent herself like any other patient. The problem arises when there is no guardian but nonetheless the physician does not deem the patient capable of giving informed consent.

There are three possible reactions, none of which is uncommon. First, the physician may nevertheless work with the patient directly. Second, the physician may consult with the patient's family, or the patient's caretaker, and proceed only if they also consent. Finally, a physician may insist on a court-appointed guardian to consent to the procedure before being willing to undertake it. The physician thereby effectively requires the patient to choose between abandoning the medical treatment and acquiring a guardian (or seeking another physician, if she is able to do that).

Physicians' responses are not uniform and hence are unpredictable. A physician may require less supervision for a prescription for birth control pills than for a sterilization or an abortion, although it is not clear that the theory of informed consent can account for that difference. The response also turns on how risk-averse the particular physician is. Many, without regard to the written law, will go ahead with a parent, even if there is no guardian, as long as no one is objecting. The response also will be affected by the law of the particular jurisdiction; some statutes appear to allow family members to participate in and consent to medical procedures even without going through guardianship.[4] Others are explicit about requiring that there be a guardian to consent to particular procedures—for example, the administration of psychotropic (antipsychotic) medication.[5]

The story of Jane R., mentioned earlier, involves a young woman who has retardation but no guardian and is seeking medical treatment. Other third parties may find themselves in positions similar to the physician in that case, not knowing whether to accept her choices as binding. A caretaker, for example, such as the director or staff of a community home or an institution, may consult with the woman's family when decisions are made, or may not. Like physicians, caretakers are more likely to consult consistently if there is a guardian, but many will often consult with family members even in the absence of guardianship.

So a woman with apparent retardation who does not have a guardian faces an unpredictable situation: Her own decisionmaking power may be respected, or other persons may attempt to foist their own preferences or views upon her. Having her own guardianship, as other adults do, may secure her privacy from her family members, or they may be brought into the process even when she tries to act on her own. Moreover, she may experience pressure from third parties to obtain a guardian or even an attempt by someone who believes she needs a guardian to obtain that role in a court proceeding. (To establish guardianship, a court proceeding is required; once appointed, the guardian can make most decisions other than sterilization without further court proceedings.)

In sum, there is no sharp dichotomy between those with and those without guardians, partly because a guardian can be appointed at any time. Anyone who does not meet the competence standard imposed by the somewhat amorphous tests for measuring it is only a judicial proceeding away from guardianship. If the only protection is that there must be a guardian, then a procedural hurdle has been added to arrogation of the decisionmaking role, but not a substantive one. That is why the prescription that all persons without guardians must be treated as competent except those declared incompetent in a court of law ends up not stating any meaningful protection for persons who have retardation and want to make decisions for themselves.

Imprecise Rules about When Guardianship Is Appropriate

True protection would also require clear limits on when it is possible for a guardian to be appointed—limits especially on whose decisionmaking capacity can be superseded in this way. But in fact the standards for who can be put under guardianship are not precise enough to perform a protective function. Jurisdictions differ, but Massachusetts is not atypical. There, persons with retardation can be placed under guardianship if a probate court finds the following:

1. The person is so disabled by mental retardation as to be incapable of making informed decisions about personal and financial affairs;
2. Failure to appoint a guardian would create an unreasonable risk to the person's health, welfare and property; and
3. Appointing someone with more limited powers (namely a conservator authorized to handle only financial affairs) would not be adequate.[6]

These standards concerning guardianship are typical in their generality. The crucial variable is how judges will apply the standards in individual cases. The Mental Health Legal Advisors Committee in Massachusetts has attempted to fill in the generalities by advising consideration of whether the person whose competency is being questioned can "do some of the following":

• Understand in simple terms the basic facts and implications of a decision. She must be able to appreciate, for example, that even though a medical operation entails certain risks and discomforts, it might still be desirable.
• Take care of herself by recognizing potentially harmful situations and responding appropriately.
• Understand and follow the basic laws of the community.
• Demonstrate or learn enough basic living skills to live in a group residence or her one home.[7]

Significantly, the committee adds that "the person *need not* be able to read or write, or even talk, as long as she can communicate effectively her needs and preferences."[8] Furthermore, it explicitly does not require "the ability to support oneself financially."[9] The committee also warns that because an adjudication of incompetence is difficult to reverse "on the grounds of improvement . . . permanent guardianship should not be sought for someone who is likely to outgrow the need and whose immediate needs can be met by a temporary guardianship."[10]

These attempts to be more specific may be helpful to judges, who have much less experience with the realities of mental retardation than the members of the mental health committee do. Without such guidelines, or the assistance of social workers and other persons with appropriate experience, judges may be too easily persuaded to place a person who has retardation under guardianship, and the generality of the legal standards makes that possible.

Interactions between Guardian and Ward

While clearer rules as to the scope of the guardian's authority might be helpful to a guardian who wants to play that role appropriately, it is doubtful that the interactions between guardian and ward—as distinct from those involving third parties—are greatly affected by the legalities of guardianship. A ward with retardation is likely to have a number of adults with whom she interacts, and the particular relationship she establishes with them may not differ greatly because of guardianship.

Questions such as whether the ward can go out at night, or can go for a walk by herself or with her boyfriend, will often be dictated by a caretaker, whether the caretaker has guardianship or not. An absent guardian is likely to be consulted, but when the guardian is dealing directly with the ward— when, for example, the ward lives with the guardian, who is also a parent— the existence of guardianship probably does not have much effect on the power relationship between the two. A parent who is not guardian can lay down strict rules and attempt to enforce them. Whether the young woman has any ability to resist is not likely to be affected substantially by guardianship.

One context in which this scenario may be played out is the administration of birth control pills. As we have seen, this example actually involves *both* third-party supervision, with the guardian as intermediary between physician and ward when a prescription is obtained, and direct interaction between a guardian-caretaker and ward when the medication is administered. In obtaining a prescription for birth control pills or any other prescription medication, as we have seen, a guardian will be consulted by physicians, and even if the patient does not have a guardian (and is thus legally presumed to be competent), some physicians will not allow her to act for herself because of evident retardation. Once medication has been obtained, it is either up to the young woman herself or to her caretaker to make sure she uses it. And with over-the-counter medications, caretakers are in a position to administer them, or at least to attempt to, without third-party supervision even from physicians.

Of course, one can argue it is not within the scope of the caretaker's (or parent's) authority to administer medicine if the young woman is legally her own decisionmaker. Similarly, one could argue about whether the right to make choices about birth control should be inferred from general guardianship or whether, like the right to marry, the subject is sufficiently personal that it should be presumed to rest with the ward herself.[11] But regardless of one's view, those inquiries are solely theoretical. The ward is unlikely to be in a position to know her rights, and it is highly unlikely that she could organize a legal action to protect them. The usual situation is that if the caretaker decides to administer a particular medication, it will be done, without regard to any legalities and despite the fact that the young woman is an adult.

While it may seem far-fetched to imagine a young woman with retardation resisting through a court proceeding, or indeed to imagine anyone bringing a proceeding to adjudicate authority over birth control, it is not unimaginable that the woman would resist taking birth control, or other medication, more directly. If she does resist, whether or not her will triumphs is unlikely to depend on legalities. If there is a clash of wills—whether or not there is actually a guardianship—the question will be whether she has the wherewithal effectively to resist or whether the caretaker is able to persuade or coerce her.

It is entirely likely that, without being appointed guardian, someone will make such decisions for her. Indeed, that may take place even if she does have the capacity to understand and give informed consent on this subject, because no supervision exists. A caretaker may have her take birth control, informing her of what she is taking, or even without informing her. If she takes other regular medication, for example, the birth control pills may be fed to her with other pills without explanation.

Such practices are all too often engaged in by caretakers, whether they are guardians or not. The young woman may in fact be better off if she does have a guardian who believes in informing her of what is going on, or in consulting her, because such a guardian can stand between the ward and a separate caretaker or other third parties. If there is a guardian other than the caretaker, that reduces the likelihood that the caretaker will administer medicine without telling the guardian and receiving the guardian's permission, since liability could result if a caretaker or another third party knowingly bypasses the guardian and that action is discovered.

If the young woman is informed and actively resists medication, should it ever be fed to her over her opposition? Although the issue is not likely to be determined in court, it is still of interest. Indeed, the same question arises with regard to sterilization, where court proceedings are a norm, and to abortion as well.

Strangely, the issue of guardians' authority is often discussed without any attention paid to whether or not the ward is resisting. Surely the patient's resistance should at least be relevant to the propriety of a procedure. With both abortion and sterilization, decisions are sometimes made without heeding even active opposition from the ward. Even when courts are exercising their vigilance, the patient's resistance is not determinative. Indeed some state statutes explicitly contemplate imposing those operations on unwilling subjects.[12] It is not difficult to imagine that if the ward's resistance can be (and frequently is) overlooked or minimized where there is judicial oversight, similar disregard of her desires can be commonplace in contexts like birth control where there is presently no judicial oversight.

The same lack of supervision that leaves the relationship between guardian and ward largely ungoverned also means that limitations on guardianship may exist only on paper. Especially if the guardian lives with the ward, the relative scope of authority is likely to be defined by the reality of their general power relationship rather than by legal rules. The reality is that there is no one to check even whether limits placed on a limited guardian are being observed. The ward is not likely to be in a position to insist on her rights and probably does not know what they are. An important variable therefore is whether effective oversight of the guardian is provided—which usually, when required, takes the form of mandatory judicial proceedings (as is common with sterilization).

CHAPTER 10

The Peculiar Problem of Abortion

Even if one is content to draw a line between sterilization and contraception and require significantly stricter procedures for third-party consent to sterilization than for contraception, that does not resolve the issue of how abortion is to be treated. Is abortion to be available at the request of a parent or guardian, or must the decision be reviewed and sanctioned by courts? If the latter, what standards should courts follow for elective (as distinguished from medically necessary) abortion? Even if judicial supervision is not imposed, what considerations should guide the well-intended guardian?

There is little law on the question of third-party consent to abortion, although there is significantly more than there is on contraception. Those judicial decisions that exist involving abortion are in conflict. The few jurisdictions that have taken positions do not agree, and in most states, "the law" with respect to third-party consent in this context remains wholly undefined. In short, the issue is an open one.

The problem is important, and someday it will have to be resolved. Although there is little law to date, the problem must be common. In contrast, cases involving abortion for minors are manifold, and the lack of litigation concerning abortion for other "incompetents" suggests that abortions are in fact taking place without court involvement.

Many would prefer to continue in this legal twilight zone and put off indefinitely judicial or legislative elucidation of the issues. They believe in what they are doing (as parents or health care workers, for example), but they are not certain it will withstand judicial scrutiny or be allowed under legislatively formulated rules. Those decisionmakers, in turn, may put off resolving the problem, because it is difficult to decide what resolution is appropriate.

One could confront the issue by asking whether abortion is more like sterilization (where judicial supervision is the norm) or other forms of contraception (where there may be no supervision of the caretaker), assuming that the current resolution of those two subjects is acceptable. But this inquiry is not really helpful, because abortion has elements of both. On the one hand, when a young woman has an abortion, that does not mean she can never have any children; in that respect, the abortion seems less intrusive than sterilization is and more like other forms of contraception. On the other hand, it is wrong to equate abortion with contraception, because it is a final, irreversible procedure in one sense: It ends the fetus's potential life. To many women the idea that they can (perhaps) have *another* child is almost beside the point, and surely the law cannot enforce the point of view that fetuses are fungible.

Even more problematic, some women—many women—believe that life commences at the time of conception, and for them abortion is morally repugnant. Certainly government should avoid forcing individuals to violate their deeply felt moral principles, just as, under prohibition from the U.S. Supreme Court,[1] government declines to impose any one view of when life begins.

Because many women view abortion as termination of life, a decision to abort is even more offensive and more permanent in one sense than is a decision to sterilize. And for the state to make a decision to abort *for* a woman is much more extreme than allowing women to decide for themselves whether to end their pregnancy, as the U.S. Supreme Court in Roe v. Wade and in Planned Parenthood v. Casey required the states to do. In the *Casey* argument, as the U.S. Solicitor General argued unsuccessfully to curtail drastically the right to choose, Justice O'Connor pointed out that a government that could deny abortion could also impose it. The Solicitor General, in reply, disclaimed any support for government-coerced abortion.

Abortion can also effectively be permanent in another sense. When contrasted with sterilization, the reversibility of abortion and contraception like birth control pills is stressed. But in fact if the caretaker is going continually to supervise and to opt for abortion or contraception, the effect on the subject's ability to reproduce is the same.

In short, there are strong reasons to protect against forcing any woman to abort against her will—even stronger than with respect to forcing contraception on her. At the same time, there often seems to be both more necessity and more urgency for abortion than sterilization. When the issue is sterilization, there usually are many alternatives. After a woman is pregnant, the options are much more limited. If abortion is not available, the young woman will soon be a mother and may not be in a position to care for the child. This consequence is an extreme one for the government to foist upon her, as it would if it did not let anyone consent to her abortion.

It would not be appropriate to bar abortion in order to punish the young woman for improper sexual conduct or to deter extramarital sex by others. Even in circumstances involving fully competent adults, where a punitive stance toward extramarital sex might seem more appropriate than it does for persons who are considered incompetent, the U.S. Supreme Court has indicated that motherhood should not be used as punishment. In Eisenstadt v. Baird, Justice Brennan said that even if fornication (sex outside marriage) can constitutionally be made a crime, he did not believe that any state would consider childbirth a suitable punishment: "It would be plainly unreasonable to assume that Massachusetts has prescribed pregnancy and the birth of an unwanted child as punishment for fornication . . . Aside from the scheme of values that assumption would attribute to the State, it is abundantly clear that the effect of the ban on distribution of contraceptives to unmarried persons has at best a marginal relation to the proffered objective."[2] The same could be said of requiring childbirth for pregnant young women, if in fact they will not be allowed any relationship with their child. Whether or not one believes that they have "done anything wrong" that deserves punishment, childbirth is an inappropriate penalty.

If these mothers-to-be were really incapable of continuing a relationship with a child, perhaps abortion should not be prevented unless it is their *personal* belief that it is immoral to undergo abortion or their *personal* choice to proceed with the pregnancy. (And attempting to determine at this stage which young women could be parents has problems of its own.)[3]

Whether one stresses that abortion is even more necessary or that it is even more dire than sterilization and contraception, it is clear that the range of strongly felt moral views will differ greatly. There are many controversial questions concerning both abortion and the Supreme Court's methodology in establishing it as a constitutional right. The important issue for women with retardation is whether they have the same rights as other women, whatever those rights happen to be. Since 1973 women who are considered competent have had the constitutional right to choose abortion without undue state interference, up until approximately the time that the fetus might be viable; under this test, states currently must make elective abortion available for the first twenty to twenty-two weeks of pregnancy.

Even if abortion is to be available for as long as it is to others, the question must still be confronted whether judicial approval should be required for abortion by third-party consent. In those instances where the parties opt to go ahead with a pregnancy, often no judicial oversight occurs. But judicial oversight may be appropriate when the choice is for abortion. It is still open to debate in many states whether judicial approval is required or whether a physician can safely proceed with the operation. And those states that have explicitly answered the question, in judicial decision or more commonly in legislation, have reached different results.

If a court were always required to oversee abortions agreed to by third parties rather than the patient, there would be significant effects. For example, fewer operations would be performed on persons without their being given full information. There would be other consequences as well: As the sterilization cases show, such proceedings provide opportunities to ensure that the person consenting actually is a guardian and is the appropriate decisonmaker; to elicit the preferences of the patient, if possible; and to see that the substituted judgment or best interests tests, as set out or applied in the particular state, are properly followed.

Should judicial process be required to approve abortion at the behest of a third party, or is the abortion decision somehow within the powers of the family, guardian, or physician? Either alternative seems unsatisfactory. If *no* process is required, effectively then there are no rules, even concerning who can be subjected to abortion at a third party's request. The possibilities and even probabilities for abuse are evident, including not informing the patient or proceeding from interests other than the patient's own. The only policing would be done by the medical profession, motivated by attempts to enforce informed consent requirements and also by physicians' desires to avoid liability. But if process *is* required, the government intrudes into what may be considered a family matter in order to prevent an abuse that may not exist, with inevitable delay of a possibly urgent procedure.

In short, it can make a big difference in the end result whether a judicial proceeding is required. But the question of policy is a close one. Accordingly it is not surprising that disagreement exists.

Two Differing Legal Approaches

Is it necessary for a guardian, parent, or physician to seek judicial approval to perform an elective abortion on a subject who is not herself considered competent to consent? While there is emerging consensus concerning sterilization and conventional contraception, it is much less clear what the law is with respect to abortion. Two differing legal approaches exist.

Some states provide by statute that a guardian alone may make medical decisions for the ward. Among states probably granting guardians the authority to consent to abortion are the more than a dozen that have adopted the 1969 original or 1989 revised Uniform Probate Code (UPC) provisions on substituted consent for minors and other incompetent persons. The original provision empowers a guardian either to "give any consents or approvals that may be necessary to enable the ward to receive medical or other professional care, counsel, treatment or service."[4] The revised provision permits "consent to medical or other professional care, treatment, or advice for the ward without liability by reason of the consent for injury to the ward resulting from the negligence or acts of third persons unless a parent would have been liable in the circumstances."[5] Of course these provisions do not expressly include abortion, but there are indications that abortion is intended to be included as a proper subject of the provisions' "medical treatment" clause. Some state legislators have thought so and adopted an amended version of the UPC text specifically excluding abortion.[6] Moreover, in another context, at least one court has interpreted "medical treatment" to include abortion.[7] Finally, an absence of reported cases in UPC jurisdictions suggests that women who have retardation are having abortions without judicial intervention.

Given the lack of judicial scrutiny, it is impossible to know whether guardians are fulfilling their fiduciary responsibilities to their wards.[8] The danger is that guardians do not even contemplate their fiduciary duty to their ward in these circumstances. Some guardians also fail to consider either their ward's best interests or their ward's wishes, whether expressed or unarticulated.

Other state legislation apparently requires the guardian to seek judicial guidance before making treatment decisions. Arkansas law expressly denies the guardian power to make a nontherapeutic abortion or sterilization decision without court approval.[9] Other statutes are vaguer about whether abortion is covered. A Colorado provision, for example, requires the guardian to resort to judicial guidance concerning matters not included in the original guardianship decree; but the all-important question is whether abortion is included, an issue on which Colorado law is unclear.[10] Massachusetts statutory consent provisions also do not refer specifically to abortion,[11] though Massachusetts common law now does. Other states do have provisions explicitly covering abortion, but the provisions themselves are not clear: they simply prohibit the guardian from making an abortion decision, but they fail to indicate who, if anyone, shall have this power.[12]

There is thus a fair amount of statutory law, though only Arkansas's statute is absolutely clear.[13] The case law, however, is sparse indeed. As of this writing, only three cases squarely face the issue. (In two of the three, the woman involved has severe retardation; in the other, her retardation is moderate.) In each, the final decisionmaker, an intermediate state court, came out in favor of the guardian's authority to opt for abortion. But none was reviewed by its state's supreme court, and in some cases a trial court decision had adopted a very different approach.

Clearly there is not yet any firm consensus about the appropriate rules. The following three cases show the conflict that exists on the fundamental issue of whether any judicial scrutiny is necessary.

In *In re* Barbara C., the director of the Brooklyn Developmental Center, which ran Barbara's group home, asked a court to approve a second-trimester abortion for Barbara, who was twenty-five years old, was nonverbal, and had profound mental retardation. Barbara C. suffered from acute tuberous sclerosis, which had caused her retardation and also caused epileptic seizures.[14]

The state had initially requested an abortion as medically necessary, saying that the pregnancy constituted a threat to Barbara's life. The court denied that petition because the evidence of medical danger was "woefully inadequate."[15] At a new hearing the state argued, instead, that because the pregnant woman was unable either to give or withhold consent, her father's consent to abortion was sufficient.[16] New York law required patient consent for any major medical procedure or surgery. Moreover, it guaranteed to each patient in a Department of Mental Hygiene facility "the same right to abortion as any other citizen."[17] But the same statutory scheme provided that, if a patient "does not have sufficient mental capacity to give consent, authorization for the procedure in question must be obtained from the patient's spouse, parent, adult child, or a court of competent jurisiction."[18]

In a strikingly brief and tautological opinion, the trial court approved the father as a substitute decisionmaker, noting only that the statute authorizes parental consent and that Barbara's father was indeed her parent. The trial court did not assume for itself any role in deciding on the appropriateness of abortion or the standards that would allow it.

On appeal, Barbara's guardian *ad litem* sought to except abortion from the above statutory provision for substitute consent and to establish a rule requiring prior judicial review of every abortion decision involving an incompetent patient. Parental consent could not, according to this argument, remove the issue from the judiciary. The guardian *ad litem* argued that the "special and fundamental nature of an abortion" authorizes a court "to ignore parental consent and determine what the incompetent woman herself would have done had she been competent."[19] The argument was for an approach to abortion similar to that developed for sterilization, making full use of judicial oversight to keep the guardian or parent within appropriate bounds.

The appeals court rejected the guardian *ad litem*'s suggestion, saying it would require a judge to "invoke his or her own moral, philosophical, theological and sociological precepts in deciding whether the operation should take place."[20] Declining that invitation, the court held that, under New York's statutory scheme, the sole role of the judiciary is to resolve any disputes that arise concerning the patient's ability to grant consent. Once the patient's incapacity to consent has been established in a judicial proceeding, the consent of the incompetent patient's prescribed relative is sufficient.[21] Only the absence of such a relative would trigger the court's *parens patriae* jurisdiction "to determine whether the interests of the patient warrant the performance of the proposed procedure."[22]

In most states, unlike New York, the issue of whether a relative can decide without judicial supervision is not yet settled. The next two cases illustrate sharply different answers to the question, with Illinois' court coming close to the New York position, and Massachusetts' appeals court adopting a very different approach.

In *In re* Estate of D. W., the mother of an eighteen-year-old woman with severe retardation sought guardianship to authorize her daughter's abortion.[23] The trial court found D. W. incompetent and appointed her mother temporary guardian to make medical decisions related to D. W.'s pregnancy. But the court also ruled that under Illinois's Probate Act only medically necessary abortion was permissible, not nontherapeutic, elective abortion. Accordingly, it refused to let D. W.'s mother approve an abortion, because there was no evidence that abortion was necessary to protect D. W.'s life or health.

The appellate court reversed, saying, "[p]lainly, there is no legal requirement that a medical necessity exist before a guardian can consent to an abortion for a ward." Although the question of judicial intervention before every abortion was not directly presented, the court said that the Probate Act vests a guardian with broad authority to act in the best interests of the ward. Clearly, the court stated, the sole constraint on the guardian's discretion is the ward's best interests. "The court's duty in this regard is to ensure that the acts and decisions of the guardian reflect the best interest of the ward by judicially interfering if the guardian is about to do some act that would cause harm or threaten harm to the ward."[24]

Yet how, as a practical matter, is the court to "judicially interfere" or otherwise to police guardians? Who will raise the issue of whether their decisions are in their ward's best interests? Unless there is a system of prior judicial review, those limitations on the guardian's authority exist only in theory.

The appeals court in *D. W.* interpreted the mandate of Illinois's guardianship statute as not barring an abortion decision by a guardian as long as no evidence existed that the guardian was not acting in the ward's best interests. That statute provides in relevant part: "To the extent ordered by the court and under the direction of the court, the guardian of the person shall . . . procure for [the ward] and shall make provision for [the ward's] support, care, comfort, health, education and maintenance and such professional services as are appropriate."[25] The trial court, said the appellate judge, interpreted the statute in "a manner that unduly limits an appointed guardian's exercise of judgment on behalf of a ward" when it held that the abortion must be "medically necessary."[26]

Notwithstanding the appeals court decision in *D. W.*, it is not at all clear that the Illinois legislature wanted the fundamental right to choose abortion left in the total discretion of a third party, operating on that person's own unreviewable evaluation of the ward's best interests. But the court's approach apparently allows hospitals and doctors to rely on a guardian's consent to abortion without seeking judicial approval.

In re Jane A. is one of the most recent examples of judicial involvement in an abortion decision. In January 1994, when Jane A. was thirty years old, the Massachusetts Department of Mental Retardation sought appointment of a guardian in order to have Jane's pregnancy ended. Unlike New York and Illinois, which seem to vest decisions with guardians, Massachusetts requires courts to make substituted judgments for persons adjudicated incompetent.[27]

The first difficulty with the *Jane A.* decision is the ease with which the trial court found her incompetent to decide for herself. At the time of the petition, Jane resided with three other clients in an apartment. The group had twenty-four-hour supervision by employees of a private corporation operating the facility under contract with the Department of Mental Retardation. Jane had resided in special care facilities since the age of sixteen but, as is common, she had never been placed under guardianship. Nevertheless, the Probate and Family Court assumed that she was incompetent to decide for herself because she had moderate retardation, saying "she has an IQ in the mid-fifties and functions mentally at the level of a three to four-year-old child, although a four year old would have more cognitive energy for problem solving."[28] Judging her incompetent, it appointed a temporary guardian for her, designated by the Department.[29]

Having found her incompetent, the next step was to utilize substitute decisionmaking. Accordingly, the court asked whether "Jane, if competent, would choose to terminate her pregnancy by abortion."[30] It appointed five people to serve in the case: a temporary guardian for Jane; counsel for her; a guardian *ad litem* "to investigate and report on the substituted judgment question with respect to the abortion"; a guardian *ad litem* "to oppose a determination that [the ward], if competent, would choose to have an abortion"; and counsel to represent the fetus.[31] In addition, the judge appointed a psychologist, whose specialty was the psychiatric aspects of developmental disability. Finally, the judge interviewed Jane in his chambers in the presence of her counsel, a worker from Jane's residence, and a stenographer.

This elaborate process did not yield any clear answers. In the words of the probate court judge, the interview with Jane was "fruitless." He was unable to discern whether she had a preference with regard to the abortion question: "She varyingly acknowledged and denied that there [was] a 'baby inside [her]' and stated preferences both 'to keep the baby inside [her] belly' and have the 'baby stop growing inside [her] belly.'"[32] Moreover, Jane's family "offered no guidance regarding . . . a religious faith that might offer clues to [Jane's] inclinations."[33] The psychologist did take a clear position that there "was nothing positive in going through with the pregnancy for [Jane.]"[34] It was the psychologist's "'very, very strong' opinion . . . that continuing the pregnancy would be harmful to Jane psychologically . . . [because she] had no tolerance for discomfort and, in the past, had reacted to physical or psychological stress by being violent, throwing herself down, destroying property, and attacking others."[35] She also testified that abortion also posed some risk to Jane's mental health—it might cause her to "disinte-grate into a psychotic state"—but that the "trauma" of it would be "greatly reduced" if the "abortion were performed under general anesthesia."[36]

Despite this psychologist's opinion, the judge decided not to order the abortion, reasoning that "we cannot presuppose that [Jane], if competent, would disregard the fetus as an important factor in her decision."[37] The Mas-sachusetts appeals court reversed, reasoning that absent evidence that Jane would view the fetus as an important or dispositive factor in her decision, uncontested evidence showed that she would not choose to continue with the pregnancy. It said:

> the assaults on [Jane's] fragile mental state from continuation of the preg-nancy would be repetitive, for each additional day she is pregnant, and in-creasing in severity and danger. Normal discomforts of pregnancy such as bladder pressure, an increasingly bulky body, and backache would be felt as unendurable by Jane because she would not fully understand their cause or meaning. From what has been found about Jane's reactions to frustration, changes in her diet to conform with wise prenatal practices might be an oc-casion for violent encounters. Birth labor would be horrifying and danger-ous, again because she could not be prepared for what was happening. In comparison to those difficulties, which would be of an accelerating nature, there is the alternative of one occasion of medical intervention, which can be achieved with a minimum of discomfort and the likelihood of much de-creased risk to the ward's psychic makeup. By the very nature of her mental impairment, the ward is self-centered and concerned about how she feels physically, but, in exercising judgment on her behalf, we must take her compassionately as we find her. Only in that way can we determine as best we can the ward's wants, needs, and choices . . . That choice would be to end the pregnancy she did not seek, barely begins to understand, and which will increasingly cause her greater discomfort and pain.[38]

Accordingly, the abortion was performed.

The trial judge's reasoning may have been speculative, but the appeals court's seems equally an exercise in imagination. Its description of Jane as "self-centered," for example, relies wholly on feelings that the court has at-tributed to her. The court patently demonstrates that, in attributing feelings and sentiments to a potential patient, it can come to any conclusion that it wants. The decisions it makes under substituted judgment doctrine actually reflect the preferences and policy views of the decisionmaker more than the patient's wishes. Moreover, the different perspectives of the lower and intermediate courts in *Jane A.* illustrate the malleability of the substituted judgment doctrine. It is hard to conclude which outcome was preferred by Jane, even though both courts took pains to gain enlightenment on this point.

Jane A. thus suggests that judicial interference in the abortion decision may not be productive. But is it preferable to follow the usual alternative—leaving the decision within the private domain of guardians or other third parties?

In *Valerie N.*, the sterilization case discussed previously, the justices of the California Supreme Court divided on the question whether a guardian ("conservator" in the language of that state) has authority to consent to abortion without judicial approval. All agreed that the conservator can choose birth control without consulting any outside authority, but Justice Rose Bird doubted that having an abortion or giving up a child for adoption (absent parental unfitness) could or should be forced.[39] The majority opinion implied, however, that abortion *can* be forced, and even Valerie's guardian *ad litem* had conceded that point at trial. The majority stated:

> The state has not asserted an interest in protecting the right of the incompetent to bear children. Neither the "involuntary imposition" of other forms of contraception, nor abortion, has been banned. A [guardian] is permitted to exercise his or her own judgment as to the best interests of the [ward] in these matters, excepting only the election of sterilization as a means of preventing conception.[40]

Justice Rose Bird, in her dissent, maintained:

> The majority make several unsupported assumptions which suggest that they recognize Valerie's right to procreate for purposes of conceptual symmetry only. They do not regard it as a real right, entitled to meaningful protection.
>
> For example, the majority assert without citation to any authority that Valerie's conservators may legally compel her to undergo an abortion or to surrender custody of any child she might bear . . . Indeed, having incorrectly cast Valerie's fundamental right to procreate as a right of procreative choice, the majority summarily conclude that she will never have the right to bear children because she will never be competent.[41]

The disagreement is of interest in illustrating the unsettled nature of the law, even though it was expressed only in dicta, because that case actually involved sterilization. (In legal practice, a court's dicta are not entitled to the same weight as statements the court makes that are essential to its decision in the case. Lawyers refer to these essential decisions as "the holding"; it reflects the central precedential value of the case.)

Does Practice Accord with the Law?

As the paucity of case law reflects, legal rights in this situation are unclear. A cautious attorney, if asked by a client-physician whether to perform an abortion on a person whom the physician does not consider capable of giving informed consent, would have to reply, in a state whose law is not certain, that the physician might conceivably be held liable for malpractice, violation of informed consent requirements, or battery, and that it would be dangerous for the physician to presume that the parent or even the guardian has authority to consent for the ward. Yet the prevalent practice is not to seek judicial review, or even necessarily guardianship. In circumstances in which physicians do not foresee any possibility of anyone objecting after the fact to an abortion, they do provide them for legally incompetent persons— both minors and persons with mental disabilities—with the family's consent and without any judicial process. They also perform them on women who have never been declared incompetent but whom the physician does not consider capable of giving informed consent. One reason case law is largely absent is that most of these procedures are performed outside judicial scrutiny. What oversight there is typically comes from physicians, hospitals, and possibly even medical ethics committees, rather than courts.

As with other medical procedures, the precise reaction of a particular physician or health care provider and the degree of oversight exercised on the patient's request, or that of her parent or guardian, is not highly predictable. Physicians are likely to exercise more supervision of abortion requests than of requests for conventional birth control prescriptions, but still they are likely to perform an abortion at the request of family members as well as guardians. Caution would dictate requiring at least a guardian, unless in that state the law is clear that family members have authority to consent, but discussions with numerous families confirm that even guardianship is often not in practice required, as long as no one is raising objections to the abortion.

As the system works now in most states, therefore, a family can get an abortion for a relative who has retardation if they can get a physician or clinic to go along. Of course, it can be difficult to find physicians to perform

abortions in general, especially in some areas of this country—a problem
that affects all women seeking abortions, not just persons with retardation.
If they can transcend that common problem, families have a good chance of
finding a physician or clinic that will cooperate without requiring judicial
participation, as long as the physician is not aware of anyone opposed to the
procedure who might later sue.

Some physicians or others might rationalize this result by characterizing
the abortion as "medically necessary." That characterization is often used to
allow abortions with which physicians are sympathetic even though no real
medical necessity exists. For example, late-term abortions are sometimes allowed as medically necessary when a fetus has been diagnosed as having a
handicap, even though the mother's physical health is in no way at issue.
Similarly, the characterization of abortion for a young woman with retardation as medically necessary because the caretakers or physician do not believe persons with retardation should have children is not unusual. Indeed,
in *Barbara C.* that was the rationale initially put forward to justify the abortion although no medical necessity even arguably existed. In Colorado law
also, the concept of medical necessity has been stretched very far.[42]

In *Barbara C.* the court rejected the medical necessity rationale. It is worth
noting, however, that without court review that rationale could have carried the day. Without judicial oversight some abortions will be performed on
persons with retardation under the medical necessity rubric when no true
medical necessity exists. Indeed any motivation can prevail as long as parent-guardian and physician are in agreement.

In most states the question whether a relative or guardian can decide
without judicial supervision remains unanswered. Even in the three states
that have case law, the decisions have come only from intermediate courts
and not from the state supreme court. The issue whether judicial review is
necessary is an important one, although it is rarely addressed. But other
difficult questions—legal or ethical—are also involved.

Standards for Abortion

It is useful to contemplate not only whether judicial process should be required for the abortion decision but also what the standards should be for allowing or disallowing abortion, if a judge were to pass on the question. First,
that inquiry shows us whether or not judges have anything useful to contribute. Second, even if judicial intervention is not required, decisionmakers

need standards to guide them in making choices for a pregnant "incompetent" woman, as a moral and practical matter. Removal of judges and government from the process still leaves the private decisionmaker with ethical dilemmas concerning what is the right thing to do.

One possible standard evident in a few cases is a requirement that the abortion be medically necessary to save the mother's life or health. Another standard that will be suggested here is that an abortion not be performed over the resistance of the patient.

Barbara C. and *D. W.*, above, are not the only cases discussing whether nontherapeutic abortion is permissible for "incompetents." *In re* Mary Moe, a Massachusetts case decided before *Jane A.*, is yet another case in which a trial court attempted to limit abortion by third-party consent to cases of medical necessity but the appeals court disagreed. The case also illustrates a tendency to elide and confuse the various tests; the trial court's position was essentially that unless there is medical necessity, substituted judgment doctrine prohibits abortion. Both *Mary Moe* and *D. W.* show that even when judicial supervision is mandated, and progressive and sensitive procedures to establish substitute decisionmaking are in place, problems persist in the context of abortion.

Mary Moe was a twenty-four-year-old divorced woman who had been pregnant five times, given birth twice, had three abortions, and happened to have retardation. She was under guardianship at the time her mother-guardian petitioned to have her sixth pregnancy aborted at nineteen and a half weeks. One of Mary's previous three abortions had apparently occurred without the guardian's knowledge, and two had occurred before Mary was placed under guardianship.

In deciding on the abortion petition, the trial court determined that Mary was incompetent to make the abortion decision for herself because she had "already been determined to be incompetent and in need of guardianship due to her mental retardation. She has 'borderline cognitive function' with an I.Q. of around high 70/low 80s."[43]

The court then applied the substituted judgment doctrine to deny the guardian's petition to abort: "Because there are no compelling medical reasons for the abortion from either the maternal or fetal standpoint, and given the weight of the evidence to the other facts . . . the Court cannot state with clarity that it would be the ward's substituted judgment to assent to the recommended treatment, *i.e.* abortion."[44]

The Massachusetts appeals court rejected the lower court's threshold finding that Mary was "not competent to make the decisions on the proposed [abortion]."[45] As a result, it ordered that the petition for the abortion be granted; that was clearly Mary's wish. The appeals court also admonished the trial court (in dicta) that even if Mary had been incompetent to decide for herself, the substituted judgment doctrine would have required allowing the abortion; the trial court had given inadequate weight to Mary's stated preferences:[46] "The ward . . . has clearly stated that she wants to have an abortion. Her rationale is that she does not want, nor could she handle, any more children. She presently lives with her parents, upon whom she depends heavily for help and support in caring for her young daughter."[47]

Resistance from the Patient

Unlike the appeals court in *Mary Moe,* courts deciding whether third-party decisionmakers have authority over abortion or other decisions often pay little attention to whether the patient wants or is resisting the procedure. Similarly, statements of guardianship rules often do not distinguish between those situations where the patient agrees with the guardian and those in which she makes her disagreement clear. The failure to focus on this seemingly relevant factor is especially apparent for out-of-court decisions, but it can also occur when there is judicial review. The trial court decision in *In re Romero* attempted to override the patient's personal resistance to sterilization, where court approval of third-party decisions are generally required; and the trial court decision in *Mary Moe* ignored the patient's desires to undergo abortion, which the guardian also desired.

What is the relevance of resistance by the patient? A cautious physician most certainly should not be willing to perform an operation, including an abortion, without court approval, if the patient is resisting. If court approval is obtained, the physician can proceed without risk and will be immune from liability (as will the court). But it clearly is appropriate for a judge to become involved before an operation whenever there is conflict between the person consenting and the person who will be subjected to the procedure. In that (admittedly somewhat unusual) situation, many important legal questions can be at stake, such as whether the subject herself can give or withhold consent.

In theory, such disagreement and resistance should trigger judicial review at the insistence of the physician, even if the issue is not an operation but a prescription for birth control. Practice does not, however, consistently follow the legally cautious route. Some physicians proceed even in the face of resistance from the patient to abortion or sterilization, and no harm befalls them, because there is no one able effectively to complain.

In cases involving third-party consent to medical procedures, such resistance is not, of course, the common scenario. Instead, the patient usually does not resist but accepts the decision that is being made for her. Such "agreement" may result from real agreement or at least acceptance based on some understanding of what is transpiring. But too frequently it reflects instead the subject's lack of awareness—she may not have been consulted or even informed. That scenario is easy to imagine in the case of administration of birth control pills; they may sometimes be given as part of daily medication, without any disclosure of their function. But even in contexts like abortion or sterilization, a young woman can be subjected to the procedure, if the physician permits it, without being asked her opinion or even told what is occurring. In the famous (and infamous) case of Stump v. Sparkman, for example, the young woman who was sterilized at her mother's behest had been informed by her mother and her physician that she was undergoing an appendectomy. Only years later, when she and her husband tried to have children, did they find out that she had been sterilized.

It is worth noting that in *Stump,* and in most cases where disagreements between guardians or parents and young women with retardation are observable, the disagreement arises when the guardian wants abortion or sterilization and the young woman does not want the medical procedure. Of course, that is not the only possible disagreement. The ward may want abortion and the guardian may not. This is the typical situation in litigation involving abortions for minors, but not in cases involving persons with mental retardation.

A Proposal for
Self-Determination

CHAPTER 11

Self-Determination Explained and Evaluated

So far, with respect to sterilization, other contraception, and abortion, we have scrutinized who should make the decision when the subject of the decision cannot; whether a third-party decision should be subject to outside supervision; and what standards, if any, should govern. Almost all the formulated law concerning procreation by persons with mental retardation is directed to these issues; indeed almost all of it is directed to the issues in the context of sterilization.

The issues are important ones. There must be rules to govern persons who cannot consent for themselves, and there are many different possibilities to debate, as we have seen. But the more important point, and one more often avoided than addressed, is whom we are talking about. Who are these people who cannot consent for themselves?

Some people clearly cannot express or refuse consent. A newborn baby and a person in a coma are obvious examples. In addition, there are others who literally cannot express a preference, including some persons with mental retardation. They also must be included in the category where either state regulation or substituted judgment is required. It is not clear, however, who if anyone other than persons who literally cannot express preferences should be included in this category.

Persons with retardation are not alone in having been denied legal authority to make their own decisions. Children and psychiatric patients also face third-party decisionmaking, and how the law should confine that approach is relevant to those groups as well. (Although many decisionmaking issues are common to these three groups, it is not clear that the resolution is or should be.)[1]

This book takes the position, with respect to adults who have retardation, that the *only* persons who should be subject to third-party decisionmaking over elective medical procedures are those who literally cannot express their own preferences. There should be no explicit category for persons with retardation. All persons who can communicate should be treated one way, differently from all persons who cannot. The important reform for persons with retardation is that all persons who can express a preference must be involved in the decisionmaking process. Like other patients, they will be subject to persuasion, but the preference they express will ultimately determine the decision.

Accordingly, the rules worked out in cases like *Valerie N., Grady,* and *Hayes*—whatever those rules might be—would apply only to a tiny fraction of the population labeled "retarded." Moreover, the persons they would apply to—persons wholly unable to express their own preferences—are the least likely to need reproductive services, because they are most likely to be sheltered and the least likely to be sexually active. The vast majority of persons labeled "retarded" should not be subject to substitute decisionmaking at all. Instead they should have the legal authority to make their own elective decisions.

The limitations of substitute decisionmakers and other considerations lead to the conclusion that it is best to leave medical decisionmaking, especially nontherapeutic medical decisionmaking, to the patient herself, in consultation with her physician. This general principle, readily accepted for most people, applies also when the patient has significant retardation. The patient with retardation may not be a perfect decisionmaker, even for elective procedures, but as long as she can make a preference known, she is a better decisionmaker than anyone else.

The Necessity for Self-Determination

This proposal for self-determination would alter the law of every state, in many states drastically. Why should it be pursued?

There are inherent advantages in involving a person in her own life decisions. But before exploring those, it is important to acknowledge candidly that an important reason for favoring self-determination is the shortcomings of other alternatives. The subject of the decision will often not be a perfect decisionmaker, and it will be necessary to guard against pitfalls. But because she will be a better decisionmaker than any other, self-determination is the best available alternative. It is worth changing the laws to place self-determination at the heart of every state's policy.

In the choice between available alternatives, there are three possibilities to consider:

1. denying access to procedures that require informed consent, as was attempted by the California legislature and rejected by the California court in *Valerie N.*; this approach was also followed in the abortion context by the trial courts (but not the appellate courts) in *Barbara C., D. W.,* and *Mary Moe*, denying access to elective procedures.
2. allowing access through substitute decisionmaking—the prevalent approach in the United States at this time; and
3. relying on the patient to decide, the approach that this book suggests.

The first two alternatives are unsatisfactory. The first has even been held unconstitutional, as we have seen (by the California Supreme Court, but not the U.S. Supreme Court, so the holding is not binding nationally). The equivalent result does, however, obtain—without apparent constitutional objection—in states like Texas and Missouri, whose courts decline to authorize sterilization absent legislative action.[2] And state statutes in Maryland, South Dakota, and Kansas prohibiting sterilization without informed consent have not yet been challenged.

The first two alternatives, but not the third, require drawing a line between "persons who are retarded" or "persons who cannot give informed consent" and other people, a line that in practice can be destructive of normalization. And an extremely troubling aspect of the second alternative, which reflects prevalent U.S. law, is that it appears upon reflection uncomfortably close to the forced sterilization of the past.

Granted, there are some differences between third-party consent and the forced sterilization of earlier times. Courts and policymakers now rarely talk of protecting society and talk instead of protecting and enabling the person considered "retarded." Nonetheless the result remains court-ordered sterilization.[3] Whenever the law allows sterilization of those labeled "retarded" through consent of third parties who may or may not be acting out of their own private motives, it bears elements of forced sterilization.[4] If substituted consent can support sterilization, any boundary between voluntary and involuntary sterilization is blurred.

In one sense the very issue is whether sterilization through substitute decisionmaking should be characterized as voluntary or involuntary. In fact, it is voluntary for the substitute decisionmaker but not for the subject of the sterilization.

When the patient is actively resisting, the fictional quality of patient consent is most apparent.[5] Usually involuntariness is better disguised, because the patient does not resist. She may realize that resistance is futile, or she may not understand what is happening—sometimes because no one has informed her about what is happening. Sometimes, of course, the patient does understand and does agree, but it is unusual for either statutes or judge-made law to require such agreement as a condition of the procedure.

State Agenda Promoting Sterilization for This Group

In attempts to differentiate the present system from that of the past, the decision to sterilize is characterized as a private decision today, made by parents and guardians. The role of courts is simply to limit these private decisions and to oversee and enforce them. According to this vision, the state plays a neutral role, allowing private actors to initiate sterilization petitions and not pursuing a pro-sterilization policy of its own.

In fact, however, the state has a thinly disguised substantive agenda, disfavoring reproduction by persons with retardation. It is less blatant than in the days of old, but it still exists and it still controls outcomes.

The dissenters in *Hayes* noticed this fact. They pointed out that there is an inherent contradiction between respecting procreative integrity and allowing judges, even in limited circumstances, to order sterilization of persons who do not or cannot consent for themselves.[6] In molding the law to allow for such sterilizations, the state is imposing its own and society's agenda. One judge frankly described the issue, to be decided by courts or legislatures, as "whether compulsory sterilization of mentally retarded persons should or should not be permitted and if so under what limitations, if any."[7] That description is more straightforward than most and reflects a realistic view of the process.

The endorsement of a third-party decisionmaking procedure necessarily reflects a substantive agenda on the part of the state. To some extent the best interests and substituted judgment doctrines serve to disguise that agenda and thereby to postpone the debate about whether it is legitimate to disfavor persons considered "retarded" as parents. Because the state's agenda is not acknowledged, it has been neither clearly thought out nor consistently applied. But even though not articulated and developed, state policy clearly operates through third-party decisionmaking to deny procreative and parenting experience to persons who have retardation.

One illustration of the state's substantive bias is the pervasive expectation that parents, making substitute decisions, will opt for sterilization, birth control, or abstinence from sex.[8] The dissenter in *Moe* noted that attitude in his fellow justices, pointing out the court's "bias . . . heavily in favor of contraception,"[9] and the majority's portrayal of pregnancy (for persons thought to have mental retardation) as "an evil to be avoided."[10]

With respect to persons with retardation, state authorities from social workers to judges to legislators widely cite other birth control methods or supervision as the alternatives to sterilization, without seeming to contemplate childbirth as an option. Even when written law does not embody a presumption against parents with retardation, these attitudes of those who administer the law and make the decisions achieve the same result. Moreover, the law itself shows this bias in many of the requirements for sterilization discussed above: for example, the many state statutes and judicial decisions allowing evaluation of the parenting ability of children thought to have retardation and allowing sterilization even of minors. The same states' laws would not allow sterilization of other minors, regardless of their apparent ability or inability to act as an effective parent. If those children's parents requested sterilization of their offspring, physicians and courts would deny the request, even though they are the legal guardians of their child.

The very common assumption of both private guardians and public policymakers that women with retardation will not (maybe should not) be mothers may reflect wise policy. It may also be defended as simply accepting the reality of life for people with retardation, instead of stressing theoretical rights that the real life situation of those persons will not allow (most of) them to exercise anyway. Many might defend it also as operating in the women's best interests. Even if so, it may be not the choice of the woman to be sterilized but that of a third party, and a decision that the state facilitates and encourages. Moreover, it is peculiarly in relation to persons with mental retardation—the same group forcibly sterilized in the past—that the state is allowing third parties to impose sterilization.

If we put aside the opinions of the subjects who have retardation themselves, most people today probably do believe that it is preferable to weight the scales against reproduction by persons diagnosed as retarded, or at least some subset of those persons. Before giving too much weight to popular opinion, however, it is important to remember that forced sterilization also accorded with contemporary public perceptions and prejudices. Most people today do not believe that that made it right.

Comparing Reproductive Decisionmaking for Minors and for Persons with Retardation

Nothing demonstrates the existence of a state agenda more conclusively than a comparison of the legal treatment of persons who have mental retardation with that of others usually deemed legally incompetent, such as children.

One arena in which attitudes have changed considerably over the last decades concerns minors' "rights" to make their own decisions and acceptance of a sex life for minors. Society remains very far from consensus on these issues, but most persons' attitudes have moved in the direction of acceptance over the last thirty years. Because many of the same issues are being addressed in relation to minors, and because most minors, like some persons with retardation, are "legally incompetent," it is instructive to compare what is being discussed or done with respect to minors and what is being discussed or done with respect to minor and adult persons with retardation.

The comparison yields striking results. The issues and answers concerning minors are entirely different from those concerning persons who have retardation. In the first place, minors have no problem getting an abortion when their parents are informed and do consent, yet that is the issue the cases involving persons with retardation address.[11] Minors' litigation has concerned quite a different set of issues: when minors can get abortions without informing their parents that they are pregnant or that they are aborting. Parental blocking of abortion is at issue, and somewhat protected.[12] Parental forcing of abortion is not. No successful parental forcing of abortion shows up in case law except with respect to subjects who have mental retardation. This trend suggests again that minors and persons with retardation are subject to drastically different state policies concerning procreation.

Even cases involving unsuccessful parental attempts to force abortions on "normal" minors are rare. In *In re* Mary P. the mother had tried to make her fifteen-and-a-half-year-old daughter have an abortion. When the daughter refused, the mother sought to have her declared "a Person in Need of Supervision" under state law.[13] The court refused, instead ordering the mother not to interfere with her daughter's decision to give birth.

Similarly, in *In re* Smith the Special Appeals Court of Maryland held that a mother could not force abortion upon her sixteen-year-old child, reversing a juvenile court order which had suggested that the minor might be compelled to follow her mother's wishes. The reviewing court held it was not within the intent of the legislature that a parent be able to compel abortion, for Maryland law expressly provided that no person should be required to participate in a procedure to terminate pregnancy. Moreover, since 1971, the state statute concerning minors' consent to medical treatment had provided that "a minor shall have the same capacity to consent to medical treatment as an adult" in certain circumstances, including when "[t]he minor seeks treatment or advice concerning venereal disease, pregnancy or contraception not amounting to sterilization." The court in *Smith* quite understandably interpreted the provision allowing minors to consent to medical treatment when seeking "treatment or advice concerning . . . pregnancy" to encompass consent to abortion.[14]

This is not to suggest that the law should generalize from its treatment of minors in devising rules to apply to persons who have mental retardation. It is interesting to consider that possibility, partly because both groups are treated through a concept of legal *in*competence and also because there have been a great many cases concerning minors—many more than those concerning disability. Especially in the context of abortion, the U.S. Supreme Court has developed a jurisprudence during the last twenty-five years concerning minors' constitutional rights of access to health care, even without the consent or knowledge of their parents. A string of decisions has established that states can require parental consent as a prerequisite to a minor's abortion, but there must be an opportunity for the minor to avoid informing her parents by showing a court that abortion is in her best interests or that she is sufficiently mature to make the decision herself. Parental consent or notification provisions without the availability of confidential judicial bypass is unconstitutional.

But that "mature minor" approach that has been adopted to resolve these issues for minors would not transfer easily to the context of mental retardation. When the triggering event that requires judicial participation is age— that the young woman be under the age of eighteen or sixteen or whatever the minors' statute provides—it is apparent who falls within the category where parental or judicial consent is required. Most important, the fact that makes such substitute consent required—age—is not stigmatizing. A comparable procedure could not work well for retardation: When the event that triggers the need for scrutiny is retardation instead of age, requiring a special procedure itself is stigmatizing. It is that fact that makes it so difficult to put into effect protections for people who have retardation who need them.

It is not desirable for a young adult who comes to a physician for an abortion to be told that her competence to consent must be determined in a judicial proceeding because it appears to someone that she may have retardation; even if it is later found that she is "mature" enough to make decisions for herself, the harm to her is done because another's view of retardation has caused her to be treated differently from people considered "normal." In the mental retardation context, at least one concern is to avoid categorizing persons as "mentally retarded" at all.[15]

But it is not just the unsuitability of the particular techniques used for minors that has made rules different for persons with retardation. There are respects in which those formulating policies regarding persons with retardation might appropriately learn from the treatment that law affords to minors and other "legal incompetents." A statute similar to the Maryland law quoted above could be applied to persons with mental retardation, transferring decisionmaking ability to them, at least over certain types of decisions as was done for minors, rather than making them legally incompetent. Here the reason the rules differ is simply that substantive policies are different for minors and for persons with retardation. Unlike minors, the latter group sometimes is subject to third-party decisions that abortion should be performed.

Moreover, it is noteworthy that statutes like the Maryland one prevent even the minors themselves from consenting to sterilization. Minors are protected from sterilization even with their own and their parents' consent, but sterilization by third-party consent is tolerated and perhaps encouraged for persons with retardation. And some courts have even thought that minors with retardation do not come within protections seemingly designed for all minors.[16]

The inescapable point is that states, many of which have a history of endorsing eugenic sterilization, are still pursuing an agenda, treating persons with retardation differently from others and disfavoring procreation especially for them. The agenda is less blatant than it was historically, and less relentlessly pursued, but it still exists and is an important element of state policy. The bias is apparent both in court proceedings and in the tests imposed, and the bias in all cases is against procreation. Legislators and judges in all states are willing, in this respect at least, to treat persons who have mental retardation *unlike* all others. The most blatant demonstration of that different treatment in the law is that sterilization is not heavily disfavored for children with retardation but is forbidden for other children. It is elective, but not promoted by government, for consenting adults. In fact, government encourages and promotes parenting for most members of society, but not for persons with retardation.

Failure to Take the Prerequisites to Sterilization Seriously

Just as the state's agenda is similar to government agendas of the past, so are the results. True, current policy and practice are not as systematic as the former policy of sterilization in institutions, which was wholesale. Some parents, of course, would never have their child sterilized, and judges will not grant *every* request for sterilization. Nonetheless, there is reason to be skeptical about third-party decisionmaking in the context of elective sterilization.

The system most commonly devised to protect the patient—the imposition of judicial review with high substantive as well as procedural standards—does not in fact achieve its goal of protection. It is not even clear whether its real purpose is actually to protect or simply to give the appearance of protecting. In either event, it achieves the latter goal better than the former. The hearings do not provide actual protection, because they are often nonadversarial charades, in which high standards are recited and the required findings made, but the standards are not in fact taken seriously.

Modern versions of the requirements for sterilization appear to afford protection against overuse. The expected result of applying these standards—for example, the requirement of the least restrictive alternative and the common requirement that other forms of birth control not be available—is that sterilization would almost never be ordered. Certainly if taken seriously, such requirements would preclude sterilization in the vast majority of cases, and young women would obtain an IUD, or be given birth control pills, or even be put on Norplant instead of being sterilized. Similarly a judge who took seriously the requirement that the young woman be permanently incapable of parenting regardless of her life circumstances (which might after all include a partner with some of the skills she lacks) would not order many sterilizations.

But the prerequisites often seem mere formalities and the hearing only a sham. It is not rare to find cases where all of the evidence presented is on the side of sterilization; where the guardian *ad litem* for the patient does not testify; and where, as far as it appears, no one has consulted with the patient or even informed her of the proceeding. The hearing often consists of the parent or other guardian making standard recitations ("no other birth control would be effective," "she will never be able to parent," "childbirth would be traumatic for her") with no one questioning the statements. When the judicial process is content to accept such conclusory allegations, it does not afford any substantial safeguard. Under this kind of approach even when rules have been adopted to prevent sterilization unless it is truly necessary there will be many sterilizations.

Many cases could be provided to show that even when the highest of standards exist in the law, they are applied in such a way that there is no real review of the legality of the substitute decision.[17] When the parents or other guardians, the guardian *ad litem*, and the judge all share the same attitude—presuming heavily against childbearing by persons with retardation—they have learned to recite the high standards, but what they do in practice does not accord with what they recite.

One good illustration of the emptiness of judicial hearings that take place, even when elaborate procedural safeguards are enforced, is Guardianship of K. M. The hearing was in many ways a sham, not because of loose legal standards for sterilization, but because it was ultimately nonadversarial, despite the common judicial requirement that there be a "case or controversy" before a case will be heard. Clearly, when no participant is arguing for the procreative rights of the subject (in this case, despite the appointment of a guardian *ad litem)*, the hearing can be essentially meaningless. *K. M.* shows both the problem and, through the state court of appeals' response, a way to handle it.

In this case, which was heard in 1991 by the Washington Court of Appeals, the parents of K. M., a fifteen-year-old with mental retardation, petitioned to be appointed her guardians for the purpose of having her sterilized. There were no appearances by any adversarial party, although the trial court appointed a guardian *ad litem* "to represent the best interests of K. M." and to "act as an independent examiner of any live witnesses that occur." K. M.'s guardian *ad litem* submitted a report to the court concluding that "the sterilization authorization request was 'responsible,'" and she clarified her conclusion in court, stating that "she believed K. M. would be at risk emotionally were she to get pregnant and thus her recommendation [in favor of sterilizing K. M.] was based on the best interests of K. M."[18]

Also in support of sterilization, K. M.'s mother told the court that "K. M.'s compliancy and naivety cause[d] [the mother] concern that K. M. may engage in sexual activity without the ability to make judgments regarding the consequences." For this reason, K. M.'s mother had provided her with birth control pills and now wanted her to be sterilized. K. M.'s neurologist testified that K. M. "would never be capable of exercising responsible judgment in sexual and reproductive matters or in caring for a child." His views about K. M.'s capabilities were admittedly not specific to K. M.; they were informed by "his experience" with retardation, which led him to the general conclusion that "pregnancy of a mentally retarded patient involves marked negative psychological impact on the patient." His conclusion was supported also by a child and adolescent psychiatrist who was not familiar with K. M. but who nevertheless testified "regarding the negative emotional repercussions of a pregnancy on a person with K. M.'s level of impairment."[19]

Prior to the court hearing, an independent counsel interviewed K. M. for the court "regarding reproductive issues." During the interview K. M. expressed to her "a desire not to have children because she felt she could not care for them." When K. M.'s guardian *ad litem* cross-examined the lawyer, the independent counsel testified that "she did not know whether K. M. was parroting her parents' views or expressing her own. Although K. M. testified that she understood if she were sterilized she could not have a child, her testimony was ambiguous as to whether she understood the procedure was irreversible."

Neither the judge nor K. M.'s guardian *ad litem* reexamined K. M. to clear up the ambiguities. Nor did they further attempt to understand what her thoughts were about being sterilized. K. M.'s guardian *ad litem* did not examine K. M.'s mother to explore the possibility that the sterilization actually served the mother's best interests rather than K. M.'s. Without further ado, the judge ruled that "the evidence was clear, cogent, and convincing that it was in the best interests of K. M. that she be sterilized."[20]

That would have been the end of the matter, except that the judge was prudent enough to withhold from K. M.'s parents the actual authority to have her sterilized pending the appointment of an attorney for K. M. to facilitate her right of appeal. On appeal, K. M.'s attorney claimed that her guardian *ad litem* had wrongfully "comported herself in a non-adversarial manner and waived a number of K. M.'s substantial rights":[21] the guardian *ad litem* had recommended against the appointment of independent counsel for K. M.; waived K. M.'s right to be present during portions of the trial; failed to object to the absence of notice to K. M.; failed to mail K. M. a copy of her report; and failed to appear herself during portions of the trial.

The court of appeals then considered what was still an open question in Washington state, "the nature of the role of the guardian *ad litem* upon a petition by a parent for authorization to sterilize a minor child." The court looked to other jurisdictions for guidance and concluded that because K. M.'s guardian *ad litem* had "regarded her role as nonadversarial" and failed to assume an "adversary posture" with regard to an issue that involved one of K. M.'s fundamental rights, the trial judge erred by not appointing an independent counsel for K. M.: "In such a case, independent counsel should be appointed when it becomes apparent to the trial court, either upon review of the guardian *ad litem*'s report or at any point during the hearing, that the appointment is necessary in order to ensure a thorough adversary exploration of the issues."[22]

K. M. illustrates that even if a guardian *ad litem* exists, the guardian's identification may be with the family and the court rather than with the woman to be sterilized. The original guardian *ad litem* in *K. M.* was ineffectual primarily for this reason. In that case the state appeals court corrected the lower court's error, but often guardians *ad litem* are permitted to play less than adversarial roles in sterilization proceedings. The resulting lack of an adversary "case or controversy" usually goes unquestioned by any of the participants in the proceedings, including the judge. Often there is no appeal or, even with an appeal, there is no judicial interference. Accordingly, despite high standards spelled out on paper, and despite elaborate procedural safeguards, a hearing can be nonadversarial and essentially meaningless.

The significance of this breakdown in the system cannot be overstated. It means that even supposedly strict standards will not keep third-party sterilization within defined limits. When there is no adversary hearing, sterilizations are ordered in circumstances that could not possibly measure up to the articulated tests. In many locales the request of a family member, accompanied by some evidence of retardation and no vocal opposition, is all that is necessary.

Even when safeguards have been adopted to ensure that proceedings are truly contested, courts can apply even strict requirements so as to make them meaningless. A recent case entitled Estate of C. W. is illustrative. There the Pennsylvania Superior Court affirmed a trial court's order permitting sterilization of a young woman in her twenties named Cynthia. The sterilization was sought by her mother when Cynthia was twenty and opposed by the guardian *ad litem,* who in this case *was* doing her job. The case received attention particularly because the Pennsylvania Supreme Court refused to stay the sterilization while the guardian *ad litem* sought review, and

Justice David Souter of the U.S. Supreme Court also declined a stay.[23] The case is also notable for interpreting what purport to be strict rules concerning sterilization in a way that makes involuntary sterilization widely available. It is but one example that even with a vigorous guardian *ad litem* and apparently strict rules concerning sterilization by substitute consent, judicial biases favoring sterilization of those deemed "retarded" can carry the day.

The law in Pennsylvania concerning sterilization of persons deemed "retarded" was already settled when the case arose, and all judges acting in the matter accepted it as binding. It had been established principally in a 1982 case, *In re* Terwilliger, which held that there was jurisdiction (meaning judicial power) to grant a guardian's request to allow him to consent to tubal ligation, but that, because of the permanence and the "intensely personal right of procreation, the trial judge must take the greatest care to ensure that the incompetent's rights are jealously guarded." In the same spirit, it required that the party seeking sterilization for another have the burden of proof and that the standard of proof be "clear and convincing evidence"[24] (not the lesser standard of "preponderance of the evidence" that is customary in civil cases). And it held that "appellate review of the instant type of case will be of the broadest scope, and [reviewing courts] will not be bound by the inferences or deductions of the lower court." Further important holdings included requiring appointment of a guardian *ad litem;* requiring comprehensive evaluations of the person alleged to be incompetent; and requiring that the patient's own views be elicited, including at an interview with the trial judge. All of these can be viewed as strict procedural requirements governing third-party sterilization in Pennsylvania.

Substantively, as well, the *Terwilliger* standards were highly protective of the patient and weighted the scales heavily against sterilization. The court emphasized repeatedly that only the best interests of the patient are relevant and not the interests of her parents, caretakers, or society in general. But even the patient's best interests could be considered only *after* two specific findings: (1) that the patient "lacks capacity to make a decision about sterilization and that the incapacity is unlikely to change in the foreseeable future"; and (2) that the patient is capable of reproduction. Moreover, the patient's best interests were strictly defined. To find nontherapeutic sterilization in a woman's best interests, a court must find as a factual matter that "sterilization is the only practicable means of contraception, *i.e.,* all less drastic contraceptive methods, including supervision, education and training are unworkable and detailed medical testimony must show that the sterilization procedure requested is the least significant intrusion necessary to protect the interests of the individual."[25]

In addition to these firm prerequisites to sterilization by substitute consent, the court set forth a list of guidelines to assist the court in making its decision concerning the patient's best interests. The guidelines were not exclusive and were adopted from the widely followed *Grady* decision. Two of the factors of relevance to the *C. W.* case are: (1) "the likelihood that the individual will voluntarily engage in sexual activity or be exposed to situations where sexual intercourse is imposed upon her"; and (2) "[e]vidence that scientific or medical advances may occur within the foreseeable future which will make possible either improvement of the individual's condition or alternative and less drastic sterilization procedures."[26] There are many points that could be made about the court's behavior in *C. W.*, but its treatment of these two requirements is enough to illustrate that even strict legal rules cannot and do not ensure unbiased decisionmaking.

To start with the second point, involving advances in contraception, the *C. W.* court said, "there is no evidence in the record that scientific or medical advances in the future will make possible a relevant improvement in [Cynthia's] own condition or that any relevant developments in sterilization techniques are imminent . . . [There was no] suggestion by any expert that medical science is on the brink of developing a new contraceptive or sterilization technique that would have a materially different effect on a person in [Cynthia's] difficult mental and physical condition." One physician had testified that he was "not aware of" any such advances.[27]

While the case was wending its way through the court system, however, Norplant became generally available in this country and quickly became a popular form of contraception. The guardian *ad litem* argued that fact to the appeals court, and also stressed the new availability of Depo-Provera, another hormonal contraceptive. In a footnote the court called these developments "irrelevant to our consideration of this case, since there was testimony concerning these hormonal contraceptives at the hearings in this matter and that testimony, albeit scant, revealed that such treatments have not been widely enough employed for anyone to know what effect they might have on [Cynthia's] severe medical problems."[28] Its attitude toward new and future scientific advances seems out of keeping with *Terwilliger's* guidelines.

Even more clearly unjustifiable was the court's treatment of *Terwilliger's* supposed prerequisite that there be no other practicable means of birth control. In addition to Norplant and Depo-Provera, more established methods of birth control were cavalierly dismissed. For example, the court said that an IUD might be "more intrusive than tubal ligation"[29] because it required annual replacement.

Most surprising was some of the court's reasoning in dismissing the birth control pill as a viable alternative. The problem with the pill was that it "is not administered to women over the age of 35 and therefore, it is not even potentially a permanent contraceptive approach."[30] Cynthia, however, was only twenty-four at the appeals court hearing. Surely, in the next eleven years, some new birth control methods would be a distinct possibility.

Instead of searching for the least restrictive alternative, as Pennsylvania law demanded, the court in effect created a presumption in favor of sterilization. That was apparent when it declared that "a potentially permanent solution is preferable." The trial court concluded, in the words of the appeals court, that "there was no reason to inject a new element that may further destabilize her, particularly where that element is unquestionably only a temporary solution to a problem that in all likelihood is permanent."[31]

Justifiable or not as a matter of policy, the court's preference for a permanent solution seems the opposite of *Terwilliger*'s concern to protect the rights of the patient because of the dangers of imposing a permanent solution.[32] There was a forceful dissent:

> The majority wants us to infer that any attempt to administer the birth control pill or other hormonal methods of contraception to [Cynthia] would have disastrous effects on her already tenuous physical condition . . . [yet] [t]he proponents of sterilization have not satisfied their burden of proving by clear and convincing evidence that less drastic contraceptive methods such as birth control pills and hormonal treatments are unworkable.[33]

In addition to the absence of alternative contraceptive measures, current or future, the other factor with which the court played havoc is the likelihood that the individual whose treatment is at issue will engage in sex, voluntarily or otherwise. Indeed both this legal requirement and the rule that no other contraception be available (both of which are part of the *Terwilliger-Grady* "guidelines") can be seen as equivalent to the *Terwilliger* requirement that sterilization be imposed only if it is necessary.

To evaluate how the rules were applied in *C. W.*, it is necessary to understand the context of her life. The petition to allow sterilization was filed by her mother when Cynthia was twenty years old, and she was twenty-four in

1995 when the court of appeals ruled in the case. Cynthia was then living in a community-living facility, visiting her mother every other weekend and for holidays. After the lawsuit commenced, she had finished her state-provided special education program and had begun working in a sheltered workshop.

Cynthia has organic brain damage and is mute. Since infancy she has had scoliosis, cerebral palsy, and grand mal epilepsy. The epilepsy at the time of litigation was controlled, though imperfectly, by three drugs that are commonly used to control epilepsy as well as other conditions: phenobarbital, Dilantin, and Tegretol. Cynthia also has retardation that the court dubbed "moderately severe," having "the mental age of a three to five year old child with an I.Q. of between 30–50."[34]

Cynthia can communicate, although imperfectly. The court said she "communicates in a very limited fashion through minimal signing and making certain noises that those around her have learned to interpret."[35]

One fact about Cynthia's life that seemingly reduced the need for sterilization, or indeed for any contraception, was the degree of supervision she already experienced because of her various medical needs. Her seizure disorder required her to be checked every fifteen to thirty minutes during the day. At night she was not checked, but staff could monitor noises in her room through an intercom. Moreover, at the time of the appeals court decision she was no longer living with any male residents—a fact that the guardian *ad litem* thought important but that the court found insignificant because she could still "come into contact with" men.

In its enthusiasm for sterilization, the court would not accept even supervision every fifteen minutes, in combination with education and training, as adequate to prevent "the disastrous eventuality of pregnancy." It explained, "Experts called by petitioner uniformly found this level of supervision inadequate, noting that much can be accomplished that can cause pregnancy in less than 15 minutes."[36] The court also pointed out that since no greater supervision (than every 15 minutes) was medically required, it would be constricting Cynthia's life to impose even more supervision simply to combat the possibility of pregnancy.

In some sense, the difference between the guardian *ad litem* and the petitioner did not concern whether the supervision did or did not protect against pregnancy as much as *how much* protection against pregnancy was sufficient. The guardian *ad litem* felt that existing supervision adequately protected Cynthia, even though the protection was not absolute and could not be, absent twenty-four-hour supervision of the young woman and also of her supervisors. For the petitioners, and seemingly for the court, no solution short of sterilization was adequate if *any* possibility of sexual contact remained.

Another important difference, which divided the court as well as the parties, is *what* sexual activity is relevant in assessing "likelihood of sexual activity." Is only consensual sexual activity to be considered, or is potential sexual exploitation and rape of the subject also a reason for her sterilization? In *C. W.*, the appeals court, somewhat remarkably, considered that all activity in which Cynthia engaged would be legally involuntary, in the sense that she lacked the mental capacity to "give legally sufficient consent" to any kind of sex. But it also thought that the potential for truly forced sex was relevant to the issue of sterilization.

The problem with relying on sterilization when the concern is forcible sex is that the young woman should be protected from rape as well as from pregnancy. One of the dissenting judges wrote separately to stress that the likelihood of sexual abuse was *not* an appropriate consideration: "[S]uch sterilization as a means of protection can only encourage complacency in safeguarding individuals like [Cynthia]."[37] A dissenter in the Court of Common Pleas had similarly pointed out that "[t]he protection of this woman's physical person from harm is the real issue in this case. Sterilization will not and cannot protect [Cynthia] from untoward sexual advances and abuse. It can only prevent one of the unwanted results of sexual abuse and activity, pregnancy. What about the trauma of rape? What about the death sentence of AIDS and the horrors of syphilis?"[38]

C. W. is relevant in many other respects as well. But even these illustrations of the court's mode of reasoning show that strict legal protections, procedural and substantive, do not ensure protection from unnecessary sterilization of persons unable to decide for themselves. *C. W.* is remarkable in this respect not only because the court avoided substantive requirements that appeared very exacting, but also because the hearing it afforded was extremely thorough. Whereas many sterilization petitions are granted in a routine, nonadversarial, even boilerplate fashion, that was in no way the case in *C. W.* The hearings covered seven days over a one-and-a-half-year period and included extensive testimony by witnesses from all sides. The guardian *ad litem*, appointed by the court at the outset in compliance with *Terwilliger*, had consistently opposed the sterilization, contending that it was not in Cynthia's interests. She thought that all contraception was unnecessary because Cynthia was supervised continually for medical reasons. She also took the position that *if* contraception were to be administered, some method other than sterilization would be less intrusive and thus preferable. Finally, she believed that, in the unlikely event that Cynthia were to become pregnant, abortion would be a possibility.

The guardian *ad litem*'s argument that abortion is less intrusive than sterilization is especially forceful in a case like *C. W.*, because of the *un*likelihood of abortion ever being actually necessary. Even if one does not agree that abortion is the lesser intrusion as a general matter, one might acquiesce when the likelihood of sexual contact is minimal, so that both sterilization and abortion will in all likelihood be avoided.

The guardian *ad litem* fought hard and ably and had the law on her side. Yet she lost in the court of appeals. Not only did she lose on the merits; the appeals courts even refused to postpone the sterilization while she sought review of the intermediate court's decision.

With results like these, even in the face of tough procedural and substantive standards, the question arises how one *can* protect against abuses and overbroad sterilization of persons who are not permitted to make their own decisions. Remembering the *Valerie N.* debate about the legitimacy of denying sterilization to persons who cannot consent for themselves, we can see why the California legislature might reasonably have been skeptical that substitute decisionmaking would work to curb past abuses concerning eugenic sterilization. It was not unreasonable for the California legislature (and the Massachusetts and Colorado legislatures, if they did so) to view sterilization by substitute decision as simply involuntary sterilization by another name. It was not unreasonable for those legislatures to believe that the only real means of protecting against abuses was to ban nonconsensual sterilization altogether. That position becomes even more compelling as varieties and methods of birth control other than sterilization increase.

The language of today's decisions differs from the language of Buck v. Bell, but all too often, buried beneath that fancy language and the protections we now afford, the substance is largely the same.

Not only are there involuntary sterilizations, but also, as in the past, sterilization is sometimes imposed *because of handicap*. The fact is that C. W. was sterilized because of her various handicaps and only for that reason. Each of the testifying physicians "stated that they would *not recommend* tubal ligation for a person of 'normal' intelligence with [Cynthia's] medical problems and would attempt to *discourage* such a person from pursuing such an option. Both gynecologists . . . testified that they would not personally perform a tubal ligation on a 'normal' woman of [Cynthia's] age, even if her medical problems were identical to [Cynthia's]."[39]

Sometimes the discrimination against persons with retardation, which is indeed pervasive, is apparent, but often it is cloaked. Establishing discrimination should be sufficient to invalidate such practices, because discrimination against persons with retardation or other handicaps is unquestionably illegal today under an array of state and federal statutes, most notably the Americans with Disabilities Act. That federal enactment took effect in the 1990s and is applicable nationwide. It proscribes acts of discrimination in the workplace and discrimination by providers of transportation, public accommodation, and public services, which include medical services.[40]

Probably, the clear illegality of current prevailing practices contributes to those practices' remaining out of view. Moreover, many would be content for these issues to remain hidden. The discrimination may be illegal, but it is a discrimination with which much of society sympathizes.

Judges as Substitute Decisionmakers

One advantage of relying on a judge's decision, rather than on that of other substitute decisionmakers, is that the judge is less personally interested than many other potential decisionmakers, such as parents, guardians, and caretakers. The guardian *ad litem*, or even the physician who decides whether to perform the procedure, is also usually less personally involved in the facts of the particular case than parents and caretakers are. Nevertheless, all three types of "disinterested decisionmakers" do bring to the case their own views and prejudices concerning the advisability of sterilization. They also bring, consciously or not, their own views and prejudices concerning the capacities of those labeled "retarded" and the proper role for them. Moreover, doctors, judges, and lawyers have no particular training enabling them to view persons with retardation from a realistic or humane perspective. Their prejudices are likely to reflect the prejudices of society generally.[41]

Like many in society, judges tend to favor sterilization, and case law suggests that prejudices against persons with mental retardation shape their decisionmaking. Indeed, the history of sterilization of persons labeled "retarded" is a history of sterilization performed with judicial approval.

Yet judges are uniquely able to act on their prejudices without fear of liability[42] and thus can legitimate particular sterilization decisions while shielding all involved—the hospital, the physician, the petitioning parent—from legal responsibility. Accordingly in close cases others can protect themselves by requiring judicial approval before they act, and judges can order the sterilization without any fear of liability for themselves or others.

Judges thus have enormous power and responsibility in sterilization decisions. But that power may be appropriate. If third-party decisions allowing sterilization are to be made at all and made on an individualized basis, then despite their shortcomings, judges as disinterested decisionmakers trained in dispensing fairness are probably the best available substitute decisionmaker.

Moreover, judges' discretion need not be limitless. The purpose of the strict standards that are increasingly being adopted limiting nonconsensual sterilization is to keep judges' decisionmaking within narrow bounds—bounds that in turn have been devised either by legislatures or by judges or by both. But what *C. W.* shows a court can do even when bound by a "least restrictive alternative" requirement suggests that additional means of controlling judges' discretion are necessary, if articulated policies are to be followed.

Problems with the Standards Themselves

Even apart from pervasive illegal discrimination, there are fundamental problems with the substitute decisionmaking system. Those problems go beyond the system's not adhering to the standards it articulates, such as best interests, substituted judgment, and least restrictive alternative. The most serious issue is the substitute standards themselves.

This difficulty with third-party decisionmaking is inherent. But it becomes most apparent when the subject is actually resisting the medical procedure that others have decided is appropriate for her. The law, with rare exceptions, purports to impose a guardian's decision on a person with mental retardation, even in the face of active resistance. For example, the current California statute governing the power of guardians-conservators to make medical decisions, except sterilization, for their wards-conservatees, provides:

a. If the conservatee has been adjudicated to lack the capacity to give informed consent for medical treatment, the conservator has the exclusive authority to give consent for such medical treatment to be performed on the conservatee as the conservator in good faith based on medical advice determines to be necessary *and the conservator may require the conservatee to receive such medical treatment, whether or not the conservatee objects.* In any such case, *the consent of the conservator alone is sufficient and no person is liable because the medical treatment is performed upon the conservatee without the conservatee's consent.*

b. If prior to the establishment of the conservatorship the conservatee was an adherent of a religion whose tenets and practices call for reliance on prayer alone for healing, the treatment required by the conservator under the provisions of this section shall be by an accredited practitioner of that religion.[43]

It was this statute, which was also in existence in 1985 when *Valerie N.* was decided, that the California Supreme Court majority relied on in saying that procedures like abortion can be forced on a ward.

Sometimes, as in the above statute, the law explicitly allows a guardian's wishes to be forced on the ward. Sometimes instead the law as it is set out pays no heed to what the patient may want or may be doing. Judicial decisions often do not rectify the problem by filling in the legislative void, or even by noticing the problem or inquiring about the patient's point of view. To some, the subject's own opinions and feelings become irrelevant as soon as she is characterized as being incapable of giving informed consent.

It seems remarkable that resistance by the ward, regardless of her level of intellectual functioning, should be of so little importance. Even in the extreme case, when she is not able to speak, resistance amounts to a declaration of her own choice. Her reasoning process may seem faulty, but especially when we are considering a supposedly elective procedure, the subject's actual choice should play a more central role. It should receive more attention, for example, than whether the patient has a guardian.

In discussing abortion and sterilization practices, this book takes the position that when the patient resists the proposed procedure, regardless of the guardian's or the parent's wishes, prudence would suggest that the physician insist on judicial review. Not only would that seem ethically appropriate, but also it would protect the physician against subsequent liability. Self-protection for the physician would counsel refusing to operate without a court order saying it is permissible to impose the operation on a patient who is actively resisting. (When the patient is a young child, being treated like all other young children, such review might not be required.)

This chapter carries that suggestion one step further: Resistance should not only trigger judicial review but also should determine its outcome. A judge reviewing the appropriateness of an elective medical procedure should adhere to the patient's wishes.

Respecting a Patient's Resistance

That basic proposition should be true *at least* when the patient's wishes are made apparent and when they are to refuse treatment, and nontherapeutic treatment at that. Accepting the patient's ability to *refuse* treatment would not necessarily mean that a person deemed retarded could *request* medical treatment and receive it without some third person joining in her request. The distinction between being allowed to refuse treatment (any treatment) and being able to demand whatever treatment one wants is familiar and well-accepted in the law, even if not immune from criticism. Competent adults are deemed to have a constitutional right (derived from the Due Process clause of the U.S. Constitution) to refuse unwanted medical treatment for any reason or for no reason at all.

When the procedure at issue is elective (nontherapeutic) as well, why would a judge ever decide to impose it on a person who is actively resisting? Such imposition raises the specter of the subject being held down to have an abortion or a sterilization imposed on her, or even to have Norplant or an IUD inserted. Is it permissible to tie her down or place her in a straitjacket? It is one thing for a judge to order an elective medical procedure when the patient is cooperative or even in the absence of any knowledge of the patient's wishes. But when the patient is resisting imposition of a procedure that is not medically necessary and that all other persons have a right to refuse for any reason, it should not matter whether the patient is considered "mentally competent" or not.

Resistance, of course, is not the usual scenario. Nonetheless it is disturbing that most statements of the applicable rules do not distinguish cases where it exists. Instead statutes, cases, and commentators often set out the role of third-party decisionmakers without paying attention to the patient's own attitudes, and certainly without making her resistance to elective procedures determinative. This book suggests instead a hard and fast rule that the patient's cooperation in a nontherapeutic medical procedure is central to the procedure's legitimacy. Conversely, a patient's active resistance to an elective medical procedure should always allow the patient to evade and avoid the procedure.

Even if the court majority in *Valerie N.* was correct in believing that the guardian had authority to force some nontherapeutic decisions on a ward, the statute it relied on (which is quoted above) did not pertain to sterilization. Moreover it does not represent the law in California today as pertains to sterilization. That state's sterilization law, as revised after *Valerie N.*, explicitly allows the patient who resists sterilization to avoid sterilization. Moreover it takes the logical next step and requires an inquiry into the wishes of the subject of the operation.

Under the current California sterilization statute, third-party sterilization is allowed only in narrow circumstances. The statute also is explicit in respecting the patient's resistance:

> The court may authorize the conservator of a person proposed to be sterilized to consent to the sterilization of that person only if the court finds that the petitioner has established all of the following beyond a reasonable doubt:
>
> [the statute then lists many factors, some of which are quoted in Chapter 6].
>
> (h) The person . . . has not made a knowing objection to his or her sterilization. For purposes of this subdivision, an individual may be found to have knowingly objected to his or her sterilization notwithstanding his or her inability to give consent to sterilization . . . In the case of persons who are nonverbal, have limited verbal ability to communicate, or who rely on alternative modes of communication, the court shall ensure that adequate effort has been made to elicit the actual views of the individual by the facilitator appointed [to do so] . . . or by any other person with experience in communicating with developmentally disabled persons who communicate using similar means.[44]

This book endorses the approach of disallowing sterilization whenever the subject makes a "knowing objection." Even further, it suggests, in the context of reproductive choices at least, that the patient's own wishes—whether to undergo or refuse procedures like abortion and insertion of Norplant—should be determinative. The same reasons that make us want to follow the patient's wishes to refuse treatment when they are most apparent because she is actively resisting should also make us want to follow them whenever they are known. Indeed, we should want to elicit her opinion whenever it can be known, as the California statute also contemplates in the context of sterilization.

In evaluating the proposition that the young woman should always be able to make her own decisions, it is helpful to separate out the different scenarios that can occur. The purpose is to show that in each of the four possible factual scenarios, the appropriate course is to follow the wishes of the subject of a procedure, even if she is under guardianship. If that is so, we should simply have a rule that the individual be her own decisionmaker.

If the issue is abortion, for example, four different possibilities arise: Guardian and ward may agree on what they want to do, either agreeing that abortion is the preferable course or agreeing to go ahead with the pregnancy. Alternatively, they may disagree, and here too two different scenarios are possible: the guardian may want childbirth and the ward may not; or the guardian may want abortion and the ward may want childbirth. The fourth possibility is the one we have just now been considering, in which the ward wants to resist an operation that the guardian would impose. The following discussion will show that in all four circumstances, the decision of the ward, not the guardian, should prevail.

In the first two situations, where guardian and ward agree, it is not at all revolutionary to accept the ward's wishes as binding, for by hypothesis, they are also the wishes of her guardian. Whether both want to abort, or both want to continue the pregnancy, it is not difficult to imagine law making their mutual wishes prevail. It is not clear, however, that that is always the law today.

Where both guardian and ward want abortion, a few states do not automatically allow their mutual wish to be followed but require a judicial proceeding before a physician can perform the procedure. Part of the reason for judicial oversight may of course be to determine whether they do really both want the procedure, or whether instead, for example, the ward has simply not been told what is going on. Oversight may also be used to apply other tests and standards, such as a best interests inquiry or even a rule that abortion be unavailable unless medically necessary. With respect to sterilization, mutual consent of guardian and ward alone is rarely seen as sufficient without judicial participation; with respect to abortion, a central issue is whether they together can consent or whether others must approve their choice, with some states going one way and some the other, and most states still lacking clear law on the issue.

When guardian and ward both want childbirth rather than abortion, their mutual wishes will prevail. Others might have objections, and one can even imagine a system in which their legal objections would be given weight. If the young woman is employed in a sheltered workshop or lives in community housing, for example, one of her caretakers, or officials from the Department of Mental Retardation, may strongly believe that the pregnancy is a mistake. Yet unless the objector is the guardian, it is most *unlikely* that our legal system would permit interference with the pregnancy (other than by persuasion). A court would not force the woman to undergo abortion.

This scenario shows that there are clear limitations on the control the state exercises over individuals with retardation in our current system. Officials, including the judge, may believe that abortion or sterilization is the best course. Nonetheless, those procedures will usually not be imposed without the consent of, and usually the initiative of, the guardian or parent. To that extent, the analogy of the current system to earlier regimes of forced sterilization fails, for the state does not impose procedures without a guardian's cooperation. (This safeguard is weaker than it seems, however, when one takes account of the ability to institute guardianship proceedings when no guardian yet exists.)[45]

The other two scenarios, because they are the ones in which guardian and ward disagree, would seem greater candidates for disregarding the ward's wishes. Yet considering each situation on its facts, one perceives a good case for allowing the wishes of the ward to trump those of the guardian in both circumstances.

The third situation involves a ward's request to have an abortion that the guardian resists. This is not the usual scenario in cases involving persons with retardation; it is the paradigmatic situation for litigation concerning minors seeking abortions.[46] In those cases the minor seeks an abortion either over the objection of or without the knowledge of the parent. In the rare cases in which this occurs between ward and guardian, the conflict should be resolved in favor of the wishes of the ward.

If the ward does not want to become a mother, what interest is there in foisting motherhood upon her? If she is so "incompetent" that she is not legally permitted to make her own decisions, why would anyone want to make her be a mother? Why should the guardian's interests in her becoming a mother—whether those interests are religious or otherwise—be determinative rather than hers? The insignificance of the guardian's interests in making her give birth is reinforced by the fact that our legal system does not let anyone require anyone else to become a mother.[47]

The more usual situation in the retardation context, however, if there is expressed disagreement between guardian and ward, is the fourth scenario described above, in which the guardian seeks an abortion that the ward does not want. In practice the situation may be difficult to distinguish from the second situation, which is also common, where both people opt for an abortion: The patient may not have been consulted, leaving her wishes wholly unknown; or even if she has been informed about pending procedures, her own views may not have been developed or elicited.

Resistance will not usually be apparent when the subject has retardation. But at least when there is active resistance, abortion should not be forced. It is not forced on anyone else, and it should not be forced on persons who have retardation. That result is required by the principle of treating persons with retardation like all others, as well as by principles of human dignity and respect for human integrity.

For some persons an additional reason is a "right to life" on the part of the fetus. In fact, that may be the young woman's motivation in declining an abortion. It does not take strong intellectual capacity to have moral and religious beliefs. If a young woman, albeit under guardianship, believes she should not have an abortion for moral or religious reasons, our system should not allow a third person to force abortion on her, whatever the motivations. There is no reason to deny her a right to follow her religious beliefs, when anyone else would be given that option.

If, as suggested, one accepts the view that the subject's wishes should prevail whenever she resists, the principle becomes difficult to contain. Presumably, the subject's wishes should prevail whenever they are known; surely her rights should not turn, at least as a matter of theory, on how much noise she makes. And if her wishes are determinative whenever they are known, should not the system take the further step of asking her? The preferable solution to the whole conundrum of how to treat reproductive rights may be to try to discover the subject's wishes, so that they can be followed if possible.

The central and inescapable difficulty with much current practice is that it does not legally allow, let alone promote, choice by women who have retardation. Even sterilization can still be forced on a woman without her consent, indeed over her active opposition. From the point of view of a person being sterilized against her will, it may make little difference whether the person subjecting her to the procedure is some state official or her mother acting in collusion with a judge and using legal procedures. From the perspective of the patient who does not want an operation, the operation is forced—as forced as it was at the time of Buck v. Bell—and the fact that her mother and a judge have agreed to it does not make it less so.

Even systems that manage to provide real hearings and attempt to enforce real standards to limit nonconsensual procedures cannot escape this central problem of lack of choice by the subject of the sterilization. Of course, if one hypothesizes that sterilization is usually in the interests of women who have retardation, there appears to be no conflict of interest between those women and substitute decisionmakers who favor sterilization. But the hypothesis is not always valid.

Moreover, it may be central to the young woman's interests to participate in making her own life decisions, to the fullest extent possible. With or without retardation, not many persons would want their mother to be able to make decisions—"in their best interests"—over their sex life, dating life, marital life, and procreative life. They might (or might not) follow their parent's advice, but that is another matter. Most daughters can appreciate the absurdity of defending a system of mothers' choice as the equivalent of their own. And a mother's choice does not become equivalent to her daughter's own even if the mother acts in good faith and has at heart the daughter's best interests, as the mother sees them.

The judge in *Eberhardy* appreciated that the central element of procreative decisionmaking must be making one's own decisions: It is wrong, he said, to equate "a decision made by others with the choice of the person to be sterilized. It is clearly not a personal choice, and no amount of legal legerdemain can make it so."[48]

Critique: Danger and Unworkability

Because procreative decisions seriously affect a young woman with retardation and could also bring into the world another person for whom she might be unable to provide adequate care, skepticism toward the idea of self-determination is understandable. The experience even of more "high-functioning" persons like Betty R., described in Chapter 4, shows that significant danger of exploitation and coercion can result from giving vulnerable persons authority to consent for themselves.

Betty R. was vulnerable to her physician and was ready to follow his (misguided and improper) advice to get an abortion until she consulted with her family and the physician's biases were exposed. Her own ability to consent had the potential effect of placing her at the mercy of her physician and his prejudices.

Of course, the same is true of many adults whose legal ability to consent is not called into question. Many who do not have retardation—young, middle-aged, and elderly—are vulnerable to medical practitioners and accept their bad advice along with their good. Many persons, including those with substantial intelligence as measured by IQ score, feel intimidated by physicians and accept their advice far too readily. They trust their physician to make decisions for them, with little questioning and sometimes with little understanding.

When considering the potential dangers of self-determination, it is most important to remember that it is not appropriate to remedy an abuse by restricting the options of the potential victim. Instead it is the conduct of the abuser that should be corrected. The diagnosis and behavior of the physician described in *Betty R.* was inappropriate, and the correct solution would involve educating physicians, starting in medical school and continuing in later education and training programs, to exhibit more respect for their patients. Members of the medical profession need to have contact and experience with persons with mental retardation—and other persons with disabilities or from cultural settings that differ from their own. Controlling the behavior of the physician, through sanctions if necessary as well as through education, is far more appropriate than taking away Betty's ability to decide for herself out of fear that she will be manipulated. Medical schools already are broadening students' experience through clinical training programs and are emphasizing ethics courses and training in communicative and interpersonal skills more than they did in the past. The aim in part is for physicians to learn to maximize communication and to allow patients to make their own choices.

An important part of a solution for all vulnerable people is to find ways short of guardianship to ensure that patients understand their situation and their options. One method would be to encourage patients to seek assistance and support from persons they trust. All patients need to find a balance between support that is coercive and the total absence of support. Many persons with retardation (and some other persons) may also need support that is tailored to their own needs, including helpers who have the time and the skill to learn how best to communicate with them.

There is a broad range of situations in which the patient has a potentially difficult decision to make. Abortion and sterilization are examples we have examined. A very different context, withdrawal of life-sustaining medical treatment, is also frequently viewed as governed by a "right to choose." One approach that can be helpful for all these issues—if the patient is to make her own decision as proposed—is for either the law or the medical profession to require that family members involved with the woman be included in the process, unless the patient specifically rejects their involvement. If no family members are close to the patient, a good friend or even a trusted caregiver might participate along with the patient.

Any such process should not be limited to persons with mental retardation but should include the many others who appear to need support. Those who do not have anyone, or who for whatever reason specifically reject the involvement of persons they know, may be assisted by a citizen advocate, unless that form of assistance also is refused. Moreover a human rights committee or an ethics advisory group should be available to the decisionmaker and any helper she chooses to rely on. Such a group could help the patient understand the situation and clarify the options. Of course, a patient who does not want any helpers can reject assistance.

But just as we found that strict rules and standards could not contain the biases of judges, similarly the *attitudes* of the health care providers and others are at least as important as any set of new procedures or systematic reforms in the rules. As the Massachusetts Department of Mental Retardation stated in another context:

> In applying these standards, it is important to bear in mind the long history of oppression and callous disregard for the lives of people with mental retardation. This ingrained tradition, together with the continuing societal pressure to devalue people with mental retardation, make it essential that those charged with their support and care be aware of the increased risks that persons with mental retardation continue to face and be especially vigilant to protect their autonomy and their right to equal treatment.[49]

The principle is as appropriate in the context of elective reproductive decisionmaking as in the context of life-sustaining treatment, which the policy addresses.

Even under current legal practice, there are some areas of decisionmaking where it seems clear that unless persons, including those with retardation, give their own consent, no one can consent for them. Examples are marriage and sex. Even if a guardian had authority to interfere with these acts for a ward, the guardian surely would not have legal authority to impose them. Similarly, it seems unlikely that a guardian can decide a ward should give up her child, despite the California Supreme Court's gratuitous statement to the contrary.

It is less clear as a matter of law whether there is any limit on which adults will be permitted to consent concerning subjects like marriage, sex, or giving up a baby for adoption. (Of course, the ability to communicate assent is one practical limit.) Even if anyone who can communicate were permitted to assent for herself to sex or marriage, law and society might appropriately be more skeptical in some other contexts and more willing to insist that consent be "informed" and the subject be capable of rational understanding.[50]

How the Proposed System Would Work

An entirely different basis for skepticism about self-determination as the appropriate course is confusion about how self-determination would operate in practice. Many dismiss as simply fanciful the suggestion that a young woman like Valerie N. or C. W. could be "responsible for" her own decisions.

Although most persons with retardation have mild retardation, most of the patients represented in third-party consent cases seem less like Betty R., who in many ways functioned independently in the community, than like C. W. and Valerie N. For Betty R., and for most persons with mild or moderate retardation, the paramount danger of self-determination lies in giving to a vulnerable person with limited understanding the authority to consent independently to whatever the physician proposes. But the more difficult problem with self-determination may be how to put into effect a system relying on the "consent" of persons with very limited faculties.

Obviously, the less communicative a person is, the greater the problem in ascertaining and relying on her wishes. A person who is clearly communicative in the sense of being able to assent or otherwise express herself may give one answer one moment and another the next. Even if her responses are consistent, there may be real reason to doubt that her "decision" is based on any actual understanding. Nevertheless, the proposed policy of self-determination would rely on the patient, even one with the most minimal communication skills, as the person with the legal authority to decide concerning these matters. In fact, a policy of self-determination for all expressive persons can be workable and, as we will see, will produce some good effects.

A more serious problem may be that the effects of a supposed regime of self-determination could be minimal. Since *none* of the procedures, including sterilization, would call for court supervision under this policy, favoring instead treating persons with any ability to communicate as their own decisionmaker, can one have any confidence that the patient will actually be asked for her consent, or even informed concerning the procedures to which she is subjected? In a sense, the proposal is to treat all elective procedures concerning reproduction as conventional birth control is treated today: subject to no judicial or other official supervision. Accordingly, it is unclear whether a transfer of legal decisionmaking authority to the patient would in fact promote her self-determination, or whether instead it would simply protect caretakers from any supervision and thereby allow even freer exploitation.

Effects on Current Practice

Comparatively independent persons with retardation would benefit most obviously from the change in legal decisionmaking authority that is proposed; and physicians would be able to accept their requests for treatment without fear of liability. But for many persons with retardation, there might not be any discernible change in practice. This is especially true with regard to birth control decisions. Absence of supervision means that the caretaker can administer medication, including birth control pills, without even informing the patient what she is taking. Unless the patient is in a position to insist on her legal rights, the change in decisionmaking authority does not actually put her in any better, or any different, position than before. In fact, the patient may not only lack ability to insist on her rights; she may not even know that she has any.

With respect to procedures like sterilization that have usually required judicial supervision, the proposed change in practice seems greater than with conventional birth control. Under the proposal, the patient has the legal right to decide. What may be more significant, there is no judicial supervision. In reality, therefore, the caretaker may have the same practical authority with respect to sterilization and abortion that he or she already has concerning conventional birth control: The patient may be unaware of her own legal right, and even if she knows about it, she may find it impossible to resist whatever a caretaker, family member, or physician wishes (especially if they all agree with one another). Perhaps a small justification for this lessening control over sterilization is its continuing tendency to become more like conventional birth control and vice versa. A self-determination policy would avoid having to draw a line on the slippery slope between long-lasting contraception like Norplant and reversible sterilization procedures.[51]

Without judicial supervision, the need for physician involvement is the main constraint (along with ethical constraints) on other would-be third-party decisionmakers. Obviously a physician's consent is necessary for access to sterilization or abortion, and even for access to birth control pills. The proposed approach relies heavily on the physician's responsibility to assure that the patient is fully informed about the medication or the medical procedure. The physician could and should insist that the patient personally approve the proposed course of action before it occurs.

Whether such a requirement could adequately ensure that the patient's wishes are the focus—rather than the parent's, guardian's, or caretaker's wishes—remains to be seen. The proposed approach relies on the integrity of the medical profession and the expectation that if clear rules are announced, to replace the fuzzy norms now in existence, physicians will not defy them. Surely more attention will be paid to the patient and her wishes than under the current system, where physicians do not know who has legal responsibility and know they can be liable for following the declared wishes of a person who seems to have marginal intelligence.

Nonetheless, if there is no one in the picture who seems likely to raise an objection, the absence of monitoring means a physician's own biases still can take control. Physician and caretaker together can arrange for contraception to be administered without the patient knowing; they can even get the patient to have an operation without informing her of its true nature. One hopes it would be rare for a physician to accede to such an unethical practice, even if the physician truly believes that the medication or procedure is "good for" the patient; even if the physician has little appreciation of the values of independent decisionmaking for persons with retardation; and even if it does not appear that anyone will later object. There are instances of such unethical conduct today and doubtless there will continue to be some, but adopting a clear rule that the patient is legally the decisionmaker and must be involved would reduce those abuses.

Because "enforcement" would be highly limited, the proposed standard might appropriately be considered primarily aspirational. At the very least, it instructs persons dealing with the patient—whether friend, relative, professional caretaker, or physician—that they should treat the patient as the decisionmaker, inform her as much as possible, and heed any preferences concerning these issues that she does express.

"The rules," of course, are only the beginning. Even if all the proper forms are observed, the patient can still be railroaded rather than consulted in a way that really involves and informs her. In the health care context, the objective is for the patient to be truthfully and fully informed in ways that will make her understand, to the maximum extent possible, the nature of the proposed medication or treatment. Obviously there are different levels of comprehension and many different methods of communicating, but the central point is that there should be serious effort to communicate as much as possible and as effectively as possible.

Often the communication can best be accomplished by those who know the woman well and answer to her needs on a daily basis. A caring and compassionate caretaker at least will have attempted over the course of their relationship to build communication and mutual understanding with the patient. It can often be much more difficult to understand what the patient wants on the basis of one interview, or even a series of interviews, but that format is sometimes necessary—for health care workers or those involved in the legal system, for example. Interviewing skills, sometimes especially adapted to the needs and limitations of the particular patient, will be helpful here. Some offices or clinics have members of the staff who are particularly experienced with retardation and sensitive in eliciting patients' views. But all health care workers in dealing with all patients could benefit from learning how better to elicit and listen to the patient's desires.

The starting point of the communication process is that the physician or other health care worker simply ask the woman what she wants to do and listen carefully to her answers. Another step is to help the woman explore and understand the nature of the proposed procedure and how it relates to her interests. For patients with retardation, the experience of having someone outside their immediate circle really try to communicate with them and even elicit *their* views may be dauntingly unfamiliar.

Such an interview should be central to the health care process whether or not the patient has retardation, but often it is not. It can be difficult for physicians to translate scientific, medical parlance into simple talk that lay people can understand. It also can be time-consuming, and the physician may not be trained for it; some doctors are excellent scientists but lack interpersonal skills. Another barrier to full patient-physician communication may arise from a clash of values between them. Some physicians, for example, are opposed in principle to childbearing by persons with retardation. Others may be dubious about its desirability. In any event, the ideal is for the patient to be truthfully and fully informed, in ways that will make her understand as much as possible, by health care providers as well as others. Under current or proposed law and accepted ethical norms, it is wrong to get compliance by keeping the patient ignorant of what is proceeding.

Effects on Current Law

If self-determination effects changes in practice, the greatest effect, beyond removing court supervision from sterilization, will be increasing the understanding of patients with retardation by taking the time to involve them in decisionmaking. But how would the proposal change current law?

The central, doctrinal difference between the proposed and the current approaches is that self-determination allows personal choice by anyone who can answer, while current law usually allows choice only to those persons who can give informed consent. Therefore the only persons who would be affected by the change in law are those who can express a preference but who have not been considered capable of giving informed consent.

Under present practices, insofar as one can generalize at all, many persons who have retardation, even when not eliminated as a group, cannot overcome the hurdle of informed consent. A health care worker, even if personally willing to accept the patient's own consent, may need to refuse treatment or require a substitute decisionmaker because of fears of liability for relying on her despite her retardation—or despite her inability to meet the informed consent criteria. The issue is the same fuzzy one discussed earlier: when is a guardian needed for consent to medical treatment, and when is it permissible to impose guardianship?

Informed consent standards can be difficult to satisfy. The requirement that a physician proceed only with the informed consent of the patient requires the physician to share all material facts with the patient, including benefits and risks and their general probabilities. It also requires that the consent be voluntary in the sense of it being free from "improper coercion" or "undue influence"; both of those terms also clearly are subject to many interpretations.

A third requirement for informed consent is that the person consenting have the capacity to understand what is being consented to. It is this element of the test that, under current law, prevents many persons who are considered "retarded" from making their own medical decisions. Sometimes the requirement is applied strictly by physicians to eliminate many persons from consenting for themselves; sometimes it is not so strictly applied.[52] The reality is that many persons, with or without retardation, do not fully understand the medical procedures to which they give consent. But a person's ability to give informed consent is much less likely to be questioned if that person is not considered "retarded."

The proposal would seek to eliminate this unequal application of informed consent standards, not by requiring that they be applied more uniformly to people across the board, but instead by abandoning them for everyone. The inquiry would focus on whether the patient, having been informed and brought into the process to the fullest extent possible, has expressed her preference with regard to whether to have a specific elective procedure. If she can express a preference, she will be deemed capable of consenting, whether or not a judgment is made that she fully understands it and whether or not she has retardation.

One significant result of this change in law is that a physician could safely provide a procedure when the patient asks for it, without regard to the physician's judgment about the intellectual capacities of the patient. Too often even attempts at reform instead misguidedly direct decisionmakers to pronounce judgments about who has mental disabilities as a first step in knowing what rules to follow. Thus, on its face at least, Colorado's revised provision on sterilization states a separate rule for "[a]ny person with a developmental disability." The rule allows such a person to be sterilized, even if she has given informed consent, only after an elaborate process in which doctors and other professionals pass on her competency.[53] Undoubtedly the intentions of the statute's drafters were beneficent, but the rules they came up with require pinpointing developmental disability and treating all people who appear disabled differently from everyone else, to the detriment of their efforts at normalization.

Moreover it is significant to reject substitute decisionmaking in preference for decisionmaking by the patient—even the patient who cannot give informed consent as it is often defined. Instead of eliminating the patient as decisionmaker if she does not understand fully, the approach strives to educate and contribute to her understanding. Then, at least for purposes of these elective, nontherapeutic procedures, it accepts as legal consent whatever preference she expresses.

Some clear improvements such a change will bring will not be reflected in results, either of judicial cases or medical decisionmaking. One shameful fact apparent even in judicial case reports is that many young women with retardation are not talked to regularly or even dealt with very much. One illustration occurred in *C. W.*, when Cynthia's mother testified that Cynthia "is able to change her own sanitary pads, but doesn't know when to stop wearing them. She once wore a pad for a full month."[54]

Often persons seeking sterilization for another put forth that she "does not understand the basic facts of life," but often it appears there has been no effort to impart any information to her. Evidence is rampant of the willingness of decisionmakers to put aside the subject of the decision, even when supposedly elective decisions are at issue. In *Grady*, for example, the court, after saying "Lee Ann herself can comprehend neither the problem nor the proposed solution," made clear that no efforts at explanation were contemplated: "Since Lee Ann is without the capacity for giving informed consent, any explanation of the proposed sterilization could only mislead her."[55]

The testimony in *C. W.* of a psychiatrist with a distinguished résumé provided an even more striking example. Dr. Melvin S. Heller testified that "even the most heroic and skilled efforts to provide Cynthia with 'programming for appropriate social skills' as recommended . . . is futile. 'You can't teach a person appropriate social skills if they can't communicate with you.'" Further,

> Dr. Heller was skeptical of the guardian's theories of "least restrictive alternative," "socialization," and "normalization" as applied to Cynthia. In his judgment, these concepts and policies are fine in theory; they are not effective in practice. Dr. Heller is convinced that Cynthia's learning ability is so impaired by irreversible neurological damage that her prognosis for learning substantially more than she knows now is not favorable . . . Dr. Heller was pessimistic about Cindy's chances of improvement. He concluded that she is going to be a child and remain a child vulnerable to molestation for the rest of her life.[56]

Not only was the effort to discourage habilitation. Dr. Heller was not above using scare tactics in his insistence on sterilization, as is reflected by his argument that the monitoring Cynthia already received was sufficient:

[T]his custodial approach to contraception at best is going to make this child/woman an asexual sheltered individual with no chance to relate. She is going to continue in this highly dependent, abnormal situation, which is not in her best interest. She is going to become increasingly a depressed vegetable. Her only hope is perhaps to be able to relate to other human beings, peers, appropriately, even within the parameters of how two or three or four year old children relate to each other, and this is very, very important.

And, as the trial court reported, "Dr. Heller related that he has had substantial experience and 'spent a professional lifetime prescribing supervision for people.' Yet, on occasions where he has written orders in state hospitals for one-on-one supervision as suicide precautions, or in the correctional system, where there is maximum supervision, he has nevertheless found people hanging and women in the county prison system who get pregnant."[57]

Perhaps on occasion persons with retardation really are incapable of learning and continuing to grow. To start with that assumption, however, is not only self-fulfilling, it also avoids our society's most fundamental obligations to this group. If there is one thing that persons with this particular disability need, it is to be treated as able, presumed able to the greatest extent possible, and encouraged to participate, especially where they can best do so. To start with pessimistic diagnoses without making any effort to communicate and to learn how to communicate better is patently irresponsible and inhumane.

The Best Available Solution

Allowing the woman to make her own decisions may not be problem-free, but it is the best solution available. The woman with retardation may not be an "ideal decisionmaker," even though her own body is at issue and her own reproductive future is at stake. But all possible substitutes are also problematic, and the subject of the procedure is a better decisionmaker than any other.

In addition, many of the risks are the same ones that, for everybody else, we accept as the price of allowing individual choice. The young woman may make decisions that are not sensible—but many other persons do as well. She may make decisions that are not fully informed—but other persons make such decisions all the time. She may even bring into the world a child she is unable to raise—but other persons do this as well. Until we prevent these actions by persons in general, there is no justification for preventing them by this group alone.

A central purpose of the proposal is to bring the patient fully into the procedure. But even if that is done, and her consent is made determinative, results may not differ radically from present-day outcomes. It is a common generalization that persons with retardation are particularly persuadable.[58] Moreover, if we envision a woman highly dependent on her caretakers, it would not be surprising that they could influence her to act as they thought best. In a great many cases the caretaker will persuade the patient that there is no alternative but for her to take birth control (or have an abortion or sterilization), stressing perhaps that there is no way for her to care for a baby. Resistance to the caretaker's or family members' wishes may be rare. And persons with retardation, like many others, can be heavily influenced by physicians and their views.[59]

In short, vesting legal decisionmaking power in the individual patients despite retardation will not necessarily make a very big difference in what procedures occur, especially in the short term.

If enactment of the proposal for self-determination would not lead to a new wave of pregnancies or births, is that a plus or a minus? It seems odd to make a dramatic proposal and then defend it on the ground that it may make little difference in actual results, at least in the near future. Indeed, it may leave persons with mental retardation even more vulnerable to sterilization or other procedures that others want for them.

There are instances, of course, where it will be crucial that the patient is the legal decisionmaker and where self-determination clearly will change the result. We have seen a few cases, such as LaVista Earline Romero's, in which the patient did continuously resist an operation that others wanted her to have. In cases like those, the patient's expressed wishes would control and she could not be subjected to a sterilization that she was resisting. As more patients are asked and involved in the decisions concerning their reproductive capacity, more disagreements will undoubtedly develop and surface. And as normalization proceeds apace, women with retardation will learn to assert their wishes and insist on greater options.

But even when outcomes remain largely the same, changing the rule may be entirely worthwhile and can achieve important objectives. A critical reason for the change in approach is to put the person with retardation at the center of the process. She should make her own choice if that is at all possible, and if not (so that effectively she is parroting a third party's desires) should at least be involved to the maximum extent possible. Even if involving her does not yield a change in results—because she agrees with her advisers or because her life situation is forcing her toward the same decision the caretakers would impose, for example—principles of treating persons with retardation with dignity call for thoroughly informing them (and all patients) and including them in decisionmaking as much as possible. Such treatment is also most in keeping with the societal aspiration of treating persons with retardation like other people.

The outcome may often be the same, but it will have greater legitimacy because she has participated in choosing it. The decisionmakers will no longer go around her while they decide her fate; they will have to go through her if they are to comply with the law.

One might raise other objections: If the young woman is not going to be able to parent anyway, as is sometimes the case, then it is unnecessarily cruel to involve her in the decisionmaking process. Because her situation in life does not permit real choice, there is no reason to disturb her by emphasizing to her what she is missing. If she is in fact made to understand the situation, a central message for her may be that she will never be able to have a child— not exactly a happy message. How could it possibly contribute to her fulfillment to have this subject brought up and drummed in?

It *is* painful to contemplate a woman who understands the range of choice open to women in general and might want her own child, but is made to understand that she will probably never be able to have or raise a child. It may seem reasonable to try to protect the person with retardation from confronting her limitations, and such a protective impetus undoubtedly supports some present practices, such as avoiding discussion of painful subjects. Similarly, in current practice persons with retardation are often left out of the judicial proceedings that decide their fate. The theory is that their presence will not affect the outcome, so it would be needlessly upsetting for them at worst, and pointless at best, to have them participate. On such reasoning C. W. was not present at her litigation, and Lee Ann Grady also was left out of her proceedings. In both cases the judge did conduct a brief interview (in judicial chambers in *C. W.;* in counsel's office in *Grady*), but neither claimed to have established any rapport with the subject of the proceeding. The judge in *Grady* said that the purpose was to get "a first-hand impression of her,"[60] since she would not be present at the hearing.

There is something to be said for the cruelty argument (as applied not only to persons with retardation but also to others who are forced to learn more by current informed consent requirements than they might like to hear or think about). But while a case can be made that it causes needless pain to involve the young woman in the decision and that it accordingly should just be made for her, such a protective approach is exactly what persons with retardation do not need. They need to be, and have a right to be, treated the same as others. They also need to be involved and treated as able to the greatest possible extent.

CHAPTER 12

Necessary Limitations on Self-Determination

Two limitations on the proposal for self-determination flow rather evidently from prior discussion: rules concerning substitute decision-making for persons who cannot express any opinion (including some persons with mental retardation); and rules prohibiting sterilization of minors, whether or not they have mental retardation.

Nonexpressive Persons

Even if all ambiguity is resolved in favor of the patient's making her own decisions, there will be cases where no response that anyone can understand is possible. A self-determinative approach obviously cannot work in this category of cases, which involves, among others, all newborns, all comatose persons, and a small percentage of persons who have mental retardation.

The first issue in these cases is the one examined at some length in connection with *Valerie N.:* If a person cannot consent for herself, should she be denied access to procedures that others may choose? Alternatively, should another person be permitted to consent for her, even though that might not in fact reflect her wishes?

The answer will differ with the procedure at issue. In particular, procedures that are medically indicated must surely be available, but elective, nontherapeutic procedures need not necessarily be. On the one hand, particularly when the procedure is intrusive and affects bodily integrity (as sterilization does), one can argue that it is most respectful of the woman who cannot consent for herself to pursue alternatives instead. On the other hand, the *Valerie N.* court—and the Massachusetts court in *Moe,* the Washington court in *Hayes,* the New Jersey court in *Grady,* and the Colorado court in *A. W.*—believed it important to provide even persons who have severe retardation with elective procedures like sterilization. Moreover, those courts considered access to such procedures constitutionally mandated.

If substitute decisionmaking is permitted, a second level of issues must be faced: whether "substituted judgment" or "best interests" or some other formulation is to be followed, and what the standards for sterilization should be. In addition, it must be decided whether the standards are to be enforceable rules or merely hortative guides to the third-party decisionmaker. For all these questions, the most important thing to note is that the debate and the answers apply to a very small group and that group includes only a tiny fraction of the population considered "retarded."

Limiting the Effect of Third-Party Decisionmaking

The most important contribution of the proposed self-determination policy is its clear delimiting of the range of cases to which substitute decision-making debates apply. It would have any approach to substitute decision-making that is chosen apply only to those cases involving persons, usually having quite severe retardation, who truly cannot make decisions for themselves because no one can understand them. How great a change in law this proposal represents is difficult to state, because it is not entirely clear how broadly substitute decisionmaking, as opposed to personal decisionmaking, is being used today.

In fact, most of the key cases involving substitute decisionmaking in the context of sterilization and abortion have involved children or wards with rather low IQs. Valerie N., for example, may have been nonexpressive[1] and had an IQ of 30; C. W.'s IQ was described as "30 to 50" by that court; Terwilliger had an IQ of 33; in *K. M.* the IQ had been measured as 40. In *Moe*, the IQ is not given in the opinion, but the subject was said to have "profound" retardation and also a "mental age of 4." The subject in *Hayes* was said to have "severe" retardation and a mental age of four to five; in *Eberhardy* the subject's mental age was described as two to three.

But even if courts have usually been dealing primarily with cases of severe retardation, they have not so limited their holdings. Accordingly, substitute decisionmaking is sometimes employed also for women who are not especially low-functioning. An obvious example is LaVista Earline Romero, with her IQ of 74—a case in which sterilization was ordered (over Ms. Romero's protest) but reversed on appeal. Other cases, however, attest to sterilization of women with even mild retardation. In *In re* Johnson, for instance, eighteen-year-old Tempie Johnson had mild retardation, but over her lawyer's opposition a sterilization petition was granted. The primary showing supporting sterilization was that the young woman, who had frequent sexual adventures, showed no interest in children. Her habit of sleeping much of the day cast doubt on her ability to create a suitable environment for a child, according to the court. (While the description does not sound ideal for impending motherhood, it also sounds fairly typical of many eighteen-year-olds and perhaps should not have led to sterilization as opposed to appropriate birth control.)

Other reported sterilization cases involve persons with IQs in the 60s. Moreover some cases show substantial confusion concerning factors like levels of retardation. In both *A. W.* and another case, *In re* Sallmaier, for example, the court refers to the retardation as "severe," but in *Sallmaier* the person's IQ was in the 60s. In *A. W.* no IQ number was adduced at trial, but the mother testified that A. W. attended a school for children whose IQs are below 50; in its technical meaning, severe retardation refers to persons who have much more limited abilities than it appears A. W. had. In *Sallmaier* the petition for sterilization, which was not opposed, was granted. In *A. W.* the court-appointed guardian *ad litem* opposed the parents' petition to have A. W. sterilized and successfully appealed the trial court's decision to grant the petition.

In *In re* Nilsson the adoptive parents of fourteen-year-old Rebecca Nilsson, whose IQ was between 50 and 60, were granted permission to have her sterilized by hysterectomy. The petition in that case was supported by Rebecca's guardian *ad litem* (called the "Law Guardian" in that case).

It is not, therefore, uniform current practice to reserve substitute decision-making over elective procedures for persons with extreme retardation, but even if it were, the proposed policy would break significantly from existing practice by limiting any third-party decisionmaking to that small group of persons who literally cannot express consent or lack of consent. It would both define much more clearly than has been defined before who cannot make decisions for him- or herself and would also use that definition to allow as many persons as possible to be responsible for their own decisions.

The proposal would also substitute "persons who are nonexpressive or who literally cannot convey a preference" for "persons who cannot give informed consent." It is that group which current law prevents from making decisions. The current informed consent standard is notoriously ill-defined, unpredictable, and flexible. The proposed replacement not only allows far more people to make their own choices but it also makes much clearer who will be able to decide for herself, because the line between who is and who is not expressive is far more apparent than the line between who can and who cannot give informed consent.

This is not to say that there will not be close cases, involving persons at the borderline between communicative and noncommunicative. Speech difficulties, inconsistent positions, conflicting statements, and obvious failures of understanding will continue.[2] But persons with these difficulties would nonetheless all be responsible for their own decisions under the proposed approach (although none are persons who would be likely to be making the decisions without participation from family, friends, or caretakers). Doubts about how to categorize persons are not a problem under this approach, because all close cases on the issue of whether a person is expressive or not would be resolved by presuming in favor of expressiveness and self-determination.

There are certainly cases in which accepting the patient's opinion will seem but a fiction—and others where one can worry about whether it is a fiction or not. Nonetheless, in borderline cases it remains important to follow the patient's "choice." In these extreme cases, especially, outcomes may not differ substantially because we call the decision the patient's own, but a self-determination policy will require that the patient be involved in the decisionmaking to the greatest extent possible.

The proposal cuts back on substitute decisionmaking concerning reproduction in another way as well. Not only would third-party decisionmaking be limited to a small and fairly clearly delimited group, but this group would be especially unlikely to have need for reproductive services like sterilization, abortion, and birth control. Unless it is appropriate to use those procedures to protect against sexual exploitation—and we argue it is not—there is no need for these procedures in many cases because many or most of the nonexpressive persons we are talking about have a very sheltered existence and are unlikely to have consensual sex lives.[3]

The most significant proposed change in the law comes from the redefinition of the class to whom the substitute decisionmaking rules will apply, not from any resolution of the ongoing debates about the substitute decisionmaking rules themselves. But a few points about what rules should be adopted for nonexpressive persons are in order.

Substitute Decisionmaking Is Not Constitutionally Required

Chapter 6 examined at some length whether the *Valerie N.* court was justified in imposing its view that sterilization should be available, despite an explicit legislative rule to the contrary. It took the position that the court should not have imposed its preferred solution in the guise of constitutional law. Instead, courts should allow a range of practices to occur and to evolve, and should encourage legislative responses. Some legislative responses, of course, may be so extreme as to be unconstitutional. Moreover, some rights are constitutionally compelled. This book maintains, however, that a right to substitute decisionmaking allowing access to elective procedures is not among them.

One reason states should not be constitutionally required to permit third-party decisionmaking is that there is so much wrong with it. Not only does substitute decisionmaking fail to achieve its stated goal of equality for persons who do not consent for themselves; not only is it difficult to fathom what the standards should be for allowing procedures like nonconsensual sterilization; there are also other problems inherent in relying on substitute decisionmakers, who almost invariably have interests and perspectives of their own that are not shared by the person for whom they are making decisions.

Since the *Valerie N.* and *Moe* decisions, it has become clearer that substitute decisionmaking is not required by constitutional law. In Cruzan v. Director, Missouri Department of Health, the U.S. Supreme Court passed on issues of third-party decisionmaking that are relevant in our context, even though the particular substitute decisionmaking did not concern reproductive rights. The case involved Nancy Cruzan, a young adult who had sustained injuries in an automobile accident and was left in a "persistent vegetative state," obviously unable to make any decision or give any consent for herself. Her guardians wished to discontinue artificial hydration and feeding, a decision that law entitles a person to make for oneself. That is, there is a right to refuse medical treatment, whether it has been commenced or not—a right to choose that can be exercised by persons able to express their desires, or at least by those able to give informed consent.

Because Nancy was no longer capable of making or expressing her own decisions, her guardians, who were her parents, sought to make the decision for her. They decided it was appropriate to disconnect the artificial feeding equipment after they became convinced there was virtually no chance of their daughter's regaining her cognitive functions. When the hospital declined to proceed without a court order, the parents obtained the trial court's authorization to discontinue treatment, but the Supreme Court of Missouri reversed. That court held that Missouri law respected third-party decisions to stop treatment only in limited circumstances: if the patient herself, when competent, had executed a living will mandating that result; or if "clear and convincing, inherently reliable" evidence shows that refusal of treatment was the patient's own wish. Because no living will was in existence, the *Cruzan* case revolved around the second circumstance and its requirement that proof satisfy the elevated standard of "clear and convincing, inherently reliable" evidence.

The question before the U.S. Supreme Court was whether the state's limitations on substitute decisionmaking doctrine unconstitutionally deprived Nancy Cruzan of her "right to reject unwanted medical treatment." The Court rejected the constitutional argument. It held that Missouri could limit decisionmaking by surrogates to cases in which there was clear and convincing evidence of the subject's own wishes to refuse life-sustaining treatment. It pointed out that the argument that Cruzan "should possess the same right in this respect as is possessed by a competent person" offers little guidance and indeed "begs the question: an incompetent person is not able to make an informed and voluntary choice to exercise a hypothetical right to refuse treatment or any other right. Such a 'right' must be exercised for her, if at all, by some sort of surrogate." It went on to state that Missouri had discretion over "procedural safeguards" like the clear and convincing evidence requirement that might accompany the substitute decisionmaking procedure. It saw the state's interests as both safeguarding the personal element of the choice and protecting incompetent persons from family members' sometimes conflicting interests. It also observed that the judicial proceedings in which third-party decisions were approved were frequently nonadversarial, and that the state could constitutionally presume in favor of sustaining rather than terminating life and could decline to weigh "quality of life" in the balance.

Nancy's parents argued not only that they had adequately proved that their decision to terminate treatment reflected Nancy's own wishes; alternatively, they said, the state "must accept the 'substituted judgment' of close family members even in the absence of substantial proof that their views reflect the views of the patient." Despite the Court's acceptance of the

Cruzans as loving and caring parents, the Court disagreed that substitute decisionmaking was constitutionally required:

> If the State were required by the United States Constitution to repose a right of "substituted judgment" with anyone, the Cruzans would surely qualify. But *we do not think the Due Process Clause requires the State to repose judgment on these matters with anyone but the patient herself.* Close family members may have a strong feeling—a feeling not at all ignoble or unworthy, but not entirely disinterested, either—that they do not wish to witness the continuation of the life of a loved one which they regard as hopeless, meaningless, and even degrading. But *there is no automatic assurance that the view of close family members will necessarily be the same as the patient's would have been* had she been confronted with the prospect of her situation while competent. All of the reasons previously discussed for allowing Missouri to require clear and convincing evidence of the patient's wishes lead us to conclude that the State may choose to defer only to those wishes, rather than confide the decision to close family members.[4]

The Court also said in a footnote, further repudiating the petitioners' arguments, "the differences between the choice made by a competent person to refuse medical treatment, and the choice made for an incompetent person by someone else to refuse medical treatment, are so obviously different that the State is warranted in establishing rigorous procedures for the latter class of cases which do not apply to the former class."[5]

In other words, the U.S. Supreme Court has accepted that in cases where there is no clear and convincing evidence of the patient's own wishes, state law may prohibit anyone from making elective decisions in the name of the patient; it may instead prescribe a particular outcome that makes the elective procedure unavailable. It can prescribe that outcome even though it would be unconstitutional for the law to assume that choice vis-à-vis a person with the ability to decide for herself. States may choose to allow substitute decisionmaking in a broad variety of ways, but the Constitution does not require that persons incompetent to make their own choices have access to all the same procedures that competent persons have a right to choose. In short, it is constitutionally permissible for no one to have authority to disconnect Nancy's feeding devices, even though the Constitution gives competent persons the right to refuse them in the first place and also to have them disconnected at any time.

Although the context was different from decisions involving sterilization and reproduction, the right to disconnect life-saving treatment, like the other elective procedures we have been considering, is generally defended as a right of personal "choice," not a right to a particular result. And like the choices we have considered, it is rooted in the Fourteenth Amendment's Due Process clause.[6]

Cruzan demonstrates the error of those who maintain that as a general proposition substitute decisionmaking is required by constitutional law. *Cruzan* was decided after *Moe* and after *Valerie N,* and it undermines both the reasoning of *Moe* and the outcome of *Valerie N.* What the Court said in *Cruzan* applies equally to reproduction issues: "[T]he State may choose to defer only to [the patient's] wishes, rather than confide the decision to close family members." *Cruzan* thus supports this book's suggestion that it is at least constitutionally acceptable to make elective sterilization unavailable to persons who cannot consent for themselves, and that this is true even where it is clear that parents, guardians, and other substitute decisionmakers are well-meaning.

If a person is truly nonexpressive, there has to be either a substitute decisionmaker or a state rule as to what outcome must prevail. The California legislature in the statute invalidated in *Valerie N.* attempted to avoid substitute decisionmaking by imposing a rule as to outcome, eliminating sterilization except by personal choice. *Cruzan* suggests that the legislature's rule should have been held permissible as far as the U.S. Constitution is concerned, and that the U.S. Supreme Court would so hold today. California courts could still reach the same result as an interpretation of their own California Constitution; additionally the state legislature has power to change state policy by itself deciding to allow substitute decisionmaking more broadly. Note that the U.S. Supreme Court in *Cruzan* did not say it was impermissible for states to adopt looser rules for third-party decisionmaking; it only said that they were not constitutionally required to do so.

Allowing Third-Party Consent Is Not Preferable Policy

In the context of sterilization, the California legislative choice was not only constitutionally permissible, despite the contrary holding of the California Supreme Court majority; it may indeed have been the preferable policy to pursue. A ban on nonconsensual sterilization is arguably the only real means of protecting against abuses. The prejudice that exists against people considered "retarded"—and specifically against procreation and parenting by them—makes it difficult to trust the motivation of any substitute decisionmaker. Furthermore, the increasing varieties and methods of birth control usually make sterilization unnecessary today, as well as undesirable.

Accordingly, a strong case can be made that elective sterilization should be available only to persons who truly elect it. Absent strict medical necessity, this unalterable decision should not be made for a young woman whose wishes are unknown, in preference to some less drastic means of controlling pregnancy. There is much to be said for legislation that bans altogether nontherapeutic sterilization by third-party consent.

One could in fact argue that permitting sterilization without personal consent is actually *un*constitutional—that the pre–*Valerie N.* California legislative approach was not only permissible and preferable but constitutionally required. There is much to justify that position, especially if one sees current practice as essentially forcing an unnecessary procedure on nonconsenting subjects. To adopt such a position—that sterilization by substitute decisionmaking is per se unconstitutional—would upset a lot of law. Cases we have seen that would have to be overruled include *Grady, Valerie N., Hayes,* and *Moe,* to name just a few.

Constitutionalization of a rule that no one can decide for the nonconsenting patient would arguably carry the same vice as the constitutionalization of the opposite rule that we saw in *Valerie N.:* it would prevent broad experimentation with a range of approaches, from which we may learn. No solution proposed to date is beyond reproach or without any problems. Rather than the Supreme Court at this point forcing one solution on all states, it is preferable to allow states to experiment with a range of approaches, as they are now doing. This may be the appropriate short-term solution even if the ultimate result will be the demise of formal third-party decisionmaking in the context of nontherapeutic medical decisionmaking and a general consensus that such substitute decisionmaking is unconstitutional.

The chief objection, whether to statutory or constitutional limits on substitute decisionmaking, is of course that nonexpressive persons are then denied access to procedures that are available to all others. Much is made of this fact, with the implication that this result itself is a denial of equal protection of the laws. It is not troubling, however, for an elective procedure to be available only to those who themselves elect it.

True, legislatures cannot constitutionally deny the right to choose sterilization to competent adults. But the reason the state must allow sterilization is not because sterilization is such an important procedure; it is because it has no legitimate reason to deny sterilization to persons who seek it for themselves. Protecting competent persons against their own, possibly foolish, decisions—or against their own later change of heart—may be too patronizing to be acceptable. The rationale does not apply, however, to persons not making their own decisions. The state does have a legitimate and important interest in protecting people from imposed sterilization, a policy that is arguably more important than affording the choice of sterilization to guardians and other third-party decisionmakers.

It is dangerous to conclude, with the California and Massachusetts Supreme Courts, that if the right to a choice exists it must necessarily be extended to allow third parties to make it for an "incompetent" person. There are many things that states do and arguably must allow individuals to choose to do that would clearly and appropriately fall outside the authority of a guardian to choose for a ward. For example, individuals have the right to choose to marry and to choose whom to marry, but presumably a guardian cannot make this decision for the ward. Similarly, in a state allowing individuals to choose to engage in prostitution, even though a woman would have the choice, a guardian (or judge) surely could not make that choice for a ward. Many rights of choice, including the right to sterilization and the right to die, as well as the right to engage in marriage or prostitution, are available or should be available only to those who actually choose them. Persons unable to make their own decision (only nonexpressive persons, if this book's preference were followed) would indeed be denied access to choices available to others, but that course seems preferable, and more respectful of them, than the alternative.

Using Birth Control and Abortion for Illegitimate Purposes

Once the category of persons who are not permitted to consent for themselves is limited to persons who are wholly nonexpressive, the arena for substitute decisionmaking concerning birth control and abortion is much reduced. It is rare that the expectation for a nonexpressive person is a consensual sex life; the need for birth control should be equally rare. In the past, especially in institutional settings, the practice has been to administer birth control pills more broadly than necessary—even to postmenopausal women in some cases. Such obvious overextensions of contraception must stop.

Moreover, contraception should not be administered when the only imaginable sex would constitute rape. The purpose of contraception is not to facilitate and cover up crime, and it should not be administered when that is the only purpose it can serve. The beautiful but unconscious patient should not be fed contraceptives; nor should she be sterilized.

It is extraordinarily difficult, however, to draw a line between consensual and exploitative sex. This difficulty exists for persons of intelligence and affluence as well as persons with retardation. But it has particular force with respect to the nonexpressive population. It certainly is imaginable that a person could be wholly nonexpressive in terms of being able to communicate a preference vis-à-vis reproductive choices, yet could sufficiently express interest in sex to constitute consent. Any such cases would, however, be extremely rare. In the rare cases where a consensual sex life is ongoing or imminent for an otherwise nonexpressive person, birth control by substitute decisionmaking would be appropriate.

Usually, however, a person who is truly nonexpressive would not be able to have consensual sexual relationships (and this is not an area where anyone is arguing that the guardian must be able to make a choice to participate for her). Therefore birth control should not be at issue. If rape appears to be a substantial danger, it should be protected against. Birth control should not be administered to protect against pregnancy from nonconsensual relationships;[7] instead, the caretaker has an obligation to prevent those relationships from occurring. Physicians should be taught not to prescribe medication to protect against (and cover up) exploitation.

In the presumably rare instances in which the caretaker fails to prevent rape, abortion may be an issue, and a decision whether to abort will be made by the guardian. If substitute decisions are limited to persons who are truly nonexpressive, that strengthens the case for requiring the guardian to come to court to obtain judicial sanction for the abortion decision. Something is obviously amiss if the young woman has become pregnant. It should be brought to the attention of the authorities rather than allowing the caretaker to cover up the problem in a secret abortion.

The nuances and the difficulties of these issues are well illustrated by the extraordinary story of Debra Lynn Thomas. Debra was born in 1958. She had two severe bouts with spinal meningitis as an infant, resulting in profound retardation. At the age of five she was placed by her family in a home operated by the Texas Department of Mental Health and Retardation. Her parents and five siblings visited her there only three times in the next twenty-five years.

In that home, Debra Thomas grew into an adult. She has several disabilities. She cannot walk and her arms and legs are splayed and rigid; she has use only of the right arm. She must be fed and bathed by others and must wear a diaper. In addition, Debra is epileptic, but her seizures are controlled by medication (Tegretol and Dilantin), which is given to her daily. Debra's IQ is measured at about 12. She can speak some words: "Hi," "Okay," "paint," and a few others.

In 1987 one of Debra's sisters, Dori Wooten, arranged for Debra to be moved to a state school in Lubbock, near the Wooten home, and the next year Dori became Debra's legal guardian. It became the Wooten family custom to have Debra visit for the weekend. In addition to Dori, the family included her husband Jim (age forty) and their teenage children Jason and Kathy. When she was visiting, Debra would go on outings with the family— to the mall or the grocery store, for example. She called everyone in the family "Mama."

In general, it appears that the changes in Debra's life during this period were very happy ones. The Wooten family was the first family Debra had known since she was an infant; they, and especially Dori Wooten, had served Debra well.

In June 1990, the Lubbock State School learned that Debra (then thirty-two years old) was pregnant. The pregnancy had been confirmed when school health workers performed a pregnancy test after two missed menstrual periods. The school then notified both Dori Wooten and the Lubbock police. Dori met with school officials and, among other things, she was asked to surrender her visitor's pass and informed that her sister could no longer be taken on weekend visits. The reason was that the "possible suspects" were thought to include Jim and Jason Wooten, as well as ten state school employees whose work had put them in contact with Debra during the relevant time.

The school denied that any of its employees could have been responsible because, it said, "security is complete." Nonetheless, the state system was sensitive to the charge, partly because Texas was one of a dozen states subject to federal court oversight for substandard conditions in state institutions for persons with retardation. At the Lubbock school there had been two other pregnancies in the past three years, according to the superintendent. Both had been carried to term, and the babies had been put up for adoption.

Abortion was first discussed at the June 1990 meeting. It was determined that an abdominal, not vaginal, abortion would probably be necessary. Dori Wooten gave her signed consent for abortion and for amniocentesis. At that time Debra was estimated to be seven weeks pregnant. For three weeks thereafter, Dori apparently thought that the school was making the arrangements. Her visits to her sister had been suspended, so she was less in touch than usual. By the time the school made clear to her that the responsibility was hers, Debra was ten weeks pregnant. (The school took the position that Dori Wooten should have realized from the outset that the responsibility was hers and not the school's.)

Next came the attempt to find a doctor who would perform an abortion. The problem of a lack of meaningful access to abortion, including to capable physicians willing to perform it, is one shared by many women in this country and is not at all limited to "the competent." It is a problem more pronounced in some areas of the country than in others. In any event, physicians around Lubbock, Texas, are not available to perform abortions; if they were, they would, apparently, risk losing patients.

Dori Wooten had the aid of the Lubbock Rape Crisis Center, which spent nearly a month trying to find a physician who would perform the operation within one hundred miles of Lubbock. Finally one agreed to operate but only on the condition that Debra Lynn Thomas be sterilized at the time of the abortion and on the condition that the physician's name not be revealed, even to the state school. While the first (outrageous) condition was readily accepted, the second proved problematic. Just before the operation was to be performed, the school informed the hospital it would not pay the fee. It is unclear whether this refusal was based on the doctor's anonymity or on a general assertion that abortion was not for the state to support even though it pays for all other medical procedures. In any event, the operation was delayed. Dori then raised the $1,100 necessary, and the operation was again scheduled, but when the date for the abortion came, hospital administrators said it could not proceed without a court order. Before Dori made any further arrangements, she was told to forget about abortion because the pregnancy was now too far advanced. This was in the second week of August, two months after the pregnancy had been discovered.

During the pregnancy, the Wootens and the school continued to accuse each other of misconduct concerning both the pregnancy and the failure to obtain an abortion. The Thomas-Wooten attorney announced plans to sue the state for "wrongful birth" after the baby was born and obtain support for the child throughout its life because it was wrongfully conceived. Investigations were undertaken by state and local authorities as well as the institutions themselves into security at state schools, and some lapses were identified (for example, too many employees having access to master keys).

Dori Wooten also announced that she and her family wanted to raise the baby and have the mother and baby live with them. Officials indicated that was the likely outcome, pending an examination of the Wootens for suitability and assuming that neither Jim nor Jason Wooten proved to be the baby's father. The situation was opposite from the usual one: Usually proving biological paternity strengthens a parent's claim to custody, but in this case genetic paternity would tend to prove criminality and unfitness rather than a right to custody.

On New Year's Day 1991, David Lynn Thomas was born. He appeared entirely healthy and weighed seven pounds, three and a half ounces. He was delivered by cesarean section. During the pregnancy much had been made of how hard pregnancy and especially delivery would be for Debra, but in fact she handled it rather easily. Her sister, who had worried that the delivery would be traumatic for Debra and had wanted abortion partly for this reason, stated that Debra did not even know she had given birth.

Blood samples were taken from the twelve persons identified as having possible access to Debra around the time of conception. Two weeks later, while Jim and Dori Wooten were eating dinner in a Lubbock restaurant, two Lubbock sheriffs appeared to arrest Jim Wooten for sexual assault and led him away in handcuffs. DNA tests had identified him (within a 99.99 percent probability) as the father of David Lynn Thomas and had ruled out all the other suspects. Three months later Jim Wooten pleaded no contest to charges of raping his sister-in-law. It was stipulated and made part of the record that his sister-in-law was so profoundly retarded that she could not have consented to sexual intercourse. Wooten received and began serving a fifteen-year sentence. Soon after the birth, Debra was moved from the state school to a group home. The baby lives with Dori Wooten, and Debra visits regularly.

Is the lesson of this story that Debra should have been on birth control, or even sterilized? Similarly abortion would have changed the outcome, and Jim's crime (assuming that the court was correct in denying the possibility of consent by Debra) would never had been detected. If Debra was exploited by Jim, sterilization, birth control, or abortion could have covered up that exploitation, and it could have continued indefinitely.

Minors

Another important reform that follows from the foregoing analysis is a prohibition against nontherapeutic sterilization of minors. Such a prohibition most probably is the law with respect to all minors who do not have mental retardation, and it should be for minors with retardation as well.

"Normal" children will not be sterilized for nontherapeutic reasons, even if they and their parents agree that they want the sterilization. It is difficult to imagine a case in which a court would permit the sterilization. A physician performing the sterilization without court authorization would be extremely vulnerable to court judgments, including monetary liability, and to disciplinary action. If the child and her parents request sterilization, the expected answer would be that they should wait until she becomes an adult and can consent for herself. Minors who have mental retardation should not be sterilized either.

Many petitions to sterilize persons with retardation are brought by parents or other guardians whose child or ward is barely past puberty. This is understandable in one sense: When children are that age, parents may worry particularly about pregnancy and also, in some cases, about inability to control their offspring. But it is extremely difficult to know of a person only fourteen or sixteen years old whether at any time during her life she will be able to make an adequate parent.

In fact, the substantial number of hysterectomies that are requested when the proposed sterilization is of a young girl suggests that the avoidance of menstruation is another frequent motive. Often the reason given is the alleviation of "menstrual difficulties."[8] In the case of *P. S.*, which involved a twelve-year-old autistic girl, the physician testified that due to the girl's extremely self-destructive behavior, it would be "very dangerous"—physically and psychologically—for her to menstruate.[9] In *In re* Penny N., involving a fourteen-year-old, the problems caused by menstruation were also characterized as psychological.[10] In *In re* Nilsson, also involving a fourteen-year-old, the reasons were that menstruation caused her pain, which, when most severe, caused her to miss school and be inactive, and that she was unable to "provide her own personal hygiene."[11]

In *P. S.* the request for hysterectomy was granted. In *Penny N.* the matter was remanded by the Supreme Court of New Hampshire for written findings, by clear and convincing evidence, that sterilization was in Penny's best interest, "rather than the parents' or the public's convenience."[12] In *Nilsson* the unopposed hysterectomy request was granted, as the "more extreme form of sterilization," simply on the ground that "it would also alleviate [the girl's] menstrual difficulties [and in so doing] . . . rectify one prospective difficulty [pregnancy] and one actual difficulty [menstruation]."[13]

Other cases involving requests for hysterectomies for girls include *A. W.* (age twelve), where the request was initially granted before being reversed, and Wentzel v. Montgomery General Hospital (age thirteen, with an IQ of "about 25 to 30"), where a hysterectomy was sought but not granted.

Hysterectomy requests usually are made for the benefit of the caretaker rather than the patient. Even when the reasoning of the petition carefully describes the procedure as necessary for the patient's own well-being, as in *P. S.* and *Penny N.,* the described need for an end to menstruation is usually speculative. Like so many other statements prerequisite to sterilization, the dispositive allegations are easy for petitioners to make and difficult to question or disprove. Indeed, a need for sterilization of any kind is speculative in most of these cases, for the young women are typically not yet sexually active.

Even conventional sterilization (by tubal ligation), unless truly medically necessary, should not be available to persons under eighteen years of age. Many parental predictions that they themselves will have to take responsibility and that their daughter will not be capable of caring for an infant may simply be wrong. Parents often underestimate the capacities of their offspring, especially of offspring who have retardation. Moreover, the parents may not have the imagination to foresee the range of situations in which their daughter may one day find herself. Perhaps she will marry or live with a person who is competent in ways that she is not. Perhaps also her own skills will develop, and her own interest in parenting, or both. To allow parents to sterilize, out of their understandable fears for the future, permanently affects and limits their daughter's life in ways that may not actually be necessary.

Some courts have recognized the problem. For example, the court in *Hayes* emphasized Edith's age and educability in denying her parents' petition to have her sterilized. It reasoned that although "a child in her early teens may be incapable at present of understanding the consequence of sexual activity, or exercising judgment in relations with the opposite sex, [she] may . . . have the potential to develop the required understanding and judgment through continued education and developmental programs."[14] Other courts, however, have not been so vigilant; as we have seen, they have granted petitions to sterilize children as young as twelve.

The story of Joseph Lee Moore in North Carolina illustrates the problems with making premature judgments about the capabilities of one's children. This is one of the few cases involving proposed sterilization of a man rather than a woman. Joseph was a minor in 1975 (the court did not specify his actual age) when his mother, Dora I. Moore, petitioned for a court order authorizing his sterilization.[15] He was labeled "moderately retarded" and was said to have a mental age of eight and an IQ under 40. In the petition the mother requested that Joseph be sterilized "because it is likely that unless sterilized he would procreate a child or children who would probably have serious physical, mental, or nervous diseases or deficiencies."[16] When the petition was filed, Joseph joined in the petition with his mother, but his guardian *ad litem* later objected and contended that North Carolina's sterilization statute was unconstitutional.

The trial court struck down the statute, but the North Carolina Supreme Court reversed, relying on grounds that would not usually be stated today. For example:

"[The] mother unquestionably is in a position to know what is best for the future of her child."[17]

"The interest of the unborn child is sufficient to warrant sterilization of a retarded individual."[18]

"Our research does not disclose any case which holds that a state does not have the right to sterilize an insane or a retarded person if notice and hearing are provided, . . . if it is applied to all persons, and if it is not prescribed as a punishment for a crime."[19]

The interesting facet of this case for our purposes occurred after the North Carolina Supreme Court had upheld the statute and sent the case back to the trial court so that it could pass on whether sterilization was appropriate for Joseph. Only a year had passed since the petition was first filed, but the mother now discovered that sterilization was not so necessary after all. She informed the Department of Social Services that she no longer had any need to proceed with the sterilization, because Joseph had matured beyond her earlier expectations and she no longer considered him uncontrollable. As Moore's attorney wrote in a letter: "It had a 'happy outcome' from my standpoint . . . the young man, during the approximate one-year period between the initial hearing and the dismissal, matured to such an extent that he was not the problem his mother had formerly encountered."[20]

Of course, if the mother had succeeded in the first instance, it would have been too late to undo the sterilization and Joseph would have been sterilized unnecessarily. One wonders how many other children are sterilized unnecessarily because of their parents' well-intentioned fears for the future.

Joseph Moore's story is but one illustration of the obvious proposition that life circumstances change and people develop. It is true discrimination to allow persons to be sterilized before majority solely because of retardation. A great many mothers may look at their "normal" fourteen-year-old daughter and consider it unbelievable that she could ever be an adequate mother to another human being, but miraculous transformations do take place. Just as we would not allow a mother to obtain nontherapeutic sterilization of other minor children through substitute decisionmaking or a notion that they will be inadequate parents, so should such irreversible judgments be precluded for minors who have retardation.

In short, even a jurisdiction that allows sterilizations of persons called "retarded" by substitute consent should forbid any such sterilizations of young women or men under eighteen years of age. Nontherapeutic sterilization should be barred on the basis of age, with or without personal or parental consent. The judgment would be that sterilization is not so clearly beneficial or so important that the parties cannot wait. With such a rule, states would treat all minor children the same way, without regard to whether they are considered "retarded." It would avoid the bizarre result earlier described in cases like *A. W.,* where a state statute apparently prohibiting sterilization of all persons with mental retardation is deemed not to apply to children.

Similarly, with respect to birth control and abortion, minors with mental retardation should be treated like other minors. With respect to abortion, for example, where there is developed case law concerning treatment of minors, those with retardation also should be able to request and consent without parental notification, on the same basis as other young women. Depending on the law of the particular state, that means their request would be respected, without parental notification, if they met a "mature minor" exception—or, perhaps more realistically, a best interests test in a jurisdiction that allows that as an alternative. Here as elsewhere the rules applied to minors with mental retardation should be the same as those applied to other minors.

CHAPTER 13

The Possibility of Varying the Rule

The proposal for self-determination calls for the law to treat persons with retardation who can communicate "the same as anyone else." It thereby places equality over protection. The law has to choose between the two principles; at a time when normalization is the goal, it is more suitable to favor equality. The choice is made easier because for the vast majority of persons with retardation (though not all) the equality choice is the more appropriate one. But it cannot be denied that there are risks and costs to this approach, and that some fine-tuning may be desirable. This chapter explores that possibility.

The two limitations discussed in the last chapter are firm and necessary limitations on a system relying on self-determination. The third limitation discussed here—curtailing self-determination with respect to certain unusual choices—is less clearly necessary or desirable. The choices we consider curtailing are those where both the likelihood of exploitation in obtaining consent seems especially great and the deprivation in not being offered those options seems particularly slight. Possible examples are becoming a mother for hire (a "surrogate mother") and engaging in hard-core sadomasochistic behavior with a sadist. In some states, at least, these kinds of choices are available on a consensual basis to adults deemed "competent," but even so they should not perhaps be available to persons with limited understanding.

The argument for limiting options in some areas is a protectionist one, and the difficult issue is whether it should be pursued even on this limited basis, when it entails selecting out persons who cannot give informed consent to treat in a different way from others. At least that category of "persons who cannot give informed consent" is preferable to a category referring in terms of mental retardation and applying special rules only to that group.

The Glen Ridge Rape Case

The omnipresence of risk is nowhere more clearly illustrated than in the highly publicized and very troubling Glen Ridge rape case, tried in New Jersey's criminal courts in 1993. The victim, Betty Harris, was a seventeen-year-old woman with mild retardation.[1] The perpetrators were thirteen teenage boys, some of whom were high school football heroes.

In 1989, when the rape occurred, Betty was a high school student in Glen Ridge, New Jersey, an affluent suburban community. She was good at sports, played on the high school's junior varsity basketball team, and had won gold medals in the Special Olympics for swimming. In addition she is "almost a [musical] savant," being able to hear a song on the radio and play it by ear on the piano.[2]

During the case that unfolded, Betty was characterized as having the "education level of an eight-year-old"[3] and an IQ of 64. Betty is an adopted child; when she was adopted her parents were told that she had a minor disability she would outgrow. Sadly, Betty's mother said at the time of the trial that if she had known Betty's actual condition, she would not have adopted her.[4]

On March 1, 1989, Betty met up with some neighborhood boys at a local park. The Scherzer twins and their friends promised her a date with Paul Archer if she would agree to come with them. Paul Archer's brother Christopher put his arm around Betty (this was "romantic," Betty later recalled) and steered her toward the Scherzer home. They took her down to the basement. There she saw that the boys had set up the chairs "like a movie." Surrounded by thirteen "large boys," many of them popular high school athletes, Betty was persuaded to undress and perform sexual acts. The crowd of boys, which ultimately diminished to about seven, shouted "go further, go further."[5] They got Betty to masturbate and then to perform oral sex on one of them. Then they raped her with a broomstick, a fungo bat, and, some testimony alleged, a dirty stick.

After they were finished, the boys warned Betty to keep silent. Otherwise, they threatened, either they would tell her mother about what had happened in the basement or she would get kicked out of school. That night, Betty did not get her prized date with Paul Archer. Instead, she experienced physical pain, later testifying with embarrassment, "It hurt . . . It hurt when I went to the bathroom."[6]

Betty did keep quiet. But three days later, after her swimming coach sensed that something was seriously wrong, Betty mentioned that something had happened with some boys at "a sort of party." Also, the day after the rape one of the boys asked her to return to the Scherzer basement. Betty, upset and confused about how to handle the proposition, had asked the coach how she could say no to the boys.[7]

Thus Betty inadvertently reported the original assault. The district attorney was informed, and an investigation commenced that two months later led to the arrests of three boys: the Scherzer twins and Christopher Archer. All three were immediately released on bail: Christopher Archer and Kevin Scherzer on $2,500 each, and Kyle Scherzer on $2,000. Subsequently, the grand jury returned indictments against the three and also against Bryant Grober, for whom Betty had performed oral sex.

Before discussing the main issues in the case, one interesting pretrial maneuver is worth noting because it sheds light on how society regards persons who have mental retardation and how the law treats them. The defense, almost at the outset, moved to have Essex County Assignment Judge Burrell Ives Humphreys recuse himself from the trial. The defense claimed that he would be biased because his daughter has mild retardation. At any rate, the defense argued, to have him judge the case would constitute the appearance of partiality.

It would be most interesting, and this book suggests clearly wrong, for a judge with "normal" children—perhaps even including teenage boys—to be presumed fully able to try the case, but one who cares about mental retardation, or has a child with retardation, to be eliminated as unrepresentative or biased. The defense motion was quite properly rejected by Judge Humphreys, who explained, "Understanding does not mean bias. Rather, it makes us better judges."[8] But in reality, the defense succeeded on the issue, for in order to escape any criticism Judge Humphreys assigned the case for trial to another judge, R. Benjamin Cohen.[9]

Betty's story is, unfortunately, not unique. It illustrates the difficulties with the proposal for self-determination and with accepting as determinative the consent of all persons who can communicate. It is not actually clear whether Betty did "consent" or exactly what happened. But assuming that lack of consent could not be proved, should the boys be excused—indeed told that under the law they "did nothing wrong"—because Betty was entitled to have her consent respected?

If not for her retardation, Betty would have been able to consent as an adult in New Jersey, for the age of statutory rape there is sixteen.[10] Adults can consent to a range of sexual practices, both usual and unconventional. The proposed approach indeed has problems, if it requires a verdict of innocence and the release of the defendants in this case. But before considering how cases like Glen Ridge ought to be resolved, in a society that cares about quality of life and equality for persons with retardation, let us see how the case was actually treated.

The New Jersey law governing the case was quite different from the model suggested here. Accordingly, the case revolved around a question that the proposed approach aspires to make irrelevant: whether Betty was incapable of consent because she was "mentally defective."[11]

This was perceived as the relevant question because New Jersey law provided that

> An actor is guilty of sexual assault if he commits an act of sexual penetration with another person under . . . the following circumstances: . . .
>
> (7) The victim is one whom the actor knew or should have known was physically helpless, mentally defective or mentally incapacitated.[12]

The provision does not appear unduly complicated, but its attempt to treat persons called "physically helpless, mentally defective or mentally incapacitated" differently from everybody else raised problems that the drafters had not anticipated. Most notably, the provision, read straightforwardly, allows no opportunity for a person who is "physically helpless, mentally defective or mentally incapacitated" to consent to sexual activity, regardless of the circumstances, as long as her partner knows of her condition, as would be likely of anyone with whom she has a loving relationship and with whom she would wish to have sex. All that the statute purports to require is "mental defect" (or one of the two other named conditions) and knowledge on the part of the "nondefective" participant. Such a literal reading of the statute puts it in clear conflict with professed goals of normalization and most probably with Due Process and Equal Protection as well.

The New Jersey courts had already noticed this problem and had attempted to resolve it through interpretation of the statute's definition of "mentally defective." The statute defined "mentally defective" to mean "that condition in which a person suffers from a mental disease or defect which renders that person temporarily or permanently incapable of understanding the nature of his conduct, including, but not limited to, being incapable of providing consent."[13]

Two years prior to the Glen Ridge case, the New Jersey Supreme Court applied and discussed this definition in State v. Olivio. The case involved a man convicted of "sexual assault on a mentally defective person" who on appeal claimed that the victim (M. R.) was not "mentally defective." The court then set out the following definition: "a person is mentally defective under [the statute] if, at the time of the sexual activity, he or she is unable to comprehend the distinctively sexual nature of the conduct, or is incapable of understanding or exercising the right to refuse to engage in such conduct with another."[14] That interpretation was important to the scope of New Jersey's statute concerning sexual assault, and the last phrase of the court's statement, "incapable of understanding or exercising the right to refuse to engage in such conduct," was central to the Glen Ridge case as well.

Sensitive to the problems of a statutory scheme that utterly deprives persons with mental retardation of a legal sex life, the court chose to solve the problem by applying the statute's ban to fewer people. In *Olivio* the court allowed some voluntary sexual relationships by excepting from the law's ban persons who understand the sexual nature of the acts and who understand that they can consent or refuse. Moreover, the court interpreted the change to allow consensual sexual activity for "mildly retarded persons."[15] Appreciating the conflict between the goals of preventing exploitation of a vulnerable population and allowing consensual activity, the court said that the legislature had adjusted the balance by "focus[ing] on levels of mental functioning" and by screening out "persons not genuinely in need of the laws' special protections."[16]

Such a way of differentiating between persons who will be "protected" and those who will be treated "as equals" requires sensitive factual determinations in particular cases. Accordingly, the prosecution in the Glen Ridge case focused on whether Betty was capable of consenting and on whether she had understood that she could refuse consent.

The difficulties with the approach that New Jersey's statutory and case law had created were exposed in this case. Most basic was the problem of having the central issue be Betty's mental capacity and whether she could validly consent, rather than focusing on the boys and their conduct. Moreover, making Betty's mental acumen the central issue led the prosecution to downplay her abilities in order to emphasize the egregiousness of the teenage boys' actions. The conclusion the state argued for—that she lacked the ability to refuse consent—was also problematic because a necessary corollary would be that her level of mental function also made a consensual sex life impossible for her.

Another problem was the murkiness of the issues of capacity for consent and understanding of ability to refuse, which are all-important under the New Jersey test. The evidence on such questions, moreover, is often sufficiently equivocal that it is difficult to make a factual finding with enough confidence to turn important consequences on it. The *Olivio* court's comment on the issues the jury would have to decide illustrates both the pliability of the issues and the temptation to fall back on numbers and labels:

> The evidence presented would permit a jury to find that M. R. had a rudimentary and childish understanding of some of the physical aspects of sexual conduct, but a jury could conclude also that her understanding of sexual conduct was incomplete and inadequate even with respect to the physical aspects of sex. Furthermore, even if M. R. was found to have a minimally-adequate comprehension of sex, it is not clear that a reasonable jury would determine that she understood that her body was private and that she had a right to be free from the invasions of others, and the capacity to refuse to engage in sexual activity. There was evidence that M. R. had the social maturity of only an eight-year-old child and that she functioned at a socially inactive level.[17]

This was the background of New Jersey law that both molded and governed the Glen Ridge case.

The defense portrayed Betty as clearly knowledgeable about sex and possessed of the capacity to consent. This characterization, it hoped, would take her out of the definition of "mentally defective" in the New Jersey statute, making the statute wholly inapplicable. The defense also sought to portray Betty as sexually aggressive and promiscuous, saying she "enjoyed the rape and . . . instigated it."[18] In his opening remarks, Kevin Scherzer's attorney referred to Betty as "a full breasted young lady" who was "ready, willing, and able to do what she did."[19] He also suggested that Betty's retardation produced an abnormally strong sex drive:

> Betty enjoyed seeing "the joy on a boy's face when he ejaculated . . . She thrived for affection . . . but she also thrived for the kissing, she craved the caressing, she craved the embracing, she craved the euphoria because her brain functioned in that way. You may very well find," he suggested to the jury, "in the condition she had, her feeling for sex and her drive, her genitals' signals, are greater than normal."[20]

In addition, Paul Archer, testifying for the defense, stated that the victim had enjoyed the acts performed on her; that when Kevin Scherzer pushed the broomstick inside her she "moaned with pleasure";[21] and that she even "asked for something bigger and Kevin got the baseball bat."[22] (This testimony brought about his destruction as a witness on cross-examination, and the jury reacted negatively to the defense's efforts to blame everyone but the defendants for what had happened.)

The prosecution conceded that Betty understood the sexual nature of the activity. One assistant prosecutor acknowledged that she "understood the 'bare-bones mechanics' of sex."[23] In fact, when asked during her testimony whether she knew a lot about sex, she answered, "Yeah, as a matter of fact I do," and agreed that she had previously bragged about her sexual experience.[24]

While conceding her sexual experience, the state argued for her inability to refuse consent. There were numerous ways in which Betty did not seem very capable. First, the defense had secretly tape-recorded conversations between Betty and a girlfriend of one of the defendants, in which the girlfriend talked with the victim about the crime and other matters. At one point, she asked what Betty would do if a man approached her on the street and asked her to have sex. The reply was, "I don't know." One juror later said that this equivocation helped convince him that the victim was not capable of refusing consent.[25]

Additionally, the victim's demeanor on the stand seemed to support a finding of inability to consent or refuse consent: "Over four days of testimony, the woman was easily confused, easily led, and seemed eager to please, much like a small child. She often changed her version of events, and expressed affection for some of the defendants under questioning."[26] At trial, Betty testified that she performed the acts because "I didn't want to hurt their feelings."[27] She also stated that she considered the defendants her friends, although, she said, "I know they don't give a hoot about me." All these statements were offered as evidence of the victim's inability to consent.

Even the defense emphasized Betty's incapacities, contrary to its theory of the case: that she was able to consent. First, defense counsel talked down to her, sometimes treating her like a small child (saying things like "pretty please" and wishing her Merry Christmas in lieu of conducting a cross-examination).[28] Even more surprising was the defense request for a competency hearing for Betty, with the aim of preventing her from testifying.[29] Although the defense understandably would have preferred for Betty not to appear personally, its main argument—that she could validly consent—required viewing her as competent. It would be extremely odd for a person allegedly competent to consent to sex to be barred from testifying about what had happened.

The trial judge ruled that Betty could testify and that she could help the prosecution in other ways. He also ruled that because her ability to consent was at issue, her past sexual activity could be admitted into evidence "for the limited purpose of showing her ability to consent to sexual activities." Limited purpose or not, New Jersey's rape shield law was thus avoided, and the victim's sexual history was elicited at trial and displayed in the media. Everyone with a television soon knew that she had once exposed her breasts at school; that her mother had put her on birth control pills; that she had once asked to see the penis of a boy with mental disabilities; and that she had had intercourse with a special education student.[30]

Under this judge's interpretation of New Jersey law, whenever there is a serious allegation of "mental defect," the victim can be treated significantly worse than other women are. Whenever ability to understand and consent is in question, the victim forfeits the protection of the rape shield law. Accordingly, "mentally defective" women, or those alleged to be "mentally defective," do not enjoy the same rights to sexual privacy as other persons—even when they have done nothing wrong and are the victims of a crime. (This state of affairs outraged many female legislators in New Jersey—not to mention legal scholars and others around the nation—and eventually led to amendment of New Jersey's rape shield law.)[31]

Such is the type of evidence that the jury had to rely on in finding that the victim was incapable of refusing consent and was accordingly "mentally defective" within the meaning of New Jersey's sexual assault statute. In addition to proving that "mental defect" existed, the prosecution was also required to prove that the defendants knew or should have known of it. This evidence seemed clearer, assuming that "mental defect" within the meaning of the law existed. Most of the boys had known Betty since they were small children, and the families' houses were close together. Betty's mental status was "part of the neighborhood lore."[32] A tennis coach revealed that Paul and Christopher Archer used to play tennis with the girl, and that they often made fun of her and called her "retard." The Scherzer boys had convinced her to eat dog feces when she was five years old, saying it was "candy." Summing up her impressions of the defendants' states of mind, a local psychologist said: "They pushed her buttons and they knew which buttons to push because they knew her . . . They picked her for this. They knew they could get her to do it . . . that they essentially had a small child in the body of a woman."[33] The totality of this evidence supported a conclusion that the defendants had reason to know of the "mental defect."

After extensive deliberations, the jury returned a verdict of guilty against each of the four defendants. Christopher Archer, as the "ringleader," and Kevin and Kyle Scherzer each were convicted of first-degree aggravated sexual assault by force or coercion and second-degree conspiracy to commit assault. In addition, Christopher Archer and Kevin Scherzer were convicted of first-degree aggravated assault upon a "mentally defective person." The fourth defendant, Bryant Grober, was convicted only of third-degree conspiracy to commit aggravated criminal sexual contact.

In a posttrial interview, a juror discussed how the jury applied the law to the facts:

> [The juror] says that the hardest decision for the jury was whether the defendants knew that the victim was mentally defective, and at what point they had their knowledge. "If they didn't know before the broom, they had to know after the broom . . . No human being would submit to that, period." So that's where the jurors drew the line, convicting those defendants involved in those acts, but excusing Bryant Grober, on whom the victim performed an act of fellatio prior to the assault with the wooden implements. [The juror] says Grober appeared to be the least culpable of the defendants, [as] the only defendant who had not known the victim since childhood, and lived in another part of town.[34]

While the prosecution seemingly prevailed, at least against three of the defendants, it was unable to turn the verdicts into substantial sentences. The state sought substantial imprisonment, saying that the defendants were dangerous, predatory offenders. First, an assistant prosecutor argued that Christopher Archer had raped a female college student several months before. The incident allegedly took place after his arrest on the Glen Ridge charges, while he was attending Boston College and fighting New Jersey's request to have him tried as an adult.[35] The alleged victim in that attack reported it to college officials, saying that Archer "forced her prone, stripped her, and then punched her in the crotch,"[36] but she never made an official complaint. She did provide a sealed affidavit for the New Jersey courts urging revocation of Archer's bail and providing rebuttal evidence for the prosecution, to be used if the defense presented evidence that Archer had good character.[37]

Second, the state noted for the court that Kevin Scherzer had exposed and fondled his genitals during high school classes and had once told opponents in a baseball game about "a rape we did." In addition, three days after jury deliberations began, he had been arrested for drunk driving after running a red light.[38]

What stunned many who followed the case was the defendants' total disregard for their victim. They told their friends that they were repulsed by her. The instruments of the rape were used because they did not want to touch the girl's body.[39]

Two of the defendants chose to address the court on their own behalf. Both Kevin Scherzer and Christopher Archer spoke for less than thirty seconds, and each said he was sorry. Archer said, "I used poor judgment . . . I ask you to let me learn from my mistake." Scherzer said, "I used bad moral judgment. I was very young at the time. I'm just sorry about everything."

In the end Judge Cohen handed down what were considered very lenient sentences, consistently exercising his discretion in favor of the defendants. First, he merged counts to eliminate some time. Second, he sentenced the remaining counts at the midpoints of the sentencing range. Third, he exercised his discretion to sentence the three main defendants as "young adult offenders." As a result, Archer and the Scherzer twins received indeterminate sentences of up to fifteen years, which in practice could be fulfilled in as little as twenty-two months. Alternatively, they could have received sentences of between thirty and forty years.

Furthermore, time in prison was to be served at a "campus-type prison with cottages" that had fewer restrictions than usual prisons. None of the defendants, however, was remanded into custody. Instead, the judge continued their bail, allowing all three to remain free pending appeal. The fourth defendant, Bryant Grober, was sentenced to three years of probation and two hundred hours of community service. In explaining his sentences, Judge Cohen stated that he did not believe the defendants were a danger; nor were they "hardened or vicious criminals" or "without redeeming values."[40]

Charges were later dropped against two other participants who had been awaiting trial. Richard Corcoran and John Maher were released from indictment because Betty's parents told the prosecutor's office that another trial would be detrimental to their daughter.[41] The Scherzer twins and Archer appealed their convictions, but Grober did not. On appeal, the convictions of all three were reversed on the most severe count, penetration by force or coercion, but conviction on the lesser counts was affirmed.[42] The reason for the court's reversal on the sexual assault count was the existence of a reasonable doubt about whether there was force or coercion or, instead, willing compliance: "[Betty] . . . said that she did not try to leave the basement because she wanted to stay, and that she could have left if she wanted to."[43] At the same time, the court affirmed the convictions for first-degree aggravated assault on a mentally defective person because Betty "did not understand that she could say no to a request."[44] The appeals court then remanded the case for less severe sentencing.

Finally, eight years after the rape and four years after the convictions, Judge Cohen refused to continue bail and sentenced Archer and Kevin Sherzer to "prison terms of up to 15 years in a youth correction facility; Kyle Scherzer was sentenced to a maximum of seven years. With good behavior, Kevin Scherzer and Archer could be released in two years; Kyle Scherzer could serve as little as 10 months." After sentencing, the "sheriff's deputies handcuffed the former high school athletic stars, took the belts and ties from their conservative suits, and led them away to jail, 'Justice delayed does not mean justice should be denied,' the prosecutor told the judge."[45]

Many facets of this case reflect the ways that courts and society still view persons with retardation. There were specific rulings, during all phases of the trial, that dealt directly with the subject of retardation and how the trial should be altered in view of the nature of the victim. For example, the state asked that the defense lawyers' movements be restricted during the victim's testimony to avoid confusing or intimidating her—a motion that Judge Cohen denied. The prosecution also asked that the victim be permitted to use anatomically correct dolls in her testimony, but Judge Cohen denied the request because of the "possible prejudice of 'portraying the witness in a child-like manner.'" He also denied another protection that is extended to children when they testify—testifying on closed-circuit television instead of in court—again declining to assume that persons with retardation are like children.[46]

The judge did permit the state to use replica evidence at trial and permitted the victim to help them in purchasing a replica of the bat used during the rape. The actual objects used in the attack were never recovered, and the tangibility of the replica had an important effect at the trial, especially because Paul Archer admitted it was precisely like the bat they had used.[47]

Whether or not the trial outcomes were appropriate, there is substantial reason to doubt that New Jersey's approach to the crime and the trial was the route the law should pursue. There are many ways that the law could be improved, but the main problem in this case was that the entire trial revolved around the victim's mental competence. The pain and humiliation of the proceedings for her resulted, among other things, in charges being dropped against some of the participants so that she would not have to undergo another trial.

But what is the alternative to this focus on the mental acumen of the victim? The primary thesis of this book—that persons with retardation should be treated like all others—also seems unsatisfactory if its result is that the victim is seen as having consented, thereby relieving the defendants of criminal responsibility. Few would doubt that the defendants acted wrongfully and immorally and that they were victimizing another human being. A principle that prohibits such behavior from being criminalized would indeed be suspect. Is there any way to support the conviction of the boys and also to support the right and legal ability of people like Betty to make their own decisions?

There were, in fact, different routes to conviction that could have been tried even under existing New Jersey law—routes that would not have relied on a finding that Betty was incapable of consenting to sex. Indeed, the prosecution did argue under an alternative theory—that Betty had been forced to engage in the sexual acts (and thus the rape was illegal regardless of her IQ). Under relatively new New Jersey precedent, the force necessary for rape can be satisfied by the force necessary for penetration; and the defense of consent requires an allegation of "affirmative and freely-given permission to . . . the act of sexual penetration."[48]

Prosecutors also considered, but ultimately rejected, making an argument under a New Jersey statute that prohibits consent to affirmative bodily harm. Merging the reasoning behind both of these theories, one might emphasize that no one (or certainly, almost no one) would freely consent to the acts involved. At least with respect to these acts, experience teaches us to presume against consent. Accordingly, affirmative evidence of consent could be required for a defendant to demonstrate consent to such an act.

All of these approaches have the virtue of being applicable in all cases, not just those involving women with retardation. Indeed, even the New Jersey statute's "incapable of understanding or exercising the right to refuse" standard could be applied to persons generally, not just those with "a mental disease or defect." Without the "mental defect" limitation, courts and even legislators would see that the standard is hopelessly vague and confusing.

Indeed, the legislature would never have applied such a standard to the population in general.

An alternative approach worthy of serious consideration would admit to needing sometimes to treat persons with substantial intellectual deficits differently from other people, but it would limit that different treatment to a few unusual activities, such as those involved in Glen Ridge. New Jersey's law, by contrast, required that in order for a vulnerable person to be protected from the clear exploitation that took place in the Glen Ridge case, that person must also give up her right to consensual sex. That result was surely inappropriate for Betty,[49] who, in fact, functioned at a higher level than many of the young women involved in sterilization cases such as Valerie N., Lee Ann Grady, and Cynthia W. As one doctor testified:

> [Betty] was a fairly highly-functioning retarded young adult, but "willing to do almost anything to gain some modicum of social acceptance," seeing her own sexuality as a means of pleasing others . . . "[S]he does not seem to have the concept that she should be able to choose what to do with her body sexually and should not be subject to the whims of 'friends.'"[50]

Rather than categorize persons with retardation as those able and those unable to consent (to sexual activity across the board), the focus should perhaps shift to the activity for which consent is sought. Persons like Betty Harris or Valerie N. should not have to be deprived of a consensual sex life in order to protect them from clearly exploitative behavior. Another solution, of course, would be to make the behavior—whether we are talking about sex with strange instruments or sadomasochistic behavior, to give two possible examples—illegal for *all* adults, without regard to supposed consent. But the U.S. Constitution's "right to choose" embodied in the Fourteenth Amendment, as well as some other considerations, support toleration of a wide range of consensual activity that includes activities very few would find desirable.

If such a broad range of choice continues to be respected for the population at large, perhaps persons who are particularly vulnerable need to be judged by a different standard. To minimize the impact on their freedom and their equality, however, this different standard should be applicable only to decisions to engage in extreme behavior. Sex with thirteen boys, a broom, and a bat would definitely qualify. Sadomasochism, especially consenting to play the masochistic role, would too. The fact that few persons would consent to these activities makes it more likely that the instigator (assuming it was not the "victim" herself) knowingly took advantage of her vulnerability in getting her to "consent."

A doctrine precluding consent to such unusual and generally distasteful choices need not be confined to particular sexual acts. The same approach could remove certain life choices from the range of choices available to persons who are especially vulnerable. Possibilities include consenting to serve as a surrogate mother and consenting to assisted suicide. Both are activities that a state can make available to consenting adults, and some states do. Nonetheless, the frequency with which these opportunities are pursued is small, and it will not interfere with the freedom of a young woman with retardation, in any substantial way, to be deprived of these life experiences or to be subjected to special procedures to assure the voluntariness of her choice. These activities may be viewed as ones that, especially for vulnerable groups, are much more likely to reflect exploitation than free choice. Moreover, only rarely will the individual attempt to make such a choice, so having a separate approach for persons with retardation does not mean that they will have to face different treatment on a daily or frequent basis.

Should Sterilization Be Available Only with Actual Informed Consent?

Having decided that certain exceptional choices that are available generally might not be available to women who are extremely vulnerable intellectually, should sterilization be included as one of those choices? Sterilization is both more drastic and less necessary than the other procreative choices available. Accordingly, it should perhaps be limited to persons who can give actual informed consent. Others would not be vulnerable to substitute decisionmaking but would simply not have sterilization as an option; they would be free to choose another method of birth control, including Norplant, or even abortion if that was necessary.

There is much to be said for such a solution. First, it would help with the disturbing fact that the proposed approach might otherwise result in substantially more sterilizations than under present practice; because no court proceedings are required, sterilizations will sometimes be much easier for caretakers, guardians, or parents to obtain or for physicians to encourage. Second, it limits a procedure that is not necessary, or certainly is not widely necessary.

Especially in view of the history of abuse, and the continuation of abuse even under progressive legal rules, eliminating sterilization from the range of choices that can be made without actual informed consent would not appear troublesome, absent one critical fact: the prevalence of sterilization as a method of birth control in the United States today. Sterilization is now, and projected through the year 2010 to be, the most commonly used birth control method in the United States.[51] For example, it is projected that of the 42.3 million women practicing birth control in the year 2000, 9.9 million will use oral contraceptives, 11.3 million will use other reversible forms of birth control, and 20.1 million will opt for sterilization.[52] These statistics make it difficult to argue that sterilization should be disallowed for persons with limited capabilities as an "oddball choice" (even though it is by nature a once-in-a-lifetime choice). If we are to create exceptions to the proposed general approach of self-determination for all expressive persons, perhaps it is important that the exceptions be truly exceptional.

On the other hand, surgical sterilization is not the birth control method of those segments of the population with the greatest range of options. The women most likely to be sterilized in the United States are those with low incomes, those with little education, Hispanics, and blacks.[53] Moreover sterilization is most in use by women who are married and have already had children—not women similar to those sterilized today by third-party consent. Perhaps, therefore, it would be legitimate, in view of the history of sterilization and the increasing lack of necessity for it (given alternative forms of birth control), to remove it from the agenda of choices available with less than traditional informed consent. The sterilization option—like surrogacy, assisted suicide, and masochism—would then be curtailed for the same persons the law currently precludes from consenting. But accepting consent by any expressive person would still be the norm where not clearly limited. It would continue as the norm and would apply at least for all standard activities requiring consent—sex, marriage, routine medical care, birth control, abortion, and other personal choices.

Ultimately, Betty Harris's story might be taken to reflect less about retardation and more about how society too readily accepts as "normal" sexually abusive behavior by adolescent boys and men. The social reaction of forgiving the boys was evident in Glen Ridge, where the trial was "a very personal tragedy" for the town.[54] In an article entitled "Ordinary People," a reporter for *Sports Illustrated* asked, "Were the suburban youths who raped a retarded girl 'star athletes' or just typical kids?"[55] He wrote that "[t]he town was like a closed fist." People told him things like "I would rather cut out my tongue than talk to you" and "To think of all the times I gave that girl a ride in my car!" In the final analysis, he concluded, "the boys . . . wind up expressing, rather than transgressing, the values of their community."[56]

Betty Harris's dilemma and the community's reaction cannot be isolated as relevant only to people with unusually low IQs. Many women in the normal course of their lives, for a range of reasons, occasionally consent to sexual activity that is both demeaning and unpleasant for them. The story of Kerri G., a college sophomore, is illustrative. During her first year of college, Kerri found herself pursuing the attentions of numerous fraternity boys whom she liked a great deal. Her interest in them was not reciprocated; she once heard one of them refer to her as "a dog." Nevertheless, she continued to go to their weekly fraternity parties with her friends.

On one occasion Kerri got drunk on two beers and, after her friends left the party, stayed behind and had sex with several of the boys whom she liked and some whom she did not know. She did this as a number of boys watched, cheered her on, and chanted her name. After the experience Kerri continued to be the butt of the boys' jokes; now they called her the "two-beer lay-dee."

Clearly, the boys had not grown to like or respect her as a result of what she had done. She was extremely embarrassed, depressed, and disillusioned for some time, and had even less self-esteem than before the incident. Nevertheless, Kerri survived and eventually got over the experience. Through it she learned that she had made a bad decision; she resolved not to repeat her mistake. No loving parent would want a daughter to have Kerri's experience, whether by force or choice. But the choice was Kerri's to make.

The moral—or issue—that this story raises is easy to detect. Are Betty Harris and Kerri so different and, if not, should lack of consent be presumed for both, or for neither? Should the boys' activities in both cases be illegal, regardless of the victims' consent, or is "the law" out of place in this arena and our tradition of allowing broad individual choice, even to do seemingly distasteful things, the appropriate path to follow?

Deciding which side of the protection-freedom divide to reinforce—for persons with retardation and others—is clearly very difficult and very close. Even if we are moved by the similarities between Kerri G. and Betty H., Kerri's experience seems far less relevant to persons with much more serious retardation than Betty. But issues of how to allow consensual sexual relationships and how to distinguish them from sexual exploitation are likely to be confronted by persons dubbed "mildly or moderately retarded" much more often than by persons with very low IQs. Not only are "higher-functioning" persons likely to have fuller lives, including fuller sex lives, but also the vast majority of persons with mental retardation have mild or moderate retardation and function at a level where legal authority to have a consensual sex life "like everybody else" would be the norm. Recall the Arc's statistics: 89 percent of persons with retardation have mild retardation; 7.5 percent have moderate retardation; and only 3.5 percent have severe or profound retardation.

PART IV

Parenting

CHAPTER 14

Some Underlying Rules and Issues

The legal presumption in the United States, arising from judicial interpretations of the U.S. Constitution, is that any person who produces a child has a "right" to parent that child.[1] Unlike some important occupations, and unlike marriage, the state does not license either procreation or parenthood. Nor does it require persons who wish to procreate or who become parents to be trained in child care or child rearing skills, or to have their parenting skills tested.[2] Moreover, once a parent-child relationship exists, public policy counsels strongly against state interference.

This respect for "the right to parent" reflects the high value that our society places on the relationship between birth parent and child. As a California court explained: "The relationship of natural parent to her children is a vital human relationship which has far-reaching implications for the growth and development of the child, and the involuntary termination of that relationship by state action must therefore be viewed as a drastic remedy which should be resorted to only in extreme cases of neglect [or abuse] or abandonment."[3]

As well as this basic reluctance to disrupt the parent-child bond, additional reasons are numerous for disfavoring state interference and allowing it only as a last resort. Three significant reasons are: (1) as a society, we lack a uniform image of what adequate parenting looks like; (2) our society values the diversity in family matters, including parenting, that exists in our heterogeneous culture, and is suspicious of attempts to impose governmental orthodoxy; and (3) we as a society distrust the accuracy of predictions about ability to parent and accordingly would oppose licensing on the ground that such an important part of the human experience should not be vulnerable to such official predictions.

Standards for Evaluating Parents: Adoption, Neglect and Abuse, and Custody Proceedings

Nevertheless, some in the professional child care community and elsewhere suggest that parenthood should be licensed in order to protect children from inadequate parenting.[4] Although that policy has not prevailed vis-à-vis persons who produce their own children, there are arenas of law and regulation that reflect that philosophy. Most notably, in the context of adoption, state and other agencies do assess the fitness and desirability of potential adoptive parents. Their rules often disqualify even persons who clearly would be "fit" to keep children they produced: for example, rules that the would-be adoptive parents not be older than thirty-five, or that they be married, or that they be financially stable.

Adoption is the paradigmatic arena of parental screening, but it is not the only one. Some states similarly license and screen foster parents.[5] And in the context of modern reproductive technologies like in vitro fertilization, and even surrogate motherhood, providers often screen potential parents for fitness and also apply predetermined rules to them, such as a requirement that they be married. Moreover governmental attempts to regulate these emerging areas of activity often include prerequisites for parenting or requirements of parental screening or both. These efforts contrast sharply with treatment of persons who give birth to and want to raise their own children. In that context, the government does not eliminate potential parents before the fact, or even at birth.

Instead of testing parental fitness at birth or at any other predetermined stage, the typical state system scrutinizes an individual's parenting abilities only when allegations of parental inadequacy are brought to the attention of child welfare authorities. Those authorities are trained to evaluate parental fitness, and when such allegations are made, they decide whether to interfere with an individual's parenting in order to protect the child. When the authorities do interfere, they can do so either by providing services within the home or, when necessary to protect the child, by removing the child from the home.

Such interference and removal are reserved for extreme cases, and removal is available only when the parent is considered "unfit." Another way the law describes the limited arena for coercive government intervention is to allow removal only when parental conduct amounts to "neglect or abuse." Undesirable parental behavior that falls short of actual unfitness (which is equivalent to neglect or abuse) has no impact on parental rights. Instead, parents retain decisionmaking power over their children, and the government refrains from attempting to enforce one orthodox method of child rearing or an orthodoxy for other facets of family life.

Unfitness (or neglect or abuse) could, of course, be defined either broadly or narrowly, but the tradition has been to limit it to the most extreme of cases. After all, when both parents are unfit, the child may be removed from home, possibly never to return; such a drastic change in the child's life should be imposed only when it is clear that it is necessary and that the benefits to the child outweigh the losses. Moreover the benefits of limiting state interference extend to society broadly. Families in general benefit from the stability and independence of knowing that the state will not interfere in their practices except in the most extreme and outrageous of cases.

In Adoption of Katharine and Jeptha, for example, a Massachusetts appellate court reversed a trial court decision that cocaine-addicted parents were unfit. The court pointed out the absence of actual neglect and abuse and said: "Parental unfitness, as developed in the case law, means more than ineptitude, handicap, character flaw, conviction of a crime, unusual life style, or inability to do as good a job as the child's foster parent. Rather, the idea of 'parental unfitness' means 'grievous shortcomings or handicaps' that put the child's welfare 'much at hazard' . . . [W]e do not think a cocaine habit, without more, translates automatically into legal unfitness to act as a parent."[6]

Lying between the strict unfitness approach common to neglect and abuse proceedings and the preapproved parenting approach followed with respect to adoption are the judicial determinations of custody that must be made when the legal parents are competing against each other for custody. Obviously, in those proceedings it is not possible for two fit parents both to keep full custody of the child, so a comparative evaluation of the parents must be made.

Custody conflicts between parents are very different from neglect and abuse hearings, where the state proceeds against a parent or parents. For one thing, custody disputes between parents are much more common. Moreover, unless joint custody is an option, the inquiry will focus on which parent is the "better" custodian and what custody arrangement comports with "the best interests of the child." The "better" parent will usually become the custodian, and the other parent will have visitation rights, which are sometimes minimal but can be substantial. In some states this choice between parents is avoided by presuming in favor of joint custody, but the custodian-visitor approach is still the most common, and many feel it is often preferable.[7]

Because a comparison between parents is the issue, it is common in custody disputes for courts to "award" custody based on characteristics that fall far short of unfitness. If one of the parents is unfit, of course, the other one will become the custodian (and any visitation may be strictly limited). But the usual, much more difficult, case is the one in which both parents appear fully adequate and a choice has to be made because the parents have separated or divorced.

When the choice is made in a judicial hearing (rather than by the parents' reaching some sort of settlement out of court), all the facts about the parents and about their relationships with the child(ren) are relevant. A judge then chooses between them, basing the determination on all the evidence. Inevitably, the judge's own background, upbringing, and values weigh heavily in evaluation of the better living arrangement, at least in close cases. Not only does this seem unfair, but also the approach of basing determination of the better custodian on all the evidence can lead to great uncertainty as to who will prevail, making it more difficult for parties to reach agreement without going to trial.[8] The necessity of a trial can be destructive, not only to the parties themselves and anything that remains of their relationship, but also to the child, whose custody must remain uncertain during the possibly prolonged custody battle.

Because of these inherent difficulties with custody litigation based on all the facts, some courts and legislatures have adopted a presumption for one parent over the other. Proponents of this approach aim to reduce the need to litigate over custody, as well as produce a suitable end result. In early Anglo-American common law, the presumption was for the father because of feudal conceptions of the "natural rights" of fathers as heads of households and owners of their children.

In the mid-nineteenth century, that rule was questioned and gradually replaced by courts' recognition of a "tender years presumption" that infants should not be snatched from the care of their mothers, who were considered instinctive nurturers.[9] That presumption was very widely accepted in the United States until the 1970s, but now it is deemed unconstitutional because of its gender-based discrimination.[10] A favorite replacement presumption favors whoever is the "primary caretaker" of the child, whether father or mother.[11] That rule can still replace custody litigation, or simplify that litigation when it occurs, and it also has the virtue of leaving the child with the most appropriate caretaker.

Even having a presumption does not eliminate custody contests, and some all-the-circumstances determinations will remain. Even in a primary-caretaker jurisdiction, for example, determinations based on all the facts will control when both parents have made substantial contributions to caretaking. In addition, parents may still try to eliminate each other from contention by alleging facts designed to show each other's unfitness. But even though presumptions do not entirely circumvent the difficulties with all-the-evidence custody litigation, they (especially strong presumptions) can nonetheless greatly reduce the necessity for custody litigation, largely by making it clearer who would prevail in the event of litigation.

Whether a state turns the outcome of custody contests on a presumption or on all the circumstances, the supposed legal standard for this type of child placement litigation is "the best interests of the child." That standard sounds unimpeachable, but it is important to realize that enormous assumptions are reflected in the assessment of what is in the child's best interests. Moreover, those assumptions are often disguised in best-interests language, instead of being expressed and subjected to scrutiny.

For example, the judge who believes that it is in a child's best interests to be raised by the better-educated parent may use that as a determinant; or a judge who feels that it cannot be in a child's best interests to be raised by a lesbian may make that judgment determinative without necessarily expressing it. Because so much can be packed into the concept of "best interests," with or without being expressed, and because generalized best interests determinations usually entail substantial and often destructive custody contests, adopting the best interests standard may not be the way to further the child's best interests.

Comparing the Standards

In any event, the best interests standard used in custody contests and the unfitness standard used in neglect and abuse proceedings must not be confused. In custody contests the court has to make a choice between two fit parents, both of whom have and retain parental "rights." The decree does not express any condemnation of the noncustodial parent by the state. Instead of passing judgment on the parents, the decree, in theory at least, focuses on the child's needs for both parents and how best to satisfy them.

Whereas a custody determination involves a comparison between two parents, both of whom may be fully adequate, neglect and abuse are different. Unfitness is an absolute, not comparative, standard, disqualifying a parent because of extremely negative behavior. A finding of unfitness *does* represent a condemnation by the state—a finding of inadequacy or worse. Moreover, this finding is made in the context of a state-initiated proceeding brought expressly to interfere with the legal parents, rather than at the initiative of one of the parents.[12]

The adoption standard is different still. The advance-permission, licensing approach that is used for adoption represents an affirmative judgment, by whatever organization is doing the screening, that the parents selected to adopt will be good parents. Adoptions through agencies reflect such a judgment today because there are so many more would-be adopters than there are babies to adopt (excluding special-needs infants, whom some families do not consider).

Even with too few babies available to satisfy would-be adopters, this selective adoption system is not foreordained. Instead of this licensing approach, there could be a screening system that approved anyone who met minimal standards of adequacy. Screening in the context of in vitro fertilization or surrogacy, where practiced, generally follows that essentially nonselective approach. Similarly, when licensing is required for foster homes, there is pressure not to set the standard too high, because in most areas of the United States there are too few foster homes to satisfy current needs. If such a nonselective approach were used in the adoption context, it would have to be supplemented by some other, nonjudgmental selection approach, like first-come-first-served, or a lottery system.

So how do these rules for becoming and remaining parents affect persons with mental retardation? The strong presumption that exists in favor of birth parents and the dichotomy drawn between them and adoptive parents may or may not make sense, but if those rules are followed in the context of the population in general, the same rules should apply to parents who have mental retardation as one of their characteristics. In general, the same approach should apply to parents with retardation as others.

The main impact of such a change for most persons with retardation is that they could be eliminated as parents only when actually found unfit. It would be most unusual for people with retardation to be considered as adoptive parents. In other contexts as well, parents whom adoption agencies might readily eliminate as prospects—because they are not married or are "too old," for example—are permitted without question to keep their own children, and that approach would prevail for persons with retardation as well.

Like other parents, of course, parents with retardation do sometimes find themselves in divorce and custody proceedings. It seems likely that in a custody contest between two fit parents, one of whom had retardation and the other of whom did not, the judge would award custody to the person with the higher IQ, couching that determination in the language of the best interests of the child. It would be interesting to observe how a progressive judge today would apply a primary caretaker presumption in those circumstances, if the primary caretaker in fact had retardation. A common way out for the judge would be to find the parent with retardation unfit. Otherwise, under the presumption the primary caretaker with retardation should remain custodian.

Although retardation can be a factor in custody and adoption, the major threat to parenting by persons with retardation comes from the government, in the form of neglect and abuse proceedings. On this subject, like others, the most important legal principle that supporters must work for is that this population be treated the same as others. Inadequate parenting should result in mandatory services, removal, possibly even termination of parental rights, but only on the same basis as it does for everyone else. If persons with retardation are to receive the same treatment as others, then the question addressed when their parental authority is challenged must be whether they are adequate parents judged by a rather minimal standard, not whether some competing parent or caretaker would be "better" for the child, or even in the child's "best interests."

Occasionally cases do use this strict unfitness approach even in the context of mental retardation. In Petitions of Department of Social Services to Dispense with Adoption, the trial court had ruled that the children should stay with their foster family, with whom they had an emotional bond; but the Massachusetts appeals court reversed. The lower court had stated that the mother's mental retardation did not justify a finding of unfitness, but, according to the appeals court, neither did anything else:

> On the question of the mother's fitness alone, the judge made the following findings: she had a good ability to perform repetitious tasks, and was an excellent and steady worker at her assembly line job, a job which required no abstract thinking or problem solving and was good for her self-esteem; she

had abstained from alcohol since acquiring the job; and she was able to babysit properly for a friend so long as the necessities for that task were provided. Countering these essentially positive findings . . . were findings that the mother's "natural impediments" included intelligence within the mentally retarded range "with an anxiety behavior characterized by low self-esteem"; that her long-term memory had been impaired, perhaps by alcohol abuse; that her ability to cope diminished as stress increased; that "[f]or many years [she] . . . was further hindered by an abusive, alcoholic husband"; and that "for a long period of time [she] could not and did not cooperate [with plans attempted by the department]. She always 'went along' with [the father] . . . She was aware that [he] was beating the children." The judge concluded that she "would not be able to stand the stress of the return of these children and the loss of her job (which [the judge found] she plans to leave if the children are returned)." We agree with the mother that this conclusion, drawn largely from findings of her demonstrated past unfitness with respect to raising her children, is not based on clear and convincing evidence of current unfitness.[13]

The court ordered the case remanded so that the possibility of the mother's regaining custody of her daughters could be considered before proceeding further with forced termination of her rights. In addition, the court ordered the state to institute a service plan without delay—as required by state law—to "explore fully and to encourage, if appropriate, the prospect of visitation rights."[14]

The Difficulty and Subjectivity of Defining Unfitness

Only the unfitness inquiry focuses on the minimally acceptable level of parental adequacy, and it is difficult to get a clear sense, either from current practice, or from judicial or legislative decisions, what behavior will be deemed unacceptable or inadequate. There is no definition of unfitness across the board.

The concept of unfitness draws its meaning from repeated particular application to the particular parents brought into courts and from the wide array of decisions that appellate tribunals write. In short, it is a highly fact-specific concept in which law, or even previous decisions, is rarely the dominant inquiry. Even so, the rest of this section attempts to extrapolate from child protection statutes and judicial decisions what inadequate parenting means. Additionally, it elucidates what factors judges and social workers weigh when deciding whether, in the first instance, to provide helpful services, or instead remove the children and later whether to terminate parental rights.

Rather wisely, most child protection statutes do not attempt an all-inclusive definition of unfitness. Some do list factors that judges should consider when deciding removal or termination issues. Other legislation is fairly specific about conduct considered to render parents unfit,[15] and sometimes even about what is necessary to "normal family life in a permanent home."[16] Some statutes do list certain conditions or "habits"[17] that can lead to loss of parental rights—most frequently emotional or mental illness, or use of alcohol or controlled substances[18]—but typically today these result in loss of parental rights only if they "render the parent incapable of caring for the needs of the child."[19]

In California, for example, a judicial finding of developmental disability is sufficient grounds for instituting termination proceedings if the director of mental health or director of developmental services and the superintendent of the hospital in the state or county in which the parents are hospitalized or reside certify "that the parent or parents . . . will not be capable of supporting or controlling the child in a proper manner."[20]

Child protection statutes commonly specify, as grounds for terminating parental rights, certain behaviors, such as abandoning the child;[21] torturing, otherwise abusing (emotionally or sexually), or cruelly beating the child;[22] failing to act to provide for the child's material needs (such as food, clothing, shelter, supervision, or medical care);[23] or failing to provide the child with an education or necessary discipline.[24] Other factors are a parent's having been convicted of or imprisoned for a felony,[25] the parent's creation of living circumstances "damaging" to the child's "moral"[26] or "sound character development,"[27] and the injury or death of a child's sibling "under circumstances which constitute substantial evidence that such injury or death resulted from parental neglect or abuse."[28]

Mental retardation or developmental disability in many statutes is on such lists of conditions that can result in removal of the child if they lead to incompetence. Historically, however, statutes listed retardation as sufficient for removal of children and ultimate termination of parental rights, without any requirement that incompetence to parent be independently shown. Those laws simply presumed that incompetence follows from the mental disability. Today that approach is rightly accepted as discriminatory; it lumps together all persons with retardation and on the basis of that characteristic treats them differently from others.

Judicial decisions are not significantly more informative in specifying what behaviors constitute inadequacy than statutory law is. The decisions are not consistent, and they reflect the extreme importance of the particular judge's values, social background, and images of parenting. Moreover, family court judges routinely rely on expert evaluations by social service agencies, agency-affiliated psychologists, and other child care professionals when making decisions whether and how to intervene in families. Very few judges have any substantial exposure to the family whose fate they are deciding, so they must depend on the impressions of persons who have more direct experience with the parties.

What Judith Areen observed in 1975 remains true a quarter century later:

> Parents convicted of neglect in one community might never have been brought in to court in another. Perhaps the most prevalent characteristic of families charged with neglect is poverty; this raises the troubling possibility that class or cultural bias plays a significant role in decisions to label children neglected or abused, because it is clear that child abuse occurs in families of all income levels.
>
> Just as there is little agreement on when intervention in a particular family is justified, there is little agreement about what forms of intervention are constructive. The predominant approach is to separate parent and child. [Although] separation may protect a child from being beaten by his family, the separation itself may seriously damage the child's emotional health, particularly if the child is shifted from one temporary home to another during the separation.
>
> Unfortunately, legal commentary has not emphasized the issues of when or how the state ought to intervene to protect children from their parents.[29]

It would of course be difficult or impossible to have one clear definition of what constitutes inadequate parenting, given the varieties of human behavior. Moreover, the law quite appropriately focuses on the unfitness that eliminates, rather than on the adequate parenting that allows one to continue in that role. Even though it is entirely understandable and appropriate that the concept of parental adequacy is undefined,[30] it still should be recognized that this lack of definition sometimes works to the disadvantage of persons with retardation, because it leaves such determinations to the social worker's discretion.

The nonlegal literature contains more judgments about what parenting is actually adequate. There appears to be consensus in the community of child psychologists about those features of parenting that are important for child development. Accepted dogma is that children need care, supervision, nurture, and stimulation. The consensus falls apart only when the issue is how much of these qualities is minimally acceptable or "good enough." As well as between professionals, "there is a clear discrepancy between parent and professional perspectives of parental adequacy."[31]

If further definition is deemed useful, a generalized description of adequate parenting might be attempted in the following terms: An adequate parent has sufficient cognitive and physical capabilities to take care of herself and another human being, with or without the assistance of family, friends, or other available caregivers.[32] The parent should thus be able to provide for her own and a child's material well-being, which usually entails being able to earn a living or being supported by a spouse or other family member(s) or by state entitlement programs. Whether a parent has retardation or not, if she cannot provide food, shelter, and clothing, she runs the risk of losing her children to state foster care.[33]

The parent should also be emotionally and psychologically balanced enough to avoid engaging in acts or behaviors that are seriously destructive to herself or that may be destructive to her child. She must therefore understand that a child is not self-sufficient in infancy and early childhood and indeed is particularly fragile during these years, and that she may need to learn to give him or her more care than she has learned to give herself.[34]

The lesson of this book is that *all* parents who meet this description (or whatever other standard is applied across the board) should be able to remain with their children, and it should not make any difference whether they are deemed "retarded" or what their IQ number is.

Nonetheless the language of child protection legislation is susceptible to flexible interpretation by judges and social workers. Furthermore, psychiatrists' and psychologists' evaluations of a child's needs make their personal judgment important as well. *In re* Paul E., decided in 1995 by the Court of Appeals of California, illustrates the extreme subjectivity of decisions to remove children and the unevenness of the standards that are imposed.

Paul, a four-year-old with possible autism, had been raised by his parents and his grandmother in the grandmother's home in Huntington Beach, California. He was living at home and attending a special school when the county's social workers reported that the grandmother's home was "chronically messy" and listed in addition several specific hazards as the basis for petitioning to remove Paul from his home. They had "found a propeller protruding from a boat located outside the house, a lamp socket with a short, and a small child's plastic wading pool in the backyard filled with dirty water."[35]

Supposedly given thirty days to remedy these conditions, Paul's parents rectified them in eight days. But at that point the social workers decided to take Paul away, saying that his parents' "lack of progress in recognizing the dirty condition of the house demonstrated that they were limited by their own ability."[36] In fact, one of the parents (the mother) had mild mental retardation or slight "developmental deficiency," but the father and grandmother did not.

The parents successfully appealed. Reversing the decision to remove Paul, the California appellate court had this to say:

> County social service agencies cannot cast themselves in the role of a super-OSHA for families. While we certainly hope conditions improve in Paul's household, chronic messiness by itself and apart from any unsanitary conditions or resulting illness or accident, is just not clear and convincing evidence of a substantial risk of harm . . . The specific hazards which the social service agency identified . . . and which led to Paul's removal are trivial to the point of being pretextual. A shorted lamp socket could occur in the White House. Motor boats normally have propellers on them. Children's plastic wading pools do not come with filtration systems, and if they are filled with water for any amount of time the water is going to become dirty. Worse hazards than these may be found on practically every farm in America. If such conditions were sufficient for removal from the home, generations of Americans who grew up on farms and ranches would have spent their childhoods in foster care.[37]

The case illustrates how sometimes more is demanded of vulnerable persons, including persons with retardation, than is required of families generally. The trial court had been influenced by the agency to insist on more than minimal adequacy, which the agency demanded probably because of the vulnerability of the particular parents. The agency had applied a much higher standard to Paul's family than it would have applied to many others.

Certainly the standards it required are not met in many families that have never been involved with the social service system.

Use and Misuse of Sociological Studies

This section reviews what is known from studies that have been conducted to assess whether retardation often produces unfitness to parent. In one sense, the issue of whether retardation produces unfitness seems central to what rules should govern, but in another sense it is entirely irrelevant to the legal inquiry about parental rights. For the established rule states that it is the *individual's* ability at issue, not the abilities of persons in general in some group to which the individual belongs. The Supreme Court firmly established this legal principle in Stanley v. Illinois, and it is controlling. Accordingly, on issues of parental rights, the parenting ability of persons with retardation as a group is not germane. If *some* persons with retardation have the ability to parent, those parents should be allowed to parent.

That said, it seems wise nonetheless to inform ourselves as much as possible about how persons with retardation as a group perform as parents and, especially, how they can be helped to perform better.

The Studies

Current research about parents with retardation assesses what accounts for parental shortcomings and the extent to which various teaching approaches can help. The most recent studies, discussed below, reveal that specialized training programs have enabled persons with retardation to parent adequately. As a result, the outlook of current researchers may now be ahead of public opinion, judicial awareness, and the practices of most social service agencies. The traditional and still prevalent negative views about parents with retardation are the result of more than a century of research deeply rooted in the prejudice of eugenics.

The earliest body of eugenics literature asserted that parents with mental retardation produced "defective" offspring[38] and lived degenerate lives in slums.[39] According to these "scientific" studies, they were unfit to multiply and, if left to do so, threatened the human race with "economic and biological disaster."[40] The underlying political fear in England and particularly the United States was that given the political opportunities created by universal suffrage, persons with retardation might take "control [of] the country and decide who was to govern."[41] Although some studies in the 1930s and 1940s rejected these conclusions,[42] their already widespread[43] acceptance fueled ongoing eugenics research and provided a pseudoscientific basis for continuing both social segregation and compulsory sterilization throughout the United States.[44]

During this period, some researchers dismissed the eugenicists' apocalyptic concerns as "rather wild"[45] and instead focused on the welfare of children reared by parents with retardation. Whereas the eugenicists had evaluated fitness to procreate, the new researchers looked at fitness to parent. One veteran researcher of the eugenics era explained in 1952: "Personally I do not believe that there is any truth in the idea that deterioration of the population will occur if high-grade defectives are allowed to breed naturally. However, judged from the point of view of the child, the conditions of health and nutrition depend upon the mother a great deal and I think that each case must be judged upon its merits as a medical rather than an eugenic problem."[46]

Viewing parents with retardation as a "medical problem" caused some to argue for rehabilitation rather than imprisonment for mothers who abandoned, neglected, or abused their children.[47] It also became the basis for yet another controlling, though unproven, hypothesis about parents with retardation: that they disproportionately maltreated their children. Unsurprisingly, the studies used to test this hypothesis did not escape the social-scientific biases that tainted earlier eugenics research literature. Since the 1940s, numerous studies that have drawn statistical correlations between incidences of child maltreatment and parents with low IQs have been widely criticized as methodologically flawed.[48]

Recent researchers have attempted more reliable methods to test the existence of such correlations, but most of these methods have imported the inherent flaws of earlier studies.[49] The flaws arise from (1) "subject group" bias: failures of research experiments adequately to control for variables besides mental retardation that may cause parental inadequacies; and (2) the absence of any accepted definition of adequate parenting. Consequently, to the extent that the studies answer the question "Can persons with mental retardation parent adequately?" the answers often reveal more about a researcher's own perspectives on what factors are central to adequacy than about the *actual* adequacy of parents with retardation.

A final common flaw in the studies is that many pertain to parents who have lived in state institutions, ignoring the greater number of parents with retardation living in the community. The sample groups for child maltreatment studies are often uncontrolled in this way, using parents with retardation at particularly high risk of inadequacy. Formerly institutionalized subjects may be especially likely to lack family experiences that would assist them as parents.[50]

One of the most frequently cited studies prior to the normalization movement was reported in 1947 by Phyllis Mickelson.[51] It examined the social welfare records of ninety families with "feebleminded" parents, all of whom were under the guardianship of the Minnesota commissioner of welfare. (Minnesota law during this era authorized commitment to "state guardianship" of persons with retardation who could not provide for their own needs).[52]

Mickelson created three subjective categories for rating parenting ability: "satisfactory" (parents who kept their children well fed, well clothed, and regularly in school); "questionable" (parents whose care of the children was inconsistent and marginally inadequate but did not warrant neglect proceedings); and "unsatisfactory" (parents whose care was inadequate and justified child protection proceedings). Approximately 42 percent of the families were rated as satisfactory, 32 percent as questionable, and 26 percent as unsatisfactory.

The correlation Mickelson found between parental IQ and parental inadequacy was inconsistent. A majority of mothers with IQs below 50 provided unsatisfactory care, but 30 percent of mothers in the 30–49 IQ range were rated satisfactory, as well as 46 percent of the mothers in the 50–69 IQ range. However, only 33 percent in the 70–79 range received a satisfactory rating.[53]

In a follow-up study, published in 1949, Mickelson asked the question "Can mentally retarded parents be helped to give their children better care?"[54] She reported that many parents with retardation improve when given general social service assistance, such as help with homemaking, and the group that receives assistance provides better care to their children than those who do not. Mickelson concluded that "the parent's mental status did not appear to be the sole determinant of adequacy of child care: otherwise, all of the children would have been neglected."[55]

Studies much more recent than Mickelson's have found that, as a group, children of parents with retardation have scored significantly higher than their parents on traditional measures of intelligence.[56] For example, a 1985 study by Maurice Feldman and his colleges of twelve two-year-old children raised by mothers with retardation used the Home Observation for Measurement of Environment Scale (HOME test) to determine the extent to which the home environment successfully fostered child development.[57] Even though all of the children had been deemed at risk of developmental delay, particularly language delays, they scored within the average range.

When children of low-IQ parents are not successful at school or on tests, it may be difficult to connect their problems to their parents' IQ. There are often other attending circumstances—for example, poverty or malnutrition in the home. Gwynnyth Llewellyn writes that

> a clear relationship between parental intelligence and the child's education achievement has not been established for any specified parent group. Rather, a variety of factors besides parent IQ have been identified as contributing to poor educational achievement. These factors include poverty, poor nutrition and school absence due to illness or high mobility. For many adults with intellectual disability such conditions are part of their daily lives.[58]

Moreover, parenting skills can be taught to mothers with retardation. Feldman and his colleagues conducted a key series of observational studies on parental education. The first phase, published in 1985, compared the parent-child play interactions of mothers with retardation to those of other mothers with children the same age. The second phase, published in 1986, developed training sessions for the control group (the mothers with retardation) in order to improve the two skill areas in which they had demonstrated deficiency: child praise and parental imitation of child vocalizations. Feldman's team observed in 1986 that although "applied behavior analysts have made significant contributions to both the teaching of domestic living skills and parent training, there has been little research on the teaching of parenting skills to developmentally handicapped parents."[59]

The training sessions in the 1986 study were conducted in the mothers' homes to increase the likelihood that the skills would be used by them there after training. An earlier study, conducted in 1983 by other researchers, had found that "initial increases in positive maternal interactions of six mothers . . . for the most part, were not maintained at a 1 month follow-up."[60] Earlier doubts had therefore been raised about the ability of parents with retardation to generalize parenting skills that they are taught and to maintain them in their own home environment.[61] Feldman and his colleagues, however, produced results in their 1986 study that contradicted those of earlier studies:

Developmentally handicapped people are often considered incapable of either handling the complexities of child-rearing or benefiting from training . . . Concern has been expressed about the ability of mentally handicapped people to generalize parenting skills . . .

Training results indicated that relatively brief behavioral instruction, consisting of discussion, modeling, feedback, social reinforcement, and self-recording, was effective in increasing and maintaining the positive interactional skills of low-IQ mothers when playing with their children at home. Interestingly we did not find it necessary to substantially modify or enhance standard parent training strategies to compensate for the lower intellectual functioning of the mothers . . .

We were particularly impressed by the increased frequency, richness, and responsiveness of the mothers' interactions. After training, the mothers were more likely to sit down and play with their babies, encourage new motor behaviors, and initiate verbal interchanges. Mothers became more sensitive and responsive to infant vocalizations, and new games such as "copycat" occurred more frequently. These types of stimulating and rewarding interactions were rarely if ever observed prior to training.

Training results were maintained, for the most part, up to 10 months following training; terminal levels were generally comparable to and sometimes considerably above those seen in the comparison group of nonhandicapped mothers . . . Using the performance of the nonhandicapped mothers as a "normative" guide, we found that developmentally handicapped mothers, with IQs as low as 64, could quickly learn, in a generalized way, more effective nurturing skills . . . The present data do suggest . . . that the model holds promise as a means of effectively identifying and remediating parenting deficiencies.[62]

The results of this study confirmed findings of other researchers in 1986 that also reported increased positive interactions between mother and children after parental training.[63]

Another frequently cited report on parental training, published in 1989, was written by Barbara Whitman, Betty Graves, and Pasquale Accardo. That team investigated a training program called Parents Learning Together, conducted in St. Louis, Missouri, in the late 1980s.[64] Theirs was a pilot program aimed at refining parenting skills in families where one or both parents had retardation. To qualify for this program, a family had to have at least one parent with an IQ of 69 or below, and an ongoing pregnancy or one or more pre–school-age children in the home. Referrals to the program were made by social workers employed by the state's Division of Family Services in St. Louis.

During the first two years of the program twenty-three mothers and three fathers participated. Together they had sixty-five children, averaging 2.57 children per family. The IQs of the mothers ranged from 35 to 69, averaging 50.6. Most parents in similar programs have had higher levels of IQ and have had only "borderline" retardation.[65]

At the beginning of the program, all of the participants were given a battery of tests:

- the Communicative Activities of Daily Living Scale;
- an analysis of parent-child interaction;
- an assessment of the emotional functioning of the parent;
- a sampling of language;
- hearing, dental, and articulation screening tests;
- a physical therapy evaluation;
- an initial HOME test.

The results gave the trainers data for "program planning" and helped them establish the needs of each parent for remedial attention. After the first ten months of the program, the assessments and HOME test were conducted again to measure the parent's progress on predetermined goals. "Progress was described in terms of attainment of goals ('completed' or 'in progress,' with a descriptive explanation of why the objective was not obtained)."[66]

During the first year of the program each parent worked in accordance with an individualized education plan (IEP) drawn up by program staff, which included the program's director, the parent coordinator, a speech and language therapist, a social worker, and personnel from other social service agencies involved with the parent (commonly referred to as the "client"). Each IEP contained goals for parent-child interaction, medical care and personal hygiene, and speech and language development.

In the second year of the program, the staff decided to replace the standard IEP process with a different planning mechanism for directing and assessing parental progress. Instead of presenting a prepared IEP, they negotiated contracts with the parents. They thereby "encountered less resistance and were able to give the clients a greater sense of control over their own formulated objectives. A staff meeting was held in which the terms of the contract were explained to the clients, and their questions were answered before they signed the contract."[67]

Throughout the year, program staff made hour-long biweekly home visits. In addition, the parents and children came to a designated "center" where they received interactive training four days a week. At the center parents were encouraged to work with one another so they could develop a self-help support group. Parents in groups also watched the staff perform parenting skills in modeling exercises, and at times the parents themselves performed modeling exercises in front of the group. Parents also received individualized training with a staff member, watched staff members interact with their children, and practiced the skills being learned with coaching from the staff members.

The teaching units covered the following subject matter: child development and child care, personal and child hygiene, medical care, time concepts, children's basic needs, parent-child interaction, parent-made toys, children's safety, planning of a daily routine, and good nutrition.[68] The teaching methods were creative and numerous:

role-playing, observing, practicing, and discussing—and most important, repetition. In all the teaching, a plan-do-recall strategy was modified for use with adults from the cognitively oriented curriculum for children. The strategy was critical both for the cognitive input and the model it provided; this type of strategy was precisely that which the adults were encouraged to use with their children. In every instance, whatever the task a parent was to be taught, the sequence was clearly thought out and presented. When the activity was complete, the instructor recalled aloud the steps of the activity, with whatever help the mother could give. Most sequences needed to be repeated many times. In these repetitions, the mother gradually took over more of the sequence. Some mothers learned to do tasks that they could never verbalize completely, but the plan-do-recall sequence still helped reinforce learning.[69]

The most common problems faced by this group of parents were difficulties with organizing and sequencing instructions, low self-esteem, inordinate desire to please, inability to read social cues appropriately, untreated medical and dental problems, and learning disability problems that further limited skill use:

Most of the adults in this program had only recently become "independent," often because the birth of a child had rendered them ineligible for other services. Thus most of them had never been taught self-organization or self-maintenance skills. Time schedules and organizing and sequencing of tasks were often new and overwhelming demands. Many required help with developing pictorial organizational aids centered around their most-watched television shows, their favorite radio shows, or some similar theme. For instance, one mother knew that the end of "Bewitched" meant it was time for her and her child to meet the transportation van. Another mother was able to match the position of the hands of her electric clock to know when to give her child medication.[70]

The conclusion of the two physicians and one special education teacher who studied and reported on the results of the program in 1989 confirm that fitness to parent is largely independent of IQ and more dependent on the "emotional involvements and relationship" between parent and child.[71] The authors' recommendation was balanced but unequivocal:

> There . . . may be a point at which the degree of retardation requires such a high level of support that the practicality (in a given case, not on the basis of IQ) of parenting by adults with mental retardation is questionable. But the existence and location of that cutoff point needs to be proven on a case-by-case basis, and not presumed. A doctrine of fairness does not allow such parents to be treated differently from other parents who neglect, abuse, and otherwise mistreat their children. Parents who have difficulties with child rearing should be able to expect from the community certain support services to help compensate for their deficiencies. Such support services must meet the needs of specific populations: typical parenting classes sponsored by [a state's social service agency] are not geared for parents with significant cognitive limitations.[72]

The success rate of this program was high, despite the relatively low level of the participants' IQs. By the end of the program, the parent training staff supported removal of children in only one family's case. That family, the only one deemed "abusive," had three children and, interestingly, was parented by two of the "higher-functioning retarded parents."[73]

The program's success illustrates once again that when problems additional to retardation are removed, parents who have more severe retardation may learn to parent adequately, sometimes more adequately than parents with higher IQ scores do. The study clarifies that the ability of a person with retardation to parent adequately is a function of her ability to engage the child in an emotional relationship; it is not a function of IQ.

A six-year study of a group of parents with retardation in Britain reinforces the importance of emotional factors to the parents' growth as well. In this study, published in 1994, the parents' perceptions were sought and provided. The parents attributed their success to the following "key features of good practice" by their social service providers:

- workers with a genuine liking or feeling for the families concerned, who understood their point of view, [and who] are not seen as interfering and respect them as people;
- practice support that is sustained over the longest term and directed towards teaching, maintaining or reinforcing parents' own skills;
- recognition of the emotional needs of the parents;
- mobilization of community supports, including the extended family;
- close integration of formal services and informal support networks;
- independent advice or advocacy, especially in cases where the worker is unable to represent the interests of both the parents and the child.[74]

What the Studies Teach Us

Viewed together, these studies illustrate the impossibility of drawing generalizable, scientific conclusions about the parenting abilities of persons with retardation. They also show the complexity of responsibly assessing adequate parenting, even in individual cases.

No single factor, such as IQ, has been proven determinative or predictive of actual fitness or unfitness to parent. More generally, there is no proven causal correlation between a person's level of intelligence and her ability to parent adequately.[75] The strongest statistical data found by early studies linking low parental IQ and inadequate parenting existed when the parent's IQ was between 30 and 49,[76] but even mothers with IQs as low as 35 learned to parent adequately, while parents with higher scores ("less serious retardation") could not.[77]

The lack of correlation between IQ and parenting ability was noted as early as 1949:

There is a slow but certain movement away from numerical correlations between feeblemindedness and tuberculosis, feeblemindedness and delinquency, feeblemindedness and vagrancy, feeblemindedness and temper tantrums . . . The mere fact of a coincidence of a low intelligence quotient with an illness, a character trait, or a form of activity is not of itself an indication of single cause-and-effect . . . In my twenty years of psychiatric work with thousands of children and their parents, I have seen percentually [sic] at least as many "intelligent" adults unfit to rear their offspring as I have seen such "feebleminded" adults. I have—and many others have—come to the conclusion that, to a large extent independent of the I.Q., fitness at parenthood is determined by emotional involvements and relationships.[78]

Studies of various training programs presented in this chapter suggest that when parents with retardation have initial deficiencies in caretaking (due, for example, to a history of their own institutionalization or another factor marking the absence of attention and affection in their own childhood), they can be taught to nurture their children and learn to demonstrate their parental love and affection and express it appropriately.[79] Other studies show that if parents with retardation are provided training that is specifically tailored to their learning disabilities, they may demonstrate their ability to learn the mundane but necessary skills of parenthood, such as menu planning, grocery shopping,[80] and the use of behavior management techniques to deal successfully with child tantrums.[81]

Training programs also assist parents in negotiating factors that are independent of intelligence and affect the ability to parent well, such as socioeconomic variables, experiences of racial prejudice, and substance abuse. The willingness of extended family, particularly the grandparents, to assist with parenting and the availability of other helpful support can be significant in overcoming these difficulties.[82]

However, parents with retardation may strongly resist support from either the state or a family member. One study found that their opinions strongly diverged from the views of social workers 85 percent of the time. These cases emphasize the importance of one pedagogical strategy introduced earlier in the chapter: allowing the parent who is under investigation to help create her own appropriate service plans. Even when the subjects are compliant, it is frequently more effective (and more respectful) to invite them into the negotiation:

If an important goal is to assist mothers with developmental disabilities to become self-sufficient and responsible parents and citizens, then service providers should recognize that their clients have the right and capability to participate in the selection and evaluation of service interventions. Successful self-advocacy may be potentially therapeutic in its own right (i.e. enhancing self-esteem). Also, client involvement in the selection of treatment goals and methods may enhance cooperation and program effectiveness . . . Incorporating the parents' views in designing comprehensive interventions that address both the child's and the parent's perceived needs may be more effective than focusing solely on child-rearing practices.[83]

The most recent studies of parenting by persons with retardation conclude that parents are best taught child care skills and home-management skills associated with adequate parenting if they participate in setting their own goals and planning their own training, even in cases where parental IQ is very low.[84]

This literature offers constructive agendas for overcoming the lack of parenting and homemaking skills that parents with retardation and others face.[85] As one study recently pointed out, however, most social service agencies do not yet have personnel trained to provide parents who have retardation with the services or training they need:

Many agencies are recognizing the tremendous gaps in services for these families . . . Social service workers rightly feel that they do not have the training and expertise to work with parents who are mentally retarded, although such families are appearing more frequently on their caseloads. Workers often rely on very popular, but ineffective techniques such as verbal instructions and brief demonstrations . . . Failures do not usually lead to the use of more effective strategies, but rather to removal of the child on the grounds of unchanging parental inadequacy.[86]

Studies pinpoint the need for altering the interventionist role that the family welfare system has traditionally played when parents have retardation:

The traditional response to mentally handicapped parents has been to remove the children at birth or to wait for them to fail and then remove the children. Either way there has been a reluctance to fully address ways in which to equip parents to succeed. Mentally handicapped parents are usually assessed on their current knowledge and skills in parenting rather than their capacity to learn.

This does call into question the "normal" way in which new parents are supposed to learn: through family experience, through antenatal classes, increasingly through books and peer support—all of which may be inaccessible to people with learning disabilities. Many have not had much opportunity to learn in the context of actual family life, i.e. by watching and participating. Many have problems with traditional sources which depend heavily on the written word or (like television, antenatal teaching or talking with experts such as obstetricians) which require instant assimilation of complex ideas. "Thus, the most vulnerable prospective parent has the least access to information."

Appropriate and skilled training has yet to be fully recognized as more humane, more effective and cheaper than taking children into care.[87]

The focus of child welfare is declared to be, and should be, reunification of the family; in the context of parents with retardation, as well as others, the state and its agencies need to adopt the attitude of expecting success. That attitude is especially appropriate in cases where there is no history of actual abuse or neglect.[88]

Expectations of success are likely to be self-fulfilling: they motivate social workers to use the mechanisms of parental training that have the best track record in teaching parents with retardation to parent adequately. For example, a contract negotiation with the parent would require social workers to talk with the parent, and even sometimes to accommodate the parent's viewpoint or otherwise to take the parent seriously. Such negotiations foster self-determination in the parents, which can help them when facing both the challenges of parenthood and the intervention of the state. Specialized training sessions, another teaching mechanism with a high success rate, also require the state to invest resources in a truly instructive program, rather than an unfocused program likely simply to reinforce the preconception that parents with retardation are inadequate. Meaningful instruction, which solicits the parent's views and anticipates engagement on the part of the parent, shows that cooperativeness in specialized training programs and an ability to engage the child emotionally are more important to the success of low-IQ parents than is their IQ number. The studies in this chapter also show that both variables, cooperation and emotional engagement, operate independently of retardation per se.[89]

CHAPTER 15

Written Law concerning Parenting: Important Issues for Parents with Retardation

Despite evidence that many parents with low IQs parent competently, many states still have laws that treat mental retardation as an independent factor to be considered in removal and termination decisions (like the California child protection statute set out in the last chapter). This chapter reviews written law and key current issues. It explores the evolution of the import of mental retardation—from its being a disqualifier to its being "a factor"—and suggests that it should have no relevance at all: The adequacy of parents with mental retardation should be measured in the same way and by use of the same criteria as the adequacy of other parents.[1] In addition to the question of how to view retardation, the most central issue for parents with retardation (and many other parents) is whether unfitness is always prerequisite to interference with parenting or whether instead the child's "best interest" can independently control. A final question this chapter addresses is how unfitness or inadequacy is to be measured and defined—for parents with retardation and other parents.

Historical Perspective: Per se Disqualification

As recently as 1980, an Illinois statute allowed the parental rights of persons "adjudicated mentally retarded" to be terminated in adoption proceedings without their consent and without any judicial determination that they were unfit.[2] This statute disqualified parents with mental retardation by creating an "irrebutable presumption" that they were "unable to make the decision either to retain their parental rights or to consent to termination of their parental rights, or to establish facts in a judicial proceeding tending to show that they were fit parents of their children."[3] Similarly, a contempora-

259

neous New York statutory provision allowed termination of parental rights if the parent had mental retardation and if her "child would be in danger of becoming a neglected child" if the child were in her custody.[4] As it was applied, this statute and others like it often operated to disqualify automatically parents with mental retardation. Little attention was paid at that time to the negative aspects of so interfering with the children's lives. At the time, that approach of considering only the retardation of the parent was not deemed constitutionally objectionable, either from the standpoint of the parents' or from the perspective of the children's rights.[5]

A 1979 New York case, *In re* Audrey C., illustrates the negative impact a "mental retardation" label could have. There the mother was disqualified as a parent because of her retardation. She appealed on the ground that she was not "retarded" within the meaning of New York law, because her condition had not been shown to have originated during the developmental period, which was an element of the state law's definition of mental retardation.[6]

The court should have reasoned that it did not matter whether she met this definition of mental retardation, because with or without retardation parental competence is the standard. But instead the court based its decision on a finding that the "mental retardation" label applied to her. It reasoned that because there was no evidence of a later cause for her retardation, the lower court's finding that it commenced within the developmental period could be accepted.

It is not always so self-evident that a court's use of the label "retarded" is determinative of whether a person can continue as a parent, but another example is the 1972 *McDonald* decision (described in Chapter 1). The Iowa Supreme Court, after a *de novo* review of the facts of the case, found that Diane McDonald, with an IQ of 47, and David McDonald, with an IQ of 74, were unable to give their twin daughters "proper care and attention" and that the best interests of the children required termination of parental rights.[7]

The trial court had found explicitly that "because of this mother's very low IQ she could never adequately take the proper care of these twins or at least provide them with the stimulation in her home that they must have to grow and develop into normal, healthy children."[8] But apart from the IQ numbers, little evidence of unfitness had been presented. A nurse who had seen the parents once and the babies several times testified that the mother was unable to follow instructions and was therefore unable to care for the children. A social worker who had never seen the parents and children together expressed doubts about the mother's ability to cope with the children. A probation officer who had never had any contact with either the parents or the children testified that in her opinion "a person with a low I.Q. did not have the capacity to love and show affection as does a person of normal intelligence." The children's grandmother testified that her daughter-in-law could not do "the things necessary for the children," though she could do "certain things . . . with training," and she had improved considerably.⁹ On the basis of such testimony, all parental rights were terminated.

In affirming this outcome, the Iowa Supreme Court appears also to have based its decision largely on the mother's IQ. One year later in *In re* Wardle, however, the same court, while affirming a termination of Janice Wardle's parental rights, at least said that mental disability alone would not ordinarily determine unfitness.¹⁰ The court was responding to an allegation made in *Wardle* that the state's Department of Social Services had embarked on a program of terminating parent-child relationships solely because of parental IQ score.¹¹

Similarly, in State *ex rel.* Paul, a 1965 case, the appeals court affirmed a decision to deny a mother with retardation custody of her child. The state had taken custody of the child a few days after the child's birth, and the mother moved to reverse that custody decision. The experts in psychology who examined the mother found her to be "either a low-grade moron or a high-grade imbecile." The court concluded that the mother did love her child and would be able to provide him with routine physical care. Nonetheless it denied her custody, saying that her inability to speak for or care for the child in emergency situations made her an unfit parent.

A final example of a case in which a court gave great weight to retardation is *In re* C. M., a 1976 Wyoming Supreme Court decision affirming termination of the parental status of parents with mental disabilities. The court found that the parents' neglect for their child was unintentional, but that the relevant statute authorized termination of parental rights without a finding of intent on the part of the parents. The opinion discussed at length, and in exceedingly vague terms, the "mental inability" of the parents, but it gave few concrete examples of any actual inability to raise their child. The court's lack of specificity on this point is especially interesting in light of its finding that the reports of isolated instances of uncleanliness in the family's home—one of the few concrete examples of actual shortcomings that the opinion mentioned—were not sufficient grounds for termination. The court was also unwilling to order homemaker services for the parents, although those would have cured the only actual deficiency that was cited.

The Unconstitutionality of Disqualifying Parents Because of Unfitness of Their Group

Although the label "retarded" was once sufficient to disqualify parents in Illinois and elsewhere, courts in Illinois and New York were among the first to question the constitutionality of preventing persons with mental retardation from parenting without proof that the particular parent was in fact unfit. Attention to the issue was stimulated by the 1972 U.S. Supreme Court decision in Stanley v. Illinois, which held that it violated Due Process to terminate an unwed father's custody of his children without a hearing on the particular father's fitness. The statute in *Stanley* had been based on the notion that the vast majority of unwed fathers would be unfit; accordingly, it was alleged that the probabilities of unfitness were sufficiently great that the legislature could constitutionally decide to treat them differently from other parents, without giving individualized hearings.

It is that approach, based on group status and on probabilities, that the Supreme Court held unconstitutional. Even if the vast majority of a group is unfit, according to the Court, there must be an individualized hearing concerning the particular parent's fitness before the government deprives any individual of a life experience as significant as raising his child. Similar to the Illinois unwed-father provision, many mental retardation provisions relating to parenting are based on the per se or at least presumptive unfitness of the entire group, and *Stanley* suggests it is constitutionally required to focus instead on the individual's abilities. When mental retardation is eliminated as a separate and explicit factor and the focus centers on parental adequacy, that focus will, of course, preclude some persons with retardation from parenting, but it clearly will not preclude all.

Evolution of the Standard

Illinois' statute concerning parents with mental retardation preceded *Stanley* and was typical of the per se disqualifications of its time. In 1980, however, the Illinois appellate court held the statutory provision unconstitutional. In Helvey v. Rednour the court recognized that persons who have mental retardation sometimes are able to parent and held that the Equal Protection clause required a hearing for them concerning their fitness, because Illinois required such a hearing for other parents before termination of their parental rights.[12]

Similarly, in 1980 in *In re* Gross, New York City's Family Court held it unconstitutional for parental rights to be severed upon a simple showing of mental illness or mental retardation. Bypassing any showing of fault, which was required before other parents could be found neglectful or abusive, both impermissibly punished the parents on the basis of their status and discriminated against them. To disqualify a parent on the simple basis of mental retardation or mental illness violates the Due Process and Equal Protection clauses of the Fourteenth Amendment of the U.S. Constitution, the family court held.

Other New York courts did not agree with *Gross* and upheld the statute despite its failure explicitly to require parental fault when there is mental illness or mental retardation.[13] The approach espoused by *Gross* and other cases seems the better one, and today it is recognized as the one more consistent with the demands of Equal Protection.

Statutes have changed over the last two decades and currently all states make unfitness prerequisite to severance of parental rights—whether or not the parent has retardation.[14] Many state statutes still today explicitly mention mental deficiency or retardation as a legal ground for removal of children from the family and for termination of parental rights "when the deficiency results in parental inadequacy."[15] But mental retardation is not called disqualifying unless it renders the parent permanently unable to care even minimally for the needs of the children.[16] New York's present statute governing severance of parental rights is a typical one: mental retardation remains an explicit and important factor, but it is not independently determinative. Under New York law, termination may be predicated on any of the following grounds: abandonment; inability to provide proper and adequate care for the child due to mental illness or mental retardation; permanent neglect; and severe or repeated child abuse.[17]

The position that unfitness, and not simply retardation, is prerequisite to termination of parental rights is now well settled in the law, and courts explain it with regularity.[18] It represents a significant improvement in the legal position of persons with retardation, removing a barrier between them and the opportunity to parent that others have never had to face. They will no longer be eliminated (or so the law says) just because they have retardation. Instead their abilities will be measured on an individual basis, and no more will be demanded of them than of anyone else.

The change in law is of enormous significance, even though it is insufficient alone to allow persons with retardation to parent. One persisting problem is that even when the same standard—unfitness—is used for all parents, there still exist important differences in how unfitness is assessed. Moreover, other aspects of the requirements for termination—for example, the requirement in many states that termination of parental rights cannot occur without a finding that it is in the best interests of the child—are not always applied to persons with retardation in the same way as they are to others.

Best Interests Inquiries and Determinations

Before parents could be deprived of their children in New York, starting in 1977 state law required, in addition to findings of neglect or abuse, a separate dispositional hearing on whether termination would be in the child's "best interests."[19] But even though the law required a best interests hearing for other parents, it did not set out that requirement for those with retardation or mental illness. In 1980 *Gross* held that this statutory provision too must apply equally to persons with retardation or mental illness.[20]

The courts that disagreed with *Gross* held the New York statute's distinction permissible despite its different treatment of persons with mental illness or retardation. They reasoned that the termination hearing would decide whether the parent's mental retardation or illness deprived her of the ability to parent and that inquiry would involve whether termination would serve the best interests of the child.[21] Accordingly, they reasoned, a separate dispositional hearing on best interests is not required, and the interests of persons with mental retardation or mental illness are adequately served. Besides, the judge retains discretion to hold a separate hearing in order to examine the matter more closely.

Nonetheless when other parents are threatened with termination of parental rights, two separate hearings *are* required, despite the claimed redundancy. If parents with retardation or mental illness were to be treated as others are in New York, a separate, subsequent investigation of whether termination is in the child's best interests would be required for all parents. Nevertheless, the most recent New York cases on the issue have held that it is not necessary to impute to the current statute such a requirement for parents with mental retardation, even though the separate statute governing termination of parental rights for neglect does require a best interests hearing.[22]

New York was not the only jurisdiction to consider whether best interests inquiries need be made and what their relation might be to unfitness requirements. An early federal court decision, Alsager v. District Court, even held that the best interests approach in termination decisions is mandated by the U.S. Constitution. That would require courts always to take account of the costs to the child of removal from the home.

Alsager struck down an Iowa statute as both unconstitutionally vague and unconstitutionally overbroad: the equivalent of a decision that the Constitution prohibited taking the Alsagers' child on the facts as they were developed at trial. The Iowa Supreme Court, affirming termination of the Alsagers' parental rights at an earlier phase in the litigation, had said that the facts of the case were "remarkably similar" to those in *McDonald,* except that the "tragic deficiencies" of the parents in *Alsager* resulted in more harm to their children than the McDonald children had suffered.[23] Yet, as the federal court later noted, "*McDonald* involved a parent with a clinically tested I.Q. of 47 . . . [a fact that] was heavily relied on by the *McDonald* court in concluding that the parent was unable to care for her children. In contrast, the record here reveals no intelligence testing of the Alsagers. Nor is there any evidence which suggests the Alsagers lacked the mental capacity to perform parental functions."[24] Indeed, the federal court stated that even though the Alsagers' level of intelligence was "below average," it was "by no means inadequate intelligence."[25]

Despite that evaluation, the evidence of "parental inadequacy" in *Alsager* was more substantial than in some other cases. The Alsager parents "sometimes permitted their children to leave the home in cold weather without winter clothing on, 'allowed them' to play in traffic, to annoy neighbors, to eat mush for supper, to live in a house containing dirty dishes and laundry, and to sometimes arrive late at school."[26] Nonetheless, the federal court held that "the probative termination standard to which the Alsagers were subjected . . . was simply not high enough to ensure that their fundamental parental rights would not be violated."[27]

Before the state can terminate a parent-child relationship, according to *Alsager,* it "must show that the consequences, in harm to the children, of allowing the parent-child relationship to continue are more severe than the consequences of termination."[28] This is an interesting and very important holding; if followed, it would apply to all states because of its basis in federal constitutional law.[29] But not all state and federal courts believe the best interests inquiry is constitutionally required. A determination of best interests is part of the inquiry in some states—either because the legislature has expressly imposed it or because the judiciary has interpreted state law to provide for it.[30] Other states, however, do not have a separate best interests inquiry and look only to whether the legal parent is unfit.[31]

The best interests finding that *Alsager* required and that some states also require was a supplement to unfitness findings, an extra hurdle that must be crossed by those wanting to terminate the legal parents' rights. But a different debate over the role of best interests has been central to many of the most wrenching family legal battles over the past few decades: Those cases have involved the question whether and when a best interests requirement can trump the unfitness one. Unlike *Alsager* and most cases, which accept that a finding of parental inadequacy must *precede* a finding that terminating parental rights is "in the best interests of the child," the argument in these cases is that best interests alone should be determinative, with or without unfitness.

That issue is central to our theme primarily because judges, given the choice, are likely to believe it better for a child not to live with a parent who has a low IQ. Accordingly, if best interests were independently determinative, that could effectively preclude parenting by many persons who have retardation. Moreover, the issue of terminating parental rights without findings of unfitness, under a best interests formulation, is pivotal to today's family law in many contexts besides retardation.

The drama of Baby Richard is illustrative.[32] Daniella Janikova, the birth mother, gave up the baby for a private adoption four days after birth, telling the biological father, Otakar Kirchner, that the baby had died. It was not until fifty-seven days after the birth, when the biological parents began to reconcile, that Daniella confessed that she had given the baby for adoption to Kim and Robert Warburton. The father hired an attorney and filed objections to the adoption that very day, but the Warburtons resisted, and a long and protracted court battle ensued. The child, never having known any home but the Warburtons', was four and a half years old by the time he was turned over to the biological parents (who by then had married). Much of the adoptive parents' strategy had been to hold on to Baby Richard for as long as possible in order to solidify their claim that staying with them was in the child's best interests.[33]

One reason the battle was so protracted is that trial and appellate courts both held for the Warburtons. First, they held the biological father was unfit, under Illinois law, because he had not shown reasonable interest in the child during the first thirty days of the child's life. That finding of unfitness made his consent unnecessary for adoption. Those courts also stressed that the child's best interests militated against transfer from the only home he had ever had. In June 1994, the Illinois Supreme Court reversed, holding that there was insufficient evidence to support unfitness (because the father had not known of his son's existence until the son was fifty-seven days old) and that without unfitness of the natural parent, there was no occasion to inquire into the baby's best interests. In other words, best interests is a supplemental test, coming into play only after unfitness of the parent(s) has been found, but it cannot alone support removal:

> [T]he appellate court, wholly missing the threshold issue in this case, dwelt on the best interests of the child. Since, however, the father's parental interest was improperly terminated, there was no occasion to reach the factor of the child's best interests. That point should never have been reached and need never have been discussed.
>
> . . . If best interests of the child were a sufficient qualification to determine child custody, anyone with superior income, intelligence, education, etc., might challenge and deprive the parents of their right to their own children.[34]

The Illinois Supreme Court in overturning earlier rulings also noted that the adoptive parents had colluded with the birth mother in deceiving Otakar Kirchner. Both the court and a concurring opinion emphasized that adoptive parents who act properly and follow the rules (attempting in good faith to notify the father and obtain his consent) have nothing to fear from the court's ruling.

Just as the Baby Richard drama captured public attention, so the conflict over Baby Jessica DeBoer, which took place a year earlier and involved many of the same issues and strategies, received extensive media coverage. Baby Jessica had been given up by her mother for adoption to the DeBoers when Jessica was two days old. But nine days later the mother sought Jessica's return. She also challenged the legality of the original surrender because it did not comply with the seventy-two-hour waiting period after birth that Iowa law required, and the birth and transfer took place in Iowa. The Iowa courts accordingly held in favor of the birth mother, but the DeBoers did not accept the outcome. Instead they filed suit in Michigan, where they lived, to stop execution of the Iowa order. Eventually the Michigan Supreme

Court ruled that no best interests hearing was necessary or appropriate, and Jessica was returned to her birth mother.[35]

In both of these cases, interestingly, public sentiment was overwhelmingly on the side of the would-be adoptive parents—the side that lost and whose position was contrary to long-established (and occasionally ignored) law.[36] The public thought it most reasonable to look to the child's best interests in the particular case and award custody accordingly; and it presumed best interests would lie with remaining in the current, perfectly satisfactory home. Yet if this publicly favored position were to become law, fraud would be rewarded; moreover it would make prolonging a custody battle an important strategy for parents who want to adopt; even if they learned at the outset that the adoptive placement was illegal, they would want to hold on to the child for a long time in order to build a relationship that would support custody.[37]

Public notoriety for these cases may be new, but the problem is many decades old. In Scarpetta v. Spence-Chapin Adoption Service, a New York court permitted the birth mother to withdraw her consent to adoption twenty-three days after she gave her consent and only five days after the agency had placed the child with the DiMartino family for adoption. When the court so ruled, however, the agency did not even inform the DiMartino family of the problem but instead left the baby with them for five more months before telling them that there was litigation. The birth mother's change of heart had come about when she learned that her family, who were "well to do, and devout in their religion" would be willing to help her with the baby; the judge (who under New York law had discretion whether to allow a woman to withdraw her consent to adoption before the adoption was final) ruled in her favor because he was impressed by her, and also because he presumed that it is best for a child to be with her birth mother unless the mother is unfit.

Although she won in court in New York, Scarpetta never in fact regained custody of Baby Lenore. The DiMartinos moved to Florida to avoid the decree (a strategy that would be less likely to succeed today than in 1971).[38] The Florida courts, where they instituted an action, awarded the DiMartinos custody, partly on the ground that it would cause Baby Lenore, then thirteen months old, emotional trauma to be separated from the only home she had ever known. The matter was finally resolved by the U.S. Supreme Court's refusal to review the judgment of the Florida court.[39]

Nor is the issue limited to the context of adoption. In 1966 in Painter v.

Bannister the Supreme Court of Iowa awarded custody of a seven-year-old boy to the maternal grandparents, who lived on a farm in Iowa, rather than to his father, a Californian who had an unconventional lifestyle. The father had sent his son, Mark, to stay with the grandparents after his wife and daughter were killed in an automobile accident; sixteen months later, when the father remarried and asked for his son's return, the grandparents refused. Conventional law would have allowed the father to prevail unless unfit, but the Iowa Supreme Court concluded that "Mark's better interests will be served" by remaining with his grandparents.[40]

The Iowa Supreme Court in *Painter*, like the lower courts years later in *Kirchner*, was probably wrong not to honor the biological father's superior right to custody of his child, but those courts are not alone in setting the court's view of the child's best interests above parental rights. Most of the cases that do take this tack, like *Painter*, involve parents who have voluntarily given up living with their children, at least on a temporary basis.[41]

In the Baby Richard case, the Warburtons tried to take advantage of a presumption against parents who do not live with their children, but that presumption could not help them because Kirchner had not given up custody voluntarily. The concurring opinion explained some necessary limitations on any rule that living apart from one's child will result in loss of legal custody:

> The appellate court sua sponte created an irrebuttable, per se presumption that, once a newborn child has lived with adoptive parents for at least 18 months, the child's living arrangements cannot be modified. However, the statutory provisions cited . . . pertain to prompt judicial disposition and review where foster care has been requested or ordered because of child abuse, neglect, or dependency . . . The statutes do not require, or suggest, that a newborn child's living environment cannot be modified if the child has lived with adoptive parents for a year and a half.[42]

Similarly Justice Stevens, denying the DeBoers' petition to the U.S. Supreme Court to stay the decision of the Michigan Supreme Court, said:

> Applicants' claim that Jessica's best interests will be served by allowing them to retain custody of her rests, in part, on the relationship that they have been able to develop with the child after it became clear that they were not entitled to adopt her. Neither Iowa law, Michigan law . . . nor federal law authorizes unrelated persons to retain custody of a child whose

natural parents have not been found unfit simply because they may be better able to provide for her future and her education . . . [C]ourts are not free to take children from parents simply by deciding another home appears more advantageous.[43]

It is important to remember that even when parental rights thus prevail, parents can exercise their rights by opting for continuity of care and for their child's welfare. One reminder occurred in the summer of 1998 when it was discovered that two girls had been switched as newborns three years earlier. Paula K. Johnson opted both to keep custody of Callie, the child she had raised as her own, and to allow her biological child, Rebecca, whom she had never met, to stay, for the time being at least, with the grandparents the girl knew. Oddly, the parents who had raised Rebecca had died in an automobile accident the day after the baby-switching became known.[44] Therefore if Ms. Johnson had litigated for her "rights," she might have been able to obtain both children.

Whether a best interests evaluation can alone be determinative, without regard to the unfitness requirement—and, if so, how broadly and when—is thus an issue central to parents' rights litigation generally, and not just to cases involving mental retardation; it has been a significant dilemma in family law for many years. Some cases do allow removal of children without parental unfitness; but they are exceptions to a general rule that unfitness is required for removal or termination of parental rights. Despite the apparent appeal of the best interests approach, it creates problems of its own. For example, the Nebraska Supreme Court held in 1980 that its statute allowing termination of parents' rights on the basis of "the best interests and welfare of the children," without standards specifying the disqualifying parental conduct, was unconstitutionally vague.[45] Not all states have agreed.[46]

Many courts hold that unfitness is invariably a prerequisite to removal and termination, and that is the more traditional view. The exception that is evolving in others is limited to parents voluntarily or legally separated from their children,[47] and that is an important limitation. Moreover, the exceptions for children who have bonded with longtime caretakers who are not their parents are only occasional. The general rule remains that, where a finding that terminating parental rights is in the best interests of the child is required at all, it supplements but does not displace the unfitness requirement.[48] As the Connecticut court said in *In re* Anthony D., "the determination of the child's best interests comes into play only after [a] statutory [ground] for termination of parental rights . . . [has] been established by clear and convincing evidence."[49] The trial court had erred by basing its decision solely on which living situation would be best for the children; it had not determined that the parent, who had retardation, was inadequate under the same rules that apply to everyone else.

Nonetheless statutory language in several jurisdictions calls the best interests consideration a "paramount" or "primary" consideration, and thereby lends support to arguments that the child's best interests can be sufficient to dispense with the necessity of a parent's consent to adoption. Even in Massachusetts, where case law and some other statutory provisions reveal that unfitness is clearly required, one relevant statute provides that the "best interests and welfare of the person to be adopted shall be of paramount consideration in the construction and interpretation of [the adoption] act."[50] In addition, the very existence of a best interests inquiry on occasion leads to confusion, suggesting to courts, and even more to psychologists and social workers, that the child's interests alone can govern the inquiry without regard to the adequacy of the birth parent. Because of considerable confusion concerning when unfitness as well as the best interests requirement is necessary, courts do sometimes terminate the parental rights of persons if it appears to them that the child would be "better off" with foster caretakers—or with other parents, assuming such parents can be found.[51] Such determinations seem particularly common concerning parents who have retardation.

Evaluating Divergent Approaches to Retardation

All states today (because of statutory requirements or judicial decisions) might be described as having the same law: Mental retardation is a factor in decisions concerning parenting, but not a conclusive one. The unanimity is, however, more apparent than real; approaches vary considerably. Mental retardation can weigh heavily against a parent or can be merely one factor to be weighed in the balance. Statutes may make the choice clear, but often they do not. Courts rarely discuss which approach they are following, but in some cases mental retardation seems to count very heavily against parental rights and in others it seems a less consequential factor.[52] Some state statutes mention mental retardation as a factor, together with incompetence to parent, while others do not mention retardation at all.

A review of the cases reveals one result of injecting a parent's mental retardation into the calculus: mental retardation may result in application of *higher* standards of parenting than are applied to other parents. When the parents have retardation, the state often makes it more difficult for them to succeed, both demanding more of them than is necessary and presuming that they are incapable.

In Illinois, for example, in *In re* Enis, the rights of parents were not terminated although their minor's thighs, buttocks, and genital area had been burned; and in *In re* A. C. B. an appeals court reversed an order terminating the parental rights of a mother who had allowed young children to engage in sexual behavior with one another. Neither of those cases involved parents with mental retardation. But in Ensign v. Illinois the rights of parents who had mental retardation were terminated after the father once accidentally dropped the child, without resultant injury. The father had immediately taken the child to the hospital and, in so doing, aroused the suspicion of the state, ultimately resulting in the loss of his parenthood.

The New York Court of Appeals, in *In re* Joyce T., affirmed the family court's termination of the rights of two parents who had mental retardation "in the range of mild to mild-severe"[53] (a highly ambiguous designation). Joyce and her brother Christopher were removed from their parents' home at the ages of six weeks and four years, respectively, pursuant to a finding of neglect. The court said the basis of the neglect was "not [the parents'] retardation but their 'maladaptive behavior.'"[54] The family court, as quoted by the court of appeals, discussed the parents' inadequacy as follows:

> While [keeping the floor clean] may be taught and [appellants] actually performed said tasks of removal of dangerous objects from the floor, once left alone [appellants] will permit the condition to exist. Indeed, [appellants] have no ability to plan if any change occurs even if it is expected, by virtue of the fact that independent judgment is lacking and in some instances does not exist. Because of the lack of such concrete response, [appellants] are unable to meet their children's nutritional, physical and educational needs, which is directly related to their developmental disabilities.[55]

The court's own ideas about the inadequacies of persons who have retardation, not any evidence about the particular parties, dominated the inquiry. The finding of inadequacies also seems largely based on prediction, unsubstantiated by particular facts. The family court acknowledged that "full-time support services would assist appellants in parenting their children," but "it rejected this alternative because, given [their] inability, the auxiliary homemakers would become the surrogate parents."[56]

The same disparity between the treatment of persons with mental retardation and the treatment of others can be found in other New York cases. In *In re* Jamie M. the court refused to find permanent neglect by parents of normal intelligence whose child had serious physical afflictions that required "significant" care, which the parents could not provide as effectively as could the child's foster parents.[57] In refusing to terminate parental rights, the court emphasized that the agency had not "made diligent efforts to aid [the parents] in remedying the very conditions"[58] on which the agency relied in bringing the neglect petition. Sensibly, the court required assistance to well-meaning parents before terminating their parental rights because of an inability to cope. But would the result have been the same if the parents had acted the same way and also had mental retardation?

Courts and agencies do not consistently follow this approach of requiring assistance for parents. Both courts and child care agencies have statutory duties to exercise diligent efforts to strengthen the parent-child relationship and to reunite the family if it has been separated.[59] Those purported mandates apply in proceedings concerning parents with mental retardation as well as others. Yet in *In re* Tonya Louise the court affirmed the family court's termination of the parental rights of a mother with retardation notwithstanding the report submitted by the law guardian who urged "a contrary result because 'with supportive services' respondent may be able to care for her children."[60] The reviewing court endorsed the family court's finding that "if the children were to be returned to [the mother] they would be in imminent danger of becoming neglected children."[61] The family court also observed that "the supervision which would enable respondent properly to care for her children would entail a 24 hour-a-day monitor. This the law does not require. We note that while the Law Guardian was assigned to participate in this proceeding to protect the interests of the children, his report is silent as to where the best interests of the children lie."[62]

It is difficult, of course, to prove discrimination against persons with mental retardation by comparing the outcomes of cases, since there are always differing facts, and it is never certain what role the mental retardation played in the outcome. Moreover, in cases of termination, a parent's mental retardation is frequently accompanied by another problem, such as mental illness or homelessness.[63] Nonetheless, any broad selection of opinions suggests that judges are peculiarly unacquainted with and unsympathetic to the problems of persons with mental retardation and are particularly fearful of allowing them to parent. A 1978 study reported that of homosexual, incarcerated, mentally ill, and mentally retarded parents, "the mentally retarded seem to be held by the Courts in the lowest esteem."[64] An important objective of the disability rights movement is to change that attitude—on the part of the judiciary and on the part of society in general—but it is an objective that has yet to be accomplished.

Toward an Appropriate Legal Standard, Applicable to All Parents

Removing All References to Mental Retardation

Changes in the law cannot always change practices, especially those based on deeply ingrained beliefs. Nonetheless some legal reforms are a necessary first step. For example, revision of current statutes concerning unfitness is long overdue, removing references to mental retardation as a factor or any reference to mental retardation at all.

Parents with retardation should not of course be immune from state procedures designed to protect children. But incompetence should have to be shown, rather than presumed—conclusively or otherwise—on the basis of retardation. If a statute requires a year for an abandonment charge to be successfully leveled against a parent, a parent who has retardation should not be held to have abandoned in a shorter period of time. If a parent with retardation beats her children, or does not feed them, she should be subject to the same rules as others who act the same way, but she should not be subject to harsher rules.

It is difficult to see why mental retardation or deficiency or whatever other term is used should be an explicit factor in parenting statutes at all. Modern statutes that purport to eliminate persons from parenting "if the mental retardation results in an inability to parent" are either redundant or discriminatory. An inability to parent should result in disqualification from parenting whether it stems from retardation or not, at least if the inability cannot be remedied by less drastic means. That should be the standard for all people; there is no need to mention retardation in the law. By listing inability resulting from retardation as a separate and special factor, the statutes may suggest singling out parents with retardation for scrutiny and for parental testing. They also may suggest that persons with retardation are likely to be incapable of parenting and thus facilitate courts' ordering removal or termination with only cursory findings.[65]

In short, statutes that seem to presume against persons with retardation as parents, or that make mental retardation in its own right an independent factor in the unfitness decision, cause confusion or worse and should be removed from the books. Of course mental retardation has some relation to fitness, but what effect it has in any particular case is revealed by a study of the usual criteria of fitness applied to everyone else.

Measuring Parental Fitness

Three of the factors often considered when courts evaluate parental fitness—of individuals with mental retardation and others—are the parent's ability to give love and affection to a child; to perform housekeeping tasks; and to attend to the child's physical needs.[66]

If a parent meets these (or other valid and generally applied) criteria for parenting, despite any mental retardation, she should be considered a fit parent. Mental retardation may have made it more difficult for her to achieve what she has, but that does not and should not weigh against her parental fitness. And if a parent cannot meet the criteria, whether she has mental retardation or not, she is not a fit parent.

It is helpful and important to decide on the proper standard for judging the fitness of parents with mental retardation even though the decision is simply that the standard should be the same one that applies to everyone else. Applying the same standard does not necessarily end discrimination, however, especially if discrimination exists in the standard itself.

Requirements that Parents Be Intellectually Stimulating

As well as the three criteria set out above, a fourth factor is often listed as requisite to parental fitness: a requirement that the parent have the ability to stimulate the children intellectually. Applying that part of the standard evenhandedly to persons with retardation will not eliminate discrimination. Though neutral on its face, in fact that criterion targets parents who have mental retardation.[67]

Although one recent study suggests a correlation between low levels of intellectual stimulation of children who live in poverty and their development of mental retardation,[68] any parental shortcomings in this area, once identified, can be remedied by placing children in early intervention programs. The state can thereby compensate for problems of understimulation.

After age five, children are in school, and special programs exist for children in need of stimulation or other intellectual help in the preschool years. It would not be difficult to extend such programs, which in any event are available to babies and toddlers with learning problems, to children of parents who have retardation. The current requirement is equivalent to a presumption against mental retardation itself, weighing something extra in the balance against persons with mental retardation. To impose a criterion of intellectual stimulation, especially for people with mental retardation, is peculiar; such a requirement obviously targets their deficiency.

Imposing that requirement for them is equivalent to requiring a parent in a wheelchair, but not others, to play sports with his children (even though their need for sports could be satisfied elsewhere). A trial court did just that in *In re* Marriage of Carney, which transferred custody of two boys, ages six and eight, from a father who had raised them and had become quadriplegic, to his ex-wife, who had not seen the boys in almost five years. The California Supreme Court reversed, however, saying that the trial judge focused unduly on Mr. Carney's physical limitations and his inability to bathe, dress, or cook for himself, instead of evaluating the household in which the children lived and giving weight to the "nice, loving relationship" the judge found existed between father and sons. The trial judge had expressly said he did not think any relationship between Mr. Carney and his children could be "normal" and that therefore the preferable parent was the one who had chosen to ignore the children for almost five years before asking for custody. Both *Carney* and the intellectual stimulation requirement show that facially neutral standards (like the ability to play sports or to stimulate intellectually) can be inherently discriminatory.

It is also discriminatory for any requirement of intellectual stimulation to apply principally to those parents who have retardation. Clearly if intellectual stimulation is still to be retained as a requirement for parenting, it should be imposed on everyone else as well. If the intellectual stimulation requirement were applied to all groups, and not just to those with known intellectual deficiencies, many households with parents who do not have retardation would not qualify. In some households where the parents are intellectually capable, stimulation of their children is nonetheless ignored, and the children are left to the care of the television.

If the state were truly serious about an intellectual stimulation requirement, presumably it would apply that requirement first to persons without intellectual deficiencies of their own, because those parents have a much greater chance of altering their behavior to satisfy the state's concern than do persons with retardation.[69] Instead, the requirement is mentioned almost exclusively in cases involving parental mental disability. The fact that a state does not apply the requirement across the board suggests that it does not take the requirement seriously and that the main function of the requirement is to create a barrier for parents who have mental disabilities.

Intellectual stimulation by the parents may be desirable, but it does not seem a necessity for parental fitness. Indeed, overstimulation is probably as much of a problem as understimulation in our society, and that is a problem that may be more difficult for the state to rectify. If the state is to start making judgments about proper amounts of stimulation within families for children, it is taking on a large and an intrusive task.

The intellectual stimulation factor unjustifiably discriminates against parents with mental retardation and should be eliminated. But whether one judges parenting by four factors or three, there will be some parents who will be able to parent successfully despite retardation and some who will not. Various factors besides intelligence will contribute to the success or failure of parents with mental retardation—most important, perhaps, whether there is emotional stability, financial stability, and the availability of a satisfactory living situation for a parent and child.

Appropriate Role for Best Interests Requirements

The best interests inquiry should supplement the unfitness inquiry, as it does already in many states. It is certainly conceivable that it will be in the best interests of a child to stay with his or her parent(s) even if the parents are unfit in some sense. One possibility may be that the unfitness can be corrected, with education or assistance, so that the child can receive adequate care without having to lose his family, whom he may dearly love. The attractiveness of this alternative has made it requisite to a termination of rights, at least on paper, that there first be an attempt to provide for the child's remaining in the home, if that is at all feasible.[70] Such a requirement should be retained and taken more seriously than it currently is, for parents with retardation as well as others. And even if unfitness is not correctable, it may sometimes be preferable for the child to live with the problem rather than to experience the losses that would occur from separation from the family.[71]

Of course that result would not be the correct one in every case and certainly not in cases of repeated abuse at the hands of a parent. But the advantage of having a best interests test, to weigh in after the parent has been found unfit but not before, is to take into account the disruption of the child's life and the insecurity and grief that the child might feel from the loss of the parent(s). Those negative factors must be weighed in the balance, as well as inadequacies in care, before the child is left without a family or even temporarily removed from the home. It also is of relevance that many of the children taken from their families because of parental unfitness become permanent wards of the state. There greater harms sometimes befall them than any harms likely from their parents' inadequacies.[72]

Strict unfitness should remain prerequisite to forcible removal of children or termination of parents' rights. Best interests inquiries should be required to supplement unfitness findings but should not be allowed to substitute for them. There are cases, however, where courts are sometimes tempted to rely solely on best interests, especially in order to continue a placement in which the child has bonded. When parent and child have lived apart for a long time, especially when the likelihood of the parent ever becoming able to take custody again is minimal, it may not make sense to allow the absent parents to prevent a permanent placement for the child. (But it also does not make sense to cut off the parents when no permanent home is available.)

Perhaps the best way to design an exception to strict unfitness rules for parents who do not live with their children is for a state legislature to provide that after a certain amount of time (six months? two years?) the parent separated from the child will lose the strong presumption that the unfitness standard creates; parents after that time may lose all parental rights if, because of an available permanent placement, that course is in the child's best interests.

Any such legal presumption is better designed by a legislature than a court, partly because a clear time limit must be chosen, and partly because a statute could give maximum warning to the parents and support predictable and even-handed application. Some family law scholars have long advocated that approach, and statutes in several states have adopted it.[73]

In sum, a model neglect and abuse statute would eliminate all reference to mental retardation; eliminate the ability to stimulate intellectually as a prerequisite for parenting; and require a best interests hearing after parents were found unfit. It would not allow best interests to be sufficient for termination, absent a finding of unfitness.

CHAPTER 16

The Social Welfare System in Practice

The social welfare system's intervention in the family occurs in many forms, from provision of a range of remedial family services to the temporary or even permanent removal of children from the home. Systems differ from state to state, so no generalized summary can accurately reflect any particular social service system in every detail. The following (based largely on Massachusetts) describes a typical system.

The Process for Parents in General

Typically a state has at least one social welfare department (or agency) that is responsible for protecting children from abuse and neglect at the hands of their parents. This agency also provides families with support services. Names differ, but in many states, the state agency is called the Department of Family Services or the Department of Social Services.[1]

When the Department is alerted to a case of possible abuse or neglect, it assigns a social worker to investigate the claim. The social worker has a great deal of discretion in determining what conditions constitute abuse or neglect. Often the rules allow the social worker to consider in addition whether it is in a child's best interests to be removed from the home. Discretion also governs the form that the services will take if the Department decides to expend its usually modest resources to provide the family with needed remedial services at all.

Regulations usually require at least one visit to the home, whether by the social worker who initially screens a suspected family or by another worker or team sent out to confirm initial findings. Like screeners, the home investigators can base their ultimate recommendations on any rationale.

If the investigation substantiates serious parental deficiencies, the Department typically prepares a service plan for the offending family.[2] States typically require the Department to provide supportive services to the family or to refer the family to other service providers, if the Department (or its social workers) is convinced that a family requires parenting assistance. The service plan often takes the form of an agreement between the parents and the state. It sets goals for the parents to accomplish by a certain deadline, with the aim of remedying parenting deficiencies that the social worker has identified. If the parents do not meet the goals and improve their parenting, they well may face more intrusive state action.

States typically have two different types of service agreements, voluntary and involuntary. The distinction is an important one, because voluntary agreements can be dissolved at any time by the parents who are party to them, whereas involuntary service plans remain compulsory. Involuntary agreements are imposed when the relevant state agency receives reports of suspected abuse or neglect and has substantiated them through its investigations. But the existence of voluntary agreements is still relevant in the neglect and abuse process; a parent may, for example, consent to a "voluntary" agreement because she fears that otherwise a compulsory one will be imposed on her.

Removal

Voluntary agreements removing a child from the home and even placing custody with the state agency are also common. They are typically entered when a parent places a child for adoption or in foster care, and also when a parent seeks less drastic forms of help like respite care, daycare, homemaker services, or counseling. A parent may, of course, be coerced into seeking help by life circumstances. She may, for example, initiate an agreement with the Department to place her child in foster care because she has to go into the hospital or go out of town temporarily and has nowhere else to turn; but such a parent-initiated process is still considered voluntary.

Removal is often involuntary, however, and results from state-instituted proceedings seeking temporary custody of a child. They are generally commenced when parents fail to agree to compulsory service plans; when they do not succeed in overcoming their parental problems as the service agreement requires; or when family circumstances immediately endanger the child's welfare. Under any of these circumstances, the Department may file a child protection petition and thereby trigger judicial scrutiny of parental behavior. Such scrutiny can result in transfer of the child's legal or physical custody, or both, to the Department. Except in emergency situations, a child cannot be transferred until the process of judicial review is complete (thereby avoiding the necessity of the child being moved back and forth as the judicial process unwinds).

In an emergency—for example, when a child is being subjected to physical or sexual abuse and cannot be protected within the home—the Department can remove the child prior to judicial review and without first instituting a service plan, but it must then seek judicial review immediately (within twenty-four hours in Massachusetts) and prepare a plan shortly thereafter. Sometimes the emergency exception creates too great a loophole, allowing the government to remove a child prior to judicial hearing simply by petitioning for an emergency removal (whether or not a true emergency exists). And although regulations require prompt judicial hearings after the fact, court review can be delayed if there is no one to object to the emergency removal.

Most states have designated a particular court to hear removal petitions. A family court is common, but a juvenile or even a probate court is a possibility. The court with jurisdiction conducts a proceeding to determine the temporary custody of the child. Parental evaluation procedures, often at a court clinic where parents will be interviewed by one or more psychologists or other experts, are part of the process the court employs to aid its decision. The court's determination of custody is technically independent of the Department's recommendations, but many judges are heavily influenced by the Department and the findings of its social workers.

There are fewer procedural protections at this stage than at termination proceedings, which may follow some time later. At termination, "clear and convincing evidence" is required, but that elevated standard of proof does not commonly apply to removal. Similarly, judicial review is less rigorous than in termination or indeed most judicial proceedings. The parents can obtain review of the decision to remove from custody, even though that decision is considered temporary (as compared with termination decisions, which are permanent). But judicial review of removal is often performed by the same court that made the initial ruling, and possibly even the same judge. Termination decisions, by contrast—and most judicial decisions, at least if "permanent" or "final"—are subject to appeal to a different, usually superior, court.

After the decision is made concerning removal, all parties return to court for a hearing at which the Department presents a service plan. The Department's role is to help parents care for their children as long as possible. A preferable alternative to removal, according to state and federal regulations, is to provide a full range of preventive and supportive services that will enable the children to remain in the home. Even if removal is necessary, the Department tries to arrange frequent visits in order to strengthen the parent-child relationships. Only under "extraordinary circumstances" should the Department place a child in long-term foster or community care.

The promise of these regulations is not always kept in practice. Agencies are told to provide a full range of preventive services to keep families together, but they lack sufficient funds for many kinds of supportive services. In reality, removal often appears the only available alternative.

A similar dichotomy between theory and practice permeates the issue of parental rights during the removal period. Parents are not, at this stage, expected to give up their status as parents, even though they are denied custody. As a matter of law, they retain some parental rights and responsibilities. The theory is that if the parents conform to the service plan and the home situation improves, they will be able to keep their children. Or they will be able to recover custody of their children, even if the children have been initially removed. In practice, however, it is difficult to regain custody once it has been taken away, and parents remain at the mercy of discretionary judgments of judges and social workers. Many parents find that removal of their children is effectively the end of their parenthood, even though they remain parents as a matter of law.

During the removal period, regulations mandate active state assistance in helping the parents prepare to retain custody and active assistance in arranging frequent visitation in order to strengthen the parent-child bond.[3] But these legal obligations are frequently not met. A severe shortage of funds allocated to social welfare programs means that only a fraction of the need can actually be met.

The failure of the system to provide actual services can be disastrous for parents who wish to keep their children. Many legal decisions hold that the agency's failure to provide services—such as parental training or even a service plan—does not excuse a parent's failure to learn how to parent adequately (although others reach the opposite conclusion).[4] And the failure of social workers to facilitate visitation with children in the temporary custody of the state[5] does not always excuse a parent who does not visit from failing to maintain familial bonds.

Termination

Parental inabilities to attain the objectives of the removal plan become highly relevant when the Department petitions for final severance of parental rights. Termination of parental rights is the final and most drastic form of state intervention in the family. After termination, the (former) parents have no authority over the child. In particular, the parents' consent is no longer necessary in order to place a child for adoption.

Termination proceedings are supposed to occur only after the Department has made all possible efforts to resolve the home problems, including provision of a full range of preventive services. In some states there is also a time requirement; in Massachusetts, for example, termination is not possible until the state has had custody of the child for at least one year. The evident purpose is to have a long enough temporary custody period to allow assistance to the parents to work, or otherwise to allow the parents to mend their ways.[6]

The primary U.S. Supreme Court decision concerning severance of parental rights is Santosky v. Kramer. That 1982 case held that "clear and convincing" evidence is required, rather than a mere preponderance of the evidence, for the state to prevail at termination hearings. The meaning (and importance) of the decision is ambiguous, however, because the Court did not say clear and convincing evidence *of what.* If the import is that states must now provide clear and convincing evidence of any standard they choose (subject to constitutional attack), then the holding, while affecting the burden of proof in a significant way, is of limited importance. But if the opinion means that there must be clear and convincing evidence of parental unfitness, so that those cases placing best interests above unfitness requirements are unconstitutional, it is of enormous potential significance. It would cut off any growing trend, like that explored in the last chapter, to focus on the better placement for the child and to substitute that inquiry for a strict requirement of parental unfitness. Which interpretation of *Santosky* will ultimately carry the day remains unclear.

Although the Court in *Santosky* did craft a constitutional rule for termination hearings, at least concerning the degree of proof required, in other ways termination proceedings have not been subjected to strict application of constitutional norms. For example, the U.S. Constitution does not require that indigent parents receive legal representation in trials to terminate their parental rights, according to the U.S. Supreme Court. Nonetheless the Court has said that, in their discretion, judges should appoint such counsel when necessary to assure a fair adjudication in complex cases.[7]

Yet the Supreme Court has recognized the severity of terminating parental rights. In M.L.B. v. S.L.J., it likened termination proceedings to criminal trials, such as probation revocation hearings, which can seriously limit an individual's freedom but which cannot result in incarceration: "[The parent] must defend against the state's destruction of her family bonds, and also resist the brand associated with a parental unfitness adjudication. Like the defendant resisting criminal conviction, she seeks to be spared from the State's devastatingly adverse action."[8] Accordingly, the Court views termination proceedings as somewhere between criminal cases (where counsel for indigents is required and the standard of proof is "beyond a reasonable doubt") and regular civil cases (in which no constitutional right to counsel exists and a party can prevail by a "mere preponderance" of the evidence). Some states, however, allow more procedural protections than are required by the U.S. Supreme Court—at termination, or even at removal, or both.[9]

Basing Determinations on Predictions of Parenting Ability

It is not absolutely necessary that courts give parents an opportunity to parent before terminating parental rights, regardless of the particular circumstances. Most courts have held that the infant need not be subject to actual deprivation and that a parent's unfitness can be predicted from past history. For example, a parent who has abused two children in the past may have a third removed without waiting for abuse to occur. Even a drug-addicted mother who has never had or harmed a child may lose a newborn who starts life with drugs in its system. The theory is that the mother has harmed the fetus and that her conduct demonstrates indifference to the needs of the child. Even though both these examples have predictive qualities, they also rely on past acts of the parents to determine present unfitness.

It is much rarer to find cases in which parenthood is terminated in the total absence of parental fault and when the parent-to-be has not yet had any chance to parent at all. But there are a few cases in which a wholly predictive or speculative judgment has been considered sufficient to terminate parenthood, relying not on past acts of the parent but instead on some characteristic of the parent—for example, age, homelessness, mental illness, or, most frequently, mental retardation.[10]

In *In re* Custody of a Minor the highest court in Massachusetts held that a court can remove a child on a preventive rather than a remedial basis, as long as the court exercises the utmost care, through specific and particularized findings of fact that explain the justification for the court's decision to remove the child. In that case the lower court had removed a newborn from the twenty-nine-year-old single mother on the grounds that the mother had a history of mental disorders and would be unable to care for the child. The Supreme Judicial Court, remanding for further findings, explained that removal need not be based on current custody and a history of parental neglect or mistreatment; it simply must be based on a finding of current parental unfitness.

In contexts other than mental illness or handicap, such purely predictive removals are very rare. They are not, however, unheard of. Predictive removal was approved in *In re* East, which involved a teenager without a home to which to take her baby. In *East* the mother was sixteen and the court described her as an incorrigible child with no home or means of support. Accordingly, it terminated her rights to her two-day-old infant, although the mother stated that she was willing to provide for her child. The court said that the mother's unfitness to care for a dependent child could be predicted from the mother's past history.

Even though that court was willing to remove a newborn at birth based on apparent unfitness, other courts have disagreed, stressing that women can and often do change under the influence of parenthood. The court in *In re* May refused to terminate the mother's parental rights to her newborn. Similar to *East*, *May* involved a young teenager with a history of running away from home who gave birth to a child whom the state tried to remove. The court, however, allowed the teenager to keep her infant, determining that the mother had never exhibited any cruelty, abuse, or neglect toward the child and that she had a reasonable chance of developing into a good mother with aid from the state.

The *May* court also emphasized that the teenager would be able to provide a home for the child, with the help of the child's grandmother. In comparing *East* with *May*, one central factor is the attitude of the particular judge toward motherhood for teenagers. Another key factor determining whether a mother will be allowed to keep her child may be her ability to provide a home.[11]

The Permanence of Predicted Unfitness

If unfitness is predicted from the existence of mental retardation, it is likely to be permanent because mental retardation is permanent. *In re* Fulton demonstrates that proposition and shows that predictively unfit parents who have other children can automatically lose those children as well. Moreover, their losses result less from their actions, over which they might have some control, than from their status as persons who have mental retardation.

Fulton reflects the all too prevalent attitude that when a parent has mental retardation it is unnecessary for social service agencies to work on family reunification. The government agency had already placed the couple's first child in an adoptive family when the couple gave birth to their daughter Kim. Two days after her birth, the state placed Kim Fulton in the same family that had adopted her older brother, because that family wanted to adopt her as well. Five months later, the state moved to terminate the parental rights of Mr. and Mrs. Fulton, who both had mental retardation.

The parents fought termination on the grounds that the state had failed to fulfill its statutory duty to provide them with reunification services. But the court rejected this plea. It found

> that neither parent was able to provide adequate care and nurturing for [their daughter] presently, nor in the future [that t]his inability was the result of mental retardation and personality disorders suffered by [the parents] . . . [and] that [the state's children's services agency] had made reasonable efforts to prevent continued removal . . . but that [Mr. and Mrs. Fulton's] refusal to keep [the agency] apprised of their whereabouts prevented that agency from providing the necessary services.[12]

The appeals court then affirmed the trial court's termination of parental rights, finding "that there was some competent, credible evidence supporting the adjudication of dependency." The parents' "mental disabilities," said the court, "hampered or eliminated any opportunity to learn to properly care for" their daughter. It also declared that, contrary to the Fultons' claim that the state must provide them with parenting services, "the law does not require the court to experiment with the child's welfare to see if he will suffer great detriment or harm in the future."[13]

Reunification with her parents seemed an "experiment" to the court because of the conclusion of a psychologist who had tested the couple when Kim was born. The psychologist concluded that "the provision of additional counseling or support services would probably be futile . . . based in part upon each parent's inability to perform 'conceptual abstract reasoning,' a deficiency which she testified is not subject to change over time."[14] The court's opinion cited no actual skills-based deficiencies but only deficiencies, like low IQ scores, that show up in psychological testing.

Despite the declared law in Ohio, Mr. and Mrs. Fulton were in fact prevented from parenting because of the court's views about mental retardation. Instead of allowing them to be parents, their pregnancies provided children for a would-be adoptive couple, with the state's participation and approval.

Applying the Procedures to Parents Who Have Retardation

Even in systems where parents who have retardation are in theory treated the same as other parents, without any particular mention of retardation in state statutes or regulations, their treatment may differ in practice. Standards for removal and termination are sufficiently imprecise that judges and social workers have considerable leeway to act on their subjective notions concerning retardation or on other biases. They presume too readily against parents with retardation rather than search for creative solutions that would enable the family to stay together.

Most state investigations of parents who have retardation occur because of suspicions that they are neglecting, rather than abusing, their children. Parents with mental retardation are more likely to come to the attention of state authorities than are other parents, and to come to their attention earlier. Because they may live in a state-run or -licensed facility, or work in a sheltered workshop, for example, state officials may be informed during the pregnancy. Moreover, hospital personnel may inform state officials at the birth.

If they have escaped state scrutiny at the outset, parents with retardation are likely to come to the attention of state authorities at least when their child enters school. One telephone call by a school official reporting suspected neglect or abuse is likely to trigger state attention if the official also reports that the child's parent has retardation. From the outset a de facto presumption of incompetence may operate against parents who have mental retardation, even if it is not expressed as such.

Evaluating Ability to Parent

Once a parent has come to the attention of state authorities because her fitness has been questioned, the social worker assigned to screen or investigate makes a preliminary finding about the individual's parenting ability. The finding is then used in the broader parenting evaluation process, which may be conducted either by professionals at court clinics or by teams of psychologists, mental health professionals, or others at specialized evaluation clinics. The clinics may or may not be independent of the state agency involved. Court clinics evaluate a wide range of parents,[15] but independent clinics are commonly used when parents who have mental retardation are at issue.

One such clinic that existed in Massachusetts during the mid-1980s, until it was disbanded for lack of funding, was the Developmental Support Team, a specialized, interdisciplinary evaluation team at Boston's Children's Hospital.[16] The team was designed to evaluate and support families in which one or both parents had mental retardation. It only did so, however, if the parents were prepared to cooperate as well as being considered appropriate for referral. The emphasis was on mental disabilities in general, and the team included specialists from special education, nursing, social work, and psychiatry. It also called on other health specialists within the hospital when their involvement was needed to design a comprehensive service plan for a particular parent.

The team's evaluation process was structured around the questions presented to it by the referring state agency; staff from the agency were permitted to participated in the evaluation process only if the parents consented. The evaluations took one or two mornings and were followed by a conference of team members. The following is a brief outline of the "criteria for adequate parenting" used by the team:

1. The parent's ability to meet the child's basic needs (nutrition, clothing, shelter, medical needs, and the need for a routine).
2. The parent's ability to meet the child's developmental needs: the need for stimulation of cognitive, motor, and language abilities; the need for protection from physical harm, overstimulation, and victimization; the need for appropriate limit setting, discipline, and supervision.
3. The parent's ability to relate to and emotionally nurture the child as a separate person.
4. The parent's ability to deal with the stresses of daily living without losing the ability to carry out the above tasks.
5. The parent's ability to support and manage the above tasks.

As part of the evaluation process, the team reviewed the parent's social history, as reported by the parent in a social service interview and by professionals and agencies involved with the family. The team also observed parent-child interactions during child care interviews with the nursing professionals on the team. During this process, the nurses and other team members evaluated the child's needs, developmental status, and attachment to the parent, as well as the parent's intellectual and protective capacities.

The team also took into consideration the context in which the parent had been and would be parenting, including such important variables as the parent's financial status, her ability to provide adequate housing, and the existence or absence of a family support network. The team then made recommendations regarding supportive services that the parent required to meet the child's needs. If the team felt that no amount of supportive services would make it possible for the woman to parent adequately, it could recommend removal or "alternate placement" of the child and the termination of parental rights.

Rules requiring a state to provide parents with services before it terminates parental rights were in place. Nonetheless team members reported that they sometimes recommended removal from the home without prior provision of services; they did so "only when the history of the ongoing parent-child relationship supports such a recommendation."[17]

Providing Parenting Services

After the state agency obtains an evaluation of ability to parent and a list of the special services the evaluators feel the parent needs, it is responsible for providing the parent with those services and in theory must do so before it can take steps to sever parental rights. Provision of services is legally required whenever such services could allow the family to stay together, even though the parents may be inadequate without them.[18] Various types of assistance are common, including homemaking assistance, respite care, daycare, psychological therapy, and transportation. Parental training for parents with retardation is a particularly important and much needed service about which there is a growing professional literature.[19]

One opinion from the Superior Court of Connecticut underscored the state's affirmative obligation to assist and extended it to parents who have retardation:

The contention that [the Department of Child and Youth Services and Child Foster Services] justifiably did not affirmatively assist Lisa M. with visitation (through transportation, bus passes, etc.) simply because the mother did not so request, overlooks, in the court's view, the statutory imperative requiring efforts to reunify, particularly in reference to a mother who has been described as overwhelmed and discouraged, extremely limited intellectually, and "borderline-retarded."[20]

Encouraging as such statements may sound, to date they reflect law rather than usual practice. Moreover, not all state decisionmakers share the view that persons with retardation should partake of services on an equal basis. The story of Kitty Oree Smith and Eddie Smith and their children shows that some states do not attempt to make parenting work when the parent has retardation. There the state legal system explicitly declined to provide services to parents with retardation. Nonetheless, the enterprising parents managed to receive parental training.

Kitty Oree Smith and Eddie Smith are the parents of two daughters, Chrissy and Louise, born in 1985 and 1987 respectively. Both parents had mild retardation. They raised their children until August 1990, when the government removed the children after receiving allegations that Chrissy had been sexually abused by either her aunt or her uncle. The sexual abuse charge was subsequently dropped by the state, but it retained custody of both girls "on the basis of the Parents' neglect in failing to seek medical attention for Chrissy when the allegations of abuse arose." In October 1990 a South Carolina family court awarded custody of the children to the state, "holding that due to Parents' mental retardation [the Department of Social Services] was not required to institute a treatment plan for rehabilitation."[21]

In June 1991 the state welfare agency filed an action against the parents for termination of parental rights under the applicable state statute, which like so many others provides, in pertinent part, that:

The Family Court may order the termination of parental rights upon a finding of one or more of the following grounds: . . .

(6) The parent has a diagnosable condition unlikely to change within a reasonable time such as alcohol or drug addiction, mental deficiency, mental illness, or extreme physical incapacity, and the condition makes the parent unlikely to provide minimally acceptable care of the child.[22]

The trial court's decision about the parents' inability to provide acceptable care was reached after a clinical psychologist interviewed each of them for one and a half hours. There were no home visits. The psychologist gave little or no weight to the relationships between parents and children that had developed over the five-year period during which they had served as parents. Even the guardian *ad litem* appointed to protect the parents' interests supported the termination of their parental rights.

During the trial a social worker explained that "due to the Smiths' mental retardation, no treatment or rehabilitation plan was proposed." The same social worker also testified that though the Department "had attempted to provide the Smiths with instruction on homemaking skills in the past . . . the homemaker instructors were not trained to teach mentally retarded people."

The Supreme Court of South Carolina accepted the state's position that no assistance was necessary, because South Carolina does not require "that the agency removing the child provide rehabilitative services to mentally incompetent parents prior to seeking termination, unlike in cases with competent parents." By explicitly acknowledging its discrimination in this way, the state made itself an easy target; nonetheless no argument of discrimination against persons with retardation in provision of services was pursued.

Instead, the parents produced a significant expert witness of their own: Bill Chidester, the executive director of the Charles Lea Center, a treatment and education facility for persons who have retardation. Mr. Chidester testified that his center had recently developed a special-needs program for educating parents with retardation, teaching them "parenting skills, family planning, and sexuality." He also testified that the Smiths had been accepted into it and Dr. Diehl, the clinical psychologist who evaluated the Smiths, testified that they "could benefit from such a program and should be given the opportunity to do so."

During cross-examination, Dr. Diehl was asked to respond to Mr. Chidester's testimony:

Q. Well let me ask you back to my question I started a minute ago. If you were aware that Charles Lea had started a program specifically designed to help mentally retarded parents with their parenting skills, to enhance their parenting skills and help them in general in that area, and if that program would have a considerable degree of supervision, a lot of follow-up, would you defer to Charles Lea's opinion as to whether or not these parents could be helped?

A. I would consider referral for evaluation. That would not alter my statements about prognosis.

Q. You would consider a referral?

A. Or to allow them to assist if these individuals were appropriate for the program they were offering.

Q. And if these individuals were appropriate, would you feel that based on Charles Lea's opinion, they ought to be given a chance in that program?

A. If there were a program that were available, and they felt they could help them.

Q. And do you feel like these folks if there is anything reasonable out there, they ought to be given that opportunity, shouldn't they?

A. That would be my usual approach to this type of situation, yes, sir.

Subsequently, the social worker was asked her opinion of the Charles Lea special-needs program: "I would not disagree if there was a program available that would help either Mr. or Mrs. Smith, that they should be referred to it at this time."[23]

The South Carolina Supreme Court used this testimony to show that the state had not in fact proved by clear and convincing evidence that the parents would be unable to parent because of their retardation. As a result, it reversed the termination holding and remanded the case for a new trial following the parents' participation in the parent training program.

States rarely explicitly acknowledge their discrimination in the open way that the *Smith* case demonstrates, but they still often fail to provide services that parents with retardation need. Services to families in general is limited by the severe budget constraints most state agencies face. Waiting lists for available services are very long.[24] This problem of resources affects all sorts of families, but in addition to financial problems, parents with retardation may encounter prejudice and discrimination. The following story of one family's experience with the social service system shows that state agencies can create barriers rather than bridges to parenting.

Jimmy and Tina Faye are the son and daughter of James C. and Louise C., parents whose IQ scores indicate mild retardation.[25] The couple's income consists of social security disability checks. James worked for twelve years at a firm, but the company eventually collapsed. He and Louise live independently in their own house, which James inherited from his father.

The couple's son, Jimmy, is "moderately retarded" with an IQ of 40. He was removed from his parents when he was five days old and returned to them when he was one and a half. Thereafter, he remained in their custody for four years until he was placed in foster care. Tina Faye was removed from her parents at birth because of their retardation. She was three years old and Jimmy was nine when the Circuit Court of Buchanan County, Missouri, terminated James's and Louise's parental rights to both children. On appeal, the termination was reversed with respect to Jimmy but upheld with regard to Tina Faye.

As summarized by the appeals court, the trial court record showed James was an expressive, self-sufficient, and sensible person:

> James himself testified at the hearing. His testimony was lucid, articulate and insightful. One would not suspect from reading his testimony he was of less than normal intelligence. The daily affairs of life he copes with adequately. He pays his bills, purchases household needs, has negotiated the purchase of a washer and dryer, and has had his residence repaired and improved. He can cook "some things." "I've got the Progressive Board [a homemaker service] coming in once a week. They ain't been out very long. My first dish was an oven-fried chicken, and the other one was a casserole, a tuna casserole, and the last one was a barbecued chicken." He can use the telephone. He can tell time. He travels by city bus and, even though he is unable to read, he knows which buses to ride. He knows directions. He appreciates the value of money, and Louise's extravagance is a source of distress to James and of dissension between Louise and himself. He has taken the initiative in learning to read. His tutor, the Reverend Mr. Lawson, a retired Methodist minister, testified James had faithfully attended weekly reading sessions, that he was cooperative and "very intense in trying to learn the material," and that he was making progress. James during his testimony demonstrated an elementary ability to read, then added: "That's what I have learned in the past eight weeks. There's no reason a retarded person can't learn." At one time he asked his [Department of Family Services] caseworker, Donna Blackmun, about having a vasectomy. Whether he had the vasectomy the record does not show. His testimony articulated an understanding of child discipline, the need for education, and child safety, and emergency measures. ("Well, first of all I'd dial 911 and call the ambulance right away.")[26]

Indeed, James and Louise had successfully cared for Jimmy on their own for four years.

Jimmy's removal from James and Louise at the age of five and a half was precipitated by an "abrupt regression" noticed by a social worker at the children's rehabilitation unit. As summarized by the appeals court, the social worker observed that Jimmy's attention span dropped. He became unresponsive. Whereas he had learned to put a six-piece puzzle together, he now suddenly lost that ability. Upon testing, he was found to be 17 months old mentally and developmentally. The [social] worker who testified to this sudden regression could not account for it. [The Department of Family Services] sought to solve the problem by asking, and securing, the removal of the child from his parents' home to foster care. There [was] no evidence that Jimmy's regression was caused by any condition in the parents' home, or by any act of commission or omission of the parents, or by any inadequacy on their part. Neither was there any evidence Jimmy's removal from his parents' home brought on improvement. His progress, which had preceded the period of regression, took place also while he was in his parents' custody. His school program director at the time of the hearing—when Jimmy was nine years old and had been in foster care four years—testified to a recent period of regression, which could not be traced to the parents' fault, for Jimmy during that time was in foster care.[27]

During the year before the removal hearing, Jimmy had, in fact, "been in two foster homes . . . which [according to the school program director] 'always makes a change in a child's life.'" The director also noted that Jimmy "was more nervous and high strung the day after his periodic visits with his natural parents. He has some language. He normally can follow directions."

The social worker once asked James C. "why his head drooped and why he became quiet during the visits with his children." The social worker told the court the following: "I can tell you what he said . . . He's depressed or sad because of his children, because he misses them. He loves them. He thinks they're beautiful kids. He's very proud of them."[28]

Tina Faye, whom James and Louise visited throughout the four-year period of her temporary removal, was born two months prematurely. Though James and Louise had made some plans for her arrival, they had, apparently, not cleaned house. As a result, when a social worker inspected the house just after the child's birth, she found it "unsuitable for the baby's reception because of dirt and bugs. She told James this. James said he would go home and clean it up." James followed her instructions with efficiency and determination. When the social worker drove by the house that evening she "saw James sweeping and cleaning." However, she never stopped to inspect "the results of his labors . . . for Tina was taken from her parents at the hospital and the condition of the [parents'] home became moot."[29]

James and Louise did not protest the removal of Tina Faye from their custody. They met the requirements of the state's social service plan and endeavored to meet the department's expectations of them, so that they could regain custody. Nonetheless, the state moved to terminate their parental rights to both children, citing two statutory grounds. The state alleged that the children were adjudicated abused or neglected and that each child had been removed from the home for the required one-year period, but that the deficient conditions in the home continued to persist and were likely to do so. Therefore, the state said that "the continuation of the parent-child relationship greatly diminished the child[ren's] prospects for early integration into a stable and permanent home."[30]

As the appeals court explained:

> Both statutory grounds require the court to consider and make findings with respect to any permanent and irreversible mental condition on the part of the parent "which renders the parent unable to knowing[ly] provide the child the necessary care, custody and control" . . . The presence of such a mental condition does not furnish independent grounds for termination of parental rights, but is a factor for the court's consideration.[31]

Other factors considered legally relevant were "the [child's] emotional ties to the birth parent,"[32] the "extent to which the parent has maintained regular visitation or other contact with the child,"[33] and the "parent's disinterest in or lack of commitment to the child."[34]

At the trial the social workers introduced evidence relating to the condition of the home as observed by social workers *prior* to Tina Faye's birth. The appeals court summarized the testimony as follows: "The [social] workers observed unwashed dishes, insects, dirt and disorder, and also some episodes of head lice. Jimmy was observed in urine-soaked diapers. James and Louise lived during that period in a different house, perhaps more than one, than the house they owned and occupied at the time of the hearing."[35] The trial court had accepted this testimony as evidence of James's and Louise's failure to correct the dirty house problem—presumably the basis of the allegation of neglect; but the appeals court did not see it as neglect:

> The testimony relates to the period when Jimmy was an infant and a toddler. It does not have much relevance when the child reached the age of nine years, and has passed the age of total dependency, as he had by the time of the second termination hearing . . . James testified that the house

where he and Louise now live was treated by an exterminator after they moved into it, three years before the hearing, and there were no roaches found in the house after the extermination treatment . . . [The social worker] testified only that [this house] was small [730 square feet, five rooms]; she did not testify to any filthy conditions . . . [This is the house] inherited by James from his father. James testified all furniture in the house was new. The house had undergone fairly extensive repairs and improvements since they moved into it. Other improvements were in the offing.[36]

With regard to James's and Louise's emotional ties to their children and their interest in an ongoing relationship with their children, the Reverend Groves, the couple's pastor, testified:

"I can truly say absolutely that James loves his son as much as any man has ever loved his son." The Reverend Groves testified to James's having a chain link fence installed to prevent Jimmy's getting into the street when he was three or four years old, and to James's calling on Mr. Groves to transport Jimmy to the hospital on two occasions, once because of a lump on his head from a fall, and the other for an "evaluation" . . . "Everywhere that James went, James had Jimmy with him."[37]

The social worker testified that during visitations, "[t]he parents brought small gifts to the children." When the court asked the supervising social worker whether "there appeared to be normal parent-child bonding," she answered, "I think the father and Jimmy are very close. I mean, you know, Jimmy seems to love his dad a lot. I don't see any bonding between the mother and the children at all."[38]

Addressing the effect of the parents' retardation on their ability to parent adequately, the psychologist and psychiatrists essentially testified that it disqualified them. Louise, Dr. Rhunke said, resisted all parental testing: she "would not enter the testing situation without her husband. He essentially coaxed her and led her into the testing situation. She was not very cooperative during the testing and sometimes would not respond. He sort of begged, pleaded and cajoled and instructed her to answer and be cooperative. And in general, he was kind of in charge of her functioning."[39]

After James and Louise "submitted themselves to unending tests and evaluations" the "sum and substance of the professionals' testimony," according to the court, was that

James's and Louise's parenting skills were deficient, and could not be made sufficient . . . The fact of James' mental retardation, the testifying psychologists and psychiatrists agreed, does not ipso facto disqualify him as a parent. Dr. Cox gave the opinion that James would be unable to supervise Louise (his wife) and two children; that would be too much for him. Louise, according to the psychiatrists' testimony, is at the same time childlike and obstreperous, and taxes James' patience . . . Dr. Cannon testified: "[James] does not have the capacity to be the sole provider of a child . . . [James's] limitations would aversely affect the child's care and stimulus, thus putting the child at a developmental and emotional risk . . . My concern would be that the child would not achieve his or her highest degree of functioning, versus being in a very healthy, structured, stimulating environment."[40]

On the basis of this testimony—that staying with their parents would prevent the children from reaching their "highest degree of functioning"—the lower court concluded that James and Louise were inadequate parents and unlikely, because of retardation, ever to become adequate. Accordingly, it severed their ties to Jimmy and Tina Faye.

On appeal, the court disagreed with the lower court's finding of parental unfitness and made clear that it found these parents impressive:

> We note the absence in this case of the circumstances we so often see in termination of parental rights cases—willful neglect, abuse, selfish disinterest, criminal behavior, drug abuse or alcohol abuse, immorality of various kinds. We see instead the opposite—selfless devotion, unflagging interest in the children, moral behavior, a steadfastness in the pursuit of a reunification with their children which is all the more remarkable because of an unbroken succession of frustrations and defeats.[41]

Moreover, it pointed out that the existence of a "better" placement, even if one were truly available, was not the relevant consideration:

> Two unsupported assumptions underlie the professionals' opinion testimony. One is that Jimmy, if his sonship were terminated, would be placed in a "very healthy, structured, stimulating environment." That is a dubious proposition, unsupported by any evidence. In fact, the record is devoid of any evidence that severance of Jimmy's filial relationship would serve the statutory goal of enabling him to have a "permanent and stable home." That goal is best served by preserving the parent-child relationship; there is no reason to doubt the permanency and stability of James' and Louise's home.
>
> The second unsupported assumption is that parental rights may be terminated if the child would be "better off" in some hypothetical ideal environ-

ment. No parent has to defend his parental relationship against the claim his children would be "better off" in some ideal environment.[42]

Having said this, the court reversed the lower court's termination of James's and Louise's parental rights to Jimmy. Nonetheless, it upheld termination as to Tina Faye.

The appeals court admitted that it did not know much about Tina Faye, since she was never in her parents' custody and was already three at the time of the hearing. The lower court record indicated that "James holds and hugs Tina Faye" during visits. "That there is any bonding between . . . James and Tina Faye," concluded the court, "is surprising."[43] During testimony the lower court judge asked James, "Can you tell us why it is you do not want the Court to terminate your parental rights?" He answered, "Well, because I had bonding over Jimmy. I don't know the girl, I don't know about her, but she's never been put in the home. I wouldn't know how she'd feel."[44] James and Louise made clear they wanted both their children, but ultimately the appeals court accepted the experts' view that James could not handle two children and supported the decision in part by saying that the parents' lack of opportunity to bond with their daughter made their interest in the girl "small" relative to the boy.[45]

The story of James and Louise illustrates many things. One is that regaining one's children after they are removed from custody may be possible but can be very difficult. The case surely makes clear that a system of intervention in the family can be used to impede persons from raising their child, especially parents with mental retardation.

Predictive Determinations Based on Intellectual Deficits

Investigations of parents with mental retardation occur not only in the context of an ongoing parent-child relationship, but also when the state family services agency predicts that a pregnant woman who has retardation may not be able to parent. An agency may develop this position whether or not she has previously failed in that role.[46] Such predictive disqualification of would-be parents arises occasionally in the context of other persons as well, such as teen mothers, but disqualification before a person has had any chance to learn to parent successfully remains rare. Removal on purely predictive grounds is much more common when parents have mental retardation or severe emotional problems than in other contexts.

When retardation is at issue, social workers frequently start their investigation as soon as they learn of the young woman's pregnancy. Women with retardation are especially vulnerable to predictive screening because state agencies are more aware of them than of most other women. And even if they are not, a telephone call from a health care professional, or even an interested member of the public, reporting that a woman who has retardation is pregnant can result in state interference and investigation of the woman's living situation and parenting potential.

Even before the state begins its investigation, it may already have accumulated information about the mother-to-be. Often the state has personal files compiled during the individual's childhood or early adulthood. The files may come from special-needs education providers; from state facilities where many persons who are currently adults were once institutionalized; or from community residential facilities, sheltered workshops, or other day programs with which the woman may currently be involved, to name but a few of the possibilities.

Clinics like Boston's Children's Hospital Developmental Support Team evaluate many mothers-to-be as well as actual parents. Professionals at that particular clinic reported that they did not and would not recommend predictive removal of a newborn solely because of intellectual deficits of the parents. Sometimes psychological disorders in conjunction with retardation (or even alone) do result in predictive removal. A common view in the more sophisticated parental evaluation clinics is that parental emotional problems are potentially much more threatening to children than parental intellectual deficits.

Nevertheless, many parents who have mental retardation are separated from their children, even from birth in some jurisdictions, not because the parents are suffering from any emotional illness but simply because they are (often unnecessarily) deemed intellectually incapable of parenting. Roberts v. State provides an example.[47] Dolly Ann Roberts, the parent in question, was an unmarried fourteen-year-old who lived with her grandparents, aged seventy-four and eighty-eight, and her fourteen-year-old brother. The county removed Ms. Roberts's son immediately after his birth on April 10, 1975. The juvenile court ordered a termination of parental rights for both parents (Ms. Roberts had initially claimed she was raped but then identified the putative father, whose whereabouts were never determined). Ms. Roberts appealed, and on July 16, 1976, the case was remanded with instructions that the juvenile court make specific findings of deprivation.[48]

On remand, the trial court heard the following testimony relevant to the evidentiary question of deprivation:

A psychologist testified that I.Q. tests showed [Ms. Roberts] to be borderline retarded, primarily attributable to her stuttering and her impoverished cultural and educational background. He testified further that she was normal emotionally, and that in his opinion would be able to care for the child. There was also evidence that [her] academic performance was at a third grade level and that it would take approximately four years training before she could perform on the job market.

[Ms. Roberts] testified at the hearing that she wanted to take the baby home, but she was unable to articulate her reasons, even though the judge let her counsel ask leading questions. [She] did demonstrate that she could make change and testified that she could be a maid or could clean kitchens.

[Ms. Roberts's] grandmother testified that she would like to have [her granddaughter] bring the baby home, but that, due to [the grandmother's] age and illness, she could not herself care for the baby.

The court sided with the county. It held that "the child was deprived and that the deprivation was likely to continue and would not be remedied, and by reason thereof, the child would probably suffer serious physical, mental, moral and emotional harm."[49]

On a second appeal, Ms. Roberts contended that the order should be overturned because she had "never had custody of the child since its birth, . . . there [was] no history of deprivation and . . . a finding of deprivation cannot be based on what might happen in the future." The appellate court was not persuaded:

Proof of deprivation is not limited to evidence of past experiences and relationships between the parent and child in such a parental termination hearing. The evidence here leads to the conclusion that if the child were to be placed in [Ms. Roberts's] home, where its mother would have to attend a special school for a number of years to become a minimally productive member of society, where the grandparents were too old and infirm to care for the child, and where there was no father nor any means of support other than through welfare, that the child would come within the statutory definition of deprived. That the statute uses the word "is" rather than "will be" does not mean that the court must wait for deprivation to actually occur. It is merely a question of the quality of the evidence. Past acts of deprivation are certainly stronger proof and more convincing evidence upon which to decide the issue. But there is no reason why a determination of deprivation may not be made on proof that the conditions under which the child would be raised in the parent's home strongly indicate that deprivation will occur in the future.

The determination of deprivation and the decision to terminate parental rights based thereon is an exercise of discretion by the trial court and if based upon evidence, will not be controlled by this court.[50]

Thus, although there was conflicting evidence concerning the mother's ability to learn a job skill and to provide the baby with a home, the appellate court both approved the removal and terminated Ms. Roberts's relationship with her son. This decision was issued in January 1977, twenty-one months after removal, and a petition for rehearing was denied the next month.

Some courts, however, resist predictive removals, at least when mental retardation is not involved. In Adoption of Katharine and Jeptha, the trial court predicted unfitness because of parental cocaine addiction: "[I]f the parents had to cho[o]se between future drug use and the well being of their children, the children would suffer. The rights of the children to a stable and safe environment are greatly at risk in this home. [The c]ourt, after eight months of court observation of this matter, observes no improvement or any likelihood that current parent unfitness will ever be remedied."[51]

The appellate court reversed because no actual parental unfitness was evident. It said the issue was "whether a trial judge may predict abuse and neglect on the basis of other pathology in the lives of the child's parents, notably, in this case, their use of cocaine and, on the basis of that prediction, make an order that separates children from their biological parents."[52] It answered the question by disfavoring wholly predictive determinations:

Of course, neither agencies responsible for the welfare of children nor judges sitting on these sorts of custodial questions need to wait for inevitable disaster to happen . . . They may consider past conduct to predict future ability and performance . . . It is one thing, however, to make a prognosis of damage to a child because of a previous pattern of abuse or neglect and quite another to predict catastrophe when the care of the child to date has been, on the whole, satisfactory and, certainly, free of abuse or neglect. The termination of parental bonds is, after all, an "extreme step."[53]

It was easier to dispute the predictions in that case than in cases involving newborns; the parents had actually had custody, and the children appeared well cared for.

Mental Retardation "as a Factor" in Practice

Courts tend to terminate parental rights of persons with retardation even in circumstances that would not constitute grounds for termination in other cases. For example, some courts have found that mental retardation in combination with the absence of an adequate living situation allows removal, even when it would not for a person of normal intelligence.[54] Courts might reason that a person with retardation is not as equipped to alter her situation—her homelessness—as is a teenage mother of normal intelligence. In so doing, they may be underestimating persons with retardation. Furthermore, even those people who lack an adequate living situation or competent family, friends, or other helpers can be aided by the state. Generally, states do not have affirmative obligations to help persons, although in this context some such duties are imposed by federal and state regulations. The crux of the complaint of persons with retardation, more valid in some areas of the country than others, is that even when services are offered to other parents, they are not always made available to persons who have retardation.

In addition, facts not relevant to the personal qualities of the parents can be relevant to their fitness as parents. Factors such as uncertain financial circumstances or lack of housing can contribute to unfitness on the part of all parents, whether or not they have retardation. But some of the factors that correlate with "at risk" parents are statistically more common among parents who have mental retardation than among other parents: low socioeconomic status,[55] stress,[56] and lack of self-esteem and the expectation of failure.[57] The factors are independent of mental retardation, and they certainly are not necessarily tied to it, but mental retardation can contribute to the existence of the danger factors, and in some cases retardation makes it more difficult for the parent to overcome them than it is for many parents with greater intelligence.[58] Accordingly, courts may write off parents without giving them a chance to prove themselves, and the relative powerlessness of persons with retardation makes it difficult for them to insist on the individualized determination to which the law entitles them.

Persuasion to Waive Parental Rights

When social workers and other state officials know of a pregnancy as it develops, or become aware that a mother with mental retardation has just given birth, unless that mother has a secure support system from family or friends, she will often face attempts by social workers to persuade her to forgo parenting, either through abortion or by giving up the child at birth. The state relies on "persuasion," but often the subject is coerced or does not understand her "consent." This approach is the most common way for persons with retardation to lose their children. It is favored by state agencies because it leads to decisions that at least appear to be voluntary and, most significant, it keeps a great many of the cases in which a pregnant woman does not parent from going to court and from showing up in the case law.

A state's social welfare agency can exercise control over a woman's parenting decisions in many different ways: It can influence whether she "chooses" to have an abortion, to place her child for adoption, or to fight the state's petition to terminate her right to parent. Perhaps it can be most effective when state personnel are aware of the pregnancy and can influence the young woman to have an abortion or to give up the child at birth.

The parental evaluation process can serve as a useful means of helping parents with mental retardation, but it is often used instead as a forum for persuading the woman with mental retardation to give up her parental rights. This use (or abuse) of the evaluation process is more common for pregnant women with mental retardation than others. Of course, when a woman truly cannot succeed as a parent, these practices may be salutary. The problem arises because these attempts to persuade pregnant women with retardation to avoid parenthood sometimes occur even when the women could succeed as parents.

Another problem is that many social service agencies' regulations prevent them from providing support services, or even a plan for future services, until the child is born. Under such a system, the pregnant woman not only loses lead time in which she could prepare for parenthood; she also cannot know what assistance will be available before she has to decide whether to forgo parenthood.

Clearly the tendency to take a disparaging view of parents with retardation is not only endemic to the judiciary; it also shapes the willingness of child welfare agencies to expend remedial resources on parents who have retardation. Without such assistance, the chances of parents with retardation mounting a successful defense against losing their children are significantly diminished.

CHAPTER 17

Reforming the System

There is no need to make special rules about mental retardation in parenting requirements, as opposed to simply requiring fitness and ability to perform basic tasks. Chapter 15 explored some changes that non-discrimination would require in the formal law concerning unfitness and requirements for parenting. Similarly, when that law is applied—in the investigation, removal, and termination processes—discrimination should be eradicated, where it is detectable. If predictive elimination of parents is disfavored for parents who do not have retardation, it should be also for parents with retardation. The only legal justification for subjecting persons with retardation to especially adverse treatment would be a showing that that group is predictably the most unfit—and also that the unfitness applies to all or almost all persons in the group. Neither of those propositions is provable. If services are offered to parents who do not have retardation, they should be offered to persons with retardation as well. The only legal justification for a contrary policy would be that services were substantially less useful for this group, a proposition that will not be maintainable. And if a jurisdiction has a mandatory waiting period between removal and termination, or a requirement that termination can be ordered only if the natural parent is unfit, those policies should apply to all parents, whether or not they have mental retardation.

This antidiscrimination principle is clear and relatively uncontroversial, but it is not very effective in the context of retardation. Even when the principle is accepted, discrimination is not always easy to demonstrate, especially in a system based largely on discretionary judgments. Even if it is established that persons with retardation are to be judged by the same standards as everyone else, and that they are to be disqualified only for actual, proven unfitness in the particular case, there will be countless opportunities for discrimination in application of the standards, which calls for discretionary judgments. So in practice discrimination will be difficult to deter.

Some Difficult Policy Issues

Eradicating discrimination is necessary but insufficient. In addition to discrimination, practical problems in making the necessary judgments are inevitable and difficult to resolve. Moreover, other policy issues concerning the regulation of parenting are less clear-cut than the policy against discrimination.

Persuasion and Waiver

Many cases where women with retardation give up an opportunity to parent, either through abortion or through consenting to their child's adoption, do not show up in any casebooks or records. Persuasion is the social worker's and the agency's favored tool, rather than resorting to courts. The first line of defense of many social workers learning of pregnancy in a woman with a very low IQ is to persuade her to abandon the pregnancy or the child.

Social workers are in a controlling position vis-à-vis their clients. They have powers of persuasion, and when persuasion does not work, they can often obtain waivers of parental rights by threatening women with coercive state action to remove children at birth.[1] Their position allows social workers to be insistent even when dealing with mothers who clearly wish to retain custody of their children. This dynamic creates a special problem because, to speak in generalizations, persons with mental retardation are used to complying with authority figures and can be talked into consenting comparatively easily.[2] *In re* Christina N., decided by the Connecticut Superior Court, shows some difficulties that can arise. There the parental rights of a mother with mild retardation were terminated on the basis of her supposedly voluntary consent, even though at the hearing itself the mother clearly did not want to give up her rights.

Before petitioning for termination, the state had provided the mother with services to improve her parenting skills. When the state decided nonetheless to terminate her rights, it supported its case with the mother's admission that she did not think she could care for the child and with a "voluntarily" signed consent form terminating her rights. Even though the mother had subsequently withdrawn her consent, the court rested its decision terminating her rights primarily on her voluntary consent.

When the state agency or department charged with child protection concludes that it will not support the parenting efforts of a mother-to-be, it can often amass large amounts of evidence to support its petition to terminate her rights.[3] It also tends to present its opinions in court with a presumed legitimacy that most individuals who have mental retardation cannot match. A woman who the department predicts will be unable to parent may thus not realistically be able to mount a successful defense, even in cases where she would be quite capable of parenting with some help from the department or another source. The ambiguity and discretionary nature of legal standards like unfitness and "the best interests of the child" make it difficult for parents with mental retardation successfully to contest termination.

When the state would succeed in having the pregnant woman adjudicated unfit, it really could be to the woman's advantage to consent, whether to abortion or adoption, rather than having the child removed in a court adjudication. That course would avoid litigation and also would avoid her forming a relationship with the child only to have it severed. The problem is that the woman usually is in no position to know the strength of the state's case or even to understand the issues that are involved—a problem many other parents share. Accordingly, even would-be parents who could in fact succeed are vulnerable to pressure and may be persuaded to forgo parenting.

In these circumstances, an obvious legal reform would be to allow women who have mental retardation to give consent to adoption only before a judicial officer who would have the responsibility of verifying whether the woman is truly willing to give up custody of her child. If the officer is not satisfied that her consent is genuine and uncoerced, the state should not be able to remove the child without holding a judicial hearing in which the parent would be represented by counsel, appointed if necessary.[4]

Mothers and fathers (with or without retardation) who are relinquishing custody need counsel in order to ensure that they know what they are giving up. Such a requirement would protect not only the biological parents but also the integrity of the subsequent adoption. It is important that the counsel representing the woman not be selected by the adopting parents or the adoption agency, and that the counsel have undivided loyalties to the parents who are giving up their child. One important role for counsel will be to make certain that birth parents fully understand what they are doing and that it is irreversible. Counsel also should inform the parents, when they decide voluntarily to relinquish custody, that the state might then use this voluntary termination as evidence warranting the removal of a second child at birth.

One useful by-product of this approach would be to draw a clearer line between "temporary" and permanent relinquishments. The line would be drawn because presumably the state would not provide counsel for temporary and voluntary relinquishments, and so it would become obvious which was which. Today, without such a boundary, mothers persuaded to relinquish custody only on a "temporary" basis sometimes find that the state then uses this relinquishment as evidence of abandonment and of the need for termination of parental rights.

Relinquishment of parental rights would then be one of those relatively unusual and dispositive procedures where legal intervention and supervision obtains. Judicial oversight should center not on the wisdom of the choice, but on the voluntariness of the young woman's own decisionmaking and the assurance that there is full information and assent before such a drastic event.

Provision of counsel cannot, however, be a full solution. Even though it would be appropriate to require that all parents relinquishing custody have a lawyer, it would not be possible or appropriate to make a similar requirement for decisions to abort. Any requirement that a woman seeking abortion must have counsel would likely be deemed an undue burden on her right of choice, violating the precepts that the Supreme Court laid down first in Roe v. Wade and again in Casey v. Planned Parenthood. Such a prohibition of required counsel, designed to protect against state interference with access to abortion, has the by-product, for women with retardation, of allowing government officials to be overly coercive in encouraging abortion. Persons with retardation will be especially vulnerable to such efforts, because current philosophy prevents special, protectionist rules for persons with retardation choosing or refusing nontherapeutic procedures, as developed in Parts II and III of this book. For them and others being pressured by social workers or physicians, the primary protection available is for them to decide to bring family, friends, or even counsel into the decision.

State officials have different reasons for unduly pressuring parents with mental retardation to give up their rights of parenting. They may genuinely underestimate the competence of the population with mental retardation. Furthermore, states have a financial incentive to accomplish termination of parental rights by obtaining parental consent even when a court would refuse to order such termination. Termination of pregnancy or of parental rights relieves the state of the obligation to provide costly parenting services. Once the biological parents' rights have been terminated, adoption becomes a possibility and state agencies have no further service obligation to the biological parents. Termination of parental rights at birth also results in the easiest transition to an adoptive family for the child, and many adoptive families will be available at that stage. Easily available adoption helps the state financially because adoption ends the need for costly foster care. In short, the state may predict that persons with mental retardation will fail as parents instead of giving them a chance to try. Indeed, it has the same financial incentive with respect to other vulnerable groups.

How should policymakers deal with these problems of overbearing social workers and others who try to dominate decisions of persons who have retardation? Perhaps educating the social workers and insisting continually that they treat persons with disabilities with respect would help, but this is not the type of problem where law or courts can effectively exercise oversight. Just as persons with mental retardation can be influenced to make childbearing decisions by overzealous friends, guardians, or social workers, so will they be subject to others' influence when faced with decisions about keeping their child. Part of allowing persons to make their own decisions is allowing them to decide whose advice to heed.

Of course, if the system is to work well, those talking with the young woman must try to elicit her wants and needs and not simply foist their own views on her. Social service departments are learning, however slowly, to respect their clients and not try simply to manage them. But because the behavior of those who influence the decisions of persons with retardation— whether social workers, medical personnel, family members, or others—is beyond the reach of the legal system, coercion as well as persuasion will continue to be employed and will blunt the extent to which a legal change in decisionmaker will alter results.

Nonetheless, it is appropriate for the young woman to have legal responsibility for her own decision. Surely these decisions should not be a guardian's. Just as a guardian should not be able to decide for a ward that the ward should marry, or that the ward should have sex, so the guardian should not be able to consent for the ward to the renunciation of the ward's child. If the ward wants to keep her child and the state believes her unfit, it can endeavor to prove that unfitness in court, but the consent or nonconsent of a guardian should not be the issue. The California Supreme Court majority in *Valerie N.* said otherwise, but it was in error.

Predicting Unfitness

As already demonstrated, unfitness is decided on a purely predictive basis for parents with retardation much more readily than for other parents. It is clearly discriminatory to allow predicted unfitness to be controlling for this group alone. That discrimination in current practice does not, however, answer the question whether predictive removal should be available for all parents or for none. But even apart from questions of discrimination, removal on a purely predictive basis should be heavily disfavored.

Reports of suspected abuse or neglect, which generally lead to service plan agreements, arise in one of three contexts: (1) when a parent is suspected of failing to care for her child adequately; (2) when a parent who has a history of abusing or neglecting a previous child becomes pregnant again; and (3) when a woman with mental retardation, pregnant for the first time, is suspected of being unable to parent.

Only the first category involves an ongoing relationship between parent and child that provides direct evidence for or against termination. The second category has a predictive aspect, but only the third category is based entirely on speculation. It is such purely predictive decisions, often reflected in the removal of a newborn from a first-time parent, that most starkly raise the issue about whether or not predictive decisions are defensible.

Terminating a parent-child relationship after witnessing an ongoing relationship and deciding it is not viable has problems of its own. When an ongoing relationship is at issue, there are opportunities for errors if too strict a standard is applied; or a social worker misjudges the situation; or the social worker distrusts parenting by persons with particular characteristics, like mental retardation. Moreover, the investigation into the relationship is intrusive in itself and may create as many problems as it resolves.

Despite these problems, terminating an ongoing relationship is less troublesome than is terminating parental rights on a predictive basis. At least with an ongoing relationship, some information and evidence are usually available. And at least the person who wants to parent has been given the opportunity to try. When parental rights are terminated solely on conjecture, by contrast, the qualities of the particular mother, rather than any actions of hers, effectively are used to disqualify her permanently from parenting.

Although interfering with parental rights on a *purely* predictive basis is problematic, removing a newborn from a woman who has abused or neglected a child in the past may be legitimate. In view of the possible harm to the newborn, and the possible benefits of severing the relationship at the earliest opportunity, removal may be reasonable. In the case of abuse, removal of future children could also be considered a legitimate part of the punishment for the crime.[5] And with a convincing case of neglect, as well as abuse, courts should return custody to the mother only if she can bear the burden of showing she has changed.[6]

Besides unfairness to the parents, there are other arguments against predictive disqualification. One is that it is inconsistent with the constitutionally mandated standard of clear and convincing evidence that is required for termination of parental rights. Surely it is different in tone. But since removal is at issue rather than termination, *Santosky's* requirement does not apply. Moreover, it seems logically possible that a prediction would be so clear that the evidence supporting it could be deemed clear and convincing, even though only a prediction was involved.

A greater problem with allowing predictions of unfitness to govern arises when the basis for the prediction is the parent's retardation. Such a decision amounts to per se disqualification for retardation by another name. The controversy over the placement of B. J. G. speaks to this point.

R. G. and T. G. have mild retardation (with IQs of 64 and 62, respectively). They were not given a chance to parent before their son B. J. G. was removed, shortly after his birth.

B. J. G. was born five weeks early. He and his mother were placed with a foster family a few days after his birth; the father was not included in this arrangement. The purpose was to provide mother and child with care and to provide the mother with child care training, but the arrangement lasted only for one month, ending when the baby was hospitalized for pneumonia. From the age of six weeks through eighteen months, B. J. G. was on a sleep apnea monitor and oxygen support. When he was released from the hospital at the age of about two months, the child alone was placed with the same foster family, and he was declared a "Child in Need of Services." Two months later the parents signed an agreement with the state, consenting to

B. J. G.'s placement in foster care for as long as the child needed to be on a medical monitor.

As part of their contract with the state, R. G. and T. G. agreed to "(1) gradually increased visits with B. J. G.; (2) overnight visits with B. J. G. upon recommendation from his supervising nurse; (3) participate in counseling and parent training; (4) cooperate with the Semi-Independent Living Program . . . and; (5) attend B. J. G.'s medical appointments."[7] Of the 156 supervised visits scheduled between January and November 1990, the parents made 112. Nonetheless, the social welfare agency decided to stop visits based on its determination that the parents "were not sufficiently progressing from their counseling and training." Two years later the state sought termination of their parental rights, and the petition was granted.

On appeal, R. G. and T. G. contended that "the evidence [did] not suggest that there was a reasonable probability that they would never be able to independently parent B. J. G." Indeed, they had never been given this opportunity, individually or as a couple. Moreover, they argued that there was "insufficient evidence to prove that termination . . . was in the best interests of B. J. G."[8]

The appeals court described the evidence relating to their ability to parent:

> The record indicates that Mother and Father have shown isolated areas of improvement in attending to B. J. G. during their supervised visits. The registered nurse who supervised the visits . . . testified that Mother had learned to change B. J. G.'s diapers without prompting, placed B. J. G. in his car seat without assistance, and encouraged B. J. G. to eat his meal independently with a spoon. The nurse also stated that Mother and Father were able to understand the importance of home safety and could identify several age related developments such as crawling, walking, and talking.[9]

The only actual negative reported by the nurse was that during a subsequent visit the parents failed to recall having had a discussion with the nurse about human growth and development.

Nonetheless, the social welfare nurse failed to recommend them for unsupervised visits, let alone custody of their child. The nurse had testified that they had basic parenting skills. Fears about their abilities, while perhaps understandable, were entirely speculative and not based on any concrete evidence or observation except for the parents' admission to having financial difficulties:

[T]he nurse testified that she could not recommend unsupervised visits or overnight visits between them because such visits could potentially endanger the safety of B. J. G. She indicated that during such visits, Mother and Father would be unable to meet B. J. G.'s basic needs because they would be unable to determine when B. J. G. was [experiencing a] medical emergency, whether B. J. G. was getting food properly, and whether B. J. G. needed a change in diapers . . . [S]he noted that during the supervised visitations . . . B. J. G. often ate the lunch prepared by his foster mother because Mother and Father did not have enough money to feed the child and . . . mentioned they had financial problems.[10]

Notwithstanding their admitted difficulties, both parents had minimal mathematics and writing skills. They also had jobs. The father, T. G., labeled prices in a grocery store, and the mother, R. G., worked for Goodwill. Periodically, however, she was laid off, owing to lack of available work.

The record also showed that both parents had stopped participating in the semi-independent living program because they felt confident they could manage on their own without outside help. But their social worker disagreed. She thought R. G. needed assistance in managing her finances and household duties, keeping her medical appointments, grocery shopping, and maintaining good nutrition. The case worker thought T. G. also needed to continue to participate in the program because he had problems managing his finances and "occasionally told her that they had no food."[11]

Finally, the trial court accepted the testimony of a psychologist who had performed a case analysis of the parents. The psychologist concluded that "the Mother and Father would not be able to provide even minimally sufficient care for B. J. G. and if put in their care, B. J. G. would not reach his full potential." This psychologist recommended that B. J. G. not be placed in the "Mother's and Father's exclusive care."[12]

The child himself had special health needs. He had moderate to severe retardation due to hydrocephalus and had a shunt, a mechanical device medically installed at the base of his skull to drain extra fluid off the brain. Accordingly, wherever he lived, B. J. G. needed therapy and medical care that could be provided only by professionals, not by his biological or by his foster parents. Yet the trial and appellate courts held against the biological parents their inexperience at dealing with a brain shunt. Many parents, however, lacking expertise in dealing with special-needs children, if they could, would delegate the task entirely to professionals, as these parents were prepared to do, without any question being raised about the parents' competence. Their own style of parenting would be respected, whether their reasons were because they felt incompetent to drain a child's shunt or because it made them squeamish to do so.

In what reads like a comparative evaluation of the abilities of the biological parents and the foster parents, the court also favored the foster parents because of stronger emotional bonds that had developed between them and B. J. G. It pointed out, "B. J. G.'s foster mother has worked extensively with the physical and mentally handicapped including developmentally disabled children and adults,"[13] and B. J. G. "has resided continuously with [the foster parents] since [he] was two weeks old . . . [They have] expressed their desire to adopt [him] after the parental rights of the parents are terminated . . . and plan to continue with therapy and medical treatment with [his current doctor]."[14]

The court did not acknowledge that the social welfare department had denied the biological parents access to the child. The department actions, ending supervised visitation without any court order, were entirely illegal and occurred despite "the Mother's love and affection" for the child. That illegality effectively paved the way for the greater bonding between the child and his foster parents that the court mentioned in its opinion. Nonetheless, taking into account "B. J. G.'s current lifestyle with his foster family," the court found support for "the trial court's determination that Mother and Father were unable to remedy the conditions which caused B. J. G. to be removed from their care and that termination was in B. J. G.'s best interests."[15]

The "conditions which caused B. J. G. to be removed" were both parents' retardation. That was the basis both for the removal in infancy and for the termination of parental rights:

Mother and Father concede that they have deficiencies which are brought on by their mental retardation . . . [but] argue that their "poor money management skills, occasionally forgetting diapers, [and] lack of experience in treating [B. J. G.'s] shunt are not immediate threats to the child" . . . [T]hey [therefore] contend that the court must refuse to consider these deficiencies in determining whether to terminate their rights because they do not pose an immediate threat to the child. We disagree . . . [P]arental rights may be terminated not only in instances where the parents' deficiencies pose an immediate danger to the child's life but also in instances where the child's emotional and physical development are threatened.[16]

One concurring judge disagreed with the panel majority's approach of comparing the foster and the biological parents rather than focusing on the appropriate legal question of whether the latter were unfit:

> I do not subscribe to the possible failure of the child to "reach his full potential" as a basis for termination of parental rights. Neither do I agree with the implication of the majority opinion that "the current lifestyle with his foster family" or that the foster home environment as more conducive to the child's "development," justifies termination of parental rights . . . Were it not for the individualized medical necessities required by the child and the reasonable conclusion that R. G. and T. G. are, and will be in the future, unable to recognize and deal with possible symptoms and emergencies, I would dissent.[17]

In sum, B. J. G. was removed from his parents because of their retardation; he was removed on the basis of predicted unfitness, not actual defective behavior. He was then placed in a foster family that wanted to adopt him. The ultimate termination of the parents' legal rights represents a watered-down version of the unfitness standard, at best.

Another noteworthy feature of predictive unfitness is that it can allow the state to avoid *ever* having to demonstrate unfitness before terminating a parental relationship. Sometimes the initial removal is accomplished in a rather cavalier fashion on a predictive basis, with the rationale being that "only" temporary custody is at stake. Nonetheless, as the B. J. G. case has demonstrated, there may be very limited opportunity, if any, for parents to regain custody by demonstrating their fitness.

Finally, predictive unfitness, by allowing removal of a child on speculative bases, opens the door to even greater speculation. One argument sometimes used against parenting by persons with retardation is that many of those who can function as parents adequately during the early years of a child's development will not be effective when the child becomes a teenager. If retardation makes one foresee inability to control a teenager, and that is ground for present termination of rights, this amounts to a thinly disguised argument against parenting by persons with retardation generally. It is noteworthy that there is no way to tell in advance which parents will be able to control their children and which will not. That fact holds true for parents without retardation as well as those with it.

The parenting problems of the parent with mental retardation (like those of other parents) vary considerably both with the stage of development of the child and with the particular child's personality. The teenage years, of course, may be problematic for "normal" parents as well as parents who have retardation. But the ability to control a rebellious teenager can be exacerbated by the retardation of a parent, who by this stage presumably is less intellectually capable in many respects than the child. Nevertheless, a teenager who from an early age has worked with and helped his parent may have acquired a level of maturity and compassion and may be quite capable of developing well and remaining with the birth family that he loves.

Even if the state makes a judgment that it may be necessary to remove the child during the early teenage years, does that necessitate terminating the relationship at the outset and never allowing it to develop at all?

In many ways the problem is that speculation abounds. Such a prediction, like most others made about new parents, usually cannot be made with any degree of certainty. Accordingly, decisions rarely rest squarely and centrally upon this ground. More commonly judges or lawyers simply buttress other arguments with statements about the parent's inevitable future unfitness.

Still, it seems worth considering whether, in the unlikely event that such a prediction could be made with near certainty, it would be a sufficient basis for separating children from their parents at the outset. If it were, it would have to apply equally to the mother who is likely to die of cancer within a certain number of years or who has any other terminal illness, as well as to a mother who is deemed unlikely to be able to handle her child in the future.

Perhaps from the single perspective of the child's interests, the best solution would be early separation; that could support a rule that the state remove newborns at birth from mothers with mental retardation (and mothers with cancer or other terminal illness). That way the baby, then child, would not have to build a relationship only to have it severed—and at a time when he or she will be less likely to be adopted. But the law does not allow early separation from other parents on grounds of future unfitness or even terminal illness, even though there, too, the single perspective of the infant's interests would warrant it equally. There is no plausible reason for treating parents with mental retardation differently from other "at risk" parents in this regard.[18]

Looked at from the perspective of the parent with mental retardation, and from the system that may allow her to parent for the time being at least, the question becomes whether allowing parenting for ten or twelve years is worth doing, even if one accepts that the parental relationship will not last throughout minority. From the point of view of the person who wants to serve as a parent, the answer seems obvious. Indeed, in some social circles in the United States (and elsewhere) children are frequently sent to boarding school when they are thirteen or fourteen, without their parents' feeling that they have taken no part in raising their offspring. Even if it were necessary to establish a separate living situation for the child of a woman who has retardation when the child becomes an adolescent, there is no reason to conclude that the mother could not care for her child until then and continue to keep in contact with the child even after he or she lives elsewhere.

In fact, from the adolescent's point of view, it would be important to find ways to ease the transition in his or her living situation. The possibility of continuing contact with the mother, though not as physical custodian, could be helpful here. The child could have the benefit of having lived successfully with the biological mother during the substantial period of time when, by hypothesis, she was able adequately to parent him or her. It would be troublesome to sever a parental relationship during the child's infancy because of projected parental inability far in the future.

Moreover, the problem of the mother who may be unable adequately to control her child when he or she is a teenager involves the same problems as predictive unfitness generally: Even if it is true that many parents will have difficulty parenting adequately during their child's teenage years, and even if the state takes the position that the parent-child relationship should not be permitted to develop if the parent would not be adequate during the child's teenage years, it still will not be possible to know *which* cases will involve that problem. One reason it is impossible accurately to predict future success or failure is that success would depend partly on the family's future living situation, which cannot be known ten to twelve years in advance. Nor can we know what services the state will be capable and willing to provide at that time. Obviously, it also is not possible to know what the relationship between mother and child will be ten or twelve years later.

Moreover, one cannot know how the personality of a newborn will develop. Whether removal in the teenage years is necessary will depend in part on whether the child is nurturing toward the mother or is rebellious. It is certainly possible that a child may be devoted to the parent and not be in need of greater parental control. Experience shows that children, as they grow up, can be extremely helpful to parents with retardation. They may help them with reading, telling time, navigating the subway system, caring for younger children, or simply by getting themselves to school on time.

Some believe that this role—with the child helping to take care of the parent—is an inappropriate ("not normal") one for the child to play. It is not, however, necessarily a destructive one.

In short, a powerful and sufficient reason for not allowing predicted future unfitness to be grounds for immediate removal or termination is that it is difficult, indeed impossible, to predict in particular cases whether separation at a later stage is going to be necessary. Moreover, it is noteworthy that in these situations the state's social service agency is in control of both sides of the equation, because many parents who would be unfit without state services are fit to parent when their state provides suitable supportive services. By arguing that such services will not be available and that the parent's behavior without the services will render her unfit, the state can deprive the parent of her child.

Applying Procedural Protections to Removal Proceedings

Some strict procedural protections are available to parents at termination. The Supreme Court has required clear and convincing evidence (an unusually high standard of proof), although it has not imposed a right to counsel or other exacting procedural requirements.[19] In addition, many states impose greater procedural protections for parents than the U.S. Supreme Court has required under the U.S. Constitution. For example, several state courts have held that the state must appoint counsel for indigent parents at termination hearings.[20]

But what protections there are may come too late to be of any actual use to the parents. In that way the protections provide the appearance of fairness much more than the actuality. Both for the sake of the parents and for the smooth working of the system, it would make more sense for all protections that exist to apply at the removal stage as well as at termination, months or years later.

For many parents, and perhaps particularly parents with retardation, the removal stage is in fact the most significant step in the process of state severance of their relationship with their child. It is obviously of great emotional significance: the child actually leaves the parents' home. Termination may seem less important than removal to the parent because it is a formal legal hearing that takes place long after the child has already gone. Of course, it is significant because it represents the end of all hope of regaining custody and also because the parent will have no rights to see and visit with the child after termination; but some parents have little hope and little ability to visit even before termination is ordered.

Removal is often the most significant moment in the legal process as well. Despite all the promises of the law and the occasional provision of services, it actually is quite rare for a mother with retardation to regain her child after removal. Some decisionmakers admit that they "could not take responsibility for placing" a child in the home of a parent with retardation—as they would be in returning custody—even though they will sometimes leave a child in the custody of such a home. Such an attitude is especially prevalent among judges who have little contact with persons who have retardation and, consequently, particularly fear them as parents.

In re Orlando F. shows the difficulty in practice of regaining custody.[21] Orlando was removed from his mother, Theodora, when he was three days old. The court described Theodora as "dull normal"; she had spent ten years of her life in a state institution for people with retardation. As well as keeping up contact with Orlando to the best of her ability, Theodora had another child.

When Orlando was almost three, the state sued to terminate parental rights. At a fact-finding hearing, a psychologist testified that Theodora's second child was "bright, attractive and properly cared for" and that Theodora was "physically and financially able to care for the child." She also pointed out that "people reared in an institutionalized setting require 'much more concrete structure and plan action' to deal with daily tasks than others, because of a lack of experience."

The judge deciding the case, and the appeals court the first time through, ruled that the evidence did not support termination. The family court ordered that Orlando be returned to his mother, and the appellate division, while halting the return on the grounds that it had not yet been shown that Theodora was ready, nonetheless concurred that there were not grounds for termination. But a dissenter in the court of appeals eventually carried the day. Justice Kuperman dissenting stressed that the mother had failed to plan for the future of her child and that termination was in Orlando's best interests. On a second appeal brought by the state the court of appeals agreed with that dissent and terminated Theodora's parental rights,[22] holding that Theodora had "failed for a period of more than a year to plan for the future of the child." The court had this to say about what constituted adequate planning for Orlando's future under New York's statutory requirement:

We need not formulate, under the instant facts, an exact standard which must be met in order to comply with the statutory mandate in light of [Theodora's] utter failure to exert even a minimal attempt to develop a plan for her child's future. Indeed, each factual pattern will undoubtedly reveal peculiarities of its own but the particular facts and totality of circumstances must be scrutinized and weighed carefully in rendering decisions in such delicate human affairs.[23]

Theodora's failure to plan in this case, exacerbated by the state's own delays in starting the planning process, was reflected in her inability to obtain a house and a job and her failure to attend scheduled appointments with social workers. The fact that she was successfully raising another child and had demonstrated her competence, yet could not regain the child who had been removed on the basis of prediction, underscores the difficulty that parents who are deemed slow can have in reuniting with their children once the children are taken away from them.

Surely *Orlando F.* and other cases show that "temporary" removal can easily become permanent, and that a parent desiring to keep her child should fight hard to resist removal in the first place. A parent should also fight hard to obtain services that will enable the child to stay. Even if the state provides services after a removal, as it commonly does, at least in theory, it is often a foregone conclusion that the services will not result in regained custody, especially when the parent has retardation. Besides, the parent has much more incentive to learn the skills when the child is in her custody. Learning how to parent in the abstract, as a lesson possibly useful in the future, is hard for all parents, especially those with retardation.

The problems with concentrating legal protections on the termination stage apply not just to those parents with retardation, but to all parents, though perhaps to a lesser degree. Regaining custody can be difficult for many, and there is at least a substantial threat when custody is lost that it may not be regained.[24]

Frequently the case will effectively have decided itself by the time the termination hearing is held. The parent may not have continued with her classes, may not have progressed, or may not have kept up visits with the child. And the judge may feel that whatever characteristics disqualified her in the first place might permanently endanger the child. In addition, some states now create a statutory presumption in favor of termination when enough time has elapsed, even without a showing of current unfitness; they apply strict unfitness requirements only to parents who are living with their children.[25] All these factors suggest that a parent must fight fully to prevent initial removal of her child, and after a child has been removed a parent must regain the child promptly if she is to keep the strong presumption for custody that the law purports to grant biological parents.

Clearly, the removal hearing can be the pivotal moment in a parent's loss of her child, and it should partake of all the procedural protections guaranteed at termination. Of course, in those rare cases when an emergency removal is required, a thorough hearing with full protections could be provided promptly thereafter.

Adjusting the Interval between Removal and Termination

There are important differences between removal and termination. The removal process places custody of the child with the state rather than the biological parent. The child is usually then placed in foster care that is paid for by the state and federal governments. But it is only after termination of parental rights that a child is free to be adopted without the parents' consent. One important issue, concerning which there are often conflicting interests, is how long the period between removal and termination should last.

There are reasons to doubt the wisdom of a protracted waiting period between removal and termination, even though other considerations counsel a significant period in order to allow for parental reform. Accordingly the policy questions are close, and reasonable persons differ on the appropriate resolution. But whether a long or short period is selected, clearly the same rule should apply to persons who have retardation as applies to everyone else. The pattern has been to terminate the rights of persons with retardation more readily than the rights of others. It has also been to demand more in practice of parents with retardation than of others.

Removal and termination can be part of a single process, with removal as the first step in a process leading to termination. Or the removal period can instead serve as a period of reform or help for the parents, concluding with their regaining custody. If it was possible to tell from the outset which parents would not succeed, it would be most economical to allow prompt termination of those parents' rights to their children, without any waiting period. But because it is impossible to predict reliably, and because an erroneous prediction could be so devastating to parents and families, the policy instead has been to allow parents to try to correct their behavior. Even if removal is necessary, laws usually require a reasonable period to elapse before termination—a year, perhaps—in order to give parents a chance to convince authorities that they can reform and be fit for custody. The dominant purpose of the waiting period is to allow family reunification; time is essential if instruction, reform, and reunification are to take place.

It is important, however, that the delay before termination not be too great. If possible, the child should not spend his or her entire childhood in the "interim placement" that the state provides during the removal period (usually foster care). That resolution is not in the interest of the child and arguably is the worst possible outcome. Many foster care placements are themselves marginal and do not at any rate give children the feelings of love and security that they need to develop well. Moreover, when that problem does not exist, its opposite is encountered—in cases where there is continuity of care and bonding in a "temporary" placement, which the child must now lose. These situations are paradigms for the conflict between continuity of care and best interests on the one hand, and parental rights on the other, that is so problematic in current family law.[26] The child's suspension in long-term foster care after removal sometimes results because the parents' rights have not been terminated and so the child is not free for adoption; it can also happen because no family presents itself to adopt the child, even though the child is free for adoption.

A protracted waiting period makes sense only if the hope of regaining custody is a real one. It makes little sense if decisionmakers have predetermined not to return children to parents with retardation because the decisionmakers imagine that the worst possible fate would be to have such a parent. If there exists such reluctance to move a child into his or her own home when parents have intellectual deficiencies, removal is in fact the determinative stage.

Newborns

The odds of a child being adopted increase dramatically if he or she is available for adoption at a young age—the younger the better. Moreover, a removal at birth on the basis of predictive factors, rather than allowing the mother and child to stay together and providing needed aid, typically reflects an expectation of permanent severance of parental rights. These facts are the basis for a likely conflict of interests between mothers and newborns caught up in the social services system.

From the perspective of the interests of the child, removal at birth is preferable to a later removal in several ways. We do not know the extent of a newborn's ties to the mother, nor do we fully understand their nature; but surely removal at this stage is less traumatic than removal after mother and child have lived together. An argument that the state does not serve the newborn's interest by removing a newborn at birth from a mother who is likely to lose the child after an opportunity to parent would have to turn on some very special consequence of biological ties.[27] Not only will an early separation be less traumatic and lead to more certain adoption, but also the baby will have more continuity with the adoptive parents, if placed as an infant. It is the baby's interest in having a permanent home that therefore supports prompt termination. It is likely, with the current demand for babies, that the state will be able to find another home that provides at least as good a set of life chances, if it can place the child during infancy.[28]

The state's interests coincide with those of the newborn: removal at birth is the most economical alternative. If the state can terminate the rights of a mother with mental retardation shortly after birth and have the baby adopted, the state saves the cost of providing training and educational services for the mother and compensatory services for the child. And because adoption is more likely to be available at this stage, the baby's stay in foster care is likely to be minimal. The government's interest, both financially and as protector of the child, will usually coincide with the interests of the infant and call for termination to follow as quickly as possible after removal from the parents. Because the state does not usually pursue this route of immediate removal and termination, it must be giving at least some weight to the value of family integrity and to the rights of parents who have retardation.

As well as respect for family integrity, there is another explanation for how limited removal at birth is, even though that removal can appear advantageous both to the state and to the newborn child: Even if removal at birth is of maximal advantage to a child for whom removal at a later date is the alternative, the state cannot accurately judge which parents will be unfit. This inability to make accurate predictions is the most basic reason for rejecting removal of newborns.

Moreover, suggestions supporting removal at birth go too far. The theory would allow children to be removed from the poor at birth because a well-to-do household is looking for a baby and the child's "best interests" would be maximized by placing him or her with better-situated parents. What groups other than the poor and "the mentally retarded" would be vulnerable to losing their newborns to the more advantageously situated? The very process of trying to draw the appropriate lines demonstrates the futility and the perniciousness of this approach.

Such an argument for realizing the child's best interests would not even have to be limited to situations where the biological parents could be called unfit. The best interests theory could support removal at birth anytime the biological parents of a newborn were in a particularly stressful or marginal situation and a loving couple who seemed much more secure wanted to raise the newborn as their child.

Despite anything that might be said for it, the claim that another couple could adopt simply because they seemed to the court to be potentially "much better" parents than the biological parents would not be taken seriously by any court or policymaker today. It is these dangers of the "comparative fitness" approach that have led our system to select, for the most part anyway, a requirement of strict unfitness for the termination of parenthood, rather than an approach of comparing biological parents with would-be substitutes. The parents are given a "right" to raise their children, unless they are deemed truly "unfit."

One problem with disqualifying fit parents because there are others who could provide better opportunities for a baby is that it violates our sense of fairness. It threatens to leave child rearing only to the privileged in our society and to take away other people's rights to their own children. Another problem is that the principle, if carried through, would actually *disrupt* our sense of family stability and the valuable feeling of security that the current system allows, at least to most families. The vast majority of families benefits from a system that makes family stability paramount and that discourages the state from making critical judgments about families and their modes of conducting themselves. It provides for and legitimates diversity, as well as a sense of security. While particular children's interests, narrowly defined, might be better served by removal to "better parents," the same children as adults benefit from being part of a system in which they are allowed to have and keep custody of their own children, without state evaluation of their child-rearing practices and without losing their children to others, unless they are strictly unfit.

Societal interests in family integrity and stability thus explain much of the weight given to parental rights. For even when the infant's perspective and the state's financial interests coincide in supporting early removal and quick termination, the parents' interests often lie elsewhere. Arguably, if a mother is eventually going to lose her legal parenthood, it might be better for her to know at the outset, so that she does not develop any contrary hopes or expectations or develop bonds with her child. But a parent may easily disagree, because a quick termination destroys any hope she has for parenting this child. Moreover, if rapid termination is ordered for predicted unfitness, based on factors over which the mother has little control without state aid, she may feel (quite correctly) that she is being disqualified from parenthood altogether; if she were to have another child, the same result would likely follow.

As well as retaining hope, there are two practical advantages to a mother of hanging onto her parenthood even after her child has been removed. First, removal without termination gives her some chance to do whatever she has to do to get her child back.[29] Second, without termination, she retains at least a theoretical right to visit her child. That right is lost with termination and will not be preserved through the adoption process in most jurisdictions today.

It is with respect to newborns that the interests of the parents are in starkest contrast to the state's financial interest and possibly to the child's own interests. When newborns have very marginal parents, these conflicts of interest between the parents and others give rise to undeniably difficult policy issues. Pursuit of the child's best interests might suggest easy removal of infants from marginal parents, but the dangers of discrimination inherent in predicting unfitness counsel otherwise. Whichever approach is followed, there is no justification for treating parents who have mental retardation differently from other parents.

Older Children

The conflict between at least the immediate needs of parent and child exists principally with respect to infants as distinct from older children, suggesting perhaps that different rules should apply. Whereas the seeming inevitability of termination may argue for it to take place quickly in the case of an infant, when older children are the subject of a proceeding there may be reason to be slow to sever parental ties, or never to sever them at all.

When state interference with parenting takes place later in the child's life, the various interests are more complementary. As with newborns, it is in the interest of the state, both financially and in its role as protector of the child, to terminate quickly once there has been a removal *if* termination is going to be the ultimate result *and* if that will lead to adoption. It is in the state's financial interest for the same reason as discussed above: that course will relieve the state of its obligations to both parents and child.

But in the case of an older child it is far less likely that adoption will result. Accordingly it may not be even in the state's financial interests to remove an older child in the first place. If there are services that could help the parent perform competently—or that could supplement the parent's contribution so that the child was adequately provided for—even if those services were rather extensive, it still might be less costly for the state to provide those services than to go through the process of removing the child from the home, placing him or her in an institution or in foster care, paying for and supervising the placement, and so forth.

In any event, the *most* expensive alternative for the state is for the child to *remain* in foster care. That can occur both when children are not free for adoption because their parents retain parental rights, and when children are eligible for adoption but not adopted. The difficulty in finding an adoptive home may be exacerbated by bad experiences a child has had: the parental conduct or situation that produced the finding of unfitness; emotional difficulties from losing a parent; and any traumatic situations the child encountered in foster care prior to adoption. Consequently, it is likely that a child who remains in foster care for a significant period of time will become a child with "special needs," emotional or intellectual.[30]

Even more important is the state's interest as protector of the child. Here again the situation is more complicated than the case of newborns. As with newborns, *if* the child is to be removed and *if* termination is to be the ultimate outcome, then it is often in the child's interest to have that occur as expeditiously as possible; it is better for the child to establish a new permanent home as soon as possible, and there is no chance of adoption without termination of parental rights. But this argument too is weakened when applied to older children, because it is much less clear that an adoption will occur than in the case of an infant.

Moreover, when older children are at issue, the child's emotional makeup must be taken into account and may counsel against removal in the first place; it is these cases in which a child's "best interests" may actually be to stay with a parent who is unfit.[31] Similarly, if removal takes place, the child's attachment to the parent may require maintaining ties or even being reunited with the biological family. This important independent variable of the child's attachment and feelings for the biological parent(s) does not apply in the case of newborns but can be central to questions involving custody of older children. It is increasingly accepted, even when it is not mentioned in the language of removal and termination statutes, that the child's ties with the parent(s) must be weighed in the balance against removal and termination. A well-known body of literature reminds us forcefully that staying with the "psychological parent" may be far more important to a child than being moved to a situation that to the outside world looks more ideal.[32]

Both the child's and the state's interests therefore may suggest leaving the child with the parent and providing services to aid the parent, rather than removing the child from the home. Notice that all parties' interests coincide more obviously in situations involving older children than in situations involving newborns or other very young children.

A central issue in removal and termination proceedings is how to judge the probabilities of the parent's improvement. On this issue, some conflict of interests between the parties emerges, because the marginal parent has an interest in being given a chance *even if* the odds of success are low, an interest not shared by the government or the child. The difficult question is what likelihood of success is required in order to fend off removal or termination. The problem of when a parent should be given a chance to parent is not one limited to parents with mental retardation; it is a problem for parents generally.

Despite the accepted position that long-term foster care is detrimental to the child, some judges have both declined to reunify the family and refused to terminate parental rights.[33] They thereby allow the parent and child to continue to know each other. To many, such a solution seems heartless. The period from removal to termination is not, overall, a happy one for the child. To leave children in this legal limbo is to maximize the chances of their never having a real home.[34]

In some cases, however, refusal to terminate parental rights even to children who are remaining in state care makes good sense. If there is no family to adopt the child, it is pointless, and needlessly destructive, to eradicate whatever relationship there is between parent and child. After all, these parents, though not ideal, may be the only parents the child will ever know.[35] Termination in favor of state custody usually makes much less sense than termination when an adoptive placement is imminent, although legal rules and court cases often do not take any account of this factor. A better legal approach would presume against wholly cutting off biological parents if the possibility of adoption is only speculative. For these reasons, the New York court in *In re* Mendes followed this path and continued the children in foster care without terminating the parents' rights. That case involved mental illness; such an approach would be suitable when parents have mental retardation as well, but too often in those cases courts hasten to sever all ties.

More Flexible Kinds of Adoption

Yet another way to preserve an appropriate balance of rights is to allow the biological mother to maintain contact with her child even after adoption. That is not the conventional model of adoption in the United States, but adoption of an older child because the parents have retardation is not the paradigm either. Such "open adoption" arrangements can legally be negotiated in most states today. The adoptive parents become fully legal parents, and there is no possibility of the birth mother's regaining parenthood or custody. Nonetheless the arrangement gives her a right to contact with the child, or to particular visitation, despite her lack of parental status.

If mothers (with or without retardation) were to be represented by counsel when they give up their children, such provisions would be much more common. At the time of relinquishing custody, birth mothers are in a position to insist on whatever conditions they want (other than money, of course, which would constitute illegal baby selling).[36]

An attorney might advise the mother to retain at least the right to know her child as he or she grows up. After all, this may be the only child she will ever have. In many cases, the mother will have done all that she can for her child and loves the child dearly. She may have been the child's parent and principal nurturer for years.

The amount and kind of contact between birth parent(s) and child would vary considerably with different contracts and different factual situations. Common provisions are letter contact only, a specified number of visits annually with the child in the context of his or her new family, or visitation that is significantly more frequent and less supervised, depending on the birth mother's characteristics and her relationship with the child.

Very different arrangements can work well. The most important variable is a willingness on the part of both the adoptive parents and the biological parents to work together for the benefit of the child. The permanence of the parties' respective roles in open adoption arrangements should help encourage cooperation as well as stability. (In contrast, divorcing parents feuding over custody are not in a stable legal arrangement; because their relative rights as custodian and visitor can change rather easily, they are continuing adversaries and are much more threatening to each other. The res judicata that applies to make most litigation final after judicial decision does not apply to child custody litigation, which parents can continually reopen.)[37]

A peaceful open adoption arrangement can be an optimal outcome, especially for an older child who has bonded with the original family but will not in any event be returned to it.

Providing Assistance

The Limits of Constitutional Law

Eliminating discrimination in law and in practice would be an enormous victory for persons with retardation, but full participation also requires assistance, as the normalization movement has long recognized. The U.S. Constitution is of little help here.

It is a basic tenet of U.S. constitutional law that most of the Constitution's guarantees protect individuals only from action by government. As a corollary, there is no affirmative right to services from government, despite the valiant efforts of some scholars to make it otherwise.[38] Sometimes an important issue in constitutional litigation is whether there was any state action.[39]

With the exception of the Thirteenth Amendment's prohibition of slavery (which the Supreme Court has construed narrowly),[40] the prohibitions found in those parts of the Constitution that are enforced by the judiciary are prohibitions against government action—for example, discrimination or suppression of free expression. Congress can usually enact laws extending the prohibitions more broadly,[41] but the Constitution itself—what is sometimes called the self-executing Constitution—essentially states limits only on government.

Accordingly, the Fourteenth Amendment limits discrimination by government but is not a sufficient basis for individuals to seek affirmative help from government, unless Congress has chosen to grant it, typically in legislation.

The import of this limitation on constitutional rights can be seen on the facts of Cleburne v. Cleburne Living Center, the Supreme Court case discussed in Chapter 2 that concerned the standard of review of discrimination against persons with retardation. Although the Court held it discriminatory to prohibit group homes for "the feebleminded" while allowing group homes for others, the case did not involve the more difficult claim the would-be residents would have had to make if the ordinance had prohibited group homes for everyone. In such a case, the plaintiffs would arguably be asking for a special favor—the right to live in a group home when that right was denied to others—instead of demanding an end to discrimination; it is far from clear that they could prevail in court.

Even if it is accepted that the Equal Protection clause protects only against discrimination and does not require affirmative equalizing by the state, that will not stop all claims for assistance. First, if assistance is provided to others, then it is discriminatory not to provide it to persons with retardation as well. Moreover, affirmative action and remedial services *can* be required when the object is to redress past discrimination; that principle has been well established in school desegregation and other racial discrimination cases. When affirmative action has been ordered as a remedy for unconstitutional discrimination, the justification is either that this government action puts people in a position they would have been in but for the discrimination, or that it serves as some small redress for their grievances.

This possibility of seeking affirmative help as recompense for past wrongs has not been explored for persons with retardation as a group. Those who were once institutionalized, however, have benefited from that analysis and have been afforded entitlements to remedial services in some states—creating some tension between that group and others, sometimes equally needy, who have never lived in a state facility. The previously institutionalized are much more likely to receive the limited placements that exist in residential and day programs.[42] Those without that background, who are often living with aging parents, are relegated to waiting lists that seem never to advance.[43]

In addition, it is often difficult to discern the boundary between assistance and nondiscrimination. For example, if the state provides services for everyone but the services are geared to persons who can follow written directions, is the state treating everyone equally or is it discriminating against retardation? In this and other situations, there is room for creative argument that rules that purport to be neutral are in fact discriminatory; even though persons with retardation trying to come out from under the rules may appear to be asking for special favors, arguments may show that in fact they are only demanding an end to discrimination. The demand that the intellectual stimulation requirement be abolished as prerequisite to parenting is one such argument. Similarly the following cases, involving provision of parenting services to parents with mental retardation, show that the boundary between special assistance and nondiscrimination is not always clear.

Consider Craig Mayle and Tammy Wenning, the biological parents of Jeffrey Mayle. Both parents have retardation and had their parental rights to Jeffrey terminated. On appeal, Craig and Tammy argued that they had been deprived of Equal Protection under the Ohio and U.S. Constitutions because the state terminated "their parental rights without offering them services specifically tailored to take into account their mental retardation and designed to enable them to become competent parents."[44]

The appeals court rejected the claim: "the biological parents . . . [were] both mentally retarded persons, were offered services to help them take care of themselves in order that they might subsequently take care of their child [but] . . . both parents failed at the programs designed to help them because of lack of motivation and interest in those programs."[45] On this reasoning, the court affirmed the termination of their rights and incorporated by reference a prior decision in which it had addressed the same issue: *In re* Dennis Cannon.

Dennis Cannon's mother also had retardation; and, unlike Jeffrey Mayle's parents, she was homeless. She gave birth to Dennis in front of an elementary school, and three days later the child welfare agency filed for permanent custody of Dennis because of his mother's "lack of suitable housing."[46] The trial court granted the petition, and the child's mother appealed unsuccessfully. (The state had obtained permanent custody of Ms. Cannon's other two children the month before Dennis was born.)

As well as having mild retardation ("a tested mental age of twelve") Ms. Cannon had also been diagnosed as having "a dependent personality disorder." Moreover, "her scores on tests measuring common sense and judgment suggest[ed] significant limitations in these areas."[47]

Before her parental rights to her first two children were terminated, the state had drawn up for her a

comprehensive reunification plan . . . [that] concentrated on teaching her to take care of herself. She was referred to programs . . . designed to teach her to care for herself[,] . . . attended sporadically, and was eventually discharged due to lack of interest . . . [She] made no significant progress in an infant stimulation program [and] . . . also made no significant progress in case-work counseling as to housekeeping skills, eating balanced meals, handling a baby, and appropriately feeding a baby. [She] was never referred

to or involved in parenting classes specifically designed for the mentally retarded.[48]

The crux of Ms. Cannon's Equal Protection claim was that she needed
classes she could understand. Because of her retardation she needed *different*
services than those provided to other parents, and her legal position was
that the state had an obligation to recognize that need.

The appellate court summarily rejected this argument, calling it an inver-
sion of Equal Protection logic. In its view Equal Protection meant that Ms.
Cannon should be treated as it believed she had been—"the same" as other
parents.[49] The issue seems almost impossible to resolve, but in one sense, the
dispute is simply semantic. Some courts would have seen Ms. Cannon's
claim as one for "appropriate" services, and would have held that she, like
everyone else, was entitled to appropriate services to facilitate reunification
with her children.[50]

What seems like a semantic game can thus be determinative of the legal
entitlements of persons with retardation. It is increasingly accepted, at least
in theory, that persons with retardation need services, as other parents do,
and cannot be excluded explicitly, but it is still uncertain to what extent constitutional law protects them from being excluded indirectly—by being provided with services they are not able to use.

The issue is also common in contexts besides parenting. Such an argument might support group homes for persons with retardation, even when
no such homes have been allowed for others. Persons with retardation
might stress that, unlike others, they need group homes in order to live in
the community at all.[51]

Legislative and Agency Support

The U.S. Congress has rescued the courts from difficult questions about
what "equality" requires by conferring benefits or entitlements on persons
with disabilities that surpass constitutional minimums. In the context of education, for example, it would be very difficult to define exactly what the
Constitution requires, but the courts would still be wrestling with that task if
Congress had not enacted legislation instead. The difficulty would arise, in
public school classrooms just as in parent training sessions, if the children
with special needs could not profit from the education offered to other children. In that circumstance, would the state be treating them "equally" in offering them the same classes as everyone else, or would the Constitution re-

quire the state to offer them a special alternative they could profit from?[52] And if some such accommodation were deemed constitutionally required, how would one decide what accommodations were sufficient for "equality"? Should the state have to spend the same amount of money on each, or is some other measure preferable or at least acceptable?

Congress spared the Supreme Court and other courts this quagmire by designing and providing for an elaborate system of special education, beginning in 1970. At the heart of the scheme is a guarantee to each child of "a free appropriate public education which emphasizes special education and related services designed to meet their unique needs."[53] That provision clearly grants more than the Constitution requires. The current embodiment of this policy is the Individuals with Disabilities Education Act (IDEA).[54] Neither it nor its predecessors required states to comply with these federal provisions for special education, but they offered federal funding to states that did. There are a few holdouts at the outset, but now all states participate and thus are bound by the federal statutory standards.

Just as the IDEA creates entitlements beyond what the Constitution requires, the Adoption Assistance and Child Welfare Act of 1980 required states that receive federal funding to make "reasonable efforts" to eliminate the need to remove children, rather than removing them. It also required that, if it is not possible to avert removal, reasonable steps be taken to return the child to the home.[55] The same statute also makes the provision of federal welfare funds for eligible children in foster care conditional on the state's reasonable efforts to prevent removal or accomplish reunification—provisions that apply except where the parents have voluntarily placed the child in foster care.[56]

The most far-reaching current enactment granting protections to persons with disabilities, including retardation, is the Americans with Disabilities Act (ADA). That statute both makes it unnecessary to delineate the constitutional limitations on discrimination against disability and also bestows benefits going beyond freedom from discrimination. First enacted by Congress in 1990, the ADA "prohibits discrimination against persons with disabilities in all services, programs, and activities provided or made available by state or local governments." It extends the ban on discrimination to "the activities of all state and local governments, regardless of whether they receive financial assistance."[57]

The ADA not only prohibits discrimination but also requires *reasonable modifications* of a public entity's rules, policies, or practices in order to accommodate the special needs of a person with a disability. A modification is required as long as it would not "*fundamentally alter* the nature of [the public entity's] services, program, or activity."[58]

The reasonable modifications requirement does not create new rights to personal services; but "if personal services or devices are customarily provided to the individuals served by the public entity . . . these personal services should also be provided to individuals with disabilities."[59] The main goal of the ADA is to help individuals with disabilities achieve maximal integration into mainstream society,[60] and its provisions are to be interpreted with that aim in mind.

Moreover, the ADA has particular application to state social service agencies, allowing its use in court to bring about changes beneficial to parents with retardation.[61] The ADA clearly extends to all departments and agencies of state or local governments, including child and family services agencies.[62] The statute states: "Subject to the provisions of this title, no qualified individual with a disability shall, by reason of such disability, be excluded from participation in or be denied the benefits of services, programs, or activities of a public entity, or be subjected to discrimination by any such entity."[63]

Several cases have explicitly found that the ADA does apply to parenting services, stressing particularly the reasonable accommodations requirement. For example, the New Mexico Court of Appeals ruled that an individual may "raise [the] state's failure to accommodate his or her disability in violation of the [ADA] to argue that he or she lacks responsibility for disintegration of the parent-child relationship, so as to preclude termination of parental rights based on his or her presumed abandonment of child."[64]

Such holdings applying the ADA to claims for parental services are especially important because the Supreme Court has held that the Adoption Assistance Act, even in conjunction with the Civil Rights Act (42 U.S.C. §1983), does *not* provide a cause of action for these suits.[65] Therefore, without the ADA parents could perhaps raise a failure to provide services in defense of a termination claim (though we have seen that such claims have limited success), but they could not bring lawsuits to enforce the promise of federal and state guarantees. The ADA allows affirmative as well as defensive use of guarantees for parental services and other help. Thus it provides a means for parents, perhaps in a class action, to obtain services in suits for injunctive relief or even for mandatory injunctions against government officials.

The three congressional enactments discussed are obviously not alone in granting federal entitlements. Employment, housing, welfare, and Medicaid are examples that cover all aspects of life and that are utilized by persons with mental retardation, among others. State governments and agencies also provide a range of benefits for their residents, some relating to our issue of central concern. Arkansas, for example, requires its Department of Human Services to "make reasonable accommodations in accordance with the Americans with Disabilities Act to parents with disabilities in order to allow them meaningful access to reunification and family preservation services."[66] More commonly state statutes confer the rights directly; for example, Florida's Community Resource Mother or Father Program gives rights to parents instead of a state agency. It provides parents who have retardation (as well as other parents) with a right to training when their shortcomings as parents place them "at risk" of losing their children to the state.[67] These specialized family reunification services, which many states provide, probably go beyond what the Constitution would require of its own force.[68] They have no actual effect, other than symbolic effects, unless they provide more benefits than federal constitutional and statutory law, which the state must in any case follow. But when they do extend greater benefits than federal law confers, they can be important to persons with disabilities.

Under the ADA, the success or failure of a claim for family services will likely depend on the nature of the modification sought and whether it is considered "reasonable,"[69] and predictably much ADA litigation will involve passing upon this question in differing factual contexts. In applying this standard, courts might accept as a norm of reasonableness some of the programs that already exist for assisting parents. Today, for example, there are many models for twenty-four-hour supervision in homes in the community for persons who need full-time assistance. Another possible model is foster care for parents and children. It is important for both models to offer educational programs to teach parenting skills, as well as to provide needed supervision.[70]

In the Boston area, the Department of Mental Retardation holds contracts with a range of service "vendors" that will supply services to help identified persons with retardation. Some provide services to help parents with retardation. One such vendor, Dynamic Action Residence Enterprises (DARE) Family Services, operates a community group living facility, called the Mothers Program, for mothers with retardation and their children. The facility houses three mothers at one time, with up to two children per mother. Each such family occupies one room in the house. Typically children range in age from newborn to age five.

In addition to the availability of twenty-four-hour staff, the parents receive training in a variety of areas, including basic life skills, cooking and budgeting, parenting skills, sex education, and job-related education. They are also assisted in getting jobs. Some families live at the home for as short a period as six months. Others have been there for more than three years. When a mother or family is considered "ready" to live independently, she and her children move into their own apartment and receive ongoing assistance, as needed, from a DARE social worker (as well as any other public assistance available to them under welfare or disability programs). In 1997, nine parents and their children were in the DARE Mothers Program and lived at the group home.[71] Three other parents, each with one to three children, lived in their own apartments.

Another program, operated by the Boston Children's Services, offers assistance from a social worker to parents living in their own homes with their children. Seven families are currently receiving services, such as family support and parental training. Each family consists of mothers, usually living with a husband or partner, and one to three child(ren) per family. The children range in age from newborn to twelve years old.

What is most necessary to the success of such programs is that the caretakers are wise and patient enough to teach the mothers what they need to know to function independently, and that they reinforce the mother as a parent, instead of simply taking over the parenting functions themselves. Such programs offer the advantages of ensuring adequate care for the child, allowing the mother and child to live together and to bond, and providing the opportunity for teaching the mother with her own child, and with one-on-one, continuous instruction.

There are instances of such innovative programs, but despite the apparent promise of federal and state laws, parents with retardation, other persons with retardation, and some other people have an acute, and widely unanswered, need for housing.[72] Many adults with retardation live, and have always lived, with their parents, who may be aging and very anxious about what will happen to their offspring when they die. Resolving the need for residences and assisted residences for persons with retardation in the community is of paramount importance.

The current residential waiting list for individuals with retardation is very long and is growing steadily. Ten or fifteen years without any placement for an eligible individual is a familiar tale. A need for day programs also exists, but it pales beside the need for housing. Moreover, what living arrangements are available are rarely offered to parents. Much more common than programs like the DARE program, which are dubbed "dual foster care," is a policy that forces adults living in state-supported residences in the community to lose their housing if they have a child. The rationale is the supposed inability to accommodate the presence of a newborn.[73]

When parents with retardation do become eligible for department-sponsored arrangements in the community where they can live with their child, as has occurred at least on a small scale in several states besides Massachusetts, that surely is an advance, at least for the parents with retardation who have a child. At the same time, because the waiting list for assisted living is so long, when parents with retardation are included, other needy persons are excluded. Such problems cannot be resolved unless sufficient services are made available to serve the population that needs them.[74]

Devising Solutions

Providing adequate services to all of the people who need them, is, of course, a daunting task. The perpetual shortage of supply seems even more inevitable in the current ethos of fiscal restraint. These circumstances behoove agencies to be particularly creative with the funding they do have to serve the needs of consumers. They also call for creative arguments from lawyers. For example, even if social service agencies have no obligation to assist parents with retardation, that does not mean that they are entitled to discriminate against them with the assistance they give. Or a more novel argument is that even if it is not possible to force a state to spend money, whatever money *is* spent on a family must be spent in service of holding it together, not separating it. If services can be provided more cheaply than long-term foster care, and such care is the likely prognosis, then parents should have the ability (in reality as well as in law) to demand the services that will allow the family unit to survive. The only exception should be those rare circumstances where separation is absolutely necessary for the good of the child and where both parents are unfit and no fit caretaker can be provided.

The proposition that extra money should not be spent to break up the home needlessly seems both self-evident and in keeping with government's stated goals, but following that proposition would clearly change current practices. For example, the cost of the Boston Children's Services program described above is roughly $6,000 annually per family. (The DARE program is more expensive. In addition to payments carried by federal entitlement programs, the Department of Mental Retardation pays $150 to $200 per bed daily.) A comparison of the cost of those family support services with the cost of child foster care arrangements suggests that family services (like the Boston Children's Services program) are more affordable and family place-ments (like the DARE program) are roughly comparable. The per child rate for foster care reported by Department of Social Services for fiscal year 1997 is $5,810 for a child age five or under; $6,159 for a child ages six to twelve; and $6,911 for a teenager. Accordingly, providing parents who have retarda-tion with specialized in-home care or foster family care would seem to fall within the proposition that state money should be spent to hold the family together, in preference to spending that separates the family. Moreover a court could avoid a constitutional ruling if providing a home or foster care is a "reasonable modification" of services, under the ADA and other reason-able accommodation provisions.

In addition, there are helpful measures that are actually cost-free. Social service departments are learning, however slowly, to respect their clients with retardation instead of simply trying to manage them or treat them as "problems" to be handled. Researchers have demonstrated that when social workers and other interveners in the family *do not* treat parents with respect, that often has a crippling effect on the parents' ability to meet the state's ex-pectations of them.

The 1994 British study of parents with retardation discussed in Chapter 14 compiled a list of social service delivery practices about which the parents "complained bitterly." The following items on the list reflect the parents' sense of not being taken seriously:

- usurping parents' authority in their own home;
- treating parents as less than fully adult;
- failing to involve parents in decisions affecting their lives or to respond to parents' concerns; . . .
- meddling in matters that have no bearing on the reasons for interven-tion;
- manipulation of the parents' ever-present fear that their child might be taken away in order to ensure their compliance;
- attributing deficits in the services to the inadequacies of the parents;
- taking advantage of people's learning difficulties;
- a tendency to assume too easily that all problems are caused by the par-ents' learning difficulties;
- too little acknowledgment of the impact of environmental factors on the parents' coping skills;
- an assumed lack of nurturing skills, coupled with too little acknowledg-

ment of the parents' capacity for learning ([often] evidenced by the removal of [a first child shortly after birth]);

- judgements about the adequacy of homemaking and parenting informed
by inappropriate comparisons with middle-class norms;
- inadequate recognition of the emotional bonding between parents and
child, and the trauma of separation;
- an underevaluation of the parents as people (illustrated by workers who
failed to turn up when expected and services that diminished rather than
enhanced their self-esteem).[75]

Clearly, social workers need to learn to treat their clients with respect.

Changes in attitude are as crucial as expenditures of money. Other simple
improvements could be made, yet are often overlooked. For example, court
cases suggest some difficulty, on the part of judges and social workers, in deciding how to view the presence of persons in the home who do not have retardation when the parent who is the primary caretaker is the person who
has retardation. One simple solution would be to rely on available caretakers even when the traditional caretaker—the mother—is not fully fit. That
was the situation in *In re* McDonald, where the mother had retardation and
the father's ability to participate and to have another competent adult at
home when he was away was apparently not considered in terminating the
parents' rights.[76] Clearly, attitudes of judicial decisionmakers need to be altered as well as those of social workers.

Hope for the Future

The case of W. P., Jr., did not look any more promising for parenting than
many of the other cases. It had a happy outcome because a judge was willing
both to insist on compliance with regulations and to experiment with creative solutions.

The decision, reached in late 1995, was different from most cases discussed in this book because the judges, on trial and appeal, required the
state to provide mother and child with dual foster care; by court order,
mother and child were placed together in the home of a foster family. Remarkably, the social worker recommended the placement even though the
mother's first seven children had been removed from her two years earlier
and she was homeless, had mild retardation and chemical dependencies,
and had been the victim of domestic abuse. Though "the mother suffers

from some intellectual impairment," the social worker proposed a living experiment that held out hope of keeping this mother and one of her children together, testifying at trial that the mother "might be able to parent the child if she and the child were in dual foster placement."[77]

That suggestion of "dual foster care" made all the difference for W. P.'s mother. The trial court directed the county to "amend the case plan to provide the mother with the opportunity to attempt dual foster care as a vehicle for reunification."[78] It rejected the agency's eighth termination petition, finding that "the county [had] failed to show . . . reasonable efforts . . . to rehabilitate the mother and reunited her with W. P., Jr. because the caseworker did not offer the dual foster care plan as an option."[79] On appeal, the county sought reversal, claiming (as the social welfare agency did in the *Fulton* case) that the county was not required to show that it had made "reasonable efforts towards reunification." But the appeals court affirmed the trial court. The caseworker had testified that "the foster family expressed an interest in having the mother live with them," supporting the conclusion that dual foster care was a feasible option, but "that she did not amend the case plan to include a dual family placement."[80]

Minnesota law required for termination that there be proof of "a pattern of conduct or specific conditions that will 'continue for a prolonged indefinite period and that are permanently detrimental to the welfare of the child.'"[81] The appeals court held that provision did not support termination in this case despite "the projected permanency of the parent's inability to care for her child." Instead the court allowed Ms. P. to try by forcing the state to help her live in circumstances that would satisfy her needs for assistance and the baby's needs for adequate care. Ms. P. thus avoided losing a child for the eighth time.

Some Key Suggested Reforms

Independent counsel, paid for by the state when the parent is indigent, should be provided to any parent giving up her child for adoption, in order to assure that the parent fully understands the rights that she is surrendering and that her consent to adoption is voluntary. State-funded counsel should also be available for indigent parents at termination proceedings *and* at removal proceedings. Today federal law does not require such a right to counsel, but some states provide it, at least for termination.[82] Indeed, all important procedural protections applied in termination proceedings should be provided in removal proceedings as well. Removal is often the more pivotal event in fact, and once that happens there is substantial likelihood, especially when the parent has retardation, that the parent will never again live with her children.

In addition to clarifying that a finding that accords with the child's best interests is necessary but insufficient for termination of parental rights, and possibly adopting a legislative rule abandoning the strict unfitness requirement after the child has lived away from the parent for a specified period, reformers should avoid needless terminations. Even if a child has been away from his or her mother for a long time and there is little prospect of her regaining custody, there is no benefit in severing the parent-child bond unless it is interfering with a permanent placement for the child or is proved affirmatively harmful to the child for other reasons. These are reforms that would benefit all parents caught in the neglect and abuse system, and are not especially applicable to persons with retardation.

The suggestion that, even though parent and child are living apart, parental rights should not be terminated unless and until there will be an adoption would greatly alter current practice in every state, but nonetheless that reform is worth implementing. There would be rare exceptions where the relationship with the parent was actually destructive to the child, most frequently in cases of deliberate parental wrongdoing involving physical or sexual abuse. But in general a child should have a right to be in contact with the parent and to maintain whatever parental relationship is possible, even if the child cannot live with the parent because of parental shortcomings; and the parent also should be able to have contact, as long as that is not harmful to the child. Even after the possibility of eventual reunification of parent and child has been abandoned and the state has satisfied its obligation to try to render the parent fit, it should take measures to facilitate visitation and other contact between parent and child, allowing them to have as much of a relationship as they can.

What's more, the state should encourage continued contact even after termination through open adoption arrangements. Provision of counsel at termination should be sufficient to encourage open adoption, if counsel is at all thorough in discussing with the biological mother the range of options she might agree to. After all, at the time of consent to adoption, the birth mother has a great deal of bargaining power.

Predictive decisions should be kept to a strict minimum. There should be a strong presumption against them for all parents, including those with retardation. Perhaps persons with retardation should not be encouraged to parent, and perhaps social policy would be promoted by talking persons with retardation out of exercising any parental rights they might otherwise have. Undoubtedly that course of persuasion will dominate parenting decisions for persons with retardation in the near future. Nonetheless, once persons with retardation have become parents—having avoided persuasion or having stood up to it—they, like other parents, should be permitted to try. Experience with some families in which parents have retardation has already shown that a conclusive presumption against their abilities is highly inaccurate—more inaccurate perhaps than the presumption against unwed fathers was in 1972 when Stanley v. Illinois held it unconstitutional. Presuming in favor of their parenting also would have the advantage of treating persons with retardation the same way other parents are treated.

Rather than remove even a newborn, the government should provide a suitable service plan and give the mother an opportunity to learn to be a parent. If assistance is cut back for certain groups in the population—as it was in the welfare reform plan of 1996 (called the Personal Responsibility and Work Opportunity Reconciliation Act)—then persons with retardation who are within those groups will also be cut off, but not on the ground that they have mental retardation.

Many other reforms, of varying degrees of magnitude, are suggested throughout this book, but even an abundant list will not accomplish the needed transformation without a change in societal attitudes. People need to learn that retardation does *not* render parents unable to learn the skills of adequate child care and child rearing, just as they are starting to learn about the competence of persons with retardation in other arenas of life. That change will happen gradually, as our society has more experience with persons who have retardation within the mainstream community and comes better to appreciate their gifts and their abilities. The more creative states are in assisting parents who have retardation, the more normal it will become to imagine and experience persons who happen to have retardation parenting successfully.

Conclusion

One could argue for parental rights for persons with retardation, relying on a Fourteenth Amendment liberty interest or privacy interest and resting on Supreme Court interpretations of the Due Process clause saying that parenting is a "fundamental right." That approach, arguing that the state should not be in the business of judging who can and cannot parent, has great appeal, but the analysis here does not rely on it and rests ultimately on Equal Protection rather than Due Process. For the moment at least, society has made the judgment that anyone who can have a baby can presumptively parent and that a baby or child will be removed from the biological parent only in extreme circumstances. It has also adopted processes very protective of biological parents, evaluating them, if at all, one parent at a time, without dismissing them because of their category—be it unwed fathers or gay men and lesbians or persons with mental illness. The only argument that persons with retardation need in order substantially to better their legal position and increase their legal rights is that they must be treated the same way others are. Accordingly, parents with retardation will sometimes lose their children, but when they do, it will be for the same reasons other persons do: because they have been adjudicated on an individual basis to be unfit; they will not be eliminated because of presumptions against them simply because of retardation. And while some parents with retardation will lose their child or children, others will raise children successfully, as some are already doing.

Just as the thesis does not rely on liberty interests, but instead on rights of equal treatment, it also does not rest on utilitarian arguments, although some could be made. Indeed, the biggest spur to deinstitutionalization has probably been the considerable savings in taxpayer money that it achieves. There also is utility in moving persons into the community and teaching them to hold jobs and participate in community life—both for society and for the persons who become included.

If there is a liberty interest that is central to the argument, it is not a constitutional right to parent or to procreate as much as a right to be involved. The right to be involved has often focused—in this book and in constitutional jurisprudence to date—on medical decisionmaking, partly because in other areas of life most people simply take for granted the right to make decisions that are denied many persons with retardation.

The right to live in the community is an example of such a right—taken for granted by most people but long denied to people with retardation and now of significance to them. A right to make one's basic life decisions needs to be recognized for people with retardation, as does a right to participate in the community. Because those rights are given to citizens generally, however, equal protection and anti-discrimination should be sufficient basis for obtaining them.

Some of the reforms this book puts forward—for example, the recommendation that independent counsel be required when a child is given up for adoption—would have large practical consequences. Others, like the central suggestion that informed consent doctrines not bar adults from making at least nontherapeutic medical decisions, will sometimes make more of a legal than a practical difference. Women with mental retardation may be influenced by other persons and by their circumstances, as many women are when they make childbirth and parenting decisions. But if they are talked to, and even sometimes listened to, instead of being left out of their own life decisions, this is itself an important gain.

If procreation and parenting choices are permitted to persons who have retardation—women and men—on the same basis as they are to others, it is not clear how greatly results will change, or how quickly. But the success of the change does not depend on how many babies women with retardation decide to have or to keep. The reform will have achieved its aim if persons with retardation are more fully respected, are allowed to participate, and are given some power in determining the direction of their own lives.

NOTES

BIBLIOGRAPHY

CASES

INDEX

Notes

Preface

1. Testimony of Jerry Whitburn, then Massachusetts Health and Human Services Commissioner, Governor's Commission on Mental Retardation, Wellesley, Mass., January 1996.

1. Some Families

1. See generally Ferleger (1983).
2. Gaines-Carter (1987).
3. Ibid.
4. Ciotti (1989).
5. Ibid.
6. In re McDonald, 449.
7. Golden (1990).

2. Public Policy, Past and Present

1. See Scheerenberger (1983), 118. See also Ward v. Dulaney; State v. Richards; Pettigrew v. State; Hays v. Commonwealth.
2. Dornick v. Reichenback.
3. Ferguson (1994), 36.
4. Ibid., 50.
5. Ibid., 20.
6. Scheerenberger (1983), 121.
7. Powell (1882), 268.
8. Reilly (1991), 13.
9. Tyor and Bell (1984), 111–122.
10. Reilly (1991), 18.
11. Tyor and Bell (1984), 36, 115–119.
12. P. Wald (1976), 9.

13. Kenyon (1914), 458, 465, 467.
14. See Scheerenberger (1983), 116.
15. Amory (1980), 5, 6.
16. See, e.g., Act of Sept. 29, 1919, No. 704, §6, 1919 Ala. Acts 1023, 1024; Act of March 9, 1887, ch. 57, 1887 Cal. Stat. 69; Act of Aug. 19, 1919, No. 373, §3; 1919 Ga. Laws 377, 379; Act of Apr. 15, 1919, ch. 150, §3, 1919 Tenn. Pub. Acts 561, 562.
17. U.S. Department of Commerce (1934); Bureau of the Census (1923), cited in Scheerenberger (1983), 158.
18. See Scheerenberger (1983), 158.
19. See Budd and Greenspan (1984), 478; Wolfensberger (1975).
20. One argument Justice Holmes made for sterilization of "the feeble minded" in institutions is that sterilizing them and thereby enabling them to move into the community would allow the state to admit more persons to its institutions and thus to sterilize more broadly. Buck v. Bell (1927), 208.
21. See Brakel and Rock (1971), 226–229, 240–243 (table of statutes). See also Linn and Bowers (1978); Shaman (1978).
22. See Searle (1976), 7.
23. Best (1965), cited in Scheerenberger (1983), 154.
24. See, e.g., Minn. Stat. §517.03 (1997) (persons with retardation who are under the guardianship or conservatorship of the commissioner of human services may marry only with the commissioner's permission); Neb. Rev Stat. §42-374 (1989) (retardation is ground for annulment).
25. Zablocki v. Redhail, 384; see In re Goalen.
26. Zablocki v. Redhail, 388.
27. Murdoch (1913), 37–38. In addition, many marriages are childless, some unintentionally and others by design.
28. Wolfensberger and Nirje (1972). See also Wolfensberger (1984).
29. See generally Edgerton (1979), 95–97 (starting in the mid-1960s there has been an "exodus" from institutions to smaller community residences for persons who have retardation).
30. A taxonomy of community residential facility alternatives was adapted from a study conducted by Baker, Seltzer, and Seltzer (1974). Cf. Flynn and Nitsch (1980), 221–225. See generally Tyor and Bell (1984).
31. United Nations (1971), Article IV.
32. Nirje (1980), 33.
33. Ibid., 31–34. See generally Turnbull and Schultz (1979). See also Paul, Turnbull, and Cruickshank (1979).
34. United States v. Carolene Products Co., 144, 152–153.
35. The Court strictly scrutinizes racial classifications and allows them to stand only when there is a "compelling state interest" and the legislation represents the "least restrictive alternative." Gender classifications receive "heightened" but not "strict" scrutiny; sometimes they are characterized as receiving "intermediate scrutiny." See Yick Wo v. Hopkins, 374 (race); Craig v. Boren, 218

(gender). See also United States v. Virginia (prohibiting all-male admission policy at Virginia military school).

36. See Heller v. Doe, 312; Cleburne v. Cleburne Living Ctr., 432.
37. See, e.g., Williamson v. Lee Optical, Inc.
38. Cleburne, 436–437.
39. Ibid., 450.
40. Ibid., 448.
41. See Craig v. Boren (adopting this standard of review for gender-based classifications).
42. See Williamson v. Lee Optical.
43. *Bowers* is actually both an Equal Protection holding and a Due Process holding. Sometimes *Bowers* is taken to be only a Due Process case, which is understandable both because the statute at issue punished sodomy across the board, whether between heterosexuals or homosexuals; and because the Court's discussion focuses on the Due Process clause and the asserted "right to choose." *Bowers* must be seen as an Equal Protection case as well, however, because the U.S. Supreme Court itself created a discrimination against gays in the way it decided the case, limiting its decision to the legitimacy of a ban on homosexual sodomy. The Court thereby took the position that it would be constitutionally permissible for legislation to allow precisely the same act between men and women that it prohibited between men. Cf. Loving v. Virginia (suggesting that a state rule prohibiting interracial marriage would be unconstitutional even if all races were allowed to marry only within their own race). Bowers v. Hardwick is therefore important not only for the Due Process holding for which it is known, but also for its necessary implication that discrimination against homosexuals will receive little if any judicial scrutiny.
44. Heller v. Doe, 307, 323, quoting F.C.C. v. Beach Communications, 2106.
45. See Pennhurst State Sch. and Hosp. v. Halderman. But cf. Youngberg v. Romeo (right to safety and freedom from bodily restraints of involuntarily committed patients with retardation).
46. Estate of C. W., discussed primarily in Chapter 11.
47. See generally the Americans with Disabilities Act, 42 U.S.C. §§12131 et seq. (1990) (Title II). Title II became effective in January 1992.
48. Skinner v. Oklahoma, 541.
49. Eisenstadt v. Baird, 453.
50. Carey v. Population Servs. Int'l., 685.
51. Roe v. Wade; Planned Parenthood v. Casey.
52. See Field (1991), 46–49. Chapter 8 discusses another ambiguity concerning reproductive choice: whether adults have a constitutional right to pursue consensual sexual relationships outside of marriage.
53. See Burgdorf (1983), 371.
54. See Pierce v. Soc. of Sisters, 510; Meyer v. Nebraska, 390.
55. Ginsburg v. New York, 639.
56. Wisconsin v. Yoder, 232.
57. Quilloin v. Walcott, 255, quoting Prince v. Massachusetts, 166, Cleveland Bd. of Educ. v. LaFleur, 639–640. See also Moore v. City of East Cleveland.

58. See Wisconsin v. Yoder, 233–234; Prince v. Massachusetts, 166.

59. See, e.g., Reiss (1971), 214. Other motivations for becoming a parent include the desire to perpetuate oneself through one's child and to be provided with emotional and financial support in old age.

60. See Simmel (1955) (discussing the human need to belong to a group). See also Richardson and Koller (1996) (discussing the negative impact of the stigma of mental retardation on spousal relationships, where one spouse has a history of being labeled with mental retardation).

61. Edgerton (1979), 157–160 (describing the attempts of deinstitutionalized persons with mental retardation to collect memorabilia and other material trappings of "normal" people).

62. A sheltered workshop is a government-supported workplace for people with disabilities who cannot obtain competitive employment. Many different types of work can be performed in these workshops, for example simple factory work, envelope stuffing, or arts and crafts.

63. See Robinson and Robinson (1965), 323.

64. Ibid., 337, citing Cromwell (1959), 333. See also Chapter 3, n. 7.

65. See Mandell and Fiscus (1981), 315.

66. See Part IV.

67. See generally Goldstein, Freud, and Solnit (1973, 1979).

68. States define parental fitness with varying degrees of explicitness. North Carolina, for example, specifically lists mental retardation as one ground for termination of parental rights due to incapacity. N.C. Gen. Stat. §7A-289.32(7) (1997) ("Incapability under this subdivision may be the result of substance abuse, mental retardation, mental illness, organic brain syndrome, or any other similar cause or condition"). By contrast, some states take a more generalized approach providing, for example, that the legal guardianship of a child shall be changed if a child's parents are "unsuitable persons to have the custody and tuition of such minor." Ohio Rev. Code Ann. §2111.06 (1977).

69. Many persons with retardation have previously been institutionalized and when released, find that records are still kept of their whereabouts. A social worker may continue to follow their progress. Moreover, whether once institutionalized or not, they may be receiving monetary benefits because of their disability, or services like transportation or recreational services. Persons with mental retardation may work at a sheltered workshop run in connection with the state, or they may live in a community residence supported by the state. Some persons with mental retardation do, of course, live at home and may not apply for any services. Accordingly, as they procreate and parent, they may escape state scrutiny. But even then, when their child or children attend school, the school system may become aware of the parent's disability. And mental retardation may be more readily detectable by school personnel than other conditions that are equally or more relevant to parental fitness.

70. Such fears of prejudice probably do not provide a constitutionally valid reason to deny a parent custody because of retardation. See Palmore v. Sidoti (fear of

racial prejudice was an impermissible consideration in a decision to transfer a child to her natural father from the custody of her natural mother, who was Caucasian and had married a black man).

71. See Brakel and Rock (1971), 207.

72. But see the case of Joseph Lee Moore in Chapter 12.

3. Who Are Called "Retarded"?

1. See National Institute on Disability and Rehabilitation Research (1996), sec. 1, pt. 4. Some studies placed the percentage between 2.0 and 3.5 percent. See Fryers (1993); Arc (1982). The President's Committee on Mental Retardation believes that only approximately 1 percent of the U.S. population (2–2.5 million people) is actually known to have retardation. That figure is based on the number of individuals who are receiving or who have received services. Telephone interview of George Bartholet, President's Committee on Mental Retardation, Washington, D.C., March 1997. Many persons with retardation receive no services, however, even after requesting them and waiting for many years. See Massachusetts Governor's Commission on Mental Retardation (1996).

2. See Arc (1997b). See also National Information Center on Youth and Children with Disabilities (1998); Batshaw and Perret (1992).

3. Arc (1993).

4. It is not a coincidence that the Americans with Disabilities Act, for example, was passed during an administration whose Attorney General had a son with retardation.

5. Approximately one-half of individuals with mental retardation have "dual diagnoses" of some form of mental illness in addition to mental retardation. Statistically, there is a "two- to-fourfold increase in psycho-pathology" (mental illness) among persons who have retardation. They, like the population without retardation, evidence the "full array of personality types and . . . personality disorders" known to psychiatry. Nonetheless psychological and medical disorders of persons with mental retardation are undertreated in our society because of those persons' "low self-expectations, economic limitations, and difficulties in managing complex organizational systems." Despite undertreatment, the psychiatric profession has noted with regard to this group that "there can be a remarkable degree of preservation of psychological growth." Hales, Yudofsky, and Talbott (1994), 775–776, 774.

6. See Batshaw and Perret (1992), 21–440.

7. The fourth and most recent edition of the American Psychiatric Association's *Diagnostic and Statistical Manual* (DSM-IV) for classifying and diagnosing mental disorders contains seventeen major classifications, the first of which—disorders usually first diagnosed in infancy, childhood, or adolescence—includes mental retardation. The other classes are: delirium, dementia, amnestic and other cognitive disorders; mental disorders due to general medical conditions not elsewhere classified; substance-related disorders; schizophrenia and other psy-

chotic disorders; mood disorders; anxiety disorders; somatoform disorders; factitious disorders; disassociative disorders; sexual and gender disorders; eating disorders; sleep disorders; impulse control disorders not elsewhere classified; adjustment disorder; personality disorder; and other conditions that may be a focus of clinical attention. See Hales, Yudofsky, and Talbott (1994), 237–244.

The sometimes complicated overlap between mental retardation and forms of mental illness is evidenced by the difficulty members of the psychiatric profession often experience when trying to distinguish the "primary elements of mental retardation" from its "psychiatric complications." The American Psychiatric Association's *Textbook of Psychiatry* explains: "People commonly expect individuals with mental retardation to be dull and lifeless. It is clear that depression can be a concomitant disorder or a complication [of having mental retardation] (e.g. in response to extra burdens, low self-image, and stigma). [But m]any apparent characteristics of mental retardation are not essential to the syndrome [of depression], may 'disappear' during the course of effective treatment [of depression], and are merely associated findings or developmental complications . . . Complications of mental retardation are numerous. In the care structure, a lack of aggressivity in medical care and a lack of continuity of rehabilitative care can hinder basic medical treatment. Common psychological complications include frequent experiencing of failure, low self-esteem, frustration in fulfillment of dependency needs and wishes for love, wavering parental support, regressive wishes for institutionalization, anticipation of failure (leading to avoidance of problem solving and challenges, reduced curiosity and exploration, and impaired mastery seeking and pride), defensive rigidity, and excessive caution (e.g. a resistance to dealing with new people and places, including helping professionals). Additional psychosocial complications are impaired communicational interactions, inappropriate social assertiveness, and vulnerability to being exploited. Financial complications (i.e. poverty) entail further medical complications, including impaired care-seeking (e.g. delayed treatment, excessive use of emergency facilities), rare preventative treatment (e.g. prenatal and well-baby care, periodic checkups), accidents and trauma, malnutrition, lead exposure, child abuse, prematurity, and teenage pregnancy. Institutionalization may promote passivity and excessive compliance. Societal ignorance and stigmatization may lead to avoidance by potential social companions and by professionals." Ibid., 775, 780–781.

8. Ibid., 777.
9. See Brakel and Rock (1971), 210, 222–223 (noting that eugenic sterilization laws applied to persons with mental illness as well as those who have mental deficiency).
10. Ibid.
11. The exception would be a genetic predisposition to some characteristic that later can trigger retardation—for example, a genetic predisposition to high fevers.

12. Arc (1993). See also Batshaw and Perret (1992), 259–289.
13. See Arc (1997a), citing Moser (1995), 4–6. See also Hales, Yudofsky, and Talbott (1994), 778.
14. Hales, Yudofsky, and Talbott (1994), 778 (Table 23-21).
15. See Batshaw and Perret (1992), 268, 270–271.
16. The following is a list of psychosocial factors that may cause mild mental retardation (Hales, Yudofsky, and Talbott 1994, 778):

Poverty
  Inadequate housing
  Weak hygiene
  Malnutrition
  Disease and infection
  Inadequate medical treatment
  Insufficient preventative medical care (prenatal, postnatal)
  Sociocultural deprivation

Parental factors
  IQ (impaired use of personal resources, help and agencies)
  Age (unplanned teenage pregnancies)
  Education (regarding parenting skills)
  Income and employment record
  Psychiatric disorders
  Help-seeking behavior (e.g. regarding medical care)
  Child care
    Supervision and caregiving (risks of accidents and ingestions)
    Limit setting and discipline (quality, predictability)
    Psychosocial stimulation
  Child abuse and neglect

Family variables
  Family size (may exceed parental resources)
  Family organization
  Planning for future needs and opportunities

Intrapsychic dimensions
  Self-esteem
  Personal assertiveness
  Mastery of challenges and management of failures
  Exploration and novelty seeking
  Concomitant psychiatric disorder

Community
  Housing
  Medical care
  Safety of neighborhood
  Specialized facilities for mental retardation

Funding resources

Political attitudes

Economic stability of nation

Advocacy on behalf of individuals with mental retardation

17. D'Souza (1990), 36, citing Smith (1988).

18. D'Souza (1990), 36, citing DeGrouchy and Turleau (1984). See also Suzuki et al. (1986), 159 (the carrier has an "extra chunk of chromosome 21").

19. D'Souza (1990), 36. It would seem, however, that two asymptomatic carriers could produce a child with the syndrome and that heredity would thus account for some Down's syndrome births—and more in a few generations, as more Down's syndrome mothers produce carriers. If male carriers had low testosterone counts as well as males with the syndrome, that would reduce possibilities for inherited Down's syndrome. See generally ibid.

20. See Davies (1989), 5.

21. See Hagerman and Cronister (1996), 150.

22. The "fragile site" within the X chromosome was discovered in the late 1970s, but the location of the fragile X gene within that site was not discovered until 1991. Since then, research on the syndrome, which was traditionally underfunded, has received an infusion of funds, and much has been learned about the prevalence of the syndrome, though important variables affecting its prevalence are still to be discovered.

23. See Davies (1989), 21. Since the discovery of the fragile X gene within the X chromosome in 1991, prevalence estimates in males have been revised downward, from 80 in 100,000 to between 16 and 25 in 100,000. The prevalence of females affected with the fragile X syndrome has long been presumed to be about one-half of the male prevalence. But the prevalence in females of the fragile gene alone (without the syndrome) has been estimated to be 1 in 259. See Tarleton and Saul (1998). For a discussion of difficulties with genetic counseling for the fragile X syndrome, see Chapter 8.

24. See Davies (1989), 42.

25. Hagerman and Cronister (1996), 179.

26. See Batshaw and Perret (1992), 268, 270–271.

27. Gottleib and Williams (1987), 130, citing Grossman (1973).

28. Ibid.

29. See American Association on Mental Retardation (AAMR) (1992).

30. Arc (1993).

31. See AAMR (1992).

32. Batshaw and Perret (1992), 268–269.

33. The American Psychiatric Association has adopted this feature of the AAMR's definition in its most recent criteria for diagnosing mental retardation (DSM-IV), published in 1994. See Hales, Yudofsky, and Talbott (1994), 772.

34. Hales, Yudofsky, and Talbott (1994), 780, citing Grossman (1983).

35. Ibid., 780.

36. *Merck Manual* (1987), 1982. See also *Merck Manual Home Edition* (1997), 1240.

37. Hales, Yudofsky, and Talbott (1994), 772.
38. See ibid.
39. Arc (1982). See also *American Medical Association Encyclopedia of Medicine* (1989); *Dorland's Illustrated Medical Dictionary* (1994). Now that these subcategories are no longer in fashion, the Arc's statements speak only of those "mildly affected," which for that organization includes all with IQs over 49. The Arc now claims that group is about 87 percent of the population with retardation in the United States and that 13 percent have IQs under 50 and "will have serious limitations in functioning." Arc (1993).
40. See Batshaw and Perret (1982), 268.
41. Arc (1991a).
42. Batshaw and Perret (1992), 269. At least 90 percent of "individuals with low intelligence" are identified by age eighteen. Diagnostic labeling of persons with mental retardation is rare before the age of five. It rises sharply in the child's early school years, peaking in the later school years—by about age fifteen—and declines to 1 percent during early adulthood. As the American Psychiatric Society's Textbook on Psychiatry explains: "High prevalence rates during the school years are usually attributed to the adaptive and intellectual demands of school (especially social and abstract thinking) and the high degree of supervision in classrooms (resulting in increased recognition of the child's difficulties). The decline of diagnostic labeling during adulthood is usually attributed to improving social and economic skills, less supervision at work, and perhaps (in some cases) delayed intellectual development. Typically, there is an earlier age of diagnosis for more severe levels of mental retardation." Hales, Yudofsky and Talbott (1994), 772, 776.
43. Batshaw and Perret (1992), 268.
44. Ibid., 269.
45. Gottlieb and Williams (1987), 113–114.
46. Ibid., citing Adams (1973), 587–598.
47. See Sparrow, Balla, and Cicchetti (1984).
48. Hales, Yudofsky, and Talbott (1994), 773, quoting Sparrow, Balla, and Cicchetti (1984).
49. Hales, Yudofsky, and Talbott (1994), 773.
50. Ibid.
51. See Scheerenberger (1983), 139.
52. Lubove (1971).
53. Batshaw and Perret (1992), 285.
54. Carson (1989).
55. Other factors, to name a few, include unwed fatherhood (as in Stanley v. Illinois); poverty; mental illness; and youth.
56. Gould (1981), 159.
57. Recapitulation was a second biological theory for ranking "inferior" and "superior" human groups according to race, gender, and social class. It held that the embryonic development of a human being (or any other animal) reflected,

at various stages, the biological changes in its evolutionary development. It was believed that the "intellectual traits of the uncivilized . . . are traits recurring in the children of the civilized." Spencer (1895), 89–90, quoted in Gould (1981), 117. Thus, "traits of modern children are primitive characters of ancestral adults." Gould (1981), 119. The American paleontologist E. D. Cope suggested that the theory of recapitulation proved that the following four groups of people were "lower human forms": the nonwhite races, all women, southern Europeans, and the lower-class members of the superior races. See Cope (1887), 291–293. The theory of recapitulation led the Italian physician Cesare Lombroso to postulate a theory of "anatomical stigmata" for identifying the physical features of savages and criminals. See Gould (1981), 124–145.

58. Gould (1981), 42, 112 (citations omitted).
59. Ibid., 30–72.
60. See Down (1866), 259–262, and (1887). See generally Scheerenberger (1983), 56–58.
61. See Scheerenberger (1983), 57.
62. Ibid.
63. The terms "Down's syndrome" and "Mongolism" are used interchangeably by some—see, e.g., Alberts et al. (1983), 465, 796—although in the United States today using "Mongolism" or "Mongoloid" to describe a person with Down's syndrome is considered pejorative.
64. See Ireland (1877), cited in Scheerenberger (1983), 58–59.
65. See, e.g., Esquirol (1845); Seguin (1846). See generally Scheerenberger (1983), 51–56.
66. Ireland defined "idiocy" as "mental deficiency, or extreme stupidity, depending upon malnutrition or disease before birth or before the evaluation of the mental faculties of childhood." He defined "imbecility" as "a less decided degree of mental capacity." Scheerenberger (1983), 59, quoting Ireland (1877), 1.
67. See, e.g., Esquirol (1838), discussed in Scheerenberger (1983), 51–56.
68. See Scheerenberger (1983), 59, 63.
69. Ibid.
70. Gould (1981), 147, quoting Binet (1898).
71. Ibid., 148, quoting Binet (1900), 403.
72. Three versions of the test were published during this period of time. See Binet and Simon (1916).
73. Gould (1981), 149. In the mid-1890s, Binet had explored an array of tests developed earlier by his contemporaries. See generally Scheerenberger (1983), 65.
74. Gould (1981), 149.
75. Scheerenberger (1983), 62, citing Duncan and Millard (1866).
76. Gould (1981), 151, quoting Binet and Simon (1916), 42.
77. MacMillan (1982), 170–171.
78. Gould (1981), 149 (Binet [1916]).
79. See discussion of IQ testing later in this chapter.

80. Gould (1981), 149 (quoting Binet [1916]).
81. Ibid.
82. As Gould explains, "Division is more appropriate [than subtraction] because it is the relative, not the absolute, magnitude of disparity between mental and chronological age that matters. A two-year disparity between mental age two and chronological age four may denote a far severer degree of deficiency than a two-year disparity between mental age fourteen and chronological age sixteen. Binet's method of subtraction would give the same result in both cases, while Stern's IQ measures 50 for the first case and 88 for the second. (Stern multiplied the actual quotient by 100 to eliminate the decimal point)." Ibid., 150n.
83. Ibid., 151.
84. Binet and Simon (1912), 329.
85. Gould (1981), 151.
86. Ibid. (quoting John Stuart Mill).
87. Ibid., quoting Binet and Simon (1916), 169.
88. Ibid., 153, 169 (quoting Binet and Simon [1916]).
89. Ibid., 151–152.
90. Ibid., 152, quoting Binet and Simon (1916).
91. Ibid., 154.
92. See Goddard (1913), 105–107; (1912–13), 91–94; (1917), 243–277.
93. Lubove (1971), 68–69 (citation omitted).
94. Ibid., 70–71, citing Richmond (1917), 229.
95. Ibid.
96. Ibid., 71–72.
97. Peculiarly, when Wechsler converted the raw scores to scaled IQ scores, he compared the raw scores of one age group against only those of the same group, instead of against scores from a common reference group, such as scores from, say, ages 20 to 34. Some critics suggest that Wechsler's reluctance to make inter-age group comparisons was politically, rather than psychometrically, motivated; inter-age group comparisons would have yielded an accelerating decline in the test results of older subjects, whose approval was needed for his newfangled formula to achieve professional acceptance. See Gregory (1987), 80.
98. To illustrate another type of measurement by standard deviation, imagine a room of 10 women in which the mean height is 5 feet 7 inches; those women who are 5 feet 9 will have a standard deviation of +2, and those at 5 feet 5 will have a standard deviation of −2.
99. For example, if a normal IQ score is defined as those scores falling between 85 and 115, and the mean result is 100, a normal IQ falls within one standard deviation of the mean, in which case one standard deviation would span 15 IQ points.
100. See Hales, Yudofsky, and Talbott (1994), 773.
101. See generally Fischer et al. (1996), 79–87.

102. Hales, Yudofsky, and Talbott, 773, Figure 23-8.
103. See Evans and Waites (1981), 131.
104. Ibid.
105. Batshaw and Perret (1992), 268–269.
106. 20 U.S.C. §1409−B (1986).
107. *Merck Manual* (1987), 1983; Batshaw and Perret (1992), 268.
108. *Merck Manual* (1987), 1983.
109. See Marsh (1992), 31.
110. To rely on the IQ number is like looking at yesterday's weather forecast to see if it is raining today, instead of looking out the window.
111. Jencks (1992).
112. See discussion of mental age and other labels above.
113. Gould (1981), 159. See also Kamin (1974). "Intelligence" is alternately defined as "the capacity to acquire and apply knowledge," "the faculty of thought and reason," and "superior powers of the mind." *American Heritage Dictionary* (1976), s.v.
114. See, e.g., Gould (1981), 155.
115. Peterson (1997), D1.
116. In response to such discoveries of new kinds of intelligence, many elementary school teachers are reshaping their curricula. Some also have dispensed with "gifted and talented" student programs, saying instead that "all children are gifted and talented [and now] intelligent, too." Ibid., D2.
117. Ibid., D1.
118. Ibid.
119. See Snyderman and Rothman (1986), 79–97.
120. Peterson (1997), D1.

4. Procreative Choice—But Whose?

1. Ms. Romero was not considered to have mental retardation or developmental disabilities, according to Colorado's definition of those terms, because her brain damage occurred during her adulthood and was not present at her birth. See In re Romero (1990), 820–821. See also the discussion of differing definitions of retardation in Chapter 3.
2. See In re Romero (1988), 1–2.
3. See In re Romero (1990), 820.
4. Ibid., 825.
5. The guardian *ad litem* must be a noninterested person but may or may not be a lawyer. The role of the guardian *ad litem* is to investigate and confer with the subject and inform the court of his or her opinion of the subject's interests with regard to the litigation.
6. Ibid.
7. The court held that an individual should be deemed competent to grant or withhold consent "if [she] understands the nature of the district court's pro-

ceedings, the relationship between sexual activity and reproduction and the consequences of the . . . procedure [at issue]." Ibid., 823. The fact that Ms. Romero had "testified at the district court hearing in an articulate manner" convinced the majority of the Colorado Supreme Court that "she understood the nature of the consequences" of the proposed tubal ligation. Ibid., 823–824. But there was a strong dissenting opinion arguing that an individual's ability to express her wishes does not provide "clear and convincing" evidence of her legal capacity to consent. Ibid., 825 (Mullarkey, J. dissenting). The dissent also argued that an element of legal capacity should be the ability to understand the risks of pregnancy. The majority found that Ms. Romero had this ability but declined to establish it as a necessary factor of competency.

8. The trial judge in *C.W.* used that term. See Estate of C.W., 441.
9. Buck v. Bell, 207.
10. See Danforth v. Planned Parenthood; Casey v. Planned Parenthood.
11. For purposes of the exercise of procreative rights and some other medical decisions, however, minors have increasingly been held legally competent to make their own decisions, a result that would have been surprising forty years ago. See Planned Parenthood v. Danforth; Carey v. Population Services.
12. An example of a limited guardian is one appointed for the sole purpose of managing a person's finances. See Chapter 9.
13. In some states more than mere touching is required. See Smith v. State.
14. See, e.g., Title VII, Civil Rights Act of 1964, 42 U.S.C. §§2000(e), *et seq.;* The Pregnancy Discrimination Act of 1978, 42 U.S.C. §2000 e(k). Earlier protective policy is reflected in Goesaert v. Cleary and Adkins v. Children's Hosp.
15. See, e.g., Planned Parenthood of Central Missouri v. Danforth; Conn. Gen. Stat. §45a-682 (1993).
16. This term includes caretakers of all kinds: friends, parents, institutional providers—those who have legal guardianship and those assisting persons who have their own guardianship.

5. Evolution of Policies toward Sterilization

1. By contrast, the law and policies concerning abortion, contraception, and parenting are almost indiscernible.
2. See Scheerenberger (1983), 71–73.
3. See generally Tyor and Bell (1984).
4. See Trent (1994), 251.
5. The techniques used—vasectomy for men and salpingectomy (cutting or tying of the fallopian tubes) for women—were developed in the late nineteenth century. See Brakel and Rock (1971), 207–225. For more modern techniques, see the discussion in Chapter 8 of reversible, laparoscopic sterilization.
6. See generally O'Hara and Sanks (1956).
7. See Note (1981), 603.

8. See O'Hara and Sanks (1956), 22.

9. Brakel and Rock (1971), 208, citing Challener (1952).

10. See Williams v. Smith. Nonetheless, the statute remained on the books until it was repealed in 1963. See Act of March 9, 1907, ch. 215, 1907 Ind. Acts 377 (repealed 1963).

11. Before 1925, the court overturned such statutes in the following cases: Smith v. Board of Exm'rs of Feeble-minded (New Jersey); Haynes v. Lapeer Circuit Judge (Michigan); In re Thompson (New York).

12. See Valerie N. (1985), 392. See also Comment (1927, 1929).

13. See Smith v. Command (Michigan) and Buck v. Bell (1925) (Virginia). See also Cynkar (1981), 1433.

14. Buck v. Bell (1927), 204.

15. Carrie Buck's school records indicate no retardation: in the five years she attended school, Carrie was promoted every year, reaching the sixth grade; one year before she left school, her teacher recommended her for promotion, evaluating her as "very good—deportment and lessons." This record was not produced at the trial. It would, arguably, have contradicted the testimony of the only witness in the case. That witness claimed that Carrie was "antisocial" because she had written notes to boys in school. See generally Lombardo (1985).

16. At the time of Carrie's commitment hearing she was seven months pregnant.

17. See Lombardo (1985), 31, n. 7.

18. See Note (1950), n. 12. Some of these statutes were struck down as unconstitutional because they failed to put adequate limits on the decisionmakers' discretion. See Brewer v. Valk.

19. See Note (1950), 253, nn. 12–13.

20. See generally Dowbiggin (1992).

21. Davis (1983), 214. Sanger made this statement in a radio talk show.

22. Areen (1992), 182, citing Human Betterment Association of America (1957). It has been estimated that between 1927 and 1964, 60,000 eugenic sterilizations were performed in the United States. See Robitscher (1973), apps. 1–2a.

23. In Buck v. Bell (1927), Justice Holmes dispensed with similar Equal Protection challenges to the statute there at issue. He considered the Equal Protection clause "the usual last resort of constitutional arguments." Ibid., 208. Starting with the Warren Court constitutional revolution of the 1950s and 1960s, the Equal Protection clause has become of enormous significance and has been the tool for invalidating important state rules. See, e.g., Brown v. Board of Education; Reynolds v. Sims.

24. Buck v. Bell (1927), 206. See also Comment (1927).

25. In re Guardianship of Hayes, 639.

26. See Ark. Code Ann. §§20-49-201 through 206 (1987); Cal. Prob. Code §§1953-1956 (1991); Colo. Rev. Stat. §27-10.5-130 (1993); Conn. Gen. Stat. §§45a-693 through 699 (1993); Del. Code Ann. tit. 16 §§5708-5710 (1997); Fla. Stat. ch. 744.3725 (1997); Ga. Code Ann. §31-20-3 (1992); Haw. Rev. Stat. §§560:5-604 through 607 (1986); Kan. Stat. Ann. §59-3018 (8) (1993); Me.

Rev. Stat. tit. 34-B §§7007-7013 (1988); Minn. Stat. §525.56 (4) (1996); Miss. Code Ann. §41-45-1, et seq. (1993); N.C. Gen. Stat. §§35-41 through 45 (1973); N.D. Cent. Code §25-01.2.11 (1997); N.J. Rev. Stat. §30:6D-5 (1997); Ohio Rev. Code Ann. §6123.86 (1997); Or. Rev. Stat. §§436.255(2), 436.275(2), 436.315 (1991); Utah Code Ann. §§62A-6-110 through 113 (1988); Va. Code Ann. §54.1-2976 (1997); Vt. Stat. Ann. tit. 18 §§8709(c), 8714 (1981); W.V. Code §27-16-1 through 5 (1997).

27. See, e.g., Colo. Rev. Stat. §27-10.5-128 (1993); Utah Code Ann. §62A-6-106 (1988); Vt. Stat. Ann. tit. 18 §8712 (1981); Or. Rev. Stat. §436.295 (1991).

28. Buck v. Bell (1927), 207.

29. Ibid. Justice Holmes wrongly described the Buck family (Carrie, her mother Emma, and Carrie's daughter) as "imbeciles." Neither Carrie nor Emma were so described even by the physicians and eugenicists who advocated Carrie's sterilization. Emma allegedly had a "mental age" of nine and would have been classified as a "low-grade moron," while they classified Carrie as a "middle-grade moron." On intelligence scales "imbeciles" rank below "morons." Moreover Carrie's school records suggest no retardation at all. See Lombardo (1985).

30. In this 1846 case, Chief Justice Taney held for a 7–2 majority of the Supreme Court that African Americans were not U.S. citizens and thus had no standing to sue in U.S. courts. The Dred Scott holding was corrected and overturned only by the Civil War and the subsequent adoption of the Fourteenth Amendment to the U.S. Constitution.

31. See generally Scott (1986).

32. See, e.g., Conn. Gen. Stat. §§45a-690(d) and 699 (1993); Me. Rev. Stat. tit. 34-B §7013(4) (1988); N.H. Rev. Stat. Ann. §464-A:251(c) (1997); Or. Rev. Stat. §436.225(3) and 436.305 (1991). Compare Cal. Prob. Code §1958 (1991).

33. See, e.g., Conn. Gen. Stat. §45a-690(d)(1) (1993); Ga. Code Ann. §31-20-3(c)(2) (1992); Me. Rev. Stat. Ann. tit. 34-B §7013(5)(a) (1988); Vt. Stat. Ann. tit. 18 §8711(c)(3)(E) (1982); Va. Code Ann. §54.1-2977(2) (1998); W.Va. Code §27-16-1(3) (1974). Several state courts also established this requirement. See C. D. M. v. State, 613; In re A. W., 376 (in state with statute); In re Moe, 722; In re Grady, 483; Hayes, 640.

34. Conn. Gen. Stat. §45a-690(d)(6) (1993); Vt. Stat. Ann. tit. 18 §8711(c)(3)(C) (1981); Va. Code Ann. §54.1-2977(4) (1997); W.Va. Code §27-16-1(3) (1974). Courts adopted this factor in: C. D. M. v. State, 613; In re Moe, 722; In re Grady, 483; In re Terwilliger, 1384; Hayes, 641.

35. Examples of states that seem to allow sterilization only of persons with authority to consent for themselves are: Kan. Stat. Ann. §59-3018(g)(5)(D)(b) (1993) (guardians may not consent to sterilization of wards); Md. Code Ann., Health-Gen §5-605(d)(1) (1993) (surrogate decisionmakers may not authorize sterilization). See also the discussion of Valerie N. and A. W. in Chapter 6.

36. These states include Arizona, Illinois, Louisiana, Montana, Nebraska, Nevada, New Mexico, Oklahoma, Rhode Island, South Dakota, and Wyoming.

37. See Hayes and Grady.
38. See Frazier v. Levi; In re M.K.R. A more extreme position is that courts should never allow sterilization of individuals who cannot give informed consent even when the legislature has sanctioned it. Courts could disregard statutory law in that way only on grounds that it was unconstitutional. There are indications in Chief Justice Bird's dissent in Valerie N. that this is her position. Valerie N. (1985), 781, 786–791. It is rather remarkable that the proponents on both sides of the issue should consider their position to be constitutionally compelled. It is much more common, when there is a constitutional debate, for the question to be whether one position is constitutionally required or can vary by state. See, e.g., Casey v. Planned Parenthood. When sterilization is the question, there is such evident disagreement even concerning how best to protect individuals with retardation that the legislature should have some leeway to decide.
39. See Guardianship of Matejski.
40. See Valerie N. (1985).
41. Matejski, 580.
42. Ibid., 581.
43. Ibid.
44. Ibid.
45. Hayes, 642 (Stafford, J., concurring in part and dissenting in part).
46. Ibid.
47. Ibid., 643 (Rosellini, J., dissenting); 642 (Stafford, J., concurring in part and dissenting in part).
48. Ibid., 642.
49. Matejski, 581–582.
50. See generally Note (1984); Murdock (1974); Lindman et al. (1961), 211; Ferster (1966), 603; Kamin (1974); Jensen (1974). But cf. Jensen (1972, 1974); Loehlin, Lindzay, and Spuhler (1975).
51. Hales, Yudofsky, and Talbott (1994), 783.
52. Ibid.
53. Batshaw and Perret (1992), 364. See Note (1969); Murdock (1974), 917–926.
54. Suzuki et al. (1986), 515–516. Hartl (1991), 228–230. See also Jensen (1974).
55. Merck Manual (1987), 1982.
56. Hales, Yudofsky, and Talbott (1994), 778, Table 23-41.
57. Ibid., 777.
58. Ibid., Figure 23-10.
59. See Wilson and Herrnstein (1985).
60. See Jencks (1992).
61. See Batshaw and Perret (1992), 272–278.
62. See Grace (1985).
63. But consider the imprecision in separating voluntary from involuntary sterilizations, especially sterilizations by third party consent. See Chapter 11, n. 4.
64. Miss. Code Ann. §41-45-1 (1993), et seq. Moreover California allows the "vol-

untary" sterilization of some sexual offenders. See Cal. Penal Code §645(e) (1997).

65. See, e.g., In re Moore.

66. Although some states still have statutes that allow involuntary sterilization, all but one are based on the individual's best interests, explicitly or implicitly, and not on society's best interests. See, e.g., Me. Rev. Stat. Ann. tit. 34-B, §7010 (1988). The exception is Mississippi. See Miss. Code Ann. §41-45-1 (1993).

67. See, e.g., Hagarman and Cronister (1996) (fragile X syndrome). Though promising from a standpoint of curing conditions that can cause retardation, such as PKU, much of the research raises concerns about genetic discrimination. See, e.g., Geller et al. (1996); Boyle (1995); Collins (1995); Alper and Natowicz (1993).

68. Hayes, 640.

6. Current Policy Issues concerning Sterilization

1. See Trussel and Vaughan (1992). Sterilization rather than "safe and controllable contraception" has been advocated internationally by Planned Parenthood. Gordon (1982). It is most popular in the United States among married couples.

2. The "120 rule" was "supported by the American College of Obstetricians and Gynecologists and through the 1960s amounted to the prevailing criterion for hospitals that performed sterilizations." Associated Press (1981). See also Hathaway v. Worcester City Hospital.

3. See C. D. M., 613, n. 17 (weight given the individual's preference varies according to ability of person to comprehend); A. W., 375 (person's wish not to be sterilized weighs heavily against authorizing procedure but is not determinative); Wentzel v. Montgomery Gen. Hosp., 1253 (court must allow full opportunity for individual to express her views); Grady, 482 (same); Terwilliger, 1383 (judge must meet with individual, but she need not attend the hearing); Hayes, 64 (court must elicit individual's views before ordering sterilization). The following statutes are similar: Me. Rev. Stat. Ann. tit. 34-B §7011.9 (1988) (court must consider person's attitudes and desires before ordering procedure); Utah Code Ann. §62A-6-108(3) (1988) (court must interview person to determine person's understanding of and expressed preferences regarding sterilization but those views are not controlling); Va. Code Ann. §54.1-2976(5) (1997) (court must elicit and take into account person's views on sterilization).

   In California, however, the patient's known objection is dispositive. See Cal. Prob. Code §§1957, 1958(h) (1991).

4. No one today, however, is advocating that the state make the decision and that the decision be in favor of sterilization. If state policy is to control and replace individual decisionmakers, the state policy will prohibit sterilization, not compel it.

5. There was little talk in the court's opinion about therapeutic sterilization, but it repeatedly made clear that what it was discussing was nontherapeutic,

"habilitative" sterilization (Valerie N. [1985], 389, 391, 394, 400, 401, 402) and that the interests protected by allowing sterilization are "her interests in living the fullest and most rewarding life of which she is capable" (ibid., 398). See ibid., 400, 403. Justice Lucas's opinion, concurring and dissenting, also stated that "sterilization necessitated by an incompetent's medical condition would be permissible under the present statutory scheme." Ibid., 408 n. 1.

Even though therapeutic sterilization as such was not discussed, the court did recite another provision of California law, which provides for appointment of a conservator empowered to give consent to medical treatment. The standard for such an appointment is that the conservatee be found to lack capacity to give informed consent: "When such a conservator is appointed, s/he can exercise her powers to give or withhold consent without any judicial supervision. (a) If the conservatee has been adjudicated to lack the capacity to give informed consent for medical treatment, the conservator has the exclusive authority to give consent for such medical treatment to be performed on the conservatee as the conservator in good faith based on medical advice determines to be necessary and the conservator may require the conservatee to receive such medical treatment, whether or not the conservatee objects. In any such case, the consent of the conservator alone is sufficient and no person is liable because the medical treatment is performed upon the conservatee without the conservatee's consent." Ibid., 394 n. 15, quoting Cal. Prob. Code §2355.

Note that, in the context of therapeutic procedures, the California law envisions imposing those procedures over the patient's active resistance.

6. The statute led to this result in a roundabout way, denying the probate court jurisdiction to grant conservators or guardians power to cause their wards to be sterilized. The prohibition of sterilization extends to persons in institutions, as well as others; earlier California had distinguished between those in institutions and others, and imposed sterilization most readily on persons in institutions who were deemed to have retardation.

7. The U.S. Constitution protects procreative choice as part of the liberty interest protected by the Due Process clause of the Fourteenth Amendment. The California constitution protects "the right not only to privacy, but to pursue happiness and enjoy liberty." Valerie N. (1985), 401, discussing art 1, sect 1. See ibid., 399–401.

8. Ibid., 404.

9. Ibid., 400.

10. Ibid., 398.

11. Ibid., 391, n. 6.

12. Ibid., 389. Justice Lucas pointed out the contradiction in his separate opinion in Valerie N. (1985), 405.

13. See Colo. Rev. Stat. §27-10.5-128(2) (providing that "[n]o person who is mentally retarded who has not given consent shall be sterilized"). The statute did not, however, treat persons with retardation as equals. In addition to the consent of the patient with retardation, the Colorado statute applicable to adults required the consent of the patient's parent or legal guardian, and the consent

of two consultants who interviewed the person. See Colo. Rev. Stat. §27-10.5-128(1) (1975).

14. See A. W., 368.
15. Ibid., 367.
16. Ibid., citing Colo. Rev. Stat. §13-22-103(3) (1973).
17. Ibid., 371.
18. See A. W., 375.
19. Ibid.
20. The concurring justice explained, "the [statute] states: 'No person who is mentally retarded and who has not given consent shall be sterilized.' These words have plain meaning which cannot be obscured or explained away by legislative history or statutory context. [The statutory scheme authorizes] the sterilization of consenting mentally retarded persons over eighteen years of age, pursuant to procedures designed to assure that such persons are adequately advised and that their consent is competently given." Ibid., 378 (Lohr, J., specially concurring).
21. See Colo. Rev. Stat. §27-10.5-130(1)(e) (1993).
22. See Cal. Prob. Code §1958 (1991).
23. Ibid. (emphasis added).
24. See, for example, discussion in Chapter 5, n. 33.
25. See discussion of Matejski and similar cases in Chapter 5.
26. See A. W., 370.
27. Grady, 470.
28. Ibid.
29. Ibid.
30. Ibid., 474–475.
31. Ibid.
32. Ibid., 482.
33. Ibid., 481.
34. Ibid., 484–485.
35. See Stump v. Sparkman.
36. Hayes, 637.
37. Ibid., 641.
38. Ibid.
39. Ibid., 637.
40. Ibid., 641.
41. Ibid., 642.
42. Ibid., 641.
43. Traynor (1963).

7. What Should the Standards for Sterilization Be?

1. As is characteristic of the imprecision in terms that haunts this subject, best interests is sometimes used in contradistinction to a least-restrictive-alternative formulation. So used, best interests suggests that all factors should be consid-

ered and that strict necessity is not required, as it would be under a least re-strictive alternative formulation. See Petition for Certiorari in C. W. (1995). More commonly, however, best interests analysis is seen as an alternative to substituted judgment analysis.

2. See generally Hayes; Grady; C. D. M.; Valerie N. (1985).
3. Moe, 720; 716, quoting Mass. Gen. Laws ch. 112 §112w (1977).
4. An example of a statute requiring the substituted judgment approach is Utah Code Ann. §62A-6-108(4) (1988).
5. Moe, 716, quoting Mass. Gen. Laws ch. 201 §12 (1978).
6. Moe, 716, citing Guardianship of Roe, In re Spring, and Superintendent of Belchertown State School v. Saikewicz.
7. Moe, 716–717. Cf. In re Guardianship of Eberhardy.
8. Moe, 717, 718, 720.
9. Ibid., quoting Saikewicz, 752; In re Carson, 545; and Guardianship of Roe, 40, n. 20.
10. Ibid., 720.
11. See discussion at the beginning of Chapter 11.
12. Moe, 720.
13. Ibid., 722.
14. Ibid., 720, quoting Saikewicz.
15. Ibid., 721. Similarly the language quoted earlier is consistent with allowing the known wishes of the incompetent person to control.
16. Ibid., 723, quoting Saikewicz, 752–753.
17. See also the Jane A. case, discussed in Chapter 10. The formulation quoted for Moe in the text is not original to the Moe opinion but was quoted from Saikewicz, the case in which Massachusetts first formulated its substituted test. That case involved whether to administer chemotherapy treatment to a patient who had mental illness and was deemed incompetent. Possibly the Saikewicz formulation was more appropriate to chemotherapy treatments than to steril-ization. But a strong case can be made for following the patient's own wishes, despite incompetence, when the issue is life-saving treatments, as well as when the issue is prevention of pregnancy. In any event, the issue of treat-ments that are truly medically essential falls outside the scope of this book's in-quiry.
18. Moe, 720.
19. Ibid., 722, citing C. D. M.
20. Moe, 724.
21. Ibid.; A. W., 375.
22. The factors the Massachusetts court identified in Moe are not so different from those of Grady and Hayes: (1) the ability of the patient herself, despite disabil-ity, to make an informed choice and the likelihood that she will become com-petent to make the choice in the near future; (2) her physical ability to procre-ate; (3) the possibility and effectiveness of less drastic means of birth control; (4) the medical necessity of the procedure; (5) the nature and extent of the

ward's disability, focusing on her ability to care for a child; (6) the likelihood of sexual activity; (7) the likelihood of health risks, trauma, etc., from the procedure and from its alternatives. See Moe, 720–721. As in Grady, the Moe court considered these "guiding factors," not per se requirements.

23. Accord Valerie N. (1985) (concluding that the substituted-judgment and best-interests doctrines are versions of one another because the ultimate goal of both is to do what is in the person's best interests, as defined by the court). The trial court in In re Grady required that the "primary concern [be] for the best interests of the incompetent rather than [the parent-guardian's] or the public's convenience," but it did not require an exclusive focus on the patient's interests. The New Jersey Supreme Court did not, however, endorse that approach.

24. See, e.g., A. W., 375; Grady, 481, n. 8.

25. See Berg v. Berg.

26. See Danforth v. Planned Parenthood; Casey v. Planned Parenthood.

27. If those factors are to be considered in relation to persons labeled "retarded," they should be considered in relation to others as well. If it were appropriate to proceed by consideration of groups rather than consider each individual separately, there are categories besides retardation in which the inquiry would be at least as appropriate. Homeless persons, for example, are likely to burden society when they have children, and persons who have been convicted of child abuse are much more likely to be undesirable parents than are persons with retardation. Nonetheless their right to parent has been held constitutionally protected without consideration of other interests that might be affected.

28. See Field (1993).

29. See ibid.

30. See Skinner v. Oklahoma; Developments in the Law (1980), 1296–1308; Comment (1975).

31. See, e.g., Ferster (1966); Bligh (1965); Matoush (1969).

32. An increasing number of cases are being brought for "wrongful birth," "wrongful life," or "professional negligence" leading to the birth of a child who has abnormalities. See Keeton (1984), 370.

33. Grady, 481.

34. Ibid., n. 8.

35. See, e.g., In re Simpson; North Carolina Ass'n for Retarded Children v. State.

36. See Grady, 481, n. 8.

37. In re Johnson, 808, citing N.C. Stat. §35-43 (1975).

38. Ibid.

39. Epstein et al. (1975), 240–242.

40. Davies (1989), 21.

41. Ibid.; Willey and Murphy (1991), 19–20.

42. Davies (1989), 14–15; Willey and Murphy (1991), 6.

43. Cases calling for least restrictive alternative analysis include: Wyatt v. Aderholt (Alabama); C. D. M. v. State (Alaska); A. W. (Colorado); In re Hillstrom (Min-

nesota); In re Truesdell (North Carolina); Eberhardy (Wisconsin). Statutes include: Cal. Prob. Code §1955(c) (1991); Conn. Gen. Stat. Ann. §45a-690(d)(1) (1993); Haw. Rev. Stat. Ann. §560:5-608(d)(4) (1986); Me. Rev. Stat. Ann. tit. 34-B, §7011(6) (1988); Or. Rev. Stat. §436.205(1)(c) (1991); Vt. Stat. Ann. tit. 18, §8711(c)(E) (1981); W.V. Code §27-16-1 (1974). Jurisdictions requiring a standard less strict than least restrictive alternative include Florida (Fla. Stat. Ann. §744.3215[4][e] [1997]; Indiana (In re P.S.); New Hampshire (In re Penny N.); and New Jersey (In re Grady).

44. Hayes, 641.
45. Grady, 483.
46. Guardianship of K.M., 72.
47. See the discussion in Chapter 12 of Debra Lynn Thomas's case. See also the discussion of Estate of C. W. in Chapter 11.
48. See the discussion of numerous studies in Chapter 14.
49. See In re P.S.; In re Nilsson (fourteen-year-old). Cf. In re Truesdell (case involving thirteen-year-old remanded for fact-finding); K.M. (same, in case involving a fifteen-year-old). But see Wentzel (denying petition to sterilize thirteen-year-old).
50. Hayes, 641.
51. See generally Blake (1995–1996).
52. See, e.g., In re Jane A., 1338; State v. Olivio, 606.
53. See, e.g., Jane A., 1339; Moe, 722.

8. Sex and Contraception

1. Moe, 722.
2. Grady, 470.
3. Arc (1996).
4. But cf. Eisenstadt v. Baird. Justice Stevens gave what is probably the most understandable explanation for a policy requiring access to contraception even while allowing states to criminalize sex by the recipients: "Although the State may properly perform a teaching function, . . . an attempt to persuade by inflicting harm on the listener is an unacceptable means of conveying a message that is otherwise legitimate. The propaganda technique [of denying contraception] significantly increases the risk of unwanted pregnancy and venereal disease. It is as though a State tried to dramatize its disapproval of motorcycles by forbidding the use of safety helmets. One need not posit a constitutional right to ride a motorcycle to characterize such a restriction as irrational and perverse."
5. Carey v. Population Servs., 692.
6. Ibid., 694, n. 17.
7. Ibid., 713.
8. See Griswold v. Connecticut.
9. See Carey v. Population Servs., 702.
10. See Doe v. Roe.

11. On the extreme difficulty of how to draw a line between exploitation and consent, see the discussion of the Glen Ridge rape case in Chapter 13.

12. Hendrix (1991).

13. Ibid. Another instance of these consultants influencing the show occurred in discussing Corky's use of the stove. In fact, the actor playing Corky needed help using a stove, so it was determined that the character should also have difficulty. But when, as part of a proposed story line, Corky was accidentally going to burn down his parents' business, one consultant said that she didn't want Corky "to mess with the stove" and that he could avoid the accident with proper guidance from his job coach: "Corky could avoid the accident by not hurrying: 'You have to tell yourself, "This is not a marathon. Take your time." People with Down's syndrome have to shift their gears.'" Above all, the consultants did not want such an accident caused by Corky to result in his parents' divorce. One consultant expressed the group's feelings on this point when he looked to the show's directors and quietly said, "Don't do that."

14. Ibid.

15. See Arkush (1992).

16. See Planned Parenthood v. Heckler (enjoining agency from requiring notice to parents when children seek contraception, because notice would be inconsistent with Congress's purpose of protecting patient confidentiality).

17. One issue concerning sex education, as with contraception, is who should receive it. Some take the view that it is appropriate only for those who are already sexually active and maintain that it lacks meaning to others. Others make it available to all who want to learn, or require it generally for the population with retardation.

18. See Arc (1996, 1991b); Andron (1987); Attard (1988), 6–7.

19. Arc (1991).

20. Ibid.

21. Moe, 722.

22. But see Estate of C. W.

23. See Trussel and Vaughan (1992).

24. Most of them are committed to keeping their family member in these facilities; otherwise he or she would probably already have been moved into the community. Usually the view is that staying in the state facility is in their family member's best interests and that he or she would be safer there than in the community. Many of the parents who fought successfully to improve conditions in state facilities now wish to maintain the facilities and the improvements that they won in court. See, e.g., Ricci v. Okin. In taking that position, however, they find themselves pitted against the twin forces of normalization and of cost savings for states (because humane institutions are much more expensive for government and taxpayers than is community living).

25. See, e.g., Attard (1988), 6–7.

26. This is true both of Norplant and of continuous consumption of the pill, for example.

27. The same problem increasingly exists with distinguishing contraception from

abortion. Some forms of contraception take effect after the egg and sperm have joined—for example, the IUD. Moreover in September 1998 the Food and Drug Administration for the first time approved a "three-day-after" pill, to be taken within 72 hours of impregnation. It prevents implantation of the egg in the uterine wall. See New York Times (1998).

28. The availability of Norplant means childbearing could be discouraged effectively even for groups, like persons with mental illness, whose conditions can be reversed. Implantation of Norplant could be required when a person was diagnosed with mental illness, to be removed only upon medical certification or judicial finding that the illness was under control. Such draconian measures have not been employed for persons with mental illness, as distinct from persons with retardation. Courts also have been reluctant to sanction forcible Norplant for women convicted of child abuse, or even forced abstinence from having children.

29. See the discussion in Chapter 11.

30. The state courts purported to apply their rules to sterilization generally and did not limit their holdings to the potentially reversible kind.

31. For children, parents are automatically their guardians until age eighteen, except where they give up the child or the state takes the child away or in rare instances of emancipation of the child before that age.

9. The Limited Impact of Guardianship

1. Menolascino (1977).

2. See discussions in Chapter 6.

3. In addition, some states' statutes explicitly include others as well as guardians among the group that can petition for consent to operations, for example, the New York law involved in *Barbara C.* See N. Y. Ment. Hyg. Law §80.01, et seq. (1996) (surrogate decisionmaking procedure for medical treatment of persons with mental disabilities).

4. Ibid.

5. See Rogers v. Commissioner of the Department of Mental Health, affirming a right of all involuntarily committed mental patients in Massachusetts, whether or not under guardianship, to refuse treatment with antipsychotic drugs. The Rogers rule also requires substituted judgment by a judge before a patient under guardianship can be medicated with antipsychotic drugs (even if the patient does not refuse). That rule applies to persons living in the community, not just in mental hospitals.

6. Massachusetts Mental Health Legal Advisors Committee (1993), 14.

7. Ibid.

8. Ibid. (emphasis added).

9. Ibid.

10. Ibid.

11. Whether or not she has a guardian, birth control should in theory depend on

her own decision if she has capacity to give informed consent. And without that capacity, she is vulnerable to a guardian's decision whether she has a guardian yet or not. These are the legal rules, but in practice it is unlikely that they will be respected: no one is going to court over birth control. Caretakers will administer medication to her if they think it appropriate and if they are able, as they usually are.

12. For example, Colorado's current statute speaks openly about hearings as determining whether a person with a disability "should be ordered to be sterilized." Colo. Rev. Stat. §27-10.5-130(1) (1993).

10. The Peculiar Problem of Abortion

1. See Akron v. Akron Center for Reprod. Health, 416, 444 ("a State may not adopt one theory of when life begins to justify its regulation of abortions"). See generally Roe v. Wade (1973).

2. Eisenstadt v. Baird, 448. Justice Brennan used this reasoning to explain why punishment of sex outside of marriage was not a plausible explanation for the statutory ban on contraception. See also Carey v. Population Servs., 693–695.

3. See Part IV.

4. This is the original UPC provision governing the guardianship of incompetent persons, promulgated in 1969 as UPC §5-312(a)(3) and replaced in 1989. The original provision can still be found in the following statutes (although in some cases with variations): Ariz. Rev. Stat. Ann. §14-5312(a)(3) (1997); Colo. Rev. Stat. §15-14-312(1)(c) (1997); Ga. Code Ann. §29-5-3(b)(8) (1998); Haw. Rev. Stat. §560:5-312(A)(3) (1997); Idaho Code §15-5-312(A)(3) (1989); Me. Rev. Stat. Ann. tit. §18-A §5-312(A)(3) (1998); Mont. Code Ann. §72-5-321(2)(c) (1997); Neb. Rev. Stat. §30-2628(a)(3) (1997); N.J. Rev. Stat. §§3B:12-57(c) and 3A:6-16:24(d) (1983); S.C. Code Ann. §62-5-312(3) (1997); Utah Code Ann. §75-5-312(2)(c) (1992).

5. This is the new UPC provision, adopted to replace the original when Article 5 of the UPC, governing the guardianship of incapacitated persons, was expanded and reorganized in 1989. The new provision is incorporated in Article 5 by reference from Article 2, where the same provision governs the guardianship of minors. See UPC §§5-209(c)(4) (minors) and 5-309 (incompetent persons). Statutes adopting the new provision (sometimes with variations) are: Ala. Code §26-2A-78(c)(4) (1997) (minors); Ariz. Rev. Stat. Ann. §14-5209(c)(4) (1997) (same); Colo. Rev. Stat. §15-14-209(3)(d) (1997) (same); Ind. Code §29-3-3-3(8) and §29-3-8-2(4) (minors) (1994); Ky. Rev. Stat. §387.065(3)(b) (1997) (minors and incompetent persons); N.M. Stat. Ann. §45-5-209(c)(4) (1997) (minors).

6. See, e.g., Alaska St. §13.26.150(e)(2) (1998).

7. See, e.g., In re Smith; Little v. Little.

8. A guardian must act in the ward's best interests at all times: "The guardian should not do what pleases himself or herself, or what pleases anyone else

other than the ward. The guardian's duty is to do what the ward would presumably, if able, do for himself or herself, and to act in the best interests of the
ward and only the ward." Rogers (1984), 37.

9. See Ark. Code Ann. §28-65-302(1) (1985). The statute provides an exception
   when sterilization or abortion is necessary to save the woman's life. But see
   Ark. Code Ann. §20-49-301 (1971) (allowing guardians of incompetent adults
   or minors to have wards involuntarily sterilized through direct medical chan-
   nels as an alternative to the state's statutory regime allowing involuntary sterilization with judicial oversight under Ark. Code Ann. §20-49-201, et seq.). That
   provision was held unconstitutional by the Supreme Court of Arkansas in
   1991, in McKinney v. McKinney (incompetent woman's challenge to the constitutionality of statute, after resisting her father-guardian's attempt to have
   her involuntarily sterilized), although it remains on the books. See also Ala.
   Code §26-1-2(g)(1) (1997).
10. Colo. Rev. Stat. §15-14-312(1)(c) (1997). See also Ala. Code §26-1-2(g)(1)
    (1997) (durable power of attorney statute); Me. Rev. Stat. Ann. tit. 18-A §5-
    312 (1998); Colo. Rev. Stat. §15-14-312(1)(c) (1997).
11. Mass. Gen. Laws ch. 201 §12.15.
12. See, e.g., Alaska Stat. §13.26.150(e)(2) (1998); C.D.M. (Alaska, 1981) (guard-
    ian may not consent to sterilization or abortion).
13. See Ark. Code Ann. §28-65-302(1) (1985) (guardians may not make abortion
    decision for ward without court approval except when necessary to save life of
    ward). See also Ark. Code Ann. §20-16-804(B) (1989) (when minor or incom-
    petent seeking abortion petitions for judicial relief from parent-guardian
    notification requirement but is not mature, court will make best interests deci-
    sion whether she should be permitted to undergo abortion without parent-
    guardian notification).
14. Sullivan (1982a).
15. In re Barbara C., 31. On this narrow threat-to-life argument, the state offered
    evidence that the withdrawal of anticonvulsive medication during pregnancy
    to protect the fetus from toxic effects could result in uncontrollable seizures.
    Ibid., 39.
16. Ibid., 31. The deputy first assistant attorney general commented that this argu-
    ment posed "a very complex legal issue" which he did not believe had "ever
    come up before" Sullivan (1982a). After the decision, the lawyers involved
    "said they believed the ruling was the first in New York in which parental con-
    sent for an abortion was substituted for the consent [of] a person judged legally
    not competent to make the decision." Sullivan (1982b).
17. Barbara C. (1982), 183 (quoting New York legal provisions).
18. Barbara C. (1984), 801.
19. Ibid.
20. Ibid.
21. Under the statute, which remains in effect, no judicial proceedings are re-
    quired; the Barbara C. appeals court rejected the suggestion that such a pro-

ceeding should be required in addition to parental consent. See N.Y. Mental Hyg. §33.03(6) (1996). New York is comparatively enlightened in its procedure to establish guardianship; see N.Y. Surr. Ct. Proc. Act §§1750, et seq. (1996). But the simple, general guardianship or competency hearing does not consider any of the issues that would be relevant to the patient's ability to consent to abortion.

22. Barbara C. (1984), 801 (citations omitted).
23. In re Estate of D. W., 355. The testimony of the mother's three witnesses was uncontroverted. A psychologist testified that D. W. would be unable to understand her pregnancy and the importance of diet, exercise, and the need to take physical precautions. He stated that the pregnancy would be traumatic and posed the risk of damage to her emotional health. He "observed that if a stranger asked to take the baby from D. W., she would probably cooperate because she is extremely susceptible to suggestion." She could not "make or communicate responsible decisions" about her condition, nor could she care for her child. An obstetrician gynecologist (who had never examined D. W.) testified that her condition would necessitate a general anesthetic and a cesarean section, posing a much greater risk to her health than an abortion. In "his professional judgment . . . terminating the pregnancy would be best for D. W." Finally, D. W.'s mother testified that she provided all of her daughter's basic care, and that her daughter could not take care of herself. Ibid., 356.
24. Ibid., 356–357. In 1991 a Massachusetts appeals court similarly ruled that finding that an abortion is "medically necessary" is not required before authorizing an abortion for an incompetent person." In re Mary Moe, 687.
25. D. W., 356, quoting Ill. Rev. Stat. 1983, ch. 110 1/2, ¶11a-17(a) (1983).
26. D. W., 356.
27. See generally Moe; Saikewicz.
28. In re Jane A., 1338.
29. Ibid. Compare Mary Moe, 686 (reversing trial court's threshold finding that Mary was incompetent to decide for herself whether or not to have an abortion).
30. In re Jane A., 1339.
31. Ibid., 1338.
32. Ibid., 1339.
33. Ibid.
34. Ibid.
35. Ibid.
36. Ibid., 1339–1340.
37. Ibid., 1340.
38. Ibid., 1340–1341 (citations omitted).
39. See Valerie N. (1985), 787 (Bird, C. J., dissenting) and majority opinion, 763, n. 6.
40. Valerie N. (1985), 774.
41. Ibid., 787 (quoting majority decision, 774).

42. See A. W.; Colo. Rev. Stat. §27-10.5-130 (1)(e) (1993).
43. In re Mary Moe, 684.
44. Ibid., 685 (quoting trial court opinion).
45. Ibid., 684 (quoting trial court opinion).
46. Ibid., 685–686.
47. Ibid., 684 (quoting trial court opinion).

11. Self-Determination Explained and Evaluated

1. See Chapter 12 (discussing different treatment of persons with retardation and of minors). And see Heller v. Doe (allowing different treatment of persons with mental illness and those with mental retardation, by upholding a statute establishing higher standards for involuntary commitment of persons with mental illness than for persons with retardation).
2. See Frazier v. Levi (Texas); In re M.K.R. (Missouri).
3. There are other examples of sterilizations that have questionably been characterized as voluntary. Some have been sterilized "voluntarily" because that was a condition to their release from an institution or a condition to avoiding institutionalization. P. Wald (1976), 12. In the past, sterilization has sometimes been a condition for receipt of welfare. See Relf v. Weinberger. See also Blake (1995–96).
4. This is one reason why many efforts to categorize sterilizations as voluntary or involuntary fail; there is no clear line between those categories if substituted consent is the rationale. Consequently, the count of which jurisdictions do and do not allow involuntary sterilization because of retardation varies wildly in different studies (from only one state still allowing it to a third, or even more than half, the states allowing it). Chief Justice Bird, dissenting, recognized in Valerie N. that "choice and consent are meaningless concepts when applied to" a person without capacity to consent for herself. Valerie N. (1985), 781.
5. See, e.g., McKinney v. McKinney.
6. See Hayes, 644 (Rosellini, J., dissenting): "The majority apparently assumes that sterilization is a matter of indifference to the person upon whom it is performed, provided, of course, [s]he is in fact retarded."
7. See Ibid., 642 (Stafford, J., concurring in part and dissenting in part).
8. But parents might decide otherwise. Unlike guardians who are less closely connected with their ward, and unlike institutional caretakers or directors of group homes, at least a few parents might *want* their child to reproduce. Some parents of the young adult will look with favor on the possibility of a grandchild—or even a baby who will be to them like another child of their own. Presumably if society believed that the parents of an individual with retardation who could not herself give informed consent were the proper decisionmakers here, it would enable them to order procreation as well as to prevent it.
9. Moe, 724 (Nolan, J., dissenting).
10. Ibid.

11. See, e.g., Moe; Jane A.

12. See Lambert v. Wicklund (holding that waiver of a parental notice require-ment—when notification is not in a minor's best interest—is sufficient to pro-tect the minor's right to abortion). See also Danforth v. Planned Parenthood; State v. Hodgson; Bellotti v. Baird.

13. Mary P., 546, citing N.Y. Fam. Ct. Act §712(a) (defining "Person in Need of Su-pervision" as a "male less than sixteen years of age and a female less than eigh-teen years of age who does not attend school in accord with the provisions of part one of article sixty-five of the education law or who is incorrigible, ungov-ernable or habitually disobedient and beyond the lawful control of parent or other lawful authority or who violates the provisions of section 221.05 of the penal law").

14. In re Smith, 245–246.

15. For example, a legal regime requiring or encouraging physicians to engage in special and complicated evaluative procedures to measure a person's ability to give informed consent whenever a person "appears" developmentally dis-abled, though beneficent in protective intent, would be extremely counterpro-ductive and stigmatizing for persons who appeared to have developmental dis-abilities. Cf. Colo. Rev. Stat. §27-10.5-128 (1997). Recall the story of Norma Jean set out in Chapter 4.

16. See, e.g., A. W., 366.

17. One clear example of a nonadversarial hearing is D. W., discussed in Chapter 10.

18. Guardianship of K. M., 72.

19. Ibid., 72–73.

20. Ibid.

21. Ibid.

22. Ibid., 73–75.

23. See Note (1995), 1012, n. 35.

24. Terwilliger, 1382–1384.

25. Ibid., 1383.

26. Ibid., 1384.

27. C. W. (1994), 433.

28. Ibid.

29. Ibid., 438.

30. Ibid.

31. Ibid.

32. The court had other reasons as well for not approving birth control pills. It pointed out that the pills can cause side effects in any woman but that if Cynthia experiences such symptoms, "she may not be capable of communicat-ing that fact so as to enable" corrective action. Further, "if she refused to take her medications, as she has sometimes done in the past, the pill would be ren-dered totally ineffective." Ibid. Since her other medications could not be dis-continued without the risk of great medical harm to Cynthia, it seems unlikely

that her refusing her medication would be tolerated. More justifiable is the court's point that the interaction of the pill with Cynthia's current medications was not known: sometimes it improves the conditions at issue; sometimes it worsens them; and sometimes it has no effect. Although the possibilities for improvement suggest that the pill should not be ruled out, the dangers that *might* come to Cynthia from taking the pill were sufficiently great—including status epilepticus and even death, according to some of the testimony—that decisionmakers might reasonably refuse to take that course. Nonetheless, Judge Johnson in dissent pointed out that the expert testimony on the un-known interaction was insufficient to satisfy a clear and convincing burden of proof standard. Accordingly, it seemed to him that the proponents of steriliza-tion had not satisfied the standard Terwilliger imposed. According to Judge Johnson, "[a]bsent clear and convincing evidence that all other methods of contraception are unworkable for C. W., this Court cannot uphold the trial court's authorization of C. W.'s sterilization." C. W. (1994) (Johnson, J., dis-senting), 445. He would have remanded so that other methods could be con-sidered and tried.

33. C. W. (1994), 440 (Johnson, J., dissenting).
34. Ibid., 442.
35. Ibid., 430. The trial judge, however, had described a session with Cynthia, say-ing, "She signed that she had brought her nephew, Ricky, into this world, [and] that girls differ from boys in that women carry purses. In response to questioning, she signed, without differentiation, that she would like to have a baby, that she would also like to have a puppy, that babies can be bought in a store and that her brother and sister-in-law had bought her nephew, Ricky." Ibid., 431. The court of appeals reported the exchange to show Cynthia's lack of understanding. It also shows much more than minimal signing, however, if she actually did communicate those ideas.
36. Ibid., 435.
37. Ibid., 445 (Hudock, J., dissenting).
38. Ibid., quoting C. W. (1991), 2 (Bruno, J., dissenting).
39. Ibid., 444 (Johnson, J., dissenting).
40. See discussion in Chapter 16.
41. In fact, this is an area where the well-to-do are substantially more prejudiced than the middle or lower classes.
42. See Stump v. Sparkman.
43. Cal. Prob. Code §2355 (emphasis added). The next section of the code, Cal. Prob. Code §2356(d), which was in effect in 1985 when Valerie N. was de-cided, provided that "[n]o ward or conservatee may be sterilized under the provisions of this division," quoted in Valerie N. (1985), 762, n. 2.
44. Cal. Prob. Code §1958 (1991).
45. See Chapter 9 discussing guardianship.
46. See, e.g., Bellotti v. Baird; Planned Parenthood v. Casey; State v. Hodgson.
47. See Roe v. Wade; Planned Parenthood v. Danforth; Planned Parenthood v. Casey.

48. Eberhardy, 893.
49. Massachusetts Department of Mental Retardation (1985).
50. See Chapter 13.
51. See discussion of Norplant and reversible sterilization in Chapter 10.
52. There are four different standards for determining a person's competency to give informed consent: the lowest finds competent an individual who can express a preference; the next considers whether the person's decision is rational (this standard, commonly used in psychiatric hospitals, is sometimes taken to mean a "decision to accept treatment is deemed competent; to refuse treatment suggests incompetency"); the third assesses whether her decisionmaking process is rational; and the fourth, and highest, "prevailing" standard is the so-called appreciation standard, asking if the patient has inferential as well as factual understanding or recall. Scott (1986), n. 116 (citations omitted). See generally Wikler (1979); Lidz et al. (1984); Meisel (1979).
53. Colo. Rev. Stat. §27-10.5-128 (1993).
54. C. W., Petition for Certiorari, Appendix, A-2.
55. Grady, 473.
56. C. W., Trial Court opinion, Petition for Certiorari, Appendix, A-250, A-251, A-248.
57. Ibid., A-249.
58. See Chapter 3, n. 7.
59. She may be especially persuadable if she is ambivalent. Many patients experience uncertainty about which choice is right for them, whether or not they have mental retardation. A patient may also feel uncertain that the choice she wants to make is the right one to make. It is normal for ambivalence to surround choices like abortion, even though when women with retardation do not know what they want it is often attributed to the "pathology of retardation." When third parties advising a woman have a separate agenda from her own, they may repress, rather than facilitate, a woman's own decisionmaking, even when she knows what she wants. And if she herself is doubtful, she may be particularly vulnerable to manipulation by advisers who have little or no doubt what she should do.
60. Grady, 471.

12. Necessary Limitations on Self-Determination

1. Valerie N. (1985), 763. Despite this clarification, the court stated that she "expressed her wish to continue to have her parents care for her" and that her parents had clear ideas about her likes and dislikes, suggesting that she must have been able to convey something. Compare Chapter 11, n. 35.
2. See In re Jane A., 238 ("Efforts to determine Jane's preference about having or not having a baby, the judge found, were 'fruitless.'"). See also Grady, 467 ("Our courts should accept the responsibility of providing her with a choice to compensate for her inability to exercise personally an important constitutional right").

3. This is not true of all choice issues, such as the right to die, for example, which applies to everyone. But all choice issues are not necessarily the same, and reproduction is probably less relevant to most nonexpressive persons than to other persons.

4. Cruzan v. Director, Mo. Dept. of Health, 286–287 (emphasis added).

5. Ibid.

6. The Court did rely on the "liberty" that the Due Process clause expressly protects rather than on "privacy," but the scope of the two terms may prove identical.

7. The Nilsson court, for example, considered as a relevant factor in granting a petition to sterilize, by hysterectomy, a fourteen-year-old girl, the fact that she "was becoming aware of boys and there exist[ed] the possibility that she could participate in promiscuous sexual activities or in view of her mental retardation that *sexual activities could be imposed upon her.*" Nilsson, 441 (emphasis added.). See also Truesdell (state has burden of showing "that there was substantial likelihood that respondent would voluntarily engage in sexual activity likely to cause impregnation or would engage in sexual activity which she did not initiate"); Grady, 482 (similar).

8. See, e.g., Nilsson, 439.

9. In re P. S., 971–972. In addition to psychological problems associated with her not understanding why she was bleeding, it was suggested that P. S. would not be able to "care" for herself during her periods, which must have meant "clean" herself.

10. In re Penny N., 542.

11. See, e.g., Nilsson, 440–441.

12. Penny N., 543.

13. Nilsson, 442.

14. Hayes, 640.

15. See In re Moore.

16. Ibid., 307.

17. Ibid., 315.

18. Ibid., 312.

19. Ibid., 309.

20. Letter from James Armentrout, Moore's attorney, March 14, 1977, quoted in Areen (1992), 981–982.

13. The Possibility of Varying the Rule

1. Betty Harris is the fictitious name used to refer to the victim in the case in a recent book about the trial, Laufer (1994), xvii. Court records refer to her as M. G.

2. Telephone interview with Bob Lorino, assistant prosecutor, Essex County, N.J., October 26, 1994 (hereafter "Lorino interview").

3. Laufer (1994), 30, quoting assistant prosecutor Glenn Goldberg.

4. Lorino interview.
5. *New Jersey Law Journal,* December 21, 1992.
6. Laufer (1994), 11, 126.
7. Ibid., 20, citing Coach Margaret Savage; Lorino interview.
8. Associated Press (1991).
9. See Walsh (1992).
10. See N.J. Stat. 2C:24-4 (1979).
11. The only adults this book's proposed approach would find incapable of con-senting are wholly noncommunicative persons. See Chapter 12.
12. N.J. Stat. 2C:14-2(7) (1979).
13. N.J. Stat. 2C:14-1(h) (1979).
14. Olivio, 599.
15. Ibid., 600.
16. Ibid., 601.
17. Ibid., 606.
18. Laufer (1994), 51.
19. Houppert (1993).
20. Laufer (1994), 51, quoting Michael Querques, Kevin Scherzer's attorney.
21. Ibid., 146.
22. Ibid., 145.
23. Schroth (1992b).
24. Ibid.
25. See Schroth (1993).
26. Schroth (1992b).
27. Ibid.
28. Laufer (1994).
29. Ibid., 112.
30. Ibid., 132–141; Houppert (1993).
31. See Robayo (1994), 297, n. 161; Boone (1996).
32. Laufer (1994), xvii–xviii.
33. Schroth (1992b), quoting Julie Blackman, a testifying psychologist.
34. Schroth (1993).
35. Walsh (1993).
36. Laufer (1994), 33.
37. Ibid.
38. Hanley (1993a).
39. Junod (1993).
40. Hanley (1993).
41. Hanley (1994).
42. State v. Scherzer, 404.
43. Ibid.
44. Ibid.
45. Campbell (1997).
46. See Schroth (1992a).

47. Ibid.
48. In re M. T. S., 1276, interpreting N.J. Stat. 2C:14-2(a)(3).
49. Betty attended special education classes at Columbia High School and West Orange High School because they were not offered at Glen Ridge High. She finished school at Glen Ridge at the age of twenty-one, a few months before the trial started. Laufer (1994), 20, 37.
50. In re B. G., 643 (quoting Dr. Susan Esquilin).
51. Trussel and Vaughan (1992), 1163.
52. Ibid.
53. Shapiro (1985); DeStefano (1982); Roberts (1993), 1442–43; Mosher and Bachrach (1996).
54. Kantrowitz (1993).
55. Junod (1993).
56. Ibid.

14. Some Underlying Rules and Issues

1. See discussion in Chapter 2.
2. See McIntire (1973). For the view that parents have a right to raise their children as they will, a right protected by the Due Process clause, see Robertson (1983), 410. Like most Due Process rights, however, parental autonomy is not absolute. Nonetheless, according to Robertson, government can limit it only by showing both that there is a compelling state interest and that the solution it has adopted is the least restrictive alternative. That standard states the highest form of judicial scrutiny and would place rules restricting parenting on the same level of disfavor as racial classifications. Robertson's suggestion does not reflect current law, which pays some heed to parental rights but does not protect them with strict scrutiny.
3. In re T.M.R., 292.
4. See LaFollette (1980); Frisch (1981); Mangel (1988). See also McIntire (1973).
5. See Grunwald (1995).
6. Adoption of Katharine and Jeptha, 27–28, 32–34 (citations omitted).
7. Under both approaches, both parents must usually contribute financially to the child's support. The amounts of the noncustodian's contribution will depend upon variables such as the parties' respective assets, income, and earning capacity. Despite theory, the custodian usually bears the lion's share of the child's expenses.
8. See, e.g., Mnookin and Kornhauser (1979), 950–968.
9. See generally Ex parte Devine, citing Helms v. Franciscus; Foster (1978).
10. See Ex parte Devine, citing numerous cases overturning the presumption; Foster (1978); Trenker (1976).
11. See, e.g., Garska v. McCoy. Cf. Goldstein, Freud, and Solnit (1973), 98 (discussing the somewhat different notion of "psychological parent"). See generally Chambers (1984).

12. Nevertheless, confusion abounds about the standards used in these different arenas. One reason, as Chapter 15 shows, is that many states' child protection statutes require findings of both parental unfitness and best interests to precede termination of parental rights. Best interests determinations in the child protection arena sometimes have the flavor of "comparative judgments" between potential parents, especially when would-be adoptive parents have had temporary custody of a child for a long period of time.

13. Petitions of Dep't of Soc. Servs. to Dispense with Consent to Adoption (1985), 539–540.

14. Ibid., 542.

15. See, e.g., Wash. Rev. Code §13.34.180(5)-(7) (1997).

16. N.Y. Soc. Serv. §384-b(1)(a)(i) (1992).

17. Utah Code Ann. §62A-4a-101(14)(a)(iii) (1998).

18. See, e.g., Ala. Code §26-18-7(a)(2) (1998); Cal. Fam. Code §7826-(a) (1994) and §7827(b) (1994); Mo. Rev. Stat. §211.447(3)(c) (1997).

19. Ala. Code §26-18-7(a)(2) (1998). See also Ga. Code Ann. §15-11-81(b)(4)(B)(ii) (1997); Cal. Fam. Code §7826 (1994).

20. See Cal. Fam. Code §7826 (1994).

21. See, e.g., Ala. code §26-18-7(a)(1) (1997); Cal. Fam. Code §7822 (1994); Ga. Code Ann. §15-11-81(b)(3) (1997); N.C. Gen. Stat. §7A-289.32(3) (1997); N.D. Cent. Code §27-20-44(1)(a) (1987); N.Y. Soc. Serv. §384(1)(b) (1992); Va. Code Ann. §16.1-278.2(A)(iii) (1997).

22. See, e.g., Ala. Code §26-18-7(a)(3) (1997); Cal. Fam. Code §7823(a)(1) (1994); Ga. Code Ann. §15-11-81(b)(4)(B)(4) and (A)(iv) (1997); La. Children's Code art. 1015(3)(a) (1997); Mass. Gen. Laws ch. 119 §24(d) (1996); N.M. Stat. Ann. §32A-4-18(C)(3) (1993); N.D. Cent. Code §27-20-44(b) (1987); S.C. Code Ann. §20-7-736(F) (1997); Utah Code Ann. §62A-4a-101(1) (1998); Va. Code Ann. §16.1-278.2A(i) (1997).

23. See, e.g., Ala. Code §26-18-7(b)(1) (1997); La. Children's Code art. 1015(3)(a) (1997); Ga. Code Ann. §15-11-81(b)(4) (1997); N.M. Stat. Ann. §32A-4-18(C)(1)–(5) (1993); N.Y. Soc. Serv. Law §384(b)(4)(d) (1992); N.D. Cent. Code §27-20-44(a) (1987); Utah Code Ann. §62A-4a-101(14)(a)(iv) (1998); Va. Code Ann. §16.1-278.2(A) (1997).

24. See, e.g., Ga. Code Ann. §15-11-81(b)(4)(A)(ii) (1997); Mass. Gen. Laws ch. 119 §24 (1996).

25. See, e.g., Ala. Code §26-18-7(a)(4) (1997); Ga. Code Ann. §15-11-81(b)(4)(B)(iii) (1997); La. Children's Code art. 1015(1)(a) (1997); N.Y. Soc. Serv. Law §384(b)(8)(a)(i)(B) (1992); Utah Code Ann. §62A-4a-103(1)(f) (1998).

26. N.D. Cent. Code §27-20-44(1)(b) (1987); Ga. Code Ann. §15-11-81(b)(4)(A)(iv) (1997).

27. Mass. Gen. Laws ch. 119 §24(b) (1996).

28. Ga. Code Ann. §15-11-81(b)(4)(B)(vi) (1997).

29. Areen (1975), 887–889.

30. See Dowdney and Skuse (1993), 27 ("widely divergent conclusions as to par-

ents' capacity to care adequately for their children have been reached");
Brantlinger (1988), 31–43. But see Tymchuk (1992), 174, who opines that parental adequacy must be better defined: "there is not only a need for an expanded view of what constitutes inadequacy of parenting by persons with
mental retardation and an identification of the factors that are related to such
inadequacy, but also for a definition of *adequacy of parenting* and an identification of the factors that are related to such adequacy."

31. Booth and Booth (1994), 11, citing Dowdney et al. (1985).
32. For a moving account of one woman's fight to retain custody of her children,
    despite her physical handicaps, see Mathews (1992).
33. See, e.g., Kozol (1988).
34. See Dowdney et al. (1985): Llewellyn (1990); Walton-Allen and Feldman
    (1991).
35. In re Paul E., 291.
36. Ibid.
37. Ibid., 294.
38. See generally Davenport (1911); Berry and Gordon (1931), 126; Fernald
    (1912).
39. Berry and Gordon (1931), 126.
40. Tredgold (1929), 496.
41. Brandon (1957), 710. Numerous studies reported on the considerably higher
    birth rates in "defective" families.
42. See, e.g., Penrose and Turner (1934) (describing a family history of a "defec-
    tive" brother and sister who had had two children who were not "defective").
43. Brandon (1957), 712.
44. See, e.g., Tredgold (1952) ("Mental defect is present to a varying extent in the
    parents of defectives . . . but it occurs to a much greater extent in the children
    of defectives. In general I think it may be said that these figures point to a pro-
    gressive family increase in the severity of the mental abnormality and in the
    number of persons affected"); Pantin (1957) ("of two feebleminded parents,
    nearly all the children will be feebleminded"); Laxova, Gilderdale, and Ridler
    (1973), 193. (The study surveyed 991 institutionalized women who became
    pregnant over a ten-year period, and researchers cataloged 89 live births.
    There were two terminations of parental rights after birth, and thorough ex-
    amination revealed subnormality in only 6 mother-offspring pairs—and of
    these 6 children, 2 were the product of incest. Of the 89 offspring, 67 were
    school age at the time of the investigation; only 12 attended programs for the
    "educationally subnormal.")
45. Brandon (1957), 734. See also Penrose and Turner (1934).
46. Brandon (1957), 714, quoting Penrose (1954).
47. Sheridan (1956), 93.
48. The most prominent of these studies published between 1947 and 1979 are de-
    scribed and criticized in Schilling et al. (1982), 201, 202. These include the fol-
    lowing: Mickelson (1947) (44 percent of 61 mothers with mild or moderate re-

tardation were found "unsatisfactory"; flaws arising from subjective definitions of adequate parenting, examination of previously institutionalized mothers, and lack of control in the study resulted in the researchers' inability to account for the causal effect of factors other than the mothers' retardation); Mitchell (1947) (noted poor casework outcomes for parents with IQs below 60, but assessments of parental ability were based on the impressions of social workers); Brandon (1957) (studied 150 children of 73 deinstitutionalized "mental defectives" and concluded that rearing by these parents did not "appear to depress the child's intelligence unduly"); Sheridan (1956) (found 70 of 100 neglectful mothers had below-average IQs, but study was uncontrolled and success rates were much higher when follow-up was provided after the initial training); Shaw and Wright (1960) (of 197 "mentally defective" individuals who had married, one-third of the families with children were known to the National Society for the Prevention of Cruelty to Children or had temporarily lost custody of their children; the central flaw in the study was the manner of registering "defectives"); Cameron, Johnson, and Camps (1966) (reported that 19 or 20 battering mothers and 11 of 27 battering fathers had a low intelligence level but gave no information about how intelligence was assessed); Borgman (1969) (of 50 women referred for psychological testing by child welfare workers, those with IQ scores below 60 were almost always judged inadequate mothers, though women with mental retardation were equally represented in groups of adequate and inadequate mothers; the study was flawed because the group of inadequate mothers was composed of women referred for psychological analysis to assess either their child care skills or their eligibility for sterilization by the state eugenics board; their referrals mentioned conditions that were presumed to be indicative of parental unfitness; by contrast, the group of adequate mothers was composed of women referred by the state for employment counseling or casework planning); Mattinson (1973) (examined 40 couples in which both partners had mental retardation and found that, of the 40 children born to 17 couples, 6 had been removed from their parents and 2 had died, one of which was the subject of a neglect investigation; the sampling group of previously institutionalized people was too small and controls were not used); Scally (1973) (reported that 30 percent of children being reared by parents with retardation are not subjects of state intervention, but relied on case records and was tainted by bias inherent in and incompleteness of government records tracking persons with retardation); Smith (1975) (found that 50 percent of abusing parents had low IQs, but was criticized for questionable control for social class); Oliver (1977) (concluded that 29.8 percent of 67 severely abusive parents had borderline or moderate mental retardation, but left unclear how IQ was measured and allowed the abuse group to include "probable" abusers); Hyman (1977) (in uncontrolled study of 44 battering parents found a "trend, albeit nonsignificant, for battering parents to do marginally less well on IQ tests than the population at large"); Robinson (1978) (group with mental retardation had more punitive tendencies than contrast group, but sociocultural contrast group consisted of second-year college students); Egeland, Breitbucher, and Rosenberg (1979) (fathers married to "inadequate mothers" had significantly lower IQs than a control group of fathers married to excellent care providers; intelligence was not found to be predictive of the mothers' child rearing ability; rather, the mothers' combined "knowledge, intelligence, and ability to cope with ambivalence and stress" was the most important predictor of their ability to parent; study inadequately addressed the concept of intelligence). Subsequent critiques of these studies are in Campion (1995); Booth and Booth (1994); Dowdney and Skuse (1993), 42–44; Llewellyn (1990), 369, 372; Gath (1988); Wates (1993); Tymchuk (1992).

49. See, e.g., Accardo and Whitman (1990), 69–70 (a retrospective study of hospital records over a six-year period, identifying 79 families with 226 children, 103—or 45.5 percent—of whom had been removed from home because of child abuse, neglect, unsafe living conditions, or sexual abuse).

50. See Sheridan (1956), 93.

51. Even before deinstitutionalization, some persons with retardation lived in the community, often with spouses and children. Those adults became the subjects of parental adequacy studies.

52. See Developmental Disabilities Advocacy Project (1977), 22–37.

53. See Mickelson (1947), 516–534, 645 ("One concludes that, with the exception of those with IQs between 30–49, the degree of the mother's mental retardation had no relationship to adequacy of child care").

54. Mickelson (1949), 516–534.

55. Ibid., 517. See also Ainsworth, Wagner, and Straus (1945).

56. Haavik and Menninger (1981), 74, 75–78. They did, however, find variability across the studies. For example, the children of parents with retardation were vulnerable to developmental delay themselves. But the causal correlation between parental stimulation and developmental delay in children was not clearly established.

57. See Caldwell and Bradley (1978).

58. Llewellyn (1990), 373. One important early study is Brandon (1957), which concluded that, contrary to eugenics statements, "[w]omen who have been certified as feebleminded do not appear to have large numbers of defective children. In the present survey the number of defective children [represents] 3–7 per cent."

59. Feldman et al. (1986), 23 (citations omitted). An earlier Red Cross parent training program had been modified for parents with retardation. See Madsen (1979), 195–196.

60. Feldman et al. (1986), 23, citing Peterson, Robinson, and Littman (1983), 329–342.

61. See Schilling et al. (1982).

62. Feldman et al. (1986), 35, 33, 33–35, 36.

63. See Slater (1986); Tymchuk and Andron (1988).

64. See Whitman, Graves, and Accardo (1989).

65. See Feldman et al. (1985, 1986, and 1989). In the first study, the mean IQ of the mothers with retardation was 66 (with a range between 59 and 77). In the second study, the mean IQ was 71 (with a range of 64 to 77). In the third study, the IQs of the three participating mothers were 70, 61, and 75.
66. Whitman, Graves, and Accardo (1989), 431.
67. Ibid., 432.
68. Ibid., citing Graves et al. (1986).
69. Whitman, Graves, and Accardo (1989).
70. Ibid., 433.
71. Kanner (1949), 4–5.
72. Whitman, Graves, and Accardo (1989), 433.
73. Ibid. Only 50 percent of the families in the program were under investigation by the Division of Protective Services at the outset of the study; the others were not in any evident risk of losing their children.
74. Booth and Booth (1994), 54.
75. See Campion (1995); Booth and Booth (1994); Dowdney and Skuse (1993); Llewellyn (1990); Gath (1988); Tymchuk (1992), 165–178; Tymchuk and Feldman (1991); Walton-Allen and Feldman (1991) (reporting on the service needs of twenty-two mothers with retardation and supporting conclusion of earlier studies that they could provide useful information about their life situations and recognize problematic skill areas; there was a high rate of disagreement between mothers and social workers about the kinds of services needed; they did agree, and the study found, that there is a dearth of available specialized services designed to meet the mothers' personal needs relating to vocational, social, and communication skills); Wates (1993); Wates (1991); Tymchuk (1990); Tymchuk and Andron (1990); Tymchuk, Yokota, and Rahbar (1990); Whitman and Accardo (1990); Tymchuk, Andron, and Rahbar (1988), 510–512; Tymchuk, Andron, and Unger (1987); Greenspan and Budd (1986), 116 (concluding that despite the negative bias of most survey samples, "virtually all studies have found a sizable percentage of mentally retarded parents to be functioning either within, or close to, normal limits, especially when compared to parents with similar demographic characteristics"); Unger and Howes (1986), 237–249; Feldman et al. (1985), 253, 256; Ross et al. (1985), 112–113 (noting the importance that parents who had retardation attached to the education of their children); Zetlin, Weisner, and Gallimore (1985), 86 (concluding that relative IQ is not a factor contributing to the adequacy of child care by parents with retardation); Budd and Greenspan (1985), 269–273 (concluding that parental behavior, not IQ, should be the criterion for assessing parental competence); Rosenberg and McTate (1982) (reporting that for parents with mild retardation, IQ has not proved to be a valid predictor of parenting success); Schilling et al. (1982); Haavik and Menninger (1981), 75–78 (concluding that "studies to date . . . have failed to document a relationship between I.Q. *per se* and ability to provide adequate child care" and that, as a group, children of parents with retardation have scored significantly, and sometimes substan-

tially, higher than their parents on traditional measures of intelligence); Mira
and Roddy (1980); Crain and Millor (1978) (studying one family consisting of
two parents with retardation and two children and concluding that even without intellectual deficiencies of their own, such children need services); Galliher
(1973); Shaw and Wright (1960), 273–274; Brandon (1957); Mickelson
(1949).

76. See Llewellyn (1990), 372. Dowdney and Skuse (1993) explain the role of IQ
as follows: "I.Q. does not relate in any systematic way to parenting competency until it falls below 55–60. Below this level, less competent parenting has
been reported; above it successful increments in IQ within the retarded range
are not associated with increased parenting competence." Ibid., 33–34 (citations omitted).

77. See Whitman, Graves, and Accardo (1989).

78. Kanner (1949), 4–5.

79. See, e.g., Feldman et al. (1986), 33, 36, and (1989). Both of these studies dispute the findings of earlier work suggesting that mothers with retardation
showed their children little affection. See Haavik and Menninger (1981);
Crittenden and Bonvillian (1984). See also Floor et al. (1975), 33–37 (study of
54 previously institutionalized couples concluding that "although the care of
some of the children would be questionable by middle class standards, there
are others who appear to be receiving proper medical attention and affection
from both parents"); Berry and Shapiro (1975) (although affection level was
high, child care was considered "poor" by middle-class standards).

80. See Sarber et al. (1983) (involving one mother with IQ of 57).

81. See Szykula, Haffey, and Parsons (1981), 180–190 (study involving one
woman with mild retardation).

82. See Zetlin, Weisner, and Gallimore (1982). Statistically, most parents with
mental retardation are poor, and poor people generally have lower IQs than
their culturally privileged middle- and upper-class counterparts. See Budd and
Greenspan (1984), citing Frotheringham (1980); Dowdney and Skuse (1993),
25–47.

83. Walton-Allen and Feldman (1991), 145. See also Tymchuk and Feldman
(1991); Whitman, Graves, and Accardo (1989); Lovett and Harris (1987);
Wahler (1980); Kanfer (1975); Kanfer and Grimm (1978); Wolfensberger and
Nirje (1972).

84. See Whitman, Graves, and Accardo (1989); Campion (1995); Booth and Booth
(1994); Richardson and Koller (1996); Budd and Greenspan (1984, 1985);
Espe-Sherwindt and Kerlin (1990).

85. See, e.g., Campion (1995); Booth and Booth (1994); Whitman and Accardo
(1990); Feldman et al. (1985, 1986, and 1989); Tymchuk (1990, 1991, and
1992); Tymchuk and Andron (1988, 1990); Tymchuk, Andron, and Hagelstein
(1992); Tymchuk, Andron, and Rahbar (1988); Tymchuk, Andron, and
Tymchuk (1990); Tymchuk, Andron, and Ungar (1987); Tymchuk and

Feldman (1991); Tymchuk, Hamada, Andron, and Anderson (1989, 1990a, and 1990b); Tymchuk and Keltner (1991); Tymchuk, Yokota, and Rahbar (1990); Unger and Howes (1986); Walton-Allen and Feldman (1991), 137–147.

86. Tymchuk and Feldman (1991), 491–492 (citations omitted).

87. Campion (1995), 163, quoting Valentine (1990).

88. See generally Tymchuk (1992) in which he concludes: "Given the little programmatic support for learning parenting skills, current levels of knowledge and skill cannot be taken as indicative of the capabilities to acquire new skills. At the same time, when such meager efforts are expended, there is little chance for success which then reinforces the idea that parent[s] with retardation cannot learn." See also Espe-Sherwindt and Kerlin (1990).

89. Tymchuk urged in 1992: "It is clear that people with mental retardation are becoming parents and will continue to do so. Unlike any other group of parents, the adequacy of parenting by persons with mental retardation will continue to be scrutinized despite the limited empirical information on which to base such scrutiny . . . [A] shift away from prediction of inadequacy to the prediction of adequacy of parenting should be emphasized. Shifting this focus allows for the identification of reasons for such adequacy and ways in which to maximize those reasons including moving the focus away from factors inherent in the person such as IQ to other present as well as historical environmental factors which are amenable to intervention." Tymchuk (1992), 165, 176.

15. Written Law concerning Parenting

1. A common justification for retaining mental retardation as an independent factor to assess parental fitness is that targeting retardation reasonably furthers state interests in protecting children from harm because of "recognized limitations inherent in such deficiencies as mental retardation." Payne (1992), §2(a). The assumption is that persons labeled "retarded" are necessarily inadequate. See generally Payne (1992).

2. The statute applied to persons who have "been adjudicated mentally retarded and who, at the time an adoption petition concerning their children is filed, are found to continue to be mentally retarded and to be persons who will not recover in the foreseeable future." Ill. Rev. Stat. ch. 40 §1501(1) (1977). Compare N.J. Rev. Stat. §§9:2–13 and 9:2-19(a) (1997) and Cal. Fam. Code §§7826 and 7827 (1997) (containing disqualifying classifications for parents with mental retardation but requiring findings of unfitness).

3. Helvey v. Rednour, 19.

4. N.Y. Soc. Serv. Law §384-b(6)(b). See also former N.Y. Soc. Serv. Law §384(7)(g) (permitting termination upon a finding of mental retardation that impairs adaptive behavior to such an extent that a child returned to the parent would be at risk of neglect).

5. See Wakefield (1981). See also 45 A.L.R. 2d 1379.
6. N.Y. Soc. Serv. Law §384-b(6)(b) (1976 and 1977). See the discussion of definitions of retardation in Chapter 3.
7. In re McDonald, 448.
8. Ibid., 449.
9. Ibid., 450–451.
10. In re Wardle, 558, 562–563.
11. Ibid., 502. Wardle's IQ number was 60.
12. In 1983 the Illinois legislature amended its statute to require a fitness hearing before termination of parental rights (see Ill. St. ch. 40 ¶1510 §[8][e] [1977], as amended by Pub. Act No. 83-870 [1983]), and established preponderance-of-the-evidence as the standard of proof (see Ill. St. ch. 37 ¶¶705-709[2] [1979]), amended by Pub. Act No. 82-437 [1981]). When the following year the U.S. Supreme Court held in Santosky v. Kramer that clear and convincing evidence was constitutionally required, the Illinois legislature again amended its statute to comply. See Ill. St. ch. 37 ¶¶803-830 (1988).
13. See, e.g., In re N. Children; In re Ursula P.; In re Daniel D. Compare In re Mendes (1980) (same court as in Gross) with In re Mendes (1981).
14. See, e.g., In re Welfare of P. J. K., holding that mental retardation is not, by itself, grounds for removal or termination of parental rights. In order for a parent's rights to be terminated, according to that court, the parent's mental disability must be "directly related to parenting and . . . be permanently detrimental to the physical or mental health of the child." Ibid., 290.
15. See, e.g., Ala. Code §26-18-7(a)(2) (1997); Cal. Fam. Code §§7826 and 7827 (1994); Colo. Rev. Stat. 19-5-105(3.1)(a)(1) (1998); Ga. Code Ann. §15-11-81(b)(4)(i) (1997); Mass. Gen. Laws ch. 119 §24(d) (1996); Mo. Rev. Stat. §211.447(2)(a) (1997); Mont. Code Ann. §41-3-609(2)(a) (1997); N.J. Rev. Stat. §§9:2-13 and 9:2-19(a) (1993); N.Y. Soc. Serv. Law §384(b)(4)(c) (1992); S.C. Code Ann. §20-7-1572(6) (1997); Tenn. Code Ann. §36-1-113 (1998); Utah Code Ann. §§78-3a-407(3) and 78-3a-408(2)(a) (1997); Wash. Rev. Code §13.34.180(5)(b) (1997).
16. See, e.g., N.C. Stat. §7A-289.32(7) (1997).
17. See N.Y. Soc. Serv. Law §384 (1992).
18. See, e.g., In re Anthony D.; In re J. B.; In re Angel B.; In re W. P., Jr.; Peterson v. Peterson ("courts may not properly deprive a parent of the custody of a minor child unless it is affirmatively shown that such parent is unfit to perform the duties imposed by the relationship, or has forfeited that right"). See also Petition of Dep't Soc. Servs. to Dispense with Consent to Adoption.
19. The 1976 Family Court Act, which became effective in 1977, incorporated the best interests requirement. See N.Y. Fam. Ct. Act §§611 and 623 (1983).
20. See In re Gross, 224. Compare N.Y. Soc. Serv. Law §384-b(4)(c) (pertaining to retardation) with §384-b(7) (pertaining to permanent neglect) (1992) and N.Y. Fam. Ct. Act §§611, 614, 623, 624, 625, 631, 634 (1983) (pertaining to permanent neglect).

21. See In re Daniel D.; In re N. Children; In re Ursula P.
22. See In re Joyce T. and In re Elizabeth Q.
23. State v. Alsager (1972), 727.
24. Alsager v. District Court (1975), 20. Nevertheless, journalistic reports about the Alsagers suggested that they were poor and had mental retardation, or at least that Mrs. Alsager went to a special school. See, e.g., Greene (1976).
25. Alsager v. District Court (1975), 23.
26. Ibid., 22.
27. Ibid.
28. Ibid., 23.
29. Some other courts also consider the best interests inquiry to be required by the Constitution—for example, the Massachusetts appeals court in Adoption of Katharine and Jeptha.
30. See, e.g., In re Michael G. (California); In re B. P. (Georgia); In re S. N. (Iowa); In re M. P. (Louisiana); Jonathan H. v. Margaret H. (Missouri); In re Christopher T. (New York); In re M. (New York); In re E. M. (Pennsylvania); In re Anderson (Pennsylvania); In re P.A.B. (23 Pa. C.S. §2511(a)(2,5)); Navarrette v. Texas Dept. of Human Resources (Tex. Fam. Code Ann. §15.02).
31. See, e.g., In re C.A.A.A. (Nebraska); In re Joyce T. (New York); In re Elizabeth Q. (New York). See generally Payne (1992), §VI(29).
32. Baby Richard was a pseudonym, used to protect the child's anonymity. The child, whose name is Daniel, was not informed of the conflict until it was time to turn him over to his biological parents.
33. See In re Doe (1993–1994); In re Kirschner.
34. In re Doe (1994), 182–183.
35. See In re Clausen, 662. In the U.S. Supreme Court, the case was called DeBoer v.Schmidt.
36. See, e.g., In re Doe (1994), 183; In re Clausen, 662.
37. See Goldstein, Freud, and Solnit (1973, 1979). These books set forth the notion of the "psychological parent," which has been the basis for arguing that a child's best interests may require continued custody by a nonparent, even though the biological parent who does not have custody is not unfit. See Hoy v. Willis (possibility of serious psychological harm to child may transcend all other considerations in custody decisions).
38. The Parental Kidnapping Act of 1980, 28 U.S.C.A. §1738A and 42 U.S.C.A. §663, and the Uniform Child Custody Jurisdiction Act, 9 U.L.A. 116 (1979), were enacted to prevent parents and would-be parents from obtaining custody by switching jurisdictions in this fashion.
39. See Areen (1993), 1585–86; New York Times (1977).
40. The Iowa court found that the grandparents provided a "stable, dependable, conventional, middle-class, middlewest background" and that the father's household was "unstable, unconventional, arty, Bohemian, and probably intellectually stimulating." It thought a move to the father would disrupt the child's development. Painter v. Bannister, 153.

41. The Phillip Becker case is another famous example of a court's placing the interests of a child above the authority of the parents, even without declaring them unfit; the parents had institutionalized the child since birth and were making medical and other decisions on his behalf that the court concluded were not in the child's interests. The California courts eventually allowed another family to serve as Phillip's guardians; allowed him to live with that family, whom he loved; and allowed that family to consent to an operation for him, which was necessary to save his life. See In re Phillip B. (1979); Guardianship of Phillip B. (1983). See also Mnookin (1988).

42. In re Doe (1994), 185.

43. DeBoer v. Schmidt, 1302.

44. See Associated Press (1998).

45. See Linn v. Linn.

46. Cf. Frye v. Spotte.

47. See generally Crocca (1994) (discussing courts' consideration of stable relationships between longstanding caretakers and a child as an important factor in sometimes denying biological parents' claims to regain custody).

48. See, e.g., Conn. Gen. Stat. §17a-112(b)(1) (1998) (best interests and abandonment); Tenn. Code Ann. §36-1-113 (1998). Examples of case law from other states are In re J. B.; In re Angel B.; In re W. P., Jr.; Adoption of Katharine and Jeptha; Petitions to Dispense with Consent for Adoption (1985).

49. In re Anthony D., 1.

50. 70 Ill. Comp. Stat. 50/20a (1992). See, e.g., Minn. Stat. §260.221(4) (1998); Mont. Code Ann. §§41-3-602 and 609(3) (1995); N.M. Stat. §32A-4-22 (1997). But cf. In re J.P. (requiring unfitness).

51. See, e.g., In re J. K. C., Jr.; In re Dull; In re Egly; In re Anthony D.

52. See, e.g., Petitions of the Dep't of Soc. Servs. to Dispense with Consent to Adoption; Lewis v. Davis. In In re Geiger the Pennsylvania Supreme Court emphasized that the state must meet a high burden of proof in order to terminate parental rights. The lower court had terminated the rights of a mother with retardation. The Pennsylvania Adoption Act, I.P.S. §§311(2) and 313, requires a court to find that a child is "without essential parental care, control, or subsistence necessary for his physical or mental well-being" before it orders termination of parental rights. The state did not meet its burden, according to the court, because the mother's children were amply nourished and in good health and were not physically abused.

53. In re Joyce T., 711.

54. Ibid., 707.

55. Ibid., 708.

56. Ibid., 708.

57. See In re Jamie M., 339. See also discussion of Jamie M. in Chapter 17.

58. Ibid., 340.

59. In re Viana Children, quoting In re Sheila G., 427.

60. In re Tonya Louise, 370.

61. Ibid.

62. Ibid.
63. See, e.g., Nebraska v. Wanek (involving a parent "functionally illiterate and mildly mentally retarded, with a severe alcoholism problem"); In re L. G. (parent suffering from schizophrenia and organic brain damage).
64. Note (1977–78), 816.
65. See, e.g., In re Ebony W., 740, n. 5 (urging trial courts to be more thorough in making findings of fact and conclusions of law in child abuse and neglect cases).
66. See Note (1979).
67. See, e.g., Guardianship of D. N.; In re M. T. and T. T.
68. New York Times (1995).
69. One example of a court's refusing to eliminate even pre-adoptive parents because of its concerns about the child's normal "neurological development" is In re Adoption of Richardson. The parents had hearing impairments, but not mental retardation. The lower court had refused their petition for adoption after social workers and fellow judges advised the lower court judge that "he would be remiss in his duty" if he allowed the adoption. The appellate court reversed the lower court's holding, finding judicial bias. Would reversal have come as easily if the parental deficit had been retardation rather than deafness?
70. See, for example, note 3 in Chapter 16 and the discussion of the Adoption Assistance and Child Welfare Act in Chapter 17.
71. See In re Geiger. See also the discussion of In re Mendes in Chapter 17.
72. See, e.g., M. Wald (1975).
73. See, e.g., M. Wald (1976); Mnookin (1973).

16. The Social Welfare System in Practice

1. The agency or department might also be called the Office of Children Services, Child Youth Services, or some such title. In Massachusetts, parents with retardation receive services from the Department of Mental Retardation, but it is the Department of Social Services that is responsible for the children's welfare, including the children of parents with retardation.
2. See Mass. Gen. Laws ch. 119 §51(a) (1997).
3. See, e.g., Mass. Regs. Code, tit. 110, §7.128 (department's responsibility to help maintain the child's ties to the biological parents); Adoption Assistance and Child Welfare Act of 1980 (AACWA), 42 U.S.C. §671(a)(15), requiring "reasonable efforts" to prevent the need to remove a child and, in case of removal, to facilitate prompt return. Many states took the federal funds promised by the AACWA without providing the services the statute required of them. Individuals brought private actions to enforce the statute, but in Suter v. Artist M., the U.S. Supreme Court held that type of suit unavailable. Other efforts continue, in lower courts, to find means to enforce the rights to social services that federal law purports to create. See, e.g., Marisol v. Guiliani; LaShawn v. Kelly. See Atwell (1992).

4. See, e.g., Adoption of Abigail (reasonable for department not to provide service plan to mother with retardation after removal of sixteen-day-old baby, because it would have "required a high and unreasonable measure of optimism to press ahead with a specific plan for keeping the mother and [child] together"); In re Fulton (failure to provide reunification services; failure of parents to learn). For cases requiring the agency to comply with the law by providing services, see the discussion of B. J. G. in Chapter 17.

5. See, for example, In re Fulton, discussed later in this chapter. But cases finding for parents, in part because the department had not facilitated visitation, include Petitions of Department of Social Services to Dispense with Consent to Adoption (1985) (reversing termination of parental rights partly because neither department nor the trial court facilitated visitation); and Anthony D., 7 (failing to find abandonment because the department failed to facilitate visitation).

6. This requirement of an interval before parental rights are terminated should not be confused with a different rule about passage of time that a growing number of statutes are adopting: a presumption that parental rights *should* terminate when parent and child have been apart for a specified period of time, such as one or two years. Moreover, some courts and legislatures are moving toward redefinition of "abandonment" to dispense with the traditional requirement of parental intent to abandon the child, requiring only a showing that the "parents manifest disinterest or inattention." Bodenheimer (1975). See also Pierce (1984).

7. See Gagnon v. Scarpelli; Lassiter v. Dep't of Soc. Servs.; M.L.B. v. S.L.J. In Lassiter, the U.S. Supreme Court decided that the mother was not entitled to counsel because no criminal charges had been proffered against her, no expert witness testified, the case presented no difficult issues of law, and the presence of counsel would not have had a significant impact on the outcome.

8. M.L.B. v. S.L.J., 4035.

9. Several state courts have held that the state must appoint counsel for indigent parents at termination hearings. See, e.g., State ex rel. Heller v. Miller; Department of Public Welfare v. J.K.B.; In re Chad S.; In re Myricks; Crist v. Division of Youth and Family Servs.; Danforth v. Maine Dep't of Health and Welfare; In re Friesz. Some others have held that indigent parents have a right to appointed counsel at the removal phase of child dependency or neglect hearings. Davis v. Page; Cleaver v. Wilcox (right to be decided case by case); Smith v. Edmiston.

10. In In re Campbell, the Ohio court held that a couple would not be able to provide the necessary "condition" or "environment" to raise the child adequately, since the couple lived in poverty and would be unable to provide food, hot water, and necessities for baby care. In In re J.L.P., the Florida Court of Appeals held that both neglect and abuse can be established prospectively. In this case the court terminated the rights of a mother it found to be "trainably retarded." (That term is now out of favor but is still sometimes used in professional circles

to refer to persons with moderate mental retardation. See Hales, Yudofsky, and Talbott [1994], 775, Table 23-19. Persons with milder retardation were called "educable" rather than "trainable.") The court also said the mother was hostile, impatient, and unable to think in terms of the child's welfare, and that she was living in inadequate housing, despite a court order not to. The appeals court dismissed the mother's argument that she could not be considered to have neglected a child who had been placed in foster care shortly after birth and who had therefore never been legally in her custody. See also Adoption of Abigail, involving removal of a child at birth from a mother who had retardation, and subsequent termination of parental rights.

11. See Adoption of Abigail, in which the seeming inability of a mother with retardation to provide a home for her child was an important factor in the court's termination of her parental rights. And in Petitions to Dispense with Consent to Adoption, the fact that a mother with retardation had a supportive aunt was important in obtaining reversal of a termination order.

12. In re Fulton, 2.

13. Ibid., 3.

14. Ibid., 6.

15. In Massachusetts, both the Department of Social Services and the Department of Mental Health use court clinics at the various courthouses to obtain a professional evaluation of an individual's parenting ability, especially when there is no retardation.

16. The Developmental Support Team at the Children's Hospital was a three-year project funded in the mid-1980s by a model service grant from the National Center for Child Abuse. Based in the hospital's Developmental Evaluation Clinic, the team was linked with various Massachusetts agencies, including the Departments of Social Services, Mental Health, and Public Health. Although the team has been disbanded for failure to obtain renewed funding, some of its former members still conduct psychological evaluations at the hospital; but they have considerably less contact with the Department of Social Services than they did in the 1980s. The Eunice Kennedy Shriver Center in Waltham, Massachusetts, is another sophisticated facility for evaluating the needs of individuals with disabilities.

17. See, e.g., In re J.K.C., Jr.; In re Ebony.

18. See note 3 above.

19. See discussion of parental training studies in Chapter 14. See generally Whitman and Accardo (1990), 51–110; Whitman, Graves, and Accardo (1989), 431–434; Feldman et al. (1986, 1989); Tymchuk and Feldman (1991); Tymchuk (1992). Between 1979 and 1984, the Eunice Kennedy Shriver Center offered a parent training program to mothers with retardation who had once lived in the Fernald State School (and their spouses or living companions). The program's directors reported that many of the women were free from severe emotional problems and were trained to parent successfully and to meet the needs of their children.

20. In re Anthony D., 12.
21. Dep't of Soc. Servs. v. Kitty Oree Smith, 808.
22. Ibid., quoting S.C. Code Ann. §20-7-1572(6).
23. Ibid., 809.
24. See, e.g., Massachusetts Governor's Commission on Mental Retardation, *Report on the Unserved and Underserved* (1996), 3.
25. See In re J.K.C., Jr.
26. Ibid., 201.
27. Ibid., 202.
28. Ibid.
29. Ibid., 203–204.
30. Ibid., 200.
31. Ibid., quoting Mo. Rev. Stat. §§211.447.2(2)(a) and (3)(c).
32. Ibid., 202, quoting Mo. Rev. Stat. §211.447.3(1).
33. Ibid., 203, quoting Mo. Rev. Stat. §211.447.3(2).
34. Ibid., quoting Mo. Rev. Stat. §211.447.3(5).
35. Ibid., 204.
36. Ibid.
37. Ibid., 203.
38. Ibid., 202.
39. Ibid., 204.
40. Ibid., 203; 200–201.
41. Ibid., 203.
42. Ibid., quoting Mo. Rev. Stat. §211.443(3) (citations omitted). Cf. In re P.J.K.
43. In re J.K.C Jr., 204.
44. Ibid., 205.
45. Ibid.
46. See, e.g., Adoption of Abigail.
47. Roberts v. State (1977).
48. Roberts v. State (1976).
49. Roberts v. State (1977), 269.
50. Ibid., 269–270.
51. Adoption of Katharine and Jeptha, 26.
52. Ibid., 27–28.
53. Ibid., 27–28, 32–34 (citations omitted).
54. See, e.g., Adoption of Abigail. Cf. Petition of Dept. of Social Services to Dispense with Consent to Adoption.
55. See Children's Bureau, National Center on Child Abuse and Neglect (1981); Pelton (1978); Schilling (1981); Elmer (1977); Roth (1982); Eastwood (1982).
56. See Egeland, Breitbucher, and Rosenberg (1980); Elmer (1979); Garbarino (1976); Coyne and Lazarus (1980); Conger, Burgess, and Barret (1979); Conley (1973); Robinson and Robinson (1976).

57. See Justice and Justice (1976); Cromwell (1963); Heber (1964); Burgess (1979); Parke and Collmer (1975); Bailer (1970); Young (1976).

58. See Whitman, Graves, and Accardo (1989), 431.

17. Reforming the System

1. One example of the state's using coercive tactics to induce a mother to give up her child is In re Lashawanda. Tricia Lashawanda gave birth at age fourteen while in state custody as a neglected child. Her social worker obtained Tricia's written consent to give up the baby as she was being wheeled out of the delivery room, less than half an hour after regaining consciousness and while still under the effects of anesthetic. The New York Family Court refused to terminate the mother's parental rights because "a so-called 'voluntary' placement executed by an infant unprotected by the advice of parent or guardian ad litem is void ab initio" and cannot support termination. In re Lashawanda, 298. The court also declined to sever her rights on grounds of abandonment and permanent neglect, holding that the state has a fiduciary obligation to its ward that would preclude termination of her parental rights. "What is most disturbing," said the judge, "more so than had this matter involved out and out deceit or overreaching, is the fact that the trampling of one mother's rights to her own child results here from the uninspired application of standard social-work platitudes which so often reinforce the sad but crushing reality that, all things being equal, the poor and disenfranchised have less of a chance to keep their own children than the 'haves' or the affluent." Ibid., 297–298.

2. See generally Hales, Yudofsky, and Talbott (1994), 780–781.

3. See, e.g., Mass. Regs. Code tit. 110, §§4-5, outlining the elaborate investigatory apparatus of the Department of Social Services in Massachusetts.

4. This proposed reform would significantly alter current law. In Lassiter v. Department of Social Services, the U.S. Supreme Court held that a state's obligation to provide counsel at a proceeding terminating a mother's custody of her child depends on a balancing of the state and individual interests in each case. See Lassiter, 27–33. The Court noted, however, that "[a] wise public policy . . . may require that higher standards be adopted than those minimally tolerable under the Constitution" and that (in 1981, when the case was decided) thirty-three states and the District of Columbia statutorily provide for the appointment of counsel in termination cases. Ibid., 33–34. For an example of such a law, see Mass. Gen. Laws ch. 119 §29 (1993).

5. Compare *Seattle Times* (1998) (schoolteacher imprisoned and denied any contact with the child she had produced with her thirteen-year-old student).

6. Of course, if the original removal for neglect was necessary only because the state failed to provide necessary services, and if it seems they could now be provided, the past adjudication of neglect should be irrelevant.

7. R. G. and T. G. v. Marion County Office, Dep't Family and Children, 327.
8. Ibid., 328.
9. Ibid., 328–329.
10. Ibid., 329.
11. Ibid.
12. Ibid.
13. Ibid., 330, n. 9.
14. Ibid., 329–330.
15. Ibid., 330.
16. Ibid., 330, n. 10.
17. Ibid., 330–331 (Sullivan, J., concurring).
18. Even if the argument were made that their parenting problems are "intractable," the same argument might be made about parents who suffer from drug addiction or alcoholism or the problems associated with continually impoverished lifestyles.
19. An exception is that counsel, or other form of state aid, would be required when necessary to ensure fair adjudication.
20. See, e.g., State ex rel. Heller v. Miller; Department of Public Welfare v. J.K.B.; In re Chad S.; In re Myricks; Crist v. Div. of Youth and Family Servs.; Danforth v. Maine Dep't of Health and Welfare; In re Friesz. A number of others have held that indigent parents have a right to appointed counsel in child dependency or neglect hearings. Davis v. Page; Cleaver v. Wilcox (right to be decided case by case); Smith v. Edmiston.
21. In re Orlando F. (1975 and 1976).
22. See In re Orlando F. (1976).
23. Ibid., 111–112 (citation omitted). The court of appeals also found that "the trial court abused its discretion in permitting the law guardian to withdraw as a representative of the child without appointing a replacement." Ibid., 103. As a result, new counsel was appointed for Orlando and the case was remanded for a dispositional hearing to determine his placement.
24. See Massachusetts Department of Social Services (1997), 9–10.
25. See generally Crocca (1994). See also discussion of the role of best interests requirements in Chapter 15.
26. Ibid.
27. See generally Rothman (1986).
28. In addition to the cases discussed with predictive unfitness, a newborn was removed from a parent with retardation in In re Green (1978); In re Orlando F. (1976); and Wishinsky v. Alabama Dep't of Resources.
29. See, e.g., Amadio and Deutsch (1983–84).
30. Subsidies are available to encourage adoption of special-needs children. The term "special needs" here means something much broader than it often does in the public school system: any child who is hard to place is considered to have special needs for purposes of adoption. Accordingly, sibling groups who

should stay together, for example, have special needs from this perspective, even though each sibling may be of average or higher intelligence.

31. See discussion of the appropriate role for best interests requirements in Chapter 15.

32. See generally Goldstein, Freud, and Solnit (1973, 1979) (the theory of the psychological parent). See also discussion in Chapter 15 of the tendency of courts to give weight to the role of the psychological parent in child custody determinations.

33. See, e.g., In re Mendes. See also In re Gross, 223.

34. See generally Goldstein, Freud, and Solnit (1973, 1979).

35. Many children in foster placements remain strongly attached to their biological parents, even if they see them infrequently and the placement is long-lasting. See Weinstein (1976), 672.

36. See Field (1991), 17–19.

37. See, e.g., Perrault v. Cook; Selivanoff v. Selivanoff; King v. King; In re Marriage of Elser; In re Marriage of Rosenfeld; In re Marriage of Sarsfield.

38. See Ammar and Widawsky (1992); Michelman (1969, 1973); Tribe (1977).

39. See Shelley v. Kramer; Moose Lodge v. Irvis.

40. See Palmer v. Thompson.

41. It cannot, however, cut back on them. See generally Katzenbach v. Morgan.

42. See Ricci v. Okin.

43. See Massachusetts Governor's Commission on Mental Retardation (1996).

44. In re Jeffrey Mayle, 1.

45. Ibid.

46. Ibid., 2.

47. Ibid., 4.

48. Ibid., 4–5.

49. Ibid., 7.

50. Similarly, if a school were located in a building with no wheelchair access, would it be a sufficient answer to a boy who had paralysis and could not therefore attend that he is being offered the same services in the same building as anyone else, so the state is not discriminating? After all, the state did not create his paralysis.

51. In Cleburne, if the City had prohibited *all* group homes, the would-be residents might have argued that, under the Due Process clause, they have a right to live in the community and the government should not be able to obstruct the right. At least legislation should not prohibit their primary means of living in the community, absent a compelling state need to do so, the argument would run. Without such a compelling need, cities must allow groups to live together—at least groups of people with retardation—because many of them (including, hopefully, the plaintiffs in the case) can exercise their fundamental right to live in the community only by living in such group homes.

   Although this argument is available and appealing, it still would be much

more difficult to win than a simple discrimination claim. In fact, many persons
with retardation have moved beyond this particular problem, since the current
preferred model for residences in the community is not a group home but a
much smaller residence, housing only three or four clients.

52. For a comparable example, see note 50.

53. 20 U.S.C.A. §1400(C)

54. See 20 U.S.C. 1400 et seq.

55. 42 U.S.C. §671(a)(15) (1997).

56. 42 U.S.C. §672(a)(1) (1997).

57. This antidiscrimination principle is contained in Title II, codified as 42 U.S.C.
12131-12165 (1990). See Gostin and Beyer (1993), 87. A related law, the Developmental Disabilities Assistance and Bill of Rights Act of 1982, requires
states that receive federal funding to set up advocacy systems for persons with
developmental disabilities. See 42 U.S.C. §6012, §6042. It also requires recipient states to take affirmative action to employ and promote "qualified handicapped individuals" on the same basis as required by the Rehabilitation Act of
1973, 29 U.S.C. 701.

58. *ADA Technical Assistance Manual* (ADATAM) II-3.6100 (emphasis added). For
discussion of remedies under the ADA and other federal laws, see Tucker and
Goldstein (1991).

59. ADATAM, II-3.6200.

60. See 28 C.F.R. 35.130. Separate programs are permitted under the act "where
necessary to ensure equal opportunity." Nevertheless, states cannot exclude
individuals from regular programs or "require them to accept special services
or benefits." ADATAM II-3.400. See also 28 C.F.R. 35.131.

61. See Watkins (1995).

62. 42 U.S.C. 12131 (1995).

63. 42 U.S.C. 12132 (1995).

64. In re John D. (quoting headnote).

65. See Suter v. Artist M.

66. See Parker v. Department of Human Servs. (quoting the 1995 amendment to
Ark. Code Ann. §9-27-341, Act 811 of 1995).

67. See Fla. Stat. ch. 402.45 (1997).

68. See Cal. Welf. & Inst. Code §361.5 (1997) and §§16500, 16500.55, 16500.65,
16506, 16507 (1996); Ind. Code §12-7-2-82.3 (1994); Me. Rev. Stat. tit. 22
§§4041(1)(c) and (d), 4401(3) and (5) (1997); Mass. Gen. Laws ch. 119 §1
(1993); Ohio Rev. Code Ann. §121.37 (1997). See also Cal. Welf. & Inst. Code
§4501 (1998) (Lanterman Development Disabilities Services Act); Williams v.
Macomber.

69. One such modification might be assigning the parent an aide experienced in
communicating with and teaching persons with mental disabilities. Many parents with retardation need help, especially during their child's short period of
complete dependency. Daytime home assistance by social workers experienced
in assisting persons with retardation may be necessary at that time, or even

twenty-four-hour staff for some parents. Dual foster care, discussed later in connection with the W. P. case, is another option. See, e.g., In re Anthony D., 6 ("the psychologist recommended commitment and placement . . . of mother and son 'in a stable living situation, such as a special group home or school, where she [could] learn parenting skills, homemaking skills, and be able to finish her education'"). But many parents can cope with much less assistance—for example, a training program one morning a week or a weekly visit from a homemaker. The training programs provided between 1979 and 1984 by the Eunice Kennedy Shriver Center in Waltham, Massachusetts, for example, generally occurred only one morning per week.

70. In the 1980s Boston Children's Services conducted an experimental foster care program for mothers with retardation and their children. The program aimed to provide the mothers with parent role modeling and supervision.

71. See DMR/DARE Residential Service Contract #3153, FY 1997.

72. Whitman, Graves, and Accardo (1989), 431 (during the first year of this training program, 48 percent of the families became homeless).

73. Interview with Dr. Mary Jane England, fall 1985. This is not an unusual state practice. See Whitman, Graves, and Accardo (1998), 433.

74. See Massachusetts Governor's Commission on Mental Retardation (1996).

75. Booth and Booth (1994), 54–55, 65.

76. See also In re Joyce T.; In re Maricopa County Juvenile Action; In re Wardle. See generally Note (1979); M. Wald (1975). But cf. Petition of Dept. of Social Services, discussed in Chapter 16, in which an aunt's presence in the home supported the children's remaining there.

77. In re W. P., Jr., 1.

78. Ibid.

79. Ibid., 2.

80. Ibid., 1–2.

81. Ibid., 3 (citation omitted).

82. See, e.g., Conn. Gen. Stat. §45A-717(b) (1998); Fla. Stat. chs. 39.461(1)(b) and 39.805 (1998); Iowa Code §232.113(1) (1994); Me. Rev. Stat. tit. 22, §4052(H) (1997); N.C. Gen. Stat. §7A-289.30(al) (1997); N.D. Cent. Code §14-17-18(2) (1997); W. Va. Code §49-6-1(b) (1998).

Bibliography

Abbeduto, L. 1991. "Development of verbal communication in persons with moderate to mild mental retardation." *International Review of Research in Mental Retardation*, vol. 17. New York: Academic Press.

Abery, B. H., and M. Fahnestock. 1994. "Enhancing the social inclusion of persons with developmental disabilities." In M. F. Hayden and B. H. Abery, eds., *Challenges for a Service System in Transition: Ensuring Quality Community Experiences for Persons with Developmental Disabilities*. Baltimore: Paul H. Brookes.

Accardo, P., and B. Y. Whitman. 1990. "Children of mentally retarded parents." *American Journal of Diseases of Children*, 144: 69–70.

Adams, J. 1973. "Clinical neuropsychology and the study of learning disorders." *Pediatric Clinics of North America*, 20. Philadelphia: W. B. Saunders Co.

Adcock, M., and R. White, eds. 1985. *Good Enough Parenting—A Framework for Assessment*. Practice Series no. 12. London: British Agencies for Adoption and Fostering.

Ainsworth, M. H., E. A. Wagner, and A. A. Straus. 1945. "Children of our children." *American Journal of Mental Deficiency*, 40:277–289.

Alberts, B., D. Bray, J. Lewis, M. Raff, K. Roberts, and J. D. Watson. 1983. *Molecular Biology of the Cell*. New York: Garland Publishing.

Alper, J. S., and M. R. Natowicz. 1993. "Genetic discrimination and the public entities and public accommodations titles of the Americans with Disabilities Act." *American Journal of Human Genetics*, 53:26–32.

Amadio, C., and S. L. Deutsch. 1983–84. "Open Adoption: Allowing Adopted Children to 'Stay in Touch' with Blood Relatives." *Journal of Family Law*, 22:59.

Amar, A. R., and D. Widawsky. 1992. "Child Abuse as Slavery: A Thirteenth Amendment Response to DeShaney." *Harvard Law Review*, 105:1359.

Amary, I. B. 1980. *The Rights of the Mentally Retarded–Developmentally Disabled to Treatment and Education*. Springfield, Ill.: Charles C. Thomas.

American Association on Mental Retardation (AAMR). 1992. "Mental Retardation: Definition, Classification, and Systems of Support." 9th ed. Washington, D.C.: AAMR.

American Heritage Dictionary. 1976. Boston: Houghton Mifflin.

American Medical Association Encyclopedia of Medicine. 1989. C. B. Clayman, ed. New York: Random House.

American Psychiatric Association. 1994. *Diagnostic and Statistical Manual of Mental Disorders (DSM-IV).* 4th ed. Washington, D.C.: American Psychiatric Association.

Andron, L. 1987. "Sexual dysfunction in couples with learning handicaps." *Sexuality and Disability,* 8(1):25–35.

Andron, L., and M. Sturm. 1973. "Is 'I do' in the repertoire of the retarded? A study of the functioning of married retarded couples." *Mental Retardation* 11(1):31–34.

Andron, L., and A. Tymchuk. 1987. "Parents who are mentally retarded." In A. Craft, ed., *Mental Handicap and Sexuality: Issues and Perspectives.* Turnbridge Wells: D. J. Costello.

Arc. 1982. "Prevalence of Mental Retardation." Arlington, Tex.: The ARC.

——. 1991a. "Position Statement on Protection and Advocacy." Arlington, Tex.: The ARC.

——. 1991b. "HIV/AIDS and Mental Retardation." Arlington, Tex.: The ARC.

——. 1993. "Introduction to Mental Retardation." Arlington, Tex.: The ARC.

——. 1996. "Position Statement on Sexuality of Persons with Retardation." Arlington, Tex.: The ARC.

——. 1997a. "Genetic Causes of Mental Retardation." Arlington, Tex.: The ARC.

——. 1997b. "Members of Minority Groups and Mental Retardation." Arlington, Tex.: The ARC.

Areen, J. 1975. "Intervention Between Parent and Child: A Reappraisal of the State's Role in Child Neglect and Abuse Cases." *Georgetown Law Journal,* 63:887–889.

——. 1978. *Cases and Materials on Family Law.* Westbury, N.Y.: Foundation Press.

——. 1992. *Cases and Materials on Family Law.* 3rd ed. Westbury, N.Y.: Foundation Press.

Arkush, M. 1992. "'Life' Fulfills her Dream." *Los Angeles Times.* March 28, p. F1.

Associated Press. 1981. "Voluntary Sterilization Campaign." *New York Times.* July 8, p. CI9.

——. 1991. "Judge in Sex Case Says Bias No Issue, Won't Give Up Glen Ridge Trial." *Record, Northern New Jersey,* December 18, p. A3.

——. 1998. "Test confirms baby was sent with wrong parents/DNA results for second child due this week." *Star Tribune Newspaper of the Twin Cities.* August 19, p. 4A.

Attard, M. 1988. "Mentally handicapped parents—some issues to consider in relation to pregnancy." *British Journal of Mental Subnormality,* 34(3):3–9.

Atwell, B. L. 1992. A Lost Generation: The Battle for Private Enforcement of the Adoption Assistance and Child Welfare Act of 1980." *University of Cincinnati Law Review,* 60:593.

Bailer, I. 1970. "Emotional Disturbance and Mental Retardation: Etiologic and Conceptual Relationships." In F. Menolascino, ed., *Psychiatric Approaches to Mental Retardation.* New York: Basic Books.

Baker, B. L., G. B. Seltzer, and M. M. Seltzer. 1974. *As Close as Possible.* Cambridge, Mass.: Behavioral Education Project.

Baroff, G. S. 1986: *Mental Retardation: Nature, Cause, and Management.* New York: Hemisphere Publishing.

Batshaw, M. L., and Y. M. Perret. 1992. *Children with Disabilities: A Medical Primer.* Baltimore: Paul H. Brookes.

Baumgart, D., and M. F. Giangreco. 1996. "Key lessons learned about inclusion." In D. Lehr and F. Brown, eds., *People with Disabilities Who Challenge the System.* Baltimore: Paul H. Brookes.

Bayley, N., and E. S. Schaefer. 1963. "Maternal Behavior, Child Behavior, and Their Intercorrelations from Infancy through Adolescence." *Monographs of the Society for Research in Child Development,* 28.

Berini, R. Y., and E. Kahn. 1987. *Clinical Genetics Handbook.* Oradell, N.J.: Medical Economics Books.

Berry, J. A., and R. G. Gordon. 1931. *The Mental Defective: a problem in social efficiency.* London: Kegan Paul, Trench, Trubner.

Berry, J. D., and A. Shapiro. 1975. "Married mentally handicapped patients in the community." *Proceedings of the Royal Society of Medicine,* 68:795–798.

Best, H. 1965. *Public provisions for the mentally retarded in the United States.* New York: Crowell.

Binet, A. 1898. "Historique des recherches sur les rapports de l'intelligence avec la grandeur et la forme de la tête." *L'Année psychologique,* 5:245–298.

———. 1900. "Recherches sur law technique de la mesuration de la tête vivante." *L'Année psychologique,* 7:314–429.

———. [1909] 1973. *Les idées modernes sur les enfants.* Introduction by J. Piaget. Paris: Flammarion.

Binet, A., and T. Simon. 1912. *A method of measuring the development of the intelligence of young children.* Lincoln, Ill.: Courier Company.

———. 1916. In *The Development of Intelligence in Children (The Binet-Simon scale).* Trans. E. S. Kite. Baltimore: Williams and Wikins.

Blake, M. 1995–96. "Welfare and Coerced Contraception: Morality Implications of State Sponsored Reproductive Control." *University of Louisville Journal of Family Law,* 34:311.

Blaney, B. C., and E. L. Freud. 1994. "Trying to play together: competing paradigms in approaches to inclusion through recreation and leisure." In V. J. Bradley, J. W. Ashbaugh, and B. C. Blaney, eds., *Creating Individual Supports for People with Developmental Disabilities: A Mandate for Change at many Levels.* Baltimore: Paul H. Brookes.

Bligh, R. 1965. "Sterilization and Mental Retardation." *American Bar Association Journal,* 51:1059.

Bodenheimer, B. M. 1975. "New Trends and Requirements in Adoption Law and Proposals for Legislative Change." *Southern California Law,* 49:10.

Bogdan, R., and S. J. Taylor. 1987. "The next wave." In S. J. Taylor, D. Biklen, and J.

Knoll, eds., *Community Integration for People with Severe Disabilities*. New York: Teachers College Press.

Boone, S. 1996. "New Jersey Rape Shield Legislation: From Past to Present—the Pros and Cons." *Women's Rights Law Reporter*, 17:223.

Booth, T., and W. Booth. 1994. *Parenting under Pressure: Mothers and Fathers with Learning Difficulties*. Buckingham, Eng.: Open University Press.

Booth, T., K. Simons, and W. Booth. 1990. *Outward Bound: Relocation and Community Care for People with Learning Difficulties*. Buckingham, Eng.: Open University Press.

Borgman, R. D. 1969. "Intelligence and maternal inadequacy." *Child Welfare*, 48:301.

Boyle, P. J. 1995. *Shaping priorities in genetic medicine. Hastings Report Center*, 25:52–58.

Brackel, S. J., and R. S. Rock, eds. 1971. *The Mentally Disabled and the Law*. Chicago: University of Chicago Press.

Braddock, D., R. Hemp, L. Bachelder, and G. Fujiura. 1995. *The State of the States in Developmental Disabilities*. 4th ed. Washington, D.C.: American Association on Mental Retardation.

Braddock, D., and D. Mitchell. 1992. *Residential Services and Developmental Disabilities in the United States*. Washington, D.C.: American Association on Mental Retardation.

Bradley, V. J. 1994. *Evolution of the new service paradigm. Creating Individual Supports for People with Development Disabilities: A Mandate for Change at Many Levels*. Baltimore: Paul H. Brookes.

Brandon, M. W. G. 1957. "The intellectual and social status of children of mental defectives, Parts I and II." *Journal of Medical Science*, 103:710–738.

Brantlinger, E. 1988. "Teachers' perceptions of the parenting abilities of their secondary students with mild mental retardation." *Remedial and Special Education*, 9(4):31–43.

Budd, K., and S. Greenspan. 1984. "Mentally retarded mothers." In E. Blechman, ed., *Behavior Modification with Women*. New York: Guilford Press.

————. 1985. "Parameters of successful and unsuccessful intervention for parents who are mentally retarded." *Mental Retardation*, 23(6):269–273.

Bullard, D., H. Glaser, M. Heagarty, and E. Pivchik. 1967. "Failure to Thrive in the 'Neglected' Child." *American Journal of Orthopsychiatry*. 37:680.

Bureau of the Census. 1923. *Feebleminded and epileptic in institutions*. Washington, D.C.: U.S. Government Printing Office.

Burgdorf, R. L., Jr. 1983. "Procreation, Marriage, and Raising Children." In *The Legal Rights of Handicapped Persons, Cases, Materials, and Texts* (supplement). Baltimore: Paul H. Brookes.

Burgess, R. L. 1979. "Child Abuse: A Social Interactional Analysis." In B. B. Lahey and A. E. Kasdin, eds., *Advances in Clinical Child Psychology*, 2. New York: Plenum Press.

Caldwell, B. M., and R. H. Bradley. 1978. *Home Observation for Measurement of the Environment*. Little Rock: University of Arkansas Press.

Cameron, J. M., H. R. M. Johnson, and F. E. Camps. 1966. "The Battered child syndrome." *Medicine, Science, and the Law*, 6:2.

Campbell, C. A. 1997. "Trio Jailed in Glen Ridge Rape Case; 'Enough is Enough,' Judge Declares." *Record, Northern New Jersey,* July 1, p. A1.

Campion, M. J. 1995. *Who's Fit to Be a Parent.* London: Routledge.

Cancro, R., ed. 1971. *Intelligence: Genetic and Environmental Influences.* New York: Grune and Stratton.

Carson, D. 1989. "The sexuality of people with learning difficulties." *Journal of Social Welfare Law,* 6:355–372.

Ceci, S. J. 1996. *On Intelligence: A Bioecological Treatise on Intellectual Development.* Cambridge, Mass.: Harvard University Press.

Challener, W. A., Jr. 1952. "The Law of Sexual Sterilization in Pennsylvania." *Dickinson Law Review,* 57:298.

Chambers, D. L. 1984. "Rethinking the Substantive Rules for Custody Disputes." *Michigan Law Review,* 83:477, 527–538.

Children's Bureau, National Center on Child Abuse and Neglect. 1981. "National Study of the Incidence and Severity of Child Abuse and Neglect." Washington, D.C.: U.S. Government Printing Office (DHHS publication no. OHDS 81-30329).

Ciotti, P. 1989. "Growing Up Different: when the retarded become parents, perhaps their children know best how well it works." *Los Angeles Times,* May 9, pt. 5, p. 1, col. 4.

Collins, F. S. 1995. "Evolution of a vision: Genome project origins, present and future challenges, and far-reaching benefits." *Human Genome News,* 7:3.

Comment. 1927. Constitutional Law: Sterilization of Defectives." *Southern California Law Review,* 1:73.

———. 1929. "Constitutional Law: Insane and Defective Persons." *California Law Review,* 17:270.

———. 1975. "Eugenic Sterilization Statutes: A Constitutional Re-Evaluation." *Journal of Family Law,* 14:280.

Conger, R. D., R. L. Burgess, and C. Barret. 1979. "Child Abuse Related to Life Change and Perceptions of Illness: Some Preliminary Findings." *Family Coordinator* 28:73.

Conley, R. W. 1973. *The Economics of Mental Retardation.* Baltimore: Johns Hopkins University Press.

Cope, E. D. 1887. *The origin of the fittest.* New York: Henry Schuman.

Coyne, J. C., and R. C. Lazarus. 1980. "Cognitive Style, Stress Perception, and Coping." In I. L. Kutash and L. B. Schlesinger et al., eds., *Handbook on Stress and Anxiety.* San Francisco: Jossey-Bass.

Craft, A. 1993. "Parents with learning disabilities—an overview." In A. Craft, ed., *Parents with Learning Disabilities.* Kidderminster: BILD.

Crain, Lucy S., and Georgia K. Millor. 1978. "Forgotten Children: Maltreated Children of Mentally Retarded Parents." *Pediatrics,* 61(1):130–132.

Crittenden, P. M., and J. D. Bonvillian. 1984. "The relationship between maternal risk status and maternal sensitivity." *American Journal of Orthopsychiatry,* 54:250–260.

Crocca, C. A. 1994. "Annotation: Continuity of Residence as Factor in Contest between Parent and Nonparent for Custody of Child who had been Residing with Nonparent—Modern Status." A.L.R. 5th 15:692.

Cromwell, R. L. 1959. "A Methodological Approach to Personality Research in Mental Retardation." *American Journal of Mental Deficiency,* 64:333.

———. 1963. "A Social Learning Approach to Mental Retardation." In N. R. Ellis, ed., *Handbook of Mental Deficiency: Psychological Theory and Research.* New York: McGraw Hill.

Cynkar, R. J. 1981. "Buck v. Bell, 'Felt Necessities' v. Fundamental Values?" *Columbia Law Review,* 81:1418.

Czukar, G. 1983. "Legal aspects of parenthood for mentally retarded persons." *Canadian Journal of Community Mental Handicap,* 2:57–69.

Davenport, C. B. 1911. *Heredity in Relation to Eugenics.* New York: Henry Holt and Co.

Davies, K. E. 1989. *The Fragile X Syndrome.* New York: Oxford University Press.

Davies, S. P. 1961. *Social Control of the Mentally Deficient.* Rev. ed. New York: Crowell. (Orig. pub. 1930, London: Constable.)

Davis, A. Y. 1983. *Women, race, and class.* New York: Vintage Books.

DeGrouchy, J., and C. Turleau. 1984. *Clinical atlas of human chromosomes.* New York: John Wiley and Sons.

Dembitz, N. 1974. "Book Review." *Yale Law Journal,* 83:1304.

Denno, D. W. 1997. "Sexuality, Rape, and Mental Retardation." *University of Illinois Law Review,* 1997:315.

DeStefano, F., et al. 1982. "Demographic Trends in Tubal Sterilization: United States, 1970–78." *American Journal of Public Health,* 72:480.

Developmental Disabilities Advocacy Project. 1977. "Legal Rights of Developmentally Disabled Citizens: An Advocacy Manual for Minnesota." Minneapolis, Minn.: DDAP.

Developments in the Law. 1980. "The Constitution and the Family." *Harvard Law Review,* 93:1159.

Dorland's Illustrated Medical Dictionary. 28th ed. 1994. Philadelphia: W. B. Saunders Company.

Dowbiggin, I. 1992. "The Cautionary History of Eugenics." *Toronto Star,* November 16, p. A19.

Dowdney, L., and D. Skuse. 1993. "Parenting provided by adults with mental retardation." *Journal of Child Psychology and Psychiatry,* 34(1):25–47.

Dowdney, L., D. Skuse, M. Rutter, D. Quinton, and D. Mrazek. 1985. "The nature and quality of parenting provided by women raised in institutions." *Journal of Child Psychology and Psychiatry,* 26(4):599–625.

Down, J. L. 1866. "Observations on an ethnic classification of idiots." *Rep. Obs. London Hospital,* 3.

———. 1887. *Mental affectations of children and youth.* London: J. and A. Churchill.

D'Souza, N. 1990. "Genetics and Mental Retardation." In Whitman and Accardo (1990).

Duncan, P. M., and W. Millard. 1866. *A Manual for the Classification, Training, and Education of the Feeble-Minded, Imbecile, and Idiotic.* London: Longmans, Green.

Eckelaar, J. M. 1973. "What are Parental Rights?" *Law Quarterly Review,* 89:210.

Edgerton, R. B. 1967. *The Cloak of Competence: Stigma in the Lives of the Mentally Retarded.* Berkeley: University of California Press.

Edgerton, R. B. 1979. *Mental Retardation.* Cambridge, Mass.: Harvard University Press.

Edgerton, R. B., M. Bollinger, and B. Herr. 1984. "The cloak of competence: after two decades." *American Journal of Mental Deficiency,* 88(4):345–351.

Edgerton, R. B., and M. A. Gaston. 1991. *I've Seen It All: Lives of Older Persons with Mental Retardation in the Community.* Baltimore: Paul H. Brookes.

Egeland, B., M. Breitbucher, and D. Rosenberg. 1980. "A Prospective Study of the Significance of Life Stress in the Etiology of Child Abuse." *Journal of Consulting and Clinical Psychology,* 48:195.

Egeland, B., A. Deinard, D. Brunquell, S. Phipps-Yonas, and L. Crichton. 1979. "Final Report: A Prospective Study of the Antecedents of Child Abuse." Unpublished manuscript. University of Minnesota.

Elliot, R. 1987. *Litigating Intelligence.* Dover, Mass.: Auburn House.

Elmer, E. 1977. *Fragile Families, Troubled Children: The Aftermath of Infant Trauma.* Pittsburgh: University of Pittsburgh Press.

———. 1979. "Child Abuse and Family Stress." *Journal of Social Issues,* 35:60.

Epstein, C., B. Childs, F. C. Fraser, V. McKusick, J. Miller, A. Motulsky, M. Rivas, M. Thompson, M. Shaw, and W. Sly. 1975. "Genetic Counselling." *American Journal of Human Genetics,* 27:240–242.

Espe-Sherwindt, M., and S. Kerlin. 1990. "Early intervention with parents with mental retardation: do we empower or impair?" *Infants and Young Children,* 2:21–28.

Esquirol, J. E. D. 1838. *Des Maladies mentales, considérées sous les rapports médiceux, hygiéniques, et médico-légaux.* Paris: Bailliére.

———. [1845]. 1965. *Mental Maladies: A Treatment on Insanity.* New York: Hafner (facsimile of original ed.).

Evans, B., and B. Waites. 1981. *IQ and Mental Testing: An Unnatural Science and Its Social History.* Atlantic Highlands, N.J.: Humanities Press.

Fantuzzo, J., L. Wray, R. Hall, C. Goins, and S. Azar. 1986. "Parent and Social-Skills Training for Mentally Retarded Mothers Identified As Child Maltreaters," *American Journal of Mental Deficiency,* 91:132–140.

Farmer, R., J. Rohde, and B. Sacks. 1993. *Changing Services for People with Learning Disabilities.* London: Chapman and Hall.

Feldman, M. A., L. Case, A. Rincover, F. Towns, and J. Bethel. 1989. "Parent education project III: increasing affection and responsivity in developmentally handicapped mothers." *Journal of Applied Behavior Analysis,* 22(2):211–222.

Feldman, M. A., L. Case, F. Towns, and J. Betel. 1985. "Parent education project I: development and nurturance of children of mentally retarded parents." *American Journal Mental Deficiency,* 90:253–258.

Feldman, M. A., F. Towns, J. Betel, L. Case, A. Rincover, and C. A. Rubino. 1986. "Parent education project II: increasing stimulating interactions of developmentally handicapped mothers." *Journal of Applied Behavior Analysis,* 19(1):23–37.

Ferguson, P. M. 1994. *Abandoned to Their Fate: Social Policy and Practice Toward Severely Retarded People in America, 1820–1920.* Philadelphia: Temple University Press.

Ferleger, D. 1983. "Anti-Institutionalization and the Supreme Court." *Rutgers Law Journal,* 14:595.

Fernald, W. E. 1912. "The Burden of Feeblemindedness." *Medical Communication* (Massachusetts Medical Society), 33.

Ferster, E. Z. 1966. "Eliminating the Unfit—Is Sterilization the Answer?" *Ohio State Law Review,* 27:591.

Field, M. A. 1991. *Surrogate Motherhood.* Rev. ed. Cambridge, Mass.: Harvard University Press.

———. 1993. "Killing 'the Handicapped'—Before and After Birth." *Harvard Women's Law Journal,* 16:7.

Fischer, C. S., et al. 1996. *Inequality by Design: Cracking the Bell Curve Myth.* Princeton, N.J.: Princeton University Press.

Floor, L., D. Baxter, M. Rosen, and L. Zisfein. 1975. "A survey of marriages among previously institutionalized retardates." *Mental Retardation* (April):33–37.

Flynn, R. J. 1987. "Massive IQ gains in 14 nations: What IQ tests really measure." *Psychological Bulletin,* 101(2):171–191.

Flynn, R. J., and K. E. Nitsch, eds. 1980. *Normalization, Social Integration, and Community Services.* Baltimore: University Park Press.

Foster, 1978. "Life with Father." *Family Law Quarterly,* 11:327.

Fotheringham, J. B. 1980. "Mentally Retarded Persons as Parents." Unpublished manuscript. Available from North York Hospital, 4001 Leslie St. Willowdale, Ontario, M2K 1E1; Department of Psychiatry, Queen's University, Kingston, Ontario, Canada.

———. 1981. "Mild mental retardation, poverty, and parenthood." Unpublished manuscript, Department of Psychiatry, Queen's University, Kingston, Ontario, Canada.

Frisch, L. F. 1981. "On licentious licensing: a reply to Hugh LaFollette." *Philosophy and Public Affairs,* 11(2):173.

Fryers, T. 1993. "Epidemiological Thinking in Mental Retardation: Issues in Taxonomy and Population Frequency." In N. W. Bray, ed., *International Review of Research in Mental Retardation,* vol. 19. New York: Academic Press.

Fujiura, G. T., and D. Braddock. 1992. "Fiscal and demographic trends in mental retardation services: The emergence of the family." In L. Rowitz, ed., *Mental Retardation in the Year 2000.* New York: Springer-Verlag.

Gaines-Carter, Patricia. 1987. "Retarded Persons Celebrate Rare Joy." *Washington Post,* December 6, p. B1.

Galliher, K. 1973. "Termination of the parent/child relationship: should parental IQ be an important factor?" *Law and the Social Order,* 4:855–879.

Garbarino, J. 1976. "A Preliminary Study of Some Ecological Correlates of Child Abuse: The Impact of Socioeconomic Stress on Mothers." *Child Development,* 47:178.

Gardiner, H. C. 1993. *Frames of Mind: The Theory of Multiple Intelligence.* 10th anniversary ed. New York: Basic Books.

Gath, A. 1988. "Mentally handicapped people as parents." *Journal of Child Psychology and Psychiatry,* 29(6):739–744.

Geller, L. N., J. S. Alper, P. R. Billings, C. I. Barash, J. Beckwith, and M. R. Natowicz. 1996. "Individual, family, and societal dimensions of genetic discrimination: A case study analysis." *Science and Engineering Ethics,* 2:71–88.

Ghent, J. F. 1973. "Annotation: Validity of Statutes Authorizing Asexualization or Sterilization of Criminals or Mental Defects." A.L.R. 3d 53:960.

Gilhool, T. K., and J. A. Gran. 1985. "Legal Rights of Disabled Parents." In S. Kenneth Thurman, ed., *Children of Handicapped Parents: Research and Clinical Perspectives.* New York: Academic Press.

Gillberg, C., and M. Geijer-Karlsson. 1983. "Children born to mentally retarded women: a 1–21 year follow-up study of 41 cases." *Psychological Medicine,* 13:891–894.

Goddard, H. H. 1912. *The Kallikak Family: A Study in the Heredity of Feeblemindedness.* New York: Macmillan.

———. 1912–13. "Feeble-mindedness and Immigration." *Training School Bulletin,* 9:91–94.

———. 1913. "The Binet Tests in relation to immigration." *Journal of Psychoasthenics,* 18:105–107.

———. 1917. "Mental tests and the immigrant." *Journal of Delinquency,* 2:243–277.

Golden, D. 1990. "The fate of families." *Boston Globe Magazine,* June 3, p. 26.

Goldstein, J., A. Freud, and A. Solnit. 1973. *Beyond the Best Interest of the Child.* New York: Free Press.

———. 1979. *Before the Best Interest of the Child.* New York: Free Press.

Goleman, D. 1995. *Emotional Intelligence: Why it Can Matter More Than I.Q.* New York: Bantam Books.

Gordon, L. 1982. "Why Nineteenth-Century Feminists Did not Support 'Birth Control' and Twentieth-Century Feminists Do: Feminism, Reproduction, and the Family." In B. Thorne and M. Yalom, eds., *Rethinking the Family: Some Feminist Questions.* New York: Longman.

Gostin, L. O., and H. A. Beyer. 1993. *Implementing the Americans with Disabilities Act: Rights and Responsibilities of All Americans.* Baltimore: Paul H. Brookes.

Gottleib, M. I., and J. E. Williams, eds. 1987. *Textbook of Developmental Pediatrics.* New York: Plenum Medical Book Co.

Gould, S. J. 1981. *The Mismeasure of Man.* New York: Norton.

Governor's Commission on Mental Retardation (GCMR). 1994. "Strategies for Reducing the Waiting List for Services from the Department of Mental Retardation in Massachusetts." Boston: GCMR.

Grace, N. E. 1985. *Everyone Here Spoke Sign Language: Hereditary Deafness on Martha's Vineyard.* Cambridge, Mass.: Harvard University Press.

Graves, B., D. Graves, Y. Haynes, G. B. Rice, and B. Y. Whitman. 1986. "Parents learning together: A curriculum for use with MR/DD parents." St. Louis: St. Louis Office for Mental Retardation/Developmental Disability Resources.

Green, P., and R. Paul. 1974. "Parenthood and the Mentally Retarded." *University of Toronto Law Journal*, 24:117–125.

Greenberg, M. H. 1996. "Early Issues in Implementation of the Personal Responsibility and Work Opportunity Reconciliation Act (PRWORA) of 1996." Washington, D.C.: Center for Law and Social Policy.

Greene, St. Albion. 1976. "They Lost Their Kids for Six Years: Can Their Reunion Undo the Harm of 23 Foster Homes?" *National Observer*, May 29, p. 1.

Greenspan, S. 1997. *The Growth of the Mind: And the Endangered Origins of Intelligence*. Reading, Mass.: Addison-Wesley.

Greenspan, S., and K. Budd. 1986. "Research on Mentally Retarded Parents." In J. Gallagher and P. Vietze, eds., *Families of Handicapped Persons: Research and Clinical Perspectives*. New York: Academic Press.

Greenspan, S., and G. Shoultz. 1981. "Why mentally retarded adults lose their jobs: Social competence as a factor in work adjustment." *Applied Research in Mental Retardation*, 2(1):23–28.

Gregory, R. J. 1987. *Adult Intellectual Assessment*. Boston, Mass.: Allyn and Bacon.

Grossman, H. J. 1973. "Manual on Terminology and Classification in Mental Retardation." Special publication no. 2. Washington, D.C.: American Association of Mental Deficiency.

Grunwald, M. 1995. "DSS head agrees on reforms: Broader licensing among issues raised by panel." *Boston Globe*, December 17, pp. 1, 52.

Haavik, S., and K. Menninger. 1981. *Sexuality, Law, and The Developmentally Disabled Person: Legal and Clinical Aspects of Marriage, Parenthood, and Sterilization*. Baltimore: Paul H. Brookes.

Hagerman, R. J., and A. Cronister. 1996. *Fragile X Syndrome: Diagnosis, Treatment, and Research*. 2d ed. Baltimore: Johns Hopkins University Press.

Hales, R. E., S. C. Yodofsky, and J. A. Talbott. 1994. *Textbook of Psychiatry*. 2nd ed. Washington, D.C.: American Psychiatric Press.

Hanley, R. 1993a. "Revoke Bail, Prosecutor Says to Court." *New York Times*, March 23, sec. B-6.

———. 1993b. "Three Are Sentenced to Youth Center Over Sex Abuse of Retarded Girl." *New York Times*, April 24, pt. 1, p. 1.

———. 1994. "One is Freed in Sex Attack in Glen Ridge." *New York Times*, January 29, pt. 1, p. 24.

Hanley-Maxwell, C., F. R. Rusch, J. Chadsey-Rusch, and A. Renzaglia. 1986. "Reported factors contributing to job terminations of individuals with severe disabilities." *Journal of the Association for Persons with Severe Handicaps*, 12:280–286.

Hartl, D. L. 1991. *Basic Genetics*. 2d ed. Boston: Jones and Bartlett.

Hayes, M. 1993. "Child care law: An overview." In A. Craft, ed., *Parents with Learning Disabilities*. Kidderminster: BILD.

Hayman, R. L., Jr. 1990. "Presumptions of Justice: Law, Politics, and the Mentally Retarded Parent." *Harvard Law Review*, 103:1201.

Heber, R. F. 1964. "Personality." In H. A. Stevens and R. Heber, eds., *Mental Retardation: A Review of Research.* Chicago: University of Chicago Press.

Heller, K., and R. W. Swindle. 1983. "Social networks, perceived social support, and coping with stress." In R. D. Felber, L. A. Jason, J. Montsugu, and S. S. Farber, eds., *Preventive Psychology: Theory, Research and Practice in Community Intervention.* Elmsford, N.Y.: Pergamon Press.

Hendrix, K. 1991. "Helping to Assure that Life Goes On." *Los Angeles Times,* July 18, p. E1.

Herrnstein, R., and C. Murray. 1994. *The Bell Curve: Intelligence and Class Structure in American Life.* New York: Free Press.

Highleyman, S. 1957. *Legal bibliography on Sterilization as of January 1, 1957.* New York: Human Betterment Association of America.

Hirschman, L. R. 1994. "Moral Philosophy and the Glen Ridge Rape Case." *Harvard Journal of Law and Public Policy,* 17:101.

Honzik, M. P. 1967. "Environmental Correlates of Mental Growth: Prediction from the Family Setting at 21 Months." *Child Development,* 38:337.

Houppert, K. 1993. "Glen Ridge Rape Trial: A Question of Consent." *Ms Magazine,* March–April, p. 86.

Huggins, G. R., and S. J. Sondheimer. 1984. "Complications of female sterilization: immediate and delayed." *Fertility and Sterility,* (3):337–355.

Hyman, C. A. 1977. "A Report on the Psychological test results of battering parents." *British Journal of Social and Clinical Psychology,* 16:221.

Illingworth, R. S. 1987. *The Development of the Infant and the young child: Normal and abnormal.* 9th ed. New York: Churchill Livingston.

Ireland, W. W. 1877. *On idiocy and imbecility.* London. J. A. Churchill.

Jacobson, M. 1988. "Rights of disabled parents." *Parenting with Disability,* (1):4.

Jencks, C. 1992. *Rethinking Social Policy: Race Poverty and the Underclass.* Cambridge, Mass.: Harvard University Press.

Jensen, A. R. 1972. *Genetics and Education.* London: Methuen.

———. 1974. "Kinship Correlations Reported by Sir Cyril Burt, IQ Scores: Science or Numerology?" *Behavioral Genetics,* 4:1.

Johnson, B. S. 1950. "A Study of sterilized persons from Laconia State School." *American Journal of Mental Deficiency,* 54:404–408.

Johnson, O. R. 1981. "Mildly Retarded Adults as Parents." Paper presented at the 89th Annual Convention of the American Psychological Association, Los Angeles, Calif.

Johnson, P., and S. Clark. 1982. "Service needs of developmentally disabled parents." In J. Berg and J. de Jong, eds., *Perspectives and Progress in Mental Retardation,* vol. 1. Baltimore: University Park Press.

Jorgensen, C. M. 1992. "Natural supports in inclusive schools: Curricular and teaching strategies." In J. Nisbet, ed., *Natural Supports in School, at Work, and in the Community for People with Severe Disabilities.* Baltimore: Paul H. Brookes.

Junod, T. 1993. "Ordinary People: Were the suburban youths who raped a retarded girl 'star athletes' or just typical kids?" *Sports Illustrated,* March 29, p. 68.

Justice, B., and R. Justice. 1976. *The Abusing Family.* New York: Human Science Press.

Kamin, L. J. 1974. *The Science and Politics of I.Q.* New York: Halsted Press.

Kaminar, R., and H. Cohen. 1983. "Intellectually Limited Mothers." In *Developmental Handicaps, Prevention and Treatment.* Washington, D.C.: American Association of University Affiliated Programs for Persons with Developmental Disability.

Kaminar, R., E. Jedrysek, and B. Soles. 1981. "Intellectually limited parents." *Journal of Developmental and Behavioral Pediatrics,* 2(2):39–43.

Kanfer, F. H. 1975. "Self-management methods." In F. H. Kanfer and A. P. Goldstein, eds., *Helping people change.* New York: Pergamon.

Kanfer, F. H., and L. G. Grimm. 1978. "Freedom of choice and behavioral change." *Journal of Consulting and Clinical Psychology,* 46:873–878.

Kanner, L. 1949. *A miniature textbook of feeblemindedness.* New York: Child Care Publications.

Kantrowitz, B. 1993. "Verdict After a Day of Horror." *Newsweek,* March 29, p. 27.

Katzman, S. 1981. "Parental Rights of the Mentally Retarded: The Advisability and Constitutionality of the Treatment of Retarded Parents in New York State." *Columbia Journal of Law and Social Problems,* 16:521.

Keeton, W. P., ed. 1984. *Prosser and Keeton on the Law of Torts.* 5th ed. St. Paul Minn.: West Publishing.

Kenyon, J. M. 1914. "Sterilization of the Unfit." *Virginia Law Review,* 1:458.

Koller, H. S., S. A. Richardson, and M. Katz. 1988. "Marriage in a young adult mentally retarded population." *Journal of Mental Deficiency Research,* 32:93–102.

Kopelman, L., and J. Moskop, eds. 1984. *Ethics and Mental Retardation.* Boston: D. Reidel.

Kozol, J. 1988. *Rachel and Her Children: Homeless Families in America.* New York: Crown Publishers.

LaFollette, H. 1980. "Licensing Parents." *Philosophy and Public Affairs,* 9(2):182.

Landman, J. H. 1929. "The History of Human Sterilization in the United States— Theory, Statute, Adjudication." *Illinois Law Review,* 23:463.

Laufer, P. 1994. *A Question of Consent: Innocence and Complicity in the Glen Ridge Rape Case.* San Francisco: Mercury House.

Laxova, R., S. Gilderdale, and M. Ridler. 1973. "An Aetiological Study of Fifty-Three Female Patients from a Subnormality Hospital and their Offspring." *Journal of Mental Deficiency Research,* 17:193–216.

Layzer, D. 1974. "Heritability Analysis of IQ Scores: Science or Numerology?" *Science,* 183:1259.

Lefkowitz, B. 1993. "Three Guilty in Jersey Rape, Fourth Convicted of Lesser Charge." *Newsday,* March 17, p. 5.

Lidz, C., A. Meisel, E. Zerubavel, M. Carter, R. Sestak, and L. Roth. 1984. *Informed Consent: A Study of Decisionmaking in Psychiatry.* New York: Guilford Press.

Lindman, F. T., and D. M. McIntyre. 1961. *The Mentally Disabled and the Law.* Chicago: University of Chicago Press.

Linn, B. J., and L. A. Bowers. 1978. "The Historical Fallacies Behind Legal Prohibitions of Marriages Involving Mentally Retarded Persons—The Eternal Child Grows Up." *Gonzago Law Review,* 13:625.

Llewellyn, G. 1990. "People with intellectual disability as parents: perspectives from the professional literature." *Australian and New Zealand Journal of Developmental Disabilities,* 16(4):369–380.

Loehlin, J. C., G. Lindzey, and J. M. Spuhler. 1975. *Race Difference in Intelligence.* San Francisco: W. H. Freeman.

Lombardo, P. A. 1985. "Three Generations, No Imbeciles: New Light on Buck v. Bell." *New York University Law Review,* 60:30.

Lovett, D. L., and M. Harris. 1987. "Important Skills for Adults with Mental Retardation: The Client's Point of View." *Mental Retardation,* 25:351–356.

Lubove, R. 1971. *The Professional Altruist: The Emergence of Social Work as a Career, 1880–1930.* Cambridge, Mass.: Harvard University Press.

Lynch, E., and S. Bakley. 1989. "Serving young children whose parents are mentally retarded." *Infants and Young Children,* 1(3):26–38.

Lytad, M. H. 1975. "Violence at Home: A Review of the Literature." *American Journal of Orthopsychiatry,* 45:328.

Maccoby, E. E., and R. H. Mnookin. 1992. *Dividing the Child: Social and Legal Dilemmas of Custody.* Cambridge, Mass.: Harvard University Press.

MacMillan, D. L. 1982. *Mental Retardation in School and Society.* Boston: Little, Brown.

Madsen, M. 1979. "Parenting classes for the mentally retarded." *Mental Retardation,* 17:195–196.

Mandell, C. J., and E. D. Fiscus. 1981. *Understanding exceptional people.* St. Paul, Minn.: West Publishing.

Mangel, C. 1988. "Licensing Parents: How Feasible?" *Family Law Quarterly,* 22(1):17.

Marchetti, A. G., R. S. Nathanson, and T. A. Kastner, and R. Owens. 1990. "AIDS and state developmental disability agencies: a national survey." *American Journal of Public Health,* 80(1):54.

Marsh, D. T. 1992. *Families and Mental Retardation: New Directions in Professional Practice.* New York: Praeger.

Martin, S., C. Ramey, and S. Ramey. 1990. "The Prevention of Intellectual Impairment in Children of Impoverished Families: Findings of a Randomized Trail of Educational Day Care." *American Journal of Public Health,* 80:844–847.

Massachusetts Department of Mental Retardation (MDMR). 1985. "Policy on Life-Sustaining Treatment." Boston: MDMR.

Massachusetts Department of Social Services (MDSS). 1985. "Reference Guide for Child Abuse and Neglect Investigations." Boston: MDSS.

———. 1997a. "Demographic Report on Consumer Populations, July 1996." Boston: MDSS.

———. 1997b. "Glossary of services to be provided and target populations to be served by the Massachusetts Department of Social Services." Boston: MDSS.

Massachusetts Governor's Commission on Mental Retardation (MGCMR). 1996. *Report on the Unserved and Underserved.* Boston: MGCMR.

Massachusetts Mental Health Legal Advisors Committee (MMHLAC). 1993. *The Handbook on Guardianship and the Alternatives.* Boston: MMHLAC.

Mathews, J. 1992. *A Mother's Touch: The Tiffany Callo Story.* New York: Henry Holt.

Matoush, W. R. 1969. "Eugenic Sterilization: A Scientific Analysis." *Denver Law Journal,* 46:631.

Mattinson, J. 1970. *Marriage and the Mental Handicap.* London: Duckworth.

———. 1973. "Marriage and the Mental Handicap." In F. F. de la Cruz and G. D. LaVeck, eds., *Human Sexuality and the Mentally Retarded.* New York: Brunner/Mazel.

McCandless, B. 1952. "Environment and Intelligence." *American Journal of Mental Deficiency,* 56:674.

McConachie, H. 1991. "Families and professionals: prospects for partnership." In S. Segal and V. Varma, eds., *Prospects for People with Learning Disabilities.* London: David Fulton.

McGraw, S. 1993. "Working with parents on parenting skills." In A. Craft, ed., *Parents with Learning Disabilities.* Kidderminster: BILD.

McIntire, R. W. 1973. "Parenthood Training or Mandatory Birth Control: Take Your Choice." *Psychology Today,* 34 (October).

Meisel, A. 1979. "The 'Exceptions' to the Informed Consent Doctrine: Striking a Balance Between Competing Values in Medical Decisionmaking." *Wisconsin Law Review,* 1979:413.

Menolascino, F. J. 1977. *Challenges in Mental Retardation: Progressive Ideology and Services.* New York: Human Sciences Press.

Merck Manual of Diagnosis and Therapy. 1982. 14th ed. Rahway, N.J.: Merck Sharp and Dohme Research Laboratories.

Merck Manual. 1987. 15th ed. Rahway, N.J.: Merck Sharp and Dohme Research Laboratories.

Merck Manual of Medical Information, Home Edition. 1997. Whitehouse Station, N.J.: Merck Research Laboratories.

Michelman, F. I. 1969. "The Supreme Court 1968 Term—Forward: On Protecting the Poor through the Fourteenth Amendment." *Harvard Law Review,* 83:7.

———. 1973. "In Pursuit of Constitutional Welfare Rights: One View of Rawls' Theory of Justice." *University of Pennsylvania Law Review,* 121:962.

———. 1979. "Welfare Rights in a Constitutional Democracy." *Washington University Law Quarterly,* 1979:659.

Mickelson, P. 1947. "The Feebleminded Parent: A Study of 90 Family Cases," *American Journal of Mental Deficiency,* 51:644.

———. 1949. "Can mentally deficient parents be helped to give their children better care?" *American Journal of Mental Deficiency,* 53(3):516–534.

Miller, E. L. 1965. "Ability and social adjustment at mid-life of persons earlier judged mentally deficient." *Genetic Psychology Monographs,* 72:139–198.

Minow, M. 1987. "When Difference has its Home: Group Homes for the Mentally Retarded, Equal Protection and Legal Treatment of Difference." *Harvard Civil Rights–Civil Liberties Law Review,* 22:111.

Mira, M., and J. Roddy. 1980. "Parenting competencies of retarded persons: a critical review." Unpublished manuscript. Available from Children's Rehabilitation Unit, University of Kansas Medical Center, Kansas City, Kansas 66103.

Mitchell, S. B. 1947. "Results in Family Casework with Feebleminded Clients." *Smith College Studies in Social Work,* 18:21.

Mnookin, R. H. 1973. "Foster Care—In Whose Best Interest." *Harvard Education Review,* 43:599.

———. 1988. "The Guardianship of Philip B.: Jay Spears' Achievement." *Stanford Law Review,* 40:841.

Mnookin, R. H., and L. Kornhauser. 1979. "Bargaining in the Shadow of the Law: The Case of Divorce." *Yale Law Journal,* 88:950.

Moscovitch, E. 1991. *Mental Retardation Programs: How Does Massachusetts Compare?* Boston: Pioneer Institute for Public Policy Research.

Moser, H. G. 1995. "A role for gene therapy in mental retardation." *Mental Retardation and Developmental Disabilities Reviews: Gene Therapy,* 1.

Mosher, W. D., and C. A. Bachrach, 1996. "Understanding U.S. Fertility: Continuity and Change in the National Survey of Family Growth, 1988–1995." *Family Planning Perspectives,* 28:4.

Murdoch, J. 1913. "State care for the feeble-minded." *Journal of Psycho-Asthenics,* 18:37–38.

Murdock, C. W. 1974. "Sterilization of the retarded: A problem or solution?" *California Law Review,* 62:917.

National Information Center for Children and Youth with Disabilities (NICHCY). 1998. "Fact Sheet Number 8." Washington, D.C.: NICHCY.

Newman, S. A. 1989. "Baby Doe, Congress, and the States: Challenging the Federal Treatment Standard for Impaired Infants." *American Journal of Law and Medicine,* 15(1):1.

Newton, J. R. 1984. "Sterilization." *Clinics in Obstetrics and Gynaecology,* 11(3):603–640.

New York Times. 1977. "A Miami lawyer for Olga Scarpetta says she is married and lives in New York." May 15, p. 41.

———. 1995. "Federal Study Links Some Mild Retardation to Poverty." May 31, p. A1.

———. 1998. "Contraception, Three Days After." September 4, p. A22.

Nirje, B. 1980. "The Normalization Principle." In Flynn and Nitsch (1980).

Nisbet, J., C. Jorgensen, and S. Powers. 1994. "System change directed at inclusive education." In V. J. Bradley, J. W. Ashbaugh, and B. C. Blaney, eds., *Creating Individual Supports for People with Developmental Disabilities: A Mandate for Change at Many Levels.* Baltimore: Paul H. Brookes.

Note. 1950. "Human Sterilization." *Iowa Law Review,* 35:251.

———. 1973. "Termination of the Parent-Child Relationship: Should Parental I.Q. Be an Important Factor." *Law and the Social Order,* 855 (published by *Arizona State University Law Journal*).

———. 1977. "The Right of the Mentally Disabled to Marry: A Statutory Evaluation." *Journal of Family Law,* 15:463.

———. 1979. "Retarded Parents in Neglect Proceedings: The Erroneous Assumption of Parental Inadequacy." *Stanford Law Review,* 31:785.

———. 1981. "Sterilization." *Florida State University Law Review,* 9:599.

———. 1984. "Procreation: A Choice for the Mentally Retarded." *Washburn Law Journal,* 23:359.

———. 1995. "Mental Health—Pennsylvania Superior Court Affirms Authorization to Sterilize Handicapped Woman." *Temple Law Review,* 68:1009.

Novison, S. 1983. "Post-Divorce Visitation: Untying the Triangular Knot." *University of Illinois Law Review,* 119.

O'Hara, J. B., and T. H. Sanks. 1956. "Eugenic Sterilization." *Georgia Law Journal,* 45:20.

Oliver, J. 1977. "Some Studies of families in which children suffer maltreatment." In A. W. Franklin, ed., *The Challenge of Child Abuse.* Proceedings of a conference sponsored by the Royal Society of Medicine, 2–4 June 1976. London: Academic Press.

Painz, F. 1993. *Parents with a Learning Disability.* Social Work Monographs no. 116. Norwich: University of East Anglia.

Pantin, A. 1957. "The Doctor and the Defective Child." *Journal Medical Women's Federation,* 39(1).

Parke, I., and C. W. Colmer. 1975. "Child Abuse: An Interdisciplinary Analysis." *Review of Child Development Research,* 5:509.

Paul, J. L., A. P. Turnbull, and W. M. Cruickshank. 1979. *Mainstreaming: a practical guide.* New York: Schocken Books.

Payne, A. 1978. "The law and the problem parent: custody and parental rights of homosexual, mentally retarded, mentally ill, and incarcerated parents." *Journal of Family Law,* 16:797–818.

Payne, A. T. 1992. "Annotation: Parents Mental Deficiency as Factor in Termination of Parental Rights—Modern Status." A.L.R. 5th 1:469.

Peck, J. R., and W. B. Stephens. 1965. "Marriage of young adult male retardates." *American Journal of Mental Deficiency,* 69:818–827.

Pelton, L. H. 1978. "Child Abuse and Neglect: The Myth of Classlessness." *American Journal of Orthopsychiatry,* 48:608.

Penrose, L. S. 1954. *The Biology of Mental Defect.* 4th ed. London: Sidgwick and Jackson.

Penrose, L. S., and F. D. Turner. 1934. "Contribution to genetic study of mental deficiency." *British Medical Journal,* 1:10.

Peterson, K. S. 1997. "Do new definitions of smart dilute meaning?" *USA Today,* February 18, pp. D1–2.

Peterson, S., E. Robinson, and I. Littman. 1983. "Parent-child interaction training for parents with a history of mental retardation." *Applied Research in Mental Retardation*, 4:329–342.

Pierce, W. 1984. "Survey of State Laws and Legislation on Access to Adoption Records." *Family Law Reporter* 10:3035.

Powell, F. 1882. "Status of the work—Iowa." Proceedings of the Association of Medical Officers of American Institutions for Idiotic and Feeble-Minded Persons, Columbus, June 12–15, 1877. Philadelphia: J. B. Lippincott.

President's Commission for the Study of Ethical Problems in Medicine and Biomedical and Behavioral Research. 1983. "Deciding to Forego Life-Sustaining Treatment." Commission publication no. 83-17978, pp. 217–223. Washington, D.C.: U.S.G.P.O.

President's Committee on Mental Retardation (PCMR). 1995a. *Journey to Inclusion: A Resource for State Policy Makers*. Washington, D.C.: PCMR.

———. 1995b. *Report to the President: Collaborating for Inclusion*. Washington, D.C.: PCMR.

Quinton, D., and M. Rutter. 1984a. "Parents with children in care, I. Current circumstances and parenting skills." *Journal of Child Psychology and Psychiatry*, 25:211–229.

———. 1984b. "Parents with children in care, II. Intergenerational continuities." *Journal of Child Psychology and Psychiatry*, 25:231–250.

Quinton, D., M. Rutter, and C. Liddle. 1984. "Institutional rearing, parenting difficulties and marital support." *Psychological Medicine*, 14:107–124.

Reilly, P. R. 1991. *The Surgical Solution: A History of Involuntary Sterilization in the United States*. Baltimore: Johns Hopkins University Press.

Reiss, I. L. 1971. *The Family System in America*. New York: Holt, Rinehart and Winston.

Rhoden, N. 1985. "Treatment Dilemmas for Imperiled Newborns: Why Quality of Life Counts." *Southern California Law Review*, 58:1283.

Richardson, S. A., M. Katz, and H. Koller. 1990. "The long-term influence of the family of upbringing on young adults with mild mental retardation." In W. Fraser, ed., *Key Issues in Mental Retardation Research*. London: Routledge.

Richardson, S. A., and H. Koller. 1996. *Twenty-two Years: Causes and Consequences of Mental Retardation*. Cambridge, Mass.: Harvard University Press.

Richler, D., and J. Pelletier. 1985. "Service Delivery Patterns in North America: Trends and Challenges." In M. Craft, J. Bicknell and S. Hollins, eds., *Mental Handicap: A Multi-Disciplinary Approach*. London: Bailliere Tindal.

Richmond, M. E. 1917. *Social Diagnosis*. New York: Russell Sage Foundation.

Roberts, A. R. 1973. *Educability and Group Differences*. New York: Harper and Row.

Roberts, D. E. 1993. "Punishing Drug Addicts Who Have Babies." *Harvard Law Review*, 104:1419.

Robertson, J. A. 1983. "Procreative Liberty and the Control of Conception." *Virginia Law Review*, 69:405.

Robinson, H. B., and N. B. Robinson. 1965. *The Mentally Retarded Child: A Psychological Approach*. New York: McGraw Hill.

Robinson, L. H. 1978. "Parental Attitudes of Retarded Young Mothers," *Child Psychiatry and Human Development,* 8(3):131–144.

Robinson, N. M., and H. M. Robinson. 1976. *The Mentally Retarded Child.* New York: McGraw Hill.

Robitscher, J., ed. 1973. *Eugenic Sterilization.* Springfield, Ill.: Thomas.

Rogers, P. 1984. "Understanding the Legal Concept of Guardianship." In T. Apollini and T. P. Cooke, eds., *A New Look at Guardianship: Protective Services that Support Personal Living.* Baltimore: Paul H. Brookes.

Rosen, J. W., and S. N. Burchard. 1990. "Community activities and social support networks: A social comparison of adults with and without mental retardation." *Education and Training in Mental Retardation,* 25:193–204.

Rosenberg, S., and G. McTate. 1982. "Intellectually handicapped mothers: problems and prospects." *Children Today,* 37:24–26.

Ross, D. H. 1981. "Sterilization of the Developmentally Disabled: Shedding Some Myth-Conceptions," *Florida State University Law Review,* 9:599.

Ross, R., M. Begab, E. Dondis, J. Giampiccolo, Jr., and C. Meyers. 1985. *Lives of the Mentally Retarded: A Forty-Year Follow-Up Study.* Stanford: Stanford University Press.

Roth, W. 1982. "Poverty and the Handicapped child." *Children and Youth Services Review,* 4:67.

Rothman, B. K. 1986. *The Tentative Pregnancy.* New York: Viking.

Salisbury, A. 1892. "The Education of the feeble-minded." *Proceedings of the Association of Medical Officers of American Institutions for Idiotic and Feeble-Minded Persons,* Columbus, June 12–15, 1877. Philadelphia: J.B. Lippincott.

Sarber, R. E., M. M. Halasz, M. C. Messmer, A. D. Bickert, and J. R. Lutzker. 1983. "Teaching menu planning and grocery shopping skills to a mentally retarded mother." *Mental Retardation,* 21:101–106.

Scally, B. G. 1973. "Marriage and mental handicap: some observations in Northern Ireland." In F. F. de la Cruz and G. D. LaVeck, eds., *Human Sexuality and the Mentally Retarded.* New York: Brunner/Mazel.

Scheerenberger, R. C. 1967. *A pictorial history of residential services in Wisconsin.* Madison: American Association on Mental Deficiency.

———. 1983. *A History of Mental Retardation.* Baltimore: Paul H. Brookes.

Schilling, R. 1981. "Treatment of Child Abuse." In S. P. Schinke, ed., *Behavioral Methods in Social Welfare.* Hawthorne, N.Y.: Aldine.

Schilling, R. F., S. P. Schinke, B. J. Blythe, and R. P. Barth. 1982. "Child maltreatment and mentally retarded parents: is there a relationship?" *Mental Retardation,* 20(5):201–209.

Schleien, S. J., and M. T. Ray. 1988. *Community Recreation and Persons with Disabilities: Strategies for Integration.* Baltimore: Paul H. Brookes.

Schroth, T. 1992a. "Both Sides in Glen Ridge Case Pull Out All Stops." *New Jersey Law Journal,* December 7:7.

———. 1992b. "Glen Ridge Jury to Decide the Meaning of 'No.'" *New Jersey Law Journal,* December 24:8.

————. 1993. "They Could Have Done Better." *New Jersey Law Journal,* March 22:1.

Scott, E. A. 1986. "Sterilization of Mentally Retarded Persons: Reproductive Rights and Family Privacy." *Duke Law Journal,* 1986:806.

Seagull, E. A. W., and S. L. Scheurer. 1986. "Neglected and Abused Children of Mentally Retarded Parents." *Child Abuse and Neglect,* 10:493–500.

Seagull, E., S. Scheurer, B. Blythe and R. Barth. 1986. "Child maltreatment and mentally retarded parents." *Abuse and Neglect,* 10(4):493–500.

Searle, G. R. 1976. *Eugenics and Politics in Britain, 1900–1914. Science in History* series, vol. 3. Leyden: Noordhoof International Publishing.

Seattle Times. 1998. "LeTourneau's Freedom Restricted." January 7, p. B1.

Seguin, E. 1846. *Traitment moral, hygiéne, et éducation des idiots et des autres enfants arriérés.* Paris: J. B. Bailliére.

Shaman, J. M. 1978. "Persons Who Are Mentally Retarded: Their Right to Marry and Have Children," *Family Law Quarterly,* 12:61.

Shapiro, T. M. 1985. *Population Control Politics: Women, Sterilization and Reproductive Choice.* Philadelphia: Temple University Press.

Shaw, C. H., and C. H. Wright. 1960. "The married mental defective: a follow-up study." *Lancet,* 30:273–274.

Sheridan, M. D. 1956. "The Intelligence of 100 Neglectful Mothers." *British Medical Journal,* 1:91.

Sherman, L. 1982. "Replication of a Home-Based Prevention Project for At-Risk Infants Whose Parents Are Mentally Retarded: Development and Implementation." Paper presented at the American Association on Mental Deficiency, Boston, June 2.

Sigelman, C., et al. 1981a. "Issues in interviewing mentally retarded persons: an empirical study." In R. Bruininks, C. Meyer, B. Sigford and K. Lakin, eds., *Deinstitutionalization and Community Adjustment of Mentally Retarded People.* Washington, D.C.: American Association on Mental Deficiency.

————. 1981b. "When in doubt, say yes: acquiescence in interviews with mentally retarded persons." *Mental Retardation,* April:53–58.

Sigelman, C., E. Budd, J. Winer, C. Schoenrock, and P. Martin. 1982. "Evaluating alternative techniques of questioning mentally retarded persons." *American Journal of Mental Deficiency,* 86(5):511–518.

Simmel, G. 1955. *Conflict and The Web of Group Affiliation.* Trans. Kurt H. Worlff and Reinhard Bendix. New York: Free Press.

Skeels, H. H. 1966. "Adult Status of Children with Contrasting Early Life Experiences." *Monographs of the Society for Research in Child Development,* 3:31.

Slater, M. A. 1986. "Modification of mother-child interaction processes in families with children at-risk for mental retardation." *American Journal of Mental Deficiency,* 91:257–267.

Smith, D. W. 1988. *Recognizable patterns of human malformation.* Philadelphia: W. B. Saunders.

Smith, S. M. 1975. *The battered child syndrome.* Reading, Mass.: Butterworth.

Snyderman, M., and S. Rothman. 1986. "Science, politics, and the IQ controversy." *Public Interest,* 83 (spring):79–97.

Sparrow, S. S., D. A. Balla, and D. V. Cicchetti. 1984. *Vineland Adaptive Behavior Scales.* Circle Pines, Minn.: American Guidance Service.

Spencer, H. 1895. *The principles of sociology.* 3rd ed. New York: D. Appleton.

Steinhauer, P. D. 1983. Assessing for parenting capacity. *American Journal of Orthopsychiatry,* 53(3):468–481.

Sternberg, R. J. 1990. *Handbook of Human Intelligence.* New York: Cambridge University Press.

———. 1995. *Emotional Intelligence: Why It Can Matter More Than I.Q.* New York: Bantam Books.

Strauss, P., and J. Strauss. 1974. "Review of *Beyond the Best Interests of the Child,*" *Columbia Law Review,* 74:996.

Strully, J. L., and C. F. Strully. 1992. "The struggle toward inclusion and fulfillment of friendship." In J. Nisbet, ed., *Natural Supports in School, at Work, and in the Community for People with Severe Disabilities.* Baltimore: Paul H. Brookes.

Sullivan, R. 1982a. "State Seeking Abortion for a Retarded Woman." *New York Times,* September 23, B1–3.

———. 1982b. "Abortion for Woman, 25, with I.Q. of 12 Allowed." *New York Times,* September 24, B5–1.

Suzuki, D. T., A. J. F. Griffiths, J. H. Miller, and R. C. Lewontin. 1986. *An Introduction to Genetic Analysis.* 3rd ed. New York: W. H. Freeman.

Szykula, S. A., A. P. Haffey, and D. E. Parsons. 1981. "Two treatment supplements to standard behavior modification for socially aggressive children." In M. Bryce and J. C. Lloyd, eds., *Treating Families in the Home: An Alternative to Placement.* Springfield, Ill.: C. C. Thomas.

Tarleton, J., and R. A. Saul. 1998. "Fragile X Syndrome: Diagnostic Criteria." Diagnostic update, June 10. Fullerton Genetics Center, Mission St. Joseph's Health System, Asheville, N.C., and Greenwood Genetic Center, Greenwood, S.C.

Taslitz, A. E. 1996. "Patriarchal Stories I: Cultural Rape Narratives in the Courtroom." *Southern California Review of Law and Women's Studies,* 5:387.

Thompson, A. 1984. "The assessment and remediation through play therapy of parenting competencies of mentally retarded mothers." *Dissertation Abstracts International,* 45(1):379.

Tracy, J., and E. Clark. 1974. "Treatment of Child Abusers." *Social Work,* 19:338.

Traynor, C. J. 1963. "Can you weigh a bushel of horsefeathers against next Thursday?" *Law and Contemporary Problems,* 28:754.

Tredgold, A. F. 1929. *Mental Deficiency (amentia),* vol. 9. New York: W. Wood.

———. 1952. *A Textbook of Mental Deficiency.* 8th ed. Baltimore: Wilkins and Wilkins.

Trenker, T. R. 1976. "Annotation: Modern Status of Maternal Preference Rule or Presumption in Child Custody Cases." A.L.R. 3d 79:262.

Trent, J. W. 1994. *Inventing the Feeble Mind: A History of Mental Retardation in the United States.* Berkeley: University of California Press.

Tribe, L. 1977. "Unraveling National League of Cities: The New Federalism and Affirmative Rights to Essential Government Services." *Harvard Law Review,* 90:1065.

Trussel, J., and B. Vaughan. 1992. "Contraceptive use projections: 1990–2010." *American Journal of Obstetrics and Gynecology,* 167(4, pt. 2):1160–1164.

Tucker, B. P., and B. A. Goldstein. 1991. *Legal Rights of Persons with Disabilities: An Analysis of Federal Law.* Horsham, Penn.: LRP Publications.

Tucker, M., and O. Johnson. 1989. "Competence promoting vs. competence inhibiting social support for mentally retarded mothers." *Human Organisation,* 42(2):95–107.

Tummino, L. 1994. "Implementation of the DSS Transfer of 18–22 Year Olds." Memorandum from Asst. Deputy Director, Executive Office of Health and Human Services, Massachusetts Department of Mental Retardation, to Regional Directors, May 3.

Turk, V., and H. Brown. 1992. "Sexual abuse and adults with learning disabilities." *Mental Handicap,* 20(2):56–58.

Turnbull, A. P., and J. B. Schultz. 1979. *Mainstreaming Handicapped Pupils: A Guide for the Classroom Teacher.* Boston: Allyn and Bacon.

Tymchuk, A. 1990. "Parents with Mental Retardation: A National Strategy." Paper commissioned by the President's Committee on Mental Retardation, Washington, D.C.

———. 1991. "Self-Concepts of Mothers who Show Mental Retardation." *Psychological Reports,* 68(2):503–511.

———. 1992. "Predicting adequacy of parenting by people with mental retardation." *Child Abuse and Neglect,* 16(2):165–178.

———. 1997. "Informing for Consent: Concepts and Methods." *Canadian Psychology,* 38(2):55–75.

Tymchuk, A., and L. Andron. 1988. "Clinic and home parent training of a mother with mental handicap caring for three children with developmental delay." *Mental Handicap Research,* 1:24–38.

———. 1990. "Mothers with mental retardation who do or do not abuse or neglect their children. *Child Abuse and Neglect,* 14:313–323.

———. 1992. "Project Parenting: Child interactional training for mothers who are mentally handicapped." *Mental Handicap Research,* 5(1):4–32.

Tymchuk, A., L. Andron, and M. Hagelstein. 1992. "Training mothers with mental retardation to discuss home safety and emergencies with their children." *Journal of Developmental and Physical Disabilities,* 4(2):151–165.

Tymchuk, A., L. Andron, and B. Rahbar. 1988. "Effective decision-making/problem-solving training with mothers who have mental retardation." *American Journal of Mental Retardation,* 92(6):510–512.

Tymchuk, A., L. Andron, and M. Tymchuk. 1990. "Training mothers with mental handicaps to understand behavioural and developmental principles." *Mental Handicap Research,* 3(1):51–59.

Tymchuk, A., L. Andron, and O. Ungar. 1987. "Parents with mental handicaps and adequate child care—a review." *Mental Handicap,* 15(June):49–54.

Tymchuk, A., and M. Feldman. 1991. "Parents with mental retardation and their children: a review of research relevant to professional practice." *Canadian Psychology,* 32(3):486–496.

Tymchuk, A., D. Hamada, L. Andron, and S. Anderson. 1989. "Emergency Training for Mothers who are Mentally Retarded: A Replication." *Mental Retardation and Learning Disability Bulletin,* 17(2):34–45.

———. 1990a. "Emergency Training for Mothers who are Mentally Retarded." *Child and Family Behavior Therapy,* 12(3):31–47.

———. 1990b. "Home Safety Training with Mothers who are Mentally Retarded." *Education and Training in Mental Retardation,* 25(2):142–149.

Tymchuk, A., and B. Keltner. 1991. "Advantage Profiles: A Tool for Health Care Professionals Working with Parents with Mental Retardation." *Issues in Comprehensive Nursing,* 14:151–161.

Tymchuk, A., A. Yokota, and B. Rahbar. 1990. "Decision-making abilities of mothers with mental retardation." *Research in Developmental Disabilities,* 11:97–109.

Tyor, P., and L. Bell. 1984. *Caring for the Retarded in America: A History.* Westport, Conn: Greenwood.

Unger, O., and C. Howes. 1986. "Mother-child interactions and symbolic play between toddlers and their adolescent or mentally retarded mothers." *Occupational Therapy Journal of Research,* 8(4)237–249.

United Nations. 1971. *Declaration of general and specific rights of the mentally retarded.* New York: United Nations.

U.S. Department of Commerce. 1934. *Mental defectives and epileptics in state institutions, 1929–1932.* Washington, D.C.: U.S. Government Printing Office.

Valentine, D. P. 1990. "Double Jeopardy: Child Maltreatment and Mental Retardation." *Child and Adolescent Social Work,* 7(6):487–499.

Wahler, R. G. 1980. "The insular mother: Her problems in parent-child training." *Journal of Applied Behavior Analysis,* 13:207–219.

Wakefield, W. E. 1981. "Validity of State Statute Providing for Termination of Parental Rights." A.L.R. 4th 22:774.

Wald, M. 1975. "State Intervention on Behalf of Neglected Children: A Search for Realistic Standards." *Stanford Law Review,* 27:985.

———. 1976. "State Intervention on Behalf of Neglected Children: Standards for Removal of Children from their Homes, Monitoring the Status of Children in Foster Care, and Termination of Parental Rights." *Stanford Law Review,* 28:623.

Wald, P. 1976. "Basic Personal and Civil Rights," In M. Kindred, ed., *The Mentally Retarded Citizen and the Law.* New York: Free Press.

Walker, A. 1998. "Special education overhaul may be headed for fight." *Boston Globe,* February 7, pp. A1, A16.

Wallerstein, J., and S. Blakeslee. 1989. *Second Chances: Men, Women, and Children A Decade After Divorce.* New York: Ticknor and Fields.

Walsh, D. C. 1982. "Humphreys selects judge for Glen Ridge sexual assault trial." *Newark Star-Ledger,* August 16 (1992 WL 110790671).

———. 1983. "Rape Affidavit Stokes Glen Ridge bail appeal." *Newark Star-Ledger,* March 20 (1993 WL 3454180).

Walton-Allen, N., and M. Feldman. 1991. "Perception of service needs by parents who are mentally retarded and their social service workers." *Comprehensive Mental Health Care,* 1(2):137–147.

Wates, M. 1991. "Able parents—disability, pregnancy, and motherhood." *Maternity Action,* 52:9.

———. 1993. "Images of Disabled Parents." *Disability, Pregnancy, and Parenthood International,* 2 (April).

Watkins, C. 1995. "Beyond Status: The Americans with Disabilities Act and the Parental Rights of People Labeled Developmentally Disabled or Mentally Retarded." *California Law Review,* 83:1415.

Wayne, J., and S. B. Fine. 1986. "Group Work with Retarded Mothers." *Social Casework,* 67:195.

Weinstein, E. 1976. "Study of Foster Care Children." *Stanford Law Review,* 28:623.

White, B. L., and J. C. Watts. 1973. *Experience and Environment: Major Influences on the Development of the Young Child.* Vol. 1. Englewood Cliffs, N.J.: Prentice-Hall.

Whitman, B. Y., and P. J. Accardo. 1990. *When a Parent is Mentally Retarded.* Baltimore: Paul H. Brookes.

Whitman, B. Y., B. Graves, and P. J. Accardo. 1986. "The mentally retarded parent in the community: an epidemiological study." *Developmental Medicine and Child Neurology,* supplement, 53:18.

———. 1987. "Mentally Retarded Parents in the Community: Identification Method and Needs Assessment Survey." *American Journal of Mental Deficiency,* 91:636.

———. 1989. "Training in parenting skills for adults with mental retardation." *Social Work,* September: 431–433.

———. 1990. "Parents learning together; parenting skills training for adults with mental retardation" In Whitman and Accardo (1990).

Whittemore, R. D., and P. Koegel. 1978. "Loving Alone is Not Helpful: Sexuality and Social Context Among the Mildly Retarded." Working Paper no. 7. Socio-Behavioral Group, Mental Retardation Research Center, School of Medicine, University of California, Los Angeles.

Wikler, A. 1979. "Paternalism and the Mildly Retarded." *Philosophy and Public Affairs,* 9:377.

Willey, A. M., and P. D. Murphy, eds. 1991. *Fragile X/Cancer Cytogenics: Proceedings of the 1989 Albany Birth Defects Symposium XX.* New York: Wiley–Liss.

Wilmot, D. M. 1989. "Cytogenics Detection Data Review." In Willey and Murphy (1991).

Wilson, J. Q., and R. J. Herrnstein. 1985. *Crime and Human Nature.* New York: Simon and Schuster.

Winik, L. 1981. "The Mildly Retarded as Parents: A Description and Explication of the Parenting Practices of Two Mildly Retarded Couples." Master's thesis, University of California, Los Angeles.

Wolfensberger, W. 1975. *The Origin and Nature of Our Institutional Models.* Syracuse, N.Y.: Human Policy Press.

————. 1984. "Social Role Valorization: A Proposed New Term for the Principle of Normalization." *Mental Retardation,* 21:234.

Wolfensberger, W., and B. Nirje. 1972. *The Principle of Normalization in Human Services.* Toronto: National Institute on Mental Retardation.

World Health Organization (WHO). 1980. *Internal classification of impairments, disabilities, and handicaps.* Geneva: WHO.

————. 1996. "Mental Retardation, 1995 World Population." 1996 World Health Report. August 30 Geneva: WHO.

Wyngaarden, M. 1981. "Interviewing mentally retarded persons: issues and strategies." In R. Bruininks, C. Meyer, B. Sigford, and K. Lakin, eds., *Deinstitutionalization and Community Adjustment of Mentally Retarded People.* Washington, D.C.: American Association of Mental Deficiency.

Young, M. 1976. "Lonely Parents: Observations by Public Health Nurses of Alienation in Child Abuse." Oklahoma City: Child Study Center, Oklahoma University Health Sciences Center, ERIC Document Reproduction Service no. ED 134 894.

Zetlin, A. G., and Turner, J. L. 1984. "Self Perspectives on Being Handicapped: Stigma and Adjustment." In R. B. Edgerton, ed., *Lives in Progress: Mildly Retarded Adults in a Large City.* Washington, D.C.: American Association on Mental Deficiency.

Zetlin, A. G., T. S. Weisner, and R. Gallimore. 1985. "Diversity, shared functioning, and the role of benefactors: a study of parenting by retarded persons," in S. Kenneth Thurman, ed., *Children of Handicapped Parents: Research and Clinical Perspectives.* New York: Academic Press.

Cases

Abigail, Adoption of, 499 N.E.2d 1234, 23 Mass. App. Ct. 191 (1986)

A.C.B., In re, 506 N.E.2d 360 (Ill. App. Ct. 1987)

Adkins v. Children's Hosp., 261 U.S. 525 (1923)

Akron v. Akron Center for Reprod. Health, 162 U.S. 416 (1982)

Alsager, State v., 201 N.W.2d 727 (Iowa 1972)

Alsager v. Dist. Ct., 406 F.Supp. 10 (S.D. Iowa 1975)

Anderson, In re, 464 A.2d 428 (Pa. Super. Ct. 1983)

Angel B., In re, 659 A.2d 277 (Me. 1995)

Anthony D., In re, 1993 WL 393348 (Conn. Super Ct. June 30, 1993).

Audrey C., In re, 419 N.Y.S.2d 209 (App. Div. 1979)

A. W., In re, 637 P.2d 366 (Colo. 1981)

Barbara C., In re, 455 N.Y.S.2d 182 (Sup. Ct. 1982), aff'd, 474 N.Y.S.2d 799 (App. Div. 1984)

Bartley v. State, No. 36698-0-1, 1996 WL 737308 (Wash. Ct. App. Dec. 23, 1996)

Bellotti v. Baird, 428 U.S. 132 (1976)

Berg v. Berg, 359 A.2d 354 (R.I. 1976)

B. G., In re, 589 A.2d 637 (N.J. Super. Ct. App. Div. 1991)

B. H., In re, 715 F.Supp. 1387 (N.D. Ill. 1989)

Bowers v. Hardwick, 478 U.S. 186 (1986)

Boyd v. Board of Registrars, 334 N.E.2d 629 (Mass. 1975).

B. P., In re, 427 S.E.2d 593 (Ga. Ct. App. 1993)

Brewer v. Valk, 167 S.E. 638 (N.C. 1933)

Brown v. Board of Educ. 347 U.S. 483 (1954)

Buck v. Bell, 130 S.E. 516 (Va. 1925), aff'd, 274 U.S. 200 (1927)

C.A.A., In re, 425 N.W.2d 621 (Neb. 1988)

Campbell, In re, 468 N.E.2d 93 (Ohio Ct. App. 1983)

Caresse B., In re, 1997 WL 133402 (Conn. Super. Ct. Mar. 11, 1997)

Carey v. Population Servs. Int'l, 431 U.S. 678 (1977)

Carney, In re Marriage of, 598 P.2d 36 (Cal. 1979)

Carson, In re, 39 Misc.2d 544 (N.Y. Sup. Ct. 1962)

Casey v. Planned Parenthood, 517 U.S. 1174 (1994)

Castorr v. Brundage, 674 F.2d 531 (6th Cir. 1982)

C.D.M. v. State, 627 P.2d 607 (Alaska 1981)

Chad S., In re, 580 P.2d 983 (Okla. 1978)

Children, Youth, and Families Dep't, State *ex. rel.,* v. John D., 934 P.2d 308 (N.M. Ct. App. 1997)

Christina N., In re, 1991 WL 31974 (Conn. Super. Ct. 1991)

Christopher T., In re, 467 N.Y.S.2d 691 (App. Div.), *appeal dismissed,* 469 N.E.2d 102 (1984), *aff'd,* In re Joyce T., 478 N.E.2d 1306 (1985)

Clausen, In re, 502 N.W.2d 649 (Mich. 1993), *stay denied sub. nom.,* DeBoer v. Schmidt, 509 U.S. 1301 (1993)

Cleaver v. Wilcox, 499 F.2d 940 (9th Cir. 1974)

Cleburne, City of, v. Cleburne Living Ctr., 473 U.S. 432 (1985)

Cleveland Bd. of Educ. v. LaFleur, 414 U.S. 632 (1974)

C. M., In re, 556 P.2d 514 (Wyo. 1976)

Conservatorship of. *See* name of party

Craig v. Boren, 429 U.S. 190 (1976)

Crist v. Division Youth and Family Servs., 320 A.2d 203 (N.J. Super. Ct. Law. Div. 1974)

Cruzan v. Director, Mo. Dep't of Health, 497 U.S. 261 (1990)

Custody of a Minor, In re, 5 Family Law Reporter 2868 (August 8, 1979)

C. W., Estate of, 640 A.2d 427 (Pa. Super. Ct. 1994), *cert. denied,* C. W. *ex rel.* McKinley v. Wasiek, 513 U.S. 1183 (1995)

Cynthia A., In re, 514 A.2d 360 (Conn. App. Ct. 1986)

Danforth v. State Dep't of Health and Welfare, 303 A.2d 794 (Me. 1973)

Daniel D., In re Guardianship of, 431 N.Y.S.2d 936 (Fam. Ct. 1980).

Davis v. Page, 640 F.2d 599 (5th Cir. 1981) (en banc)

DeBoer v. Schmidt, 509 U.S. 1301 (1993)

Debra B., In re, 495 A.2d 781 (Me. 1985)

Dennis Cannon, In re, 1990 WL 237462 (Ohio Ct. App. 1990)

Department of Pub. Welfare v. J.K.B., 393 N.E.2d 406 (Mass. 1979)

Department of Soc. Servs. v. Kitty Oree Smith, 429 S.E.2d 807 (S.C. 1993)

Devine, *Ex parte,* 398 S.2d 686 (Ala. 1981)

D. N., In re Guardianship of, 464 A.2d 1221 (N.J. Juv. and Dom. Rel. Ct. 1983)

Doe, In re, 627 N.E.2d 648 (Ill. 1993), *rev'd and reh'g denied,* 638 N.E.2d 181 (1994), *cert. denied,* 513 U.S. 994 (1994)

Doe v. G. D., 370 A.2d 27 (N.J. Super. Ct. 1976), *aff'd sub nom.,* Doe v. Downey, 377 A.2d 626 (1997)

Doe v. Roe, 841 F.Supp. 444 (D.D.C. 1993)

Dornick v. Reichenback, 10 Serg. and R. 84 (Pa. 1882)

Dred Scott v. Sandford, 60 U.S. (19 How.) 393 (1857)

Drummond v. Fulton County Dept. of Family and Children's Services, 408 F.Supp. 382 (N.D.Ga. 1976), *aff'd,* 563 F.2d 1200 (5th Cir. 1977) (en banc), *cert. denied,* 437 U.S. 910 (1978)

Dull v. Delaware County Dep't of Pub. Welfare, 521 N.E.2d 972 (Ind. Ct. App. 1988)

D. W., In re Estate of, 481 N.E.2d 355 (Ill. App. Ct. 1985)

East, In re, 288 N.E.2d 343 (Ohio C.P. Highland County 1972)

Eberhardy, In re Guardianship of, 307 N.W.2d 881 (Wis. 1981)

Egly v. Blackford County Dep't of Pub. Welfare, 575 N.E.2d 312 (Ind. Ct. App. 1991), *rev'd*, 592 N.E.2d 1232 (Ind. 1992)

Eisenstadt v. Baird, 405 U.S. 438 (1972)

Elizabeth Q., In re, 511 N.Y.S.2d 181 (App. Div. 1987)

Elser, In re Marriage of, 895 P.2d 619 (Mont. 1995), *overruled on other grounds by* Porter v. Galarneau, 911 P.2d 1143 (Mont. 1996)

E. M., In re, 620 A.2d 481 (Pa. 1993)

Enis, In re, 520 N.E.2d 362 (Ill. 1988)

Ensign, In re, 512 N.E.2d 140 (Ill. App. Ct. 1986), *cert. denied,* Ensign v. Illinois, 484 U.S. 962 (1987)

Estate of. *See* name of party

Ex parte. *See* name of party

F.C.C. v. Beach Communications, 508 U.S. 307 (1993)

Frazier v. Levi, 440 S.W.2d 393 (Tex. Civ. App. 1969)

Friesz, In re, 208 N.W.2d 259 (Neb. 1973)

Frye v. Spotte, 359 S.E.2d 315 (Va. Ct. App. 1987)

Fulton, In re, 1992 WL 238898 (Ohio Ct. App. Sept. 18, 1992)

Gagnon v. Scarpelli, 411 U.S. 778 (1973)

Garska v. McCoy, 278 S.E.2d 357 (W.Va. 1981)

Geiger, In re, 331 A.2d 172 (Pa. 1975)

George, In re, 414 A.2d 1063 (Super. Ct. Pa. 1979)

Ginsberg v. New York, 390 U.S. 629 (1968)

Goalen, In re, 414 U.S. 1148 (1974)

Goesart v. Cleary, 335 U.S. 464 (1948)

Grady, In re, 426 A.2d 467 (N.J. 1981)

Greco v. United States, 893 P.2d 345 (Nev. 1995)

Green, In re, 5 *Family Law Reporter* (BNA) 2173 (N.Y. Fam. Ct. Oct. 17, 1978)

Green, In re, *New York Law Journal,* Dec. 12, 1978, p. 12, col. 6 (N.Y. Fam. Ct. 1978)

Griswold v. Connecticut, 381 U.S. 479 (1965)

Gross, In re, 425 N.Y.S.2d 220 (1980)

Guardianship of. *See* name of party

Hathaway v. Worcester City Hosp., 341 F.Supp. 1385 (D. Mass. 1972)

Hayes, In re Guardianship of, 608 P.2d 635 (Wash. 1980)

Haynes v. Lapeer Circuit Judge, 166 N.W. 938 (Mich. 1918)

Hays v. Commonwealth, 33 S.W. 1104 (Ky. 1896)

Heller, State *ex rel.* v. Miller, 399 N.E.2d 66 (Ohio 1980)

Heller v. Doe, 509 U.S. 312 (1993)

Helms v. Franciscus, 2 Bland Ch. (Md) 544 (1830)
Helvey v. Rednour, 408 N.E.2d 17 (Ill. App. Ct. 1980)
Hillstrom, In re, 363 N.W.2d 871 (Minn. Ct. App. 1985)
Hodgson, State v., 204 N.W.2d 199 (Minn. 1973)
Hoy v. Willis, 398 A.2d 109 (N.J. Super. Ct. App. Div. 1978)

In re. *See* name of party

Jamie M., In re, 465 N.Y.S.2d 339 (App. Div. 1983), *aff'd,* 472 N.E.2d 311, 482 N.Y.
    Supp.2d 461 (1984)
Jane A., In re, 629 N.E.2d 1337 (Mass. App. Ct. 1994)
J. B., In re, 555 N.E.2d 1198 (Ill. App. Ct. 1990).
Jeffrey Mayle, In re, 1991 WL 100527 (Ohio App. Ct. 1991)
J.J.C.H., In re, 827 P.2d 812 (Mont. 1992)
J.K.C. Jr., In re, 841 S.W.2d 198 (Mo. Ct. App. 1992)
J.L.P., In re, 416 S.2d 1250 (Fla. Dist. Ct. App. 1982)
Johnson, In re, 263 S.E.2d 805 (N.C. Ct. App. 1980)
Johnston v. J.K.C. Sr., 841 S.W.2d 198 (Mo. Ct. App. 1992)
Jonathan H. v. Margaret H., 771 S.W.2d 111 (Mo. Ct. App. 1989)
Joyce T., In re, 478 N.E.2d 1306, 489 N.Y.S.2d 705 (Ct. App. 1985)
J.P., In re, 648 P.2d 1364 (1982)
Judy G., In re, 48 USLW 2570-71, (N.Y. Fam. Ct. NYC, Feb. 1, 1980)
Juvenile Appeal, etc., In re, 454 A.2d 1262 (Conn. 1983)

Katharine and Jeptha, Adoption of, 674 N.E.2d 256 (Mass. App. Ct. 1997)
King v. King, 333 A.2d 135 (R.I. 1975)
Kirchner, In re, 649 N.E.2d 324 (1995), *cert. denied,* 515 U.S. 1152 (1995)
K. M., In re Guardianship of, 816 P.2d 71 (Wash. Ct. App. 1991)
K.M.T., In re, 390 N.W.2d 371 (Minn. Ct. App. 1986)

Lacy v. Lacy, 553 P.2d 928 (Alaska 1976)
Lambert v. Wicklund, 520 U.S. 292 (1997)
Lashawanda M., In re, 451 N.Y.S.2d 553 (Fam. Ct. 1982)
LaShawn v. Kelly, 990 F.2d 1319 (D.C. Cir. 1993), *appeal after remand,* 69 F.3d 556
    74 F.3d 303 (D.C. Cir.), *and on reh'g en banc,* 87 F.3d 1389 (1996)
Lassiter v. Dep't of Soc. Servs., 452 U.S. 18 (1981)
Lay, In re, 539 N.E.2d 664 (Ohio Ct. App. 1987)
Lesher v. Lavrich, 632 F.Supp. 77 (N.D. Ohio 1984), *aff'd,* 784 F.2d 193
Lewis v. Davis, No. D-26437 (Sup. Ct. Chatham Cty. Georgia), July 19, 1974
Lewis v. Dukakis, 719 F.2d 508 (Mass. App. Ct. 1983)
L.F.G., In re, 598 P.2d 1125 (Mont. 1979)
Linn v. Linn, 286 N.W.2d 765 (Neb. 1980)
Little v. Little, 576 S.W.2d 493 (Texas Civ. App 1979)
Loving v. Virginia, 388 U.S. 1 (1967)
Lynch v. Dukakis, 719 F.2d 504 (1st Cir. 1983)

M., In re, 538 So.2d 1112 (La. App. 5th Cir. 1989)

Maricopa County Juvenile Action, In re, 555 P.2d 679 (Ariz. Ct. App. 1976)

Marisol v. Giuliani, 929 F.Supp. 662 (S.D.N.Y. 1996)

Mary Moe, In re, 579 N.E.2d 682 (Mass. App. Ct. 1991)

Mary P., In re, 444 N.Y.S.2d 545 (Fam. Ct. 1981)

Matejski, In re Guardianship of, 419 N.W. 576 (Iowa 1988)

Matter of. *See* name of party

May v. Anderson, 345 U.S. 528 (1953)

McDonald, In re, 201 N.W.2d 447 (Iowa 1972)

McKinney v. McKinney, 805 S.W.2d 66 (Ark. 1991)

M.E.D., In re, 436 A.2d 1158 (N.J. Juv. Ct. 1981)

Mendes, In re Guardianship of, 428 N.Y.S.2d 419 (Fam. Ct. 1980), *rev'd in part, aff'd in part*, In re Guardianship of Sylvia M., 443 N.Y.S.2d 214 (App. Div. 1981), *aff'd*, In re Guardianship of Nereida S., 439 N.E.2d 870 (1982)

Meyer v. Nebraska, 262 U.S. 390 (1923)

Michael G., In re, 194 Cal. Rptr. 745 (Ct. App. 1993)

M.L.B. v. S.L.J., 65 U.S.L.W. 4035 (U.S. Dec. 16, 1996) (No. 95-853)

Moe, In re, 432 N.E.2d 712 (Mass. 1982)

Moore v. City of East Cleveland, 431 U.S. 494 (1977)

Moore, In re, 221 S.E. 301 (N.C. 1976)

Moose Lodge v. Irvis, 407 U.S. 163 (1972)

M. P., In re, 538 S.2d 1112 (La. Ct. App. 1993)

M. T. and T. T., In re, 330 N.W.2d 247 (Wisc. Ct. App. 1982)

M.T.S., In re, 609 A.2d 1266 (N.J. 1992)

Myrics, In re, 533 P.2d 841 (Wash. 1975) (en banc)

N. Children, In re, 435 N.Y.S.2d 1018 (Fam. Ct. 1981)

Navarrette v. Texas Dept. of Human Resources, 669 S.W.2d 849 (Tex. App. El Paso 1984)

New Jersey Division of Youth and Family Servs. v. A.W. and R.W., 512 A.2d 438 (N.J. 1986)

Nilsson, In re, 471 N.Y.S.2d 439 (Sup. Ct. 1983)

North Carolina Ass'n for Retarded Children v. State, 420 F.Supp. 451 (M.D.N.C. 1976)

Olivio, State v., 589 A.2d 597 (N.J. 1991)

Opinion of Justices, In re, 162 So. 123 (Ala. 1935)

Orlando F., In re, 377 N.Y.S.2d 502 (App. Div. 1975), *modified by* 40 N.Y.2d 103, 351 N.E.2d 711 (1976)

Osborn v. Thompson, 481 F.Supp. 162 (M.D. Tenn. 1979)

P.A.B., In re, 570 A.2d 522 (Pa. Super. Ct. 1990)

Painter v. Bannister, 140 N.W.2d 152 (Iowa 1966)

Palmer v. Thompson, 403 U.S. 217 (1971)

Palmore v. Sidoti, 466 U.S. 429 (1984)

Parker v. Dep't of Human Servs., No. CA96-155, 1997 WL 50505 (Ark. Ct. App. Feb. 5, 1997)

Paul, State ex rel., v. Dep't of Pub. Welfare, 170 So. 549 (La. Ct. App. 1965)

Paul E., In re, 46 Cal.Rptr.2d 289 (Ct. App. 1995)

Pennhurst State Sch. and Hosp. v. Halderman, 465 U.S. 89 (1984)

Penny N., In re, 414 A.2d 541 (N.H. 1980)

Perreault v. Cook, 322 A.2d 610 (N.H. 1974)

Peterson v. Peterson, 399 N.W.2d 792 (Neb. 1987)

Petition of Dep't Soc. Servs. to Dispense with Consent to Adoption, 493 N.E.2d 197 (Mass. 1986)

Petition of New England Home for Little Wanderers to Dispense with Consent to Adoption, 328 N.E.2d 854 (Mass. 1975)

Petitions of Dep't Soc. Servs. to Dispense with Consent to Adoption, 482 N.E.2d 535 (Mass. App. Ct. 1985)

Pettigrew v. State, 12 Texas App. 225 (1882)

Phillip B., Guardianship of, 188 Cal. Rptr. 781 (Ct. App. 1983)

Phillip B., In re, 156 Cal. Rptr. 48 (Ct. App. 1979), *cert. denied sub nom.*, Bothman v. Warren B., 445 U.S. 949 (1980)

Pierce v. Soc'y of Sisters, 268 U.S. 510 (1925)

P.J.K., In re Welfare of, 369 N.W.2d 286 (Minn. 1985)

Planned Parenthood Fed'n v. Heckler, 712 F.2d 650 (D.C. Cir. 1983)

Planned Parenthood of Central Missouri v. Danforth, 428 U.S. 52 (1976)

Planned Parenthood of Southeastern Pennsylvania v. Casey, 505 U.S. 833, *remanded,* 978 F.2d 74 (3rd Cir. 1992)

P.L.L., In re, 597 P.2d 886 (Utah 1979)

Prince v. Massachusetts, 321 U.S. 158 (1944)

P. S., In re, 452 N.E.2d 969 (Ind. 1983)

Quilloin v. Walcott, 434 U.S. 246 (1978)

Quinlan, In re, 355 A.2d 647 (N.J. 1976), *cert. denied,* 429 U.S. 922

Relf v. Weinberger, 372 F.Supp. 1196 (D.D.C. 1974)

Renea Ebony W., In re, 452 S.E.2d 737 (W.Va. 1994)

Reynold v. Sims, 377 U.S. 533 (1964)

R. G. and T. G. v. Marion County Office, Dep't Family and Children, 647 N.E.2d 326 (Ind. Ct. App. 1995)

Ricci v. Okin, 823 F.Supp. 984 (D. Mass. 1993)

Richard M., In re, 443 N.Y.S.2d 291 (Fam. Ct. 1981)

Richards, State v., 39 Conn. 590 (1873)

Richardson, In re Adoption of, 59 Cal. Reptr. 323 (Cal. App. Ct. 1967)

Ricky Ralph M. v. Onondoga County Dep't of Soc. Servs., 451 N.Y.S.2d 41 (Ct. App. 1982)

R. J., In re, 589 P.2d 244 (Utah 1978)

Robert H., State v., 393 A.2d 1387 (N.H. 1978)

Roberts v. State, 228 S.E.2d 376 (Ga. Ct. App. 1976)

Roberts v. State, 233 S.E.2d 224 (Ga. Ct. App. 1977)

Roe, In re Guardianship of, 421 N.E.2d 40 (Mass. 1981)

Roe v. Wade, 410 U.S. 113 (1973)

Rogers v. Commissioner of the Dep't of Mental Health, 458 N.E.2d 308 (Mass. 1983)

Romero, In re, 790 P.2d 819 (Colo. 1990)

Rosenfeld, In re Marriage of, 524 N.W.2d 212 (Iowa Ct. App. 1994)

Saikewicz. *See* Superintendent of Belchertown State School v. Saikewicz

Sallmaier, In re, 378 N.Y.S.2d 989 (Sup. Ct. 1976)

Santosky v. Kramer, 455 U.S. 745 (1982)

Sarsfield, In re Marriage of, 671 P.2d 595 (Mont. 1983)

Scarpetta, People *ex rel.* v. Spence-Chapin Adoption Serv., 269 N.E.2d 787 (N.Y.
   1971), *cert denied,* Demartino v. Scarpetta, 404 U.S. 805 (1971)

Scherzer, State v., 694 A.2d 196 (N.J. Super. Ct. App. Div. 1997)

Selivanoff v. Selivanoff, 529 P.2d 486 (Wisc. App. 1974)

Sheila G., In re, 462 N.E.2d 1139 (N.Y. Ct. App. 1984)

Shelley v. Kramer, 334 U.S. 1 (1948)

Simpson, In re, 180 N.E.2d 206 (Ohio 1962)

Skinner v. Oklahoma, 316 U.S. 535 (1942)

Smith, In re, 295 A.2d 238 (Md. 1972)

Smith v. Board of Examrs of Feeble-Minded, 88 A. 963 (N.J. 1913)

Smith v. Command, 204 N.W. 140 (Mich. 1925)

Smith v. Edmiston, 431 F.Supp. 941 (W.D. Tenn 1977)

Smith v. State, 131 S.E.2d 163 (Ga. Ct. App. 1925)

S. N., In re, 500 N.W.2d 32 (Iowa 1993)

Spring, In re, 405 N.E.2d 115 (Mass. 1980)

Stanley v. Illinois, 405 U.S. 645 (1972)

State v. *See* name of party

Strausberg, Guardianship of, 400 N.Y.S.2d 1013 (Fam. Ct. 1977)

Stump v. Sparkman, 435 U.S. 349 (1978)

Superintendent of Belchertown State Sch. v. Saikewicz, 373 Mass. 728, 370 N.E.2d
   417 (1977)

Suter v. Artist M., 503 U.S. 347 (1992)

T. D., In re, 537 S.2d 173 (Fla. Dist. Ct. App. 1989)

Terwilliger, In re, 450 A.2d 1376 (Pa. Super. Ct. 1982)

Thibeault v. Larson, 666 A.2d 112 (Me. 1995)

Thompson, In re, 169 N.Y.S. 638 (Sup. Ct. 1918), *aff'd mem. sub nom.,* Osborn v.
   Thompson, 171 N.Y.S. 1094 (App. Div. 1918)

T.M.R., In re, 116 Cal. Rptr. 292 (Ct. App. 1974)

Tonya Louise M., In re, 458 N.Y.S.2d 370 (App. Div. 1982)

Truesdell, In re, 304 S.E.2d 793 (N.C. App. 1983), *aff'd as modified* 329 S.E.2d 630
   (N.C. 1985)

Index